Lecture Notes
in Business Information Pro

75

Series Editors

Wil van der Aalst
Eindhoven Technical University, The Netherlands

John Mylopoulos
University of Trento, Italy

Michael Rosemann
Queensland University of Technology, Brisbane, Qld, Australia

Michael J. Shaw
University of Illinois, Urbana-Champaign, IL, USA

Clemens Szyperski
Microsoft Research, Redmond, WA, USA

Joaquim Filipe
José Cordeiro (Eds.)

Web Information Systems and Technologies

6th International Conference, WEBIST 2010
Valencia, Spain, April 7-10, 2010
Revised Selected Papers

 Springer

Volume Editors

Joaquim Filipe
Polytechnic Institute of Setúbal
Department of Systems and Informatics
Rua do Vale de Chaves - Estefanilha
2910-761 Setúbal
Portugal
E-mail: j.filipe@est.ips.pt

José Cordeiro
Polytechnic Institute of Setúbal
Department of Systems and Informatics
Rua do Vale de Chaves - Estefanilha
2910-761 Setúbal
Portugal
E-mail: jcordeir@est.ips.pt

ISSN 1865-1348   e-ISSN 1865-1356
ISBN 978-3-642-22809-4   e-ISBN 978-3-642-22810-0
DOI 10.1007/978-3-642-22810-0
Springer Heidelberg Dordrecht London New York

Library of Congress Control Number: 2011933341

ACM Computing Classification (1998): H.3.5, J.1, K.4.4, H.5, I.2, D.2

Typesetting: Camera-ready by author, data conversion by Scientific Publishing Services, Chennai, India

Printed on acid-free paper

Springer is part of Springer Science+Business Media (www.springer.com)

Preface

The present book includes extended and revised versions of a set of selected papers from WEBIST 2010 (the 6th International Conference on Web Information Systems and Technologies), held in Valencia, Spain, in 2010, and organized by the Institute for Systems and Technologies of Information, Control and Communication (INSTICC), in cooperation with the Workflow Management Coalition (WfMC) and ACM SIGMIS.

The purpose of the WEBIST series of conferences is to bring together researchers, engineers and practitioners interested in the technological advances and business applications of Web-based information systems. The conference has four main tracks, covering different aspects of Web Information Systems, including Internet Technology, Web Interfaces and Applications, Society, e-Business and e-Government and Web Intelligence.

WEBIST 2010 received 205 paper submissions from 46 countries on all continents. A double-blind review process was enforced, with the help of more than 160 experts from the International Program Committee; each of them specialized in one of the main conference topic areas. After reviewing, 25 papers were selected to be published and presented as full papers and 50 additional papers, describing work-in-progress, as short papers. Furthermore, 43 papers were presented as posters. The full-paper acceptance ratio was 12%, and the total oral paper acceptance ratio was 36%.

The papers included in this book were selected from those with the best reviews taking also into account the quality of their presentation at the conference, assessed by the Session Chairs. Therefore, we hope that you find the papers included in this book interesting, and we trust they may represent a helpful reference for all those who need to address any of the research areas mentioned above.

We wish to thank all those who supported and helped to organize the conference. On behalf of the conference Organizing Committee, we would like to thank the authors, whose work mostly contributed to a very successful conference, and the members of the Program Committee, whose expertise and diligence were instrumental in ensuring the quality of the final contributions. We also wish to thank all the members of the Organizing Committee, whose work and commitment was invaluable. Last but not least, we would like to thank Springer for their collaboration in getting this book to print.

December 2010

Joaquim Filipe
José Cordeiro

Conference Committee

Conference Chair

Joaquim Filipe   Polytechnic Institute of Setúbal / INSTICC, Portugal

Program Chair

José Cordeiro   Polytechnic Institute of Setúbal / INSTICC, Portugal

Organizing Committee

Sérgio Brissos	INSTICC, Portugal
Helder Coelhas	INSTICC, Portugal
Andreia Costa	INSTICC, Portugal
Bruno Encarnação	INSTICC, Portugal
Bárbara Lima	INSTICC, Portugal
Raquel Martins	INSTICC, Portugal
Elton Mendes	INSTICC, Portugal
Carla Mota	INSTICC, Portugal
Vitor Pedrosa	INSTICC, Portugal
Daniel Pereira	INSTICC, Portugal
Filipa Rosa	INSTICC, Portugal
José Varela	INSTICC, Portugal
Pedro Varela	INSTICC, Portugal

Program Committee

Silvia Abrahão, Spain
Isaac Agudo, Spain
Fahim Akhter, UAE
Jacky Akoka, France
Margherita Antona, Greece
Valeria De Antonellis, Italy
Liliana Ardissono, Italy
Ismailcem Budak Arpinar, USA
Elarbi Badidi, UAE
Azita Bahrami, USA
Matteo Baldoni, Italy

Cristina Baroglio, Italy
Christine Bauer, Austria
David Bell, UK
Orlando Belo, Portugal
C. Bouras, Greece
Stéphane Bressan, Singapore
Tobias Buerger, Austria
Maria Claudia Buzzi, Italy
Jordi Cabot, Canada
Elena Calude, New Zealand
Rafael A. Calvo, Australia

Th. Tsiatsos, Greece
Michail Vaitis, Greece
Christelle Vangenot, Switzerland
Jari Veijalainen, Finland
Juan D. Velasquez, Chile
Maria Esther Vidal, Venezuela
Petri Vuorimaa, Finland

Mohd Helmy Abd Wahab, Malaysia
Manuel Wimmer, Austria
Viacheslav Wolfengagen,
    Russian Federation
Bing Wu, Ireland
Bin Xu, China
Jieh-Shan George Yeh, Taiwan

Auxiliary Reviewers

Mutaz Al-Debei, UK
Mohammad AL Asswad, UK
Paul Beskow, Norway
Duygu Celik, Turkey
Alberto Corni, Italy
Stuart Cunningham, UK
Elton Domnori, Italy
Adrián Fernández, Spain
Cristina Gomez, Spain

Carmine Gravino, Italy
Carlos Guerrero, Spain
Nigel Houlden, UK
Mehdi Khouja, Spain
Isaac Lera, Spain
Federica Sarro, Italy
Eduardo Gonçalves da Silva,
    The Netherlands

Invited Speaker

Žiga Turk   University of Ljubljana / Reflection Group,
                                  Slovenia

Table of Contents

Part III: Society, e-Business and e-Government

Part IV: Web Intelligence

How People and Stakeholders Shape Standards: The Case of IEEE 802.11

Kai Jakobs

RWTH Aachen University, Informatik 4, Ahornstr. 55, 52074 Aachen, Germany
kai.jakobs@cs.rwth-aachen.de

Abstract. Following the 'social shaping of technology' approach, this paper provides a brief discussion of the relations that exist between different stakeholders in ICT standardisation. It then discusses the impact exerted by the individuals who populate a standards body's working group, and how this body's voting rules impact its final standards. The paper primarily draws upon a qualitative empirical study. In particular, it will use the IEEE 802.11 committee as a real-world sample group to further highlight the issues discussed more theoretically above.

Keywords: Standards, Standardisation, Social shaping of technology.

1 Introduction and Motivation

Colloquially, the term 'standard' is used for specifications of very diverse origins. Windows and SAP/R3 are (industry/proprietary) standards, XML and UML are (consortium) standards, and UMTS and ISDN are (formal) standards. Yet, regardless of their respective origin, (successful) standards are crucial building blocks of all virtually all ICT systems. Think of it – the success of the Internet, for instance, may to no small amount be put down to the sheer existence, simplicity and effectiveness of its core protocols, TCP/IP.

Thus, standards now under development will be an integral part of future ICT systems, and will to no small extent define their functionality. In a way, this provides us with an opportunity for taking a glimpse into the future, albeit possibly a blurred one. What's more, there may even be a chance to pro-actively try and shape these future systems by shaping today's standards setting. After all, a standard does not come out of the blue, but is a product of standards development process and of the environment within which it emerges. Thus, if the characteristics of this environment were known this might enable an early shaping of tomorrow's ICT systems.

Perhaps a bit surprisingly, I would consider 'people' to be one of the major influencing factors in standardisation. After all, a standard originates from a technical committee or working group, where a group of individuals try to find a working solution to a given problem; it is here were the basic technical decisions are made. That is, we will need to look at the motivations, attitudes and views that influence these people's work if we want a better understanding of why a particular specification emerged the way it did.

J. Filipe and J. Cordeiro (Eds.): WEBIST 2010, LNBIP 75, pp. 1–13, 2011.
© Springer-Verlag Berlin Heidelberg 2011

The remainder of the paper is organised as follows. Some brief theoretical background on the Social Shaping of Technology (SST) is provided in chapter 2. Subsequently, chapter 4 highlights the impact an individual may have on the outcome of a standards working group, and discusses the impact of the working group's voting rights. Finally, some brief conclusions are presented in chapter 5.

2   Some Brief Theoretical Background

Technological artefacts in general, and especially such powerful representatives as ICT systems, will exert potentially strong impact on their environment. Yet, the same holds for the reverse direction. That is, complex interactions between ICT systems and their respective environments can be observed. Technology may assume both an active and a passive role; that is, technological artefacts and their environment are mutually interdependent. The environment within which technology is used and employed has, among others, social, cultural, societal, and organisational behaviours, rules and norms. It is clear that technology cannot emerge completely independent from such external influences. However, the impact ICT may have on organisations, or indeed society as a whole, has thus far attracted considerably more attention than the powers that shape this technology in the first place. Especially the impact of ICT within organisational settings (e.g. on a company's performance, or its role as an enabler of business process re-engineering) has been subject to a vast number of studies and analyses. Keywords such as 'organisational transformation' 'technology management', and 'management of change', can frequently be found in the literature, typically denoting studies on how the introduction and subsequent use of ICT have changed a particular organisational environment - for better or worse. Only recently has the reverse direction of impact been studied, i.e. the one exerted from organisational and societal conditions on technology.

2.1 Social Shaping of Technology

Two mutually exclusive schools have dominated research on technology and organisations until the early eighties (and are still in evidence). Proponents of the 'organisational choice' model consider technology as a vehicle to both reflect and foster the interests of particular groups; the process of change can be, and indeed is, shaped entirely by policy makers or organisation's managers; these actors have unlimited technological choices. *"Technology has no impact on people or performance in an organisation independent of the purposes of those who would use it, and the responses of those who have to work with it"* [1]. In contrast, 'technological determinism' in essence postulates that ICT determines the behaviour of organisations, that the consequences of manipulating a given technology will always be the same, independent of who manipulates and within which context. It follows that, according to this view, organisations have little choice but to adapt to the requirements of technology; particular paths of technological development are inevitable; like organisations, society at large also has no other choice but to adapt [2].

Research into SST largely emerged as a response to technological determinism (see e.g. [3] for an in-depth introduction). SST acknowledges that technology indeed has an impact on its environment, but that at the same time it is well framed through technical, but rather more through e.g. organisational, societal, cultural and economic factors. In particular, SST attempts to unveil the interactions between these technical and social factors. Abandoning the idea of inevitable technological developments implies that choices can be made regarding, for instance, acquisition, the use, and particularly the design of technological artefacts. There may be a broad variety of reasons upon which these choices are based. In an organisational context this may include purely technical reasons, as e.g. the need to integrate legacy systems, but decisions may also take into account company particulars, as for instance organisational or reporting structures. These choices, in turn, may lead to different impacts on the respective social or organisational environments. Thus, studying what shaped the particular technology offers a chance to proactively manipulate that very impact expected to result from this particular choice. At the same time this capability should also contribute to the prediction – and thus prevention – of undesirable side effects potentially resulting from a new technology. After all, technology tends to have other effects besides those actually intended, and these effects need to be explored as well. On the other hand, the respective environment shapes technical artefacts and systems during design and in use, i.e. at the site of the actual implementation.

2.2 Shaping Standardisation

Technological artefacts embody, and thus transfer, their respective environment of origin. The same holds for standards, which result from work in a committee. This alone implies that adaptations will subsequently be required if a system is to be exported to other markets, or user organisations, with different environments. *"The shaping process begins with the earliest stages of research and development"* [4]. This observation points to a direct link between the shaping of technology and standardisation activities. Especially since the advent of pro-active standardisation technological systems have increasingly been rooted in standards activities. In fact, the shaping of technology needs to start here.

Standards emerge through the co-operation and joint efforts of different individuals in technical committees and working groups. Whilst in theory these individuals act in their capacity as 'independent' experts, their views, beliefs, and prejudices have to a considerable degree been shaped by the environment within which they live and, especially, work. That is, various factors that may shape technology are also likely be channelled into the working groups of the international standards setting bodies. The corporate environment of the group members' respective employer, for instance, will have a major impact on the different visions of how a technology should be used, and the ideas of how this can be achieved. Therefore, they will also exert a significant impact on the work of the committees. This holds especially in the case of anticipatory, or pro-active, standards which specify new services from scratch, and thus offer the opportunity to incorporate to some (a considerable?) degree the particular presumptions, views, and ideas of the members of the originating committee (and their respective employers).

A reactive standard (i.e. one that basically just rubber-stamps an existing technology) will likewise transpose the environment from which it emerged; this will be the corporate environment (using this term very loosely) of its inventor (i.e. typically a manufacturer or a service provider) who originally specified the system upon which the standard will be based. Thus, this company's visions will implicitly be embodied in the standard specification, together with the ideas and views of its representative(s).

A first attempt to put together the individual factors that contribute to the shaping of a standard yields the following list:

1. External forces, including e.g.
   – advances in science and technology,
   – prevailing societal norms,
   – legislation.
2. The context within which a WG works, including e.g.
   – the rules and by-laws of the respective Standards Setting Body (SSB),
   – the SSB's 'culture'.
3. Individual major stakeholders' (vendors and possibly large users) preferences, including e.g.
   – technical interests
   – corporate strategies.
4. The immediate context from which a standard emerges, including e.g.
   – WG members' views, ideas, competencies, attitudes, backgrounds, etc,
   – members' communication capabilities,
   – the roles they assume.

In the following, I will look more closely first at 3 and then at 4.

3 Relations between Stakeholders

The procedures adopted by the individual SSBs may differ with respect to various criteria. In particular, the criteria upon which voting power is assigned to members differ. The options range from 'one country|company|individual – one vote' (applied by e.g., ISO/W3C/IEEE) to rather elaborate schemes with different membership levels that basically allow companies to 'buy' voting power. Here, the 'price' (i.e., the membership fee) typically also depends on the size or revenue of the company (ETSI, for instance, uses such a scheme).

At least the former, rather egalitarian approach suggests that the degree of control over, and influence on, the standards setting process is about equally distributed between the different types of stakeholders. This, in turn, yields the model of the standardisation process as depicted in Figure 51 It shows the 'ideal' situation, with all stakeholders having a (more or less equal) say in the standards setting process.

This – fairly technocratic – model still underlies many SSBs' rules and processes. Unfortunately, it ignores organisational and social aspects, and does not assume any links or interrelations between the different stakeholders.

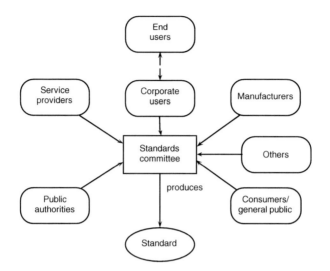

Fig. 1. A naive model of the standards setting process (adapted from [5])

As a consequence, this ideal scenario is far removed from reality – at least according to some earlier research (see e.g. [6]). In fact, it appears that so far IT standards development has almost exclusively been technology driven; with standards produced solely reflecting providers' and implementers' priorities like, for example, manageability rather than usability. This can largely be attributed to the fact that relevant standardisation committees have typically been dominated by vendors and service providers (see also [7] for a more elaborate discussion). Accordingly, a more realistic model is called for.

Obviously, there are also relations between these various stakeholders outside the standards setting process, the most obvious one being customer – supplier. Those relations may well have considerable impact on both sides' activities and conduct in standardisation. For instance, most users (except for some very large and sophisticated ones) would rather try and resolve problems locally (by e.g., enhancing a standards implementation to meet local needs). They rarely get involved in setting standards that may eventually meet their requirements.

Those entities that form the 'third estate' in standards setting are a different case altogether. Although they represent the vast majority of stakeholders these groups have extremely little say in the standards setting process. This holds despite the fact that organisations such as ANEC[1] for the consumers and NORMAPME[2] for SMEs are actively participating in selected standard working groups on behalf of their respective constituencies.

Figure 2 depicts the actual situation more realistically. Specifically, it highlights two phenomena. First, manufacturers and service providers seem to act as a sort of buffer or filter between corporate users and standards committees [6] – whether deliberately or not – in that they filter their customers' requirements. Also, in co-operation with the users they provide individual solutions to meet their respective

---

[1]   The 'European Association for the Co-ordination of Consumer Representation in Standardisation'.

[2]   The 'European Office of Crafts, Trades and SMEs for Standardisation'.

customers' needs. This way, they potentially compromise to some extent the idea of many ICT standards, i.e., to provide interoperability. This also contributes to reducing the number of users in standards setting.

Second, some sort of invisible 'shield' keeps potential input from standardisation's 'Third Estate' away from the working groups. This 'shield' is largely rooted in a lack of financial resources (actively contributing to standards setting is a costly business, see e.g., [8]) and of qualified personnel. This is frequently combined with inadequate knowledge about the value of standards in general, and of the potential value of active contributions to standards setting in particular.

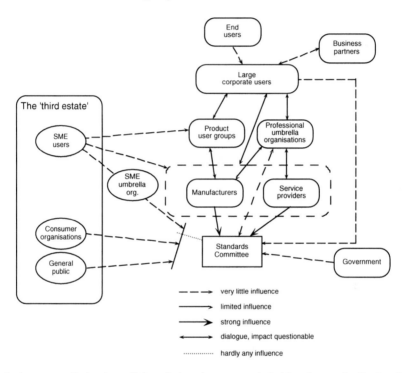

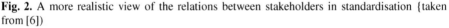

Fig. 2. A more realistic view of the relations between stakeholders in standardisation {taken from [6])

4   The Individual's Role

4.1   A Little Background

The above already suggests that different players exert varying degrees of influence over an SSB's process, depending on their respective levels of interest in a new standard, but also on rather more mundane aspects like deep pockets and market power. However, at the end of the day, a standard's specification results from the efforts of the members of an SSB's working group. Consequently, these individuals' motivations, attitudes and views are very likely to have an influence on their contributions to the standards setting process, and thus on its outcome.

Various factors, which do not necessarily bear a relation to the technology to be standardised, are channelled into an SSB's working groups (WGs), and shape the process outcome. [9] argue that the respective corporate environments of the WG members' employers, for instance, are playing a major role here. The different visions of how a technology should be used, and the ideas of how this can be achieved are shaped by these local environments, which therefore also exert an impact on the standardisation work. This holds especially in the case of anticipatory standards, which specify new services from scratch, and thus offer the opportunity to incorporate to some degree the particular presumptions of the (more outspoken) members of the originating WG. Yet, a reactive standard will likewise transpose the environment from which it originally emerged; i.e. the corporate environment of its inventor who specified the system upon which the standard will be based.

4.2 Perceived Influential Factors

To find out which such non-technical factors actually do play a role, and thus to better understand why a standard emerges the way it does, we need to have a closer look inside WGs.

In a (smallish) study of factors that influence the standards setting process at WG level within ISO and ITU-T, [7] showed that a WG's decisions are taken for a variety of reasons, a proposal's technical merits being but one of them. For example, about one out of three respondents from ISO observed that it is individuals that are most powerful.

> *"Oddly enough, it's been my experience that _individuals_ dominate ISO. Sometimes the individual will have a powerful multinational corporation or government/national interest on their side, but the bully pulpit is controlled by individuals, and only those with a strong sense of purpose survive."*

Much in line with the above observation, many respondents from ISO and ITU stress that speaking out at meetings for or against a proposal is the most important single factor influencing technical decisions. That is, even good proposals will hardly be considered if nobody is available to explain or defend them at meetings.

> *"For any given technical decision the presence of supporters/opponents weighs heavily, for in practice unless there is someone or some organization that champions a solution and pushes it forward it does not get as much consideration/exposure as alternate solutions. That is, group members typically do not delve into researching solutions that someone happened to send us unless such solution at first glance seems to be overwhelmingly good. More likely the members push the solutions that they already understand."*

Along similar lines, the influence of those who are prepared to put in extra work should not be under-estimated. These two aspects are probably linked – those with strong views are more likely to be inclined to invest time and effort to get their views through.

> *"Often the group "leaders" (including formal editors, and strong personalities who are not formal leaders) have tremendous influence. (This is not necessarily bad.)".*

Another factor identified as influential – though overall said to be of lower importance – is a proposal's technical merit; underlying company interests may also have to be taken into account.

> "Unless you are at the meeting, your view is not taken into account (no matter how technically correct it may be). This is the overwhelming factor that decides the content of the standard. Company interests (political influence at the voting level) is the next priority. Technical merit is of little importance - standards are usually a poor compromise of many strong views".
>
> "The technical viability of a decision does carry great weight. As almost all members at the technical committee meeting level are engineers, the technical prowess of the solution, tied with the credibility (knowledge) of the person presenting it are very influential. On occasion, a company which already has a product back in their labs will also prove to be a formidible opponent."

The above observations stress the importance of the rather more non-technical aspects of the standardisation process. Clearly, these aspects are strongly linked to the individual WG members' attitudes and approaches. However, as stated above, these, in turn, are to a considerable degree shaped by their respective work environments.

4.3 The Case of IEEE 802.11

In the IEEE, membership – including voting rights – in the 'international programme' is assigned to individuals (as opposed to e.g., companies). That is, here as well a closer look at the roles, views, and motivations of WG members is of interest – do WG members actually act based on their personal views and perceptions, or do other factors play a role, too? To this end, a questionnaire comprising 16 open ended questions was distributed to a number of individuals who played an important role during the development of the IEEE 802.11 set of standards [10]. The findings from this survey should be taken as a snapshot – the idea was to shed some light on different aspects associated with the IEEE's 'individual membership' approach.

Almost all respondents have a strictly technical background, with job titles such as 'communication engineer' or 'system architect'. They were all very active in the process, and typically attended almost all meetings (which gave them almost permanent voting rights; they are conferred after attendance of 3 out of 4 consecutive plenary meetings, and need to be maintained through continuing participation in both meetings and ballots). However, only very few had previous experience in standards development. Obviously, the initial motivations for attendance differed, but interest in the technology dominated (which is no big surprise considering the respondents' engineering background).

With primarily engineers populating the WGs one could be inclined to suspect that influence during deliberations is based on the respective technical merits of the proposals on the table. Yet, it appears that other factors are at least as influential here. Two typical responses:

> "Most influence came from 1/3 powerful organizations (companies), 1/3 strong technical proposals, 1/3 active and respected company representatives".
>
> "The influence came through a combination of strong technical proposals, active representatives and powerfull organizations".

Standards setting is a costly business (see e.g., [8]; things have not improved since then). Thus, a link between the economic strength of a company and its interest in a specific standard on the one hand, and the level of its representation in the body developing this standard on the other may safely be assumed. Indeed,

> *"There are active/respected representatives from most large organizations because it costs so much to commit people to creating the standard, and active/respected representatives gravitate to organizations that support the standards effort".*

Said "large organizations" were typically (chip) manufacturers:

> *"90% of all attendance was by manufacturers. Manufacturers are (and continue to be) the most influential in the committees as they are primary companies responsible for creating and distributing the technology".*

To a considerable extent, developing standards is about the distribution, and the use, of power. The above suggests that in the case of the 802.11 power was – for obvious reasons – primarily with large manufacturers. With their vested interest in the technology they were prepared to invest heavily in R&D efforts, and to send representatives who were widely respected in the industry to the WG meetings. These individuals came armed with good proposals (the results of the R&D efforts), for which they could make a strong case. Strong corporate interest, good proposals and respected and knowledgeable proponents seems to be a wining combination (whether or not two out of these would do remains an open issue). In the words of a respondent, influence in the WG.

> *" ... is a combination* [of e.g., powerful organisation, deep pockets, strong technical proposals, active/respected representatives]*, but the companies that were the strongest in the market also put most effort in the standard by means of number of people, proposals, technical knowledge, experience in the field. But there are also examples of small companies with very smart/ respected representatives who took and got a lot of bandwidth".*

These quotes seem to suggest that corporate interests were at least very visible inside 802.11. Yet, the question remains if WG members actually represented their respective employers' or clients' proposals, or if they supported other proposals they felt them to have more merits (for instance, because they considered them technically superior). If the former were the case, all representatives of a company that submitted a proposal should rally behind it. In fact, respondents agree – albeit not unanimously – that such behaviour could normally be observed. Of course, representatives of a company defending their employer's proposal is not necessarily a contradiction to 'individual membership'. After all, the developers of a corporate proposal were most likely the ones also attending standards meetings; this way, their interests and those of the employer happened to be aligned. As one respondent put it:

> *"[Different representatives of one company] mostly acted in unison based on their affiliation, and usually because they had a vested interest in their proposal or position succeeding ...."*

In addition to such vested interests, fear of reprimand and reprisal might also be behind a vote:

"In general, when a company's rep did not represent the affiliations point of view, they tended not to appear at the next meeting. There are expections to this rule, but in general, if you work for a company, you are voting for their proposal".

While most respondents agree that supporting their employer's or client's proposal was the norm, they also agreed that deviations from this behaviour could be observed as well. However (and this suggests that fear of retaliation did not just come out of the blue),

"This was not a frequent phenomenon as far as I can tell. But there are examples of individuals who did (for whatever reason, sometimes they even self did not notice that they pleaded against their own company). I can think of one succes, but the individual lost (left?) his job afterwards".

Apparently, potential reasons for rogue acting (and voting) were diverse, the ambition to standardise on the best technical solution being a comparably popular one:

"... there were a number of very good people who worked toward the creation of the best standard that could be formed regardless of their companies position and agenda".

However, acting 'politically' is also not unheard of:

"... people would purposely vote opposite to their affiliation to *appear* fair minded".

Similar behaviour can be explained by exploiting IEEE rules:

"Other times they would vote contrarily when it could be predicted, or sometimes just in case, the vote would confirm that alternate position anyway. That would ensure that the company had at least one vote on the prevailing side so that indidvual could later make a motion for reconsideration – again that's another political ploy".

The latter two reasons for 'acting individually' are really cases of 'corporate tactics'. Thus, so far, it would seem that only some cases of 'individualism' can be explained by WG members' acting as individuals (as opposed to 'company reps').

The idea of 'individual membership' also implies that voting behaviour should not change with of WG-member's new affiliation, or with a consultant's new client. No clear picture emerged here. Still, a concrete observation by one respondent:

"Yes. A change of affiliation either as an employee or consultant has caused changes in on formerly held positions. A recent case in the IEEE 802 where two companies had brought in opposing technologies resulted in a stalemate position. The larger corporation purchased the smaller opposing technology company. So there became a committee where all the members were the same as before but the purchased company voters now had a new affiliation and voted accordingly".

Even if only some respondents reported such occurrences it seems safe to assume that at least several WG-members do change views depending on those of their current employer (which is perfectly understandable).

With a group of engineers discussing technical matters one should not be surprised to find evidence of the 'Not Invented Here' syndrome; likewise clashes of egos may be suspected. Respondents do indeed report such incidences that obviously occurred quite frequently. One responded observed that

> *"Many members can not separate valid technical criticism from "your baby is ugly". This is more frequent than necessary".*

Such clashes may be over both personal and corporate views (e.g., if a company depends on a certain technology to be standardised), or over procedures. This is little surprise, as 'being outspoken' and 'having a sense of purpose' are essential attributes for successful standards setters [7]. At the same time, respondents noted that such personal clashes might well go hand in hand with clashes of corporate interests,

> *"... and it was more of a combination of both ego and money. Many clashes were driven due to big investments in company technology directions where the direction of the standard was important to the financial health of the companies involved".*

Finally, the observation that existing implementations might well have a detrimental effect on a proposal's chances of being accepted is interesting.

> *"Technical merits are important but never the most important. Implementability, time to market (for all), fairness are equally important to drive decisions".*

Obviously, the desire not to favour one company (the implementer) over others plays a role, too. This – rather striking – aspect surfaced quite frequently,

> *"Solutions already implemented did play a strong role, but could also be a strong reason to change things, to level the playing field (by forcing changes for certain vendors that already had an implementation)".*
> *"I have never seen that a decision is taken that is in the benefit of only one company (because it already has solutions/products)".*

And, even more strongly:

> *"No four organizations can make 802.11 do anything."*

Even if the latter may be a slight exaggeration, these comments suggest that (many) members of the 802.11 groups were not prepared to let their work be overly dominated by corporate interests, and also that at least some of them were actively acting against any such dominance.

Accordingly, finding as many allies as possible, and forming strong alliances is an integral part of the game ('if you scratch my back, I'll scratch yours'). This necessity is not least triggered by the IEEE balloting process, which requires a 75% level of support for a proposal to enter the next stage of the process.

> *"With respect to 802.11 DS PHY, main issues were agreed to by a coalition of companies out side of IEEE meetings and then were brought into IEEE 802.11 for debate. THis coordination between NCR/Aironet/Harris ensured sucess of 802.11b".*
> *"In the end (the important decisions) are influenced most by the strength of companies (number of voters) and coalitions between companies. I have never seen that a decision is taken that is in the benefit of only one company (because it already has solutions/products)".*

These observations suggest that once everything has been said and done the decision about success and failure burns down to a simple head-count. A number of individual voters together form a 'corporate vote' (there may be exceptions), and enough such 'corporate votes' (i.e., a strong coalition) lead to the success of a proposal.

5 Brief Summary and Analysis

The survey responses draw a somewhat ambivalent picture. On the one hand, it seems that the majority of members of the 802.11 WGs have a very strong sense of fairness – they try not to allow a single powerful company, or a group of them, to dominate the process, may well consider existing pilot implementations as an unfair advantage and accordingly reject the associated proposal. On the other hand, it is safe to say that the majority of the leading figures are coming from exactly these powerful companies – they have the means and the motivation to invest heavily in the standards setting process, as the return on investment may be enormous. In addition, their employees are likely to be motivated to assume formal roles in the process (Chair, secretary, technical editor, etc), thus getting additional influence.

Overall, it seems that WG members cast their votes at least with a view towards their respective employers' business interests. Yet, exceptions from this seem to not-so-infrequent, and typically aim at technically superior solutions. Likewise, the reports about WG members adapting their point of view to the one held by their current employer do not hint at strong personal opinions (rather at pragmatism). Thus, here again we do not see a homogeneous picture (of course, it is hard to vote against your employer's interests when you see people being fired for having done exactly that; another course of events not entirely unheard of, according to some respondents). Then again, the apparently fairly frequent clashes of egos suggest strong feelings about a proposal (there may be other reasons involved as well, though).

All in all, I do not believe that 'individual' membership is making a big difference. The responses from 802.11 members are pretty much in line with those from members of other standards bodies (ISO also prescribes that committee members "act in a personal capacity" [11]). People act differently; some may consider 'individual' membership as carte blanche to push their own proposals, others will still act exclusively on behalf of their employers, both regardless of the official membership rules.

From a theoretical perspective, one could argue that research into the role of the individual in the development of standards (probably not so much in the development of technology) is called for. Specifically, it would appear that one cannot necessarily assume that the professional background of a WG member, or the specifics of his/her employer have an immediate impact on the work done in the WG, or the views represented there.

And in more practical terms: what can the interested companies do about this situation? After all, companies would like to see their corporate strategy and/or technology being promoted by the people they send to SSBs' working groups.

Companies would be well advised to educate the people they are sending to SSBs' working groups. This education primarily needs to cover relevant corporate strategies and goals that need to be observed. After all, it is a huge difference if a company's goal is to have a standard – any standard – in order to broaden or even create a market, or if they want to push their own technical solution. But education must not stop there – it should also cover more mundane aspects like SSBs' regulations and bylaws, as well as negotiation and diplomatic skills. Likewise, companies should manage their standards activities very carefully; this includes whom to send to which body. For instance, it may not always be advisable to send R&D people who may tend to push their brainchildren rather than support the corporate strategy.

Unfortunately, whatever they do will hardly guarantee success – we are dealing with the human nature here…..

References

1. Buchanan, D.A., Huczynski, A.A.: Organizational Behaviour. Prentice-Hall, Englewood Cliffs (2004)
2. Williams, R.: The Social Shaping of Information and Communications Technologies. In: Kubicek, H., et al. (eds.) The Social Shaping of the Information Superhighways. Proceedings of International Conference, COST A4, European Commission DGXIII, Luxembourg (1997)
3. Williams, R., Edge, D.: The Social Shaping of Technology. Research Policy 25, 856–899 (1996)
4. Williams, R.: The Social Shaping of Technology: Research Concepts and Findings in Great Britain. In: Dierkes, M., Hoffmann, U. (eds.) New Technologies at the Outset – Social Forces in the Shaping of Technological Innovations. Campus/Westview (1992)
5. Egyedi, T., Jakobs, K., Monteiro, E.: Helping SDOs to Reach Users. Report for EC DG ENT, Contract No, 20010674 (2003),
   `http://www-i4.informatik.rwth-aachen.de/~jakobs/grant/`
   `Final_Report.pdf`
6. Jakobs, K. (E-Business & ICT) Standardisation and SME Users – Mutually Exclusive? In: Proc. Multi-Conference on Business Information Systems Track 'E - Business - Standarisierung und Integration. Cuviller Verlag, Göttingen (2004)
7. Jakobs, K., Procter, R., Williams, R.: The Making of Standards. IEEE Communications Magazine 39(4) (2001)
8. Spring, M.B., Weiss, M.B.H.: Financing the Standards Development Process. In: Kahin, B., Abbate, J. (eds.) Standards Policy for Information Infrastructure. MIT Press, Cambridge (1995)
9. Jakobs, K.: Shaping User-side Innovation Through Standardisation – The Example of ICT. Technological Forecasting and Social Change 73(1) (2006)
10. Jakobs, K., Lemstra, W., Hayes, V., Tuch, B., Links, C.: Towards a Wireless LAN Standard. In: Lemstra, W., Groenewegen, J., Hayes, V. (eds.) The Innovation Journey of WiFi. Cambridge University Press, Cambridge (2010) (to be published)
11. ISO: ISO/IEC Directives, Part 1 – Procedures for the technical work (2008),
    `http://www.iec.ch/tiss/iec/Directives-Part1-Ed6.pdf`

Semantic Building Information Model and Multimedia for Facility Management

Christophe Nicolle and Christophe Cruz

LE2I UMR CNRS 5158, University of Bourgogne, BP 47870, 21078 Dijon Cedex, France
{cnicolle,christophe.cruz}@u-bourgogne.fr

Abstract. In the field of civil engineering, the proliferation of stakeholders and the heterogeneity of modeling tools detract from the quality of the design process, construction and building maintenance. In this paper, we present a Web-based platform lets geographically dispersed project participants—from facility managers and architects to electricians to plumbers—directly use and exchange project documents in a centralized virtual environment using a simple Web browser. A 3D visualization lets participants move around in the building being designed and obtain information about the objects that compose it. This approach is based both on a semantic architecture called CDMF and IFC 2x3. Our framework, based on Building Information Modeling features, facilitates data maintenance (data migration, model evolution) during the building lifecycle and reduces the volume of data.

Keywords: Interoperability, 3D collaborative platform, Industry foundation classes (IFC), Building information modeling (BIM), Semantic web.

1 Introduction

For twenty years, the construction sector makes a profound challenge. This is due to several causes such as: evolution of standards, evolution of methodologies and pressure on controlling costs and delays. The building lifecycle management requires the development of a specific environment solving at the same time the problems of syntactic and semantic heterogeneity [14, 15]. Moreover, the environment should also allow the required extensibility and the flexibility in order to guarantee the coherent evolution of the collaborative processes developed in this field. The information in an AEC project is generated during all the building lifecycle. It is essential to structure the information in a relevant way for a better management. The activities in an AEC project generate a huge variety of data and information. Consequently, the management and the communication of these data by various participants are complex. The process of information sharing requires a framework in which computer programs can exchange data automatically regardless of the software and data location. Moreover, in this field, the use of tools for 3D visualization of the buildings is crucial. Towards this goal the IAI proposed a standard called IFC that specifies object representations for AEC projects [5]. Industry foundation classes (IFCs) include object specifications, or classes, and provide a structure for data sharing among applications.

J. Filipe and J. Cordeiro (Eds.): WEBIST 2010, LNBIP 75, pp. 14–29, 2011.

From a collaborative point of view the IFCs form the basis of a building description. This basis is enriched during the building's lifecycle with elements related to facilities management: financial data, maintenance rules, evacuation procedures and so on. The quantity of information becomes exponential and then a relevant organization of these elements becomes very complex. Today, "Building Information Modeling (BIM)" is promising to be the facilitator of integration, interoperability and collaboration in the future of building industry. The term BIM has been recently pointed to demarcate the next generation of Information Technologies (IT) and Computer-Aided Design (CAD) for buildings.

The remainder of this paper is structured in 3 parts. The first part presents a brief description of the concept of BIM. The second part presents the principles of our approach using semantic graphs to describe the objects of the building. The third part presents the industrial platform derived from our work and examples to illustrate our point.

2 Building Information Modeling

The term BIM marks the transition from conventional CAD applications for construction and recent developments in computer science. It is the process of generating, storing, managing, exchanging and sharing building information in an interoperable and reusable way. A BIM system is a tool that enables users to integrate and reuse the information of a building and the domain knowledge throughout the lifecycle of a building [16]. A BIM system is a central system that manages various types of information, such as enterprise resource planning, resource analysis packages, technical reports, meeting reports, etc. However, the main feature of a BIM is the 3D modeling system with data management, data sharing and data exchange during the lifecycle of the building. As a matter of fact, a building is composed of geometrical elements which are the basis of a building's design. Furthermore, parametric modeling provides powerful mechanisms that can automate the generation of the building information. Especially those mechanisms, in conjunction with the behavior of building object and an object-based system, facilitate the maintenance and the validity of the building's designs. Several definitions of BIM can be found in the specialized literature. The NBIMS [17] divides BIM categories in three axes which are Product, Collaborative Process and Facility. The Product is an intelligent digital representation of the building. The Collaborative Process covers business drivers, automated process capabilities and open information standards used for information sustainability and fidelity. The Facility concerns the well understood information exchanges, workflows, and procedures which are used by the different teams as a repeatable, verifiable and sustainable information-based environment throughout the building's lifecycle. According to [18], a BIM is a computable representation of all the physical and functional characteristics of a building and it is related to the project information, which is intended to be a repository of information for the building owner/operator to use and maintain throughout the lifecycle of the building. According to Autodesk [19], BIMs have three main features: They create and operate on digital databases for collaboration. They manage change through those databases so that a change to any part of the database is coordinated in all other parts. They capture and preserve information for reuse by adding industry-specific applications.

By analyzing the BIM definition we index a set of features common to BIM systems [20, 21, 22, 23, 24, 25, 27]. (1) The main feature of BIM is the ability to store, share and exchange data. Many methods are used to realize those processes like files or databases. Concerning data exchange, BIMs are developed with the aim to keep open non-proprietary data format exchange. (2) Data managed in BIM processes concerns building geometries which are most of the time 3D data. 3D data is more helpful for designers for the visualization of complex construction conditions than 2D while it communicates at the same time design intentions. AEC industry visualizes the design using stereoscopic projection tools to create an immersive experience [26]. Spatial relationships between building elements are managed in a hierarchical manner. (3) BIMS are data rich and comprehensive as they cover all physical and functional characteristics of a building. BIMs are also rich semantically as they store a high amount of semantic information about building elements. Moreover, the data model is fully object oriented to facilitate data management and process definition. (4) Some of the BIMs are extensible to cover unimplemented information domains. For instance, the development of IFC 2.X went though a major change in order to extend progressively the range and the capability of IFCs by using modules. (5) BIMs play a central role in the building lifecycle. In order to ease data exchange, a data format has to be widely used. By definition, BIMs enable interoperability among diverse applications using a shared universal information standard. (6) The lifecycle of the project in AEC is composed of several phases which have to be validated by the corresponding AEC engineering designer. BIMs cover several lifecycle phases. The state of these phases is processed by BIMs in order to sequence and schedule the process. BIMs support 4D analysis, where activities from the project schedule can be simulated and studied to optimize the sequence of construction.

Our research aims at solving the problem linked to the constant IFC evolution (4). The definition of a complete framework that allows to manage knowledge around the building process requires an extensible and generic formalism to represent both specific data describing building information and connected information defined by the user during the building's lifecycle. It requires also tools to handle and query the corresponding modeled data, and it requires also tools to manage the data evolution during the building's lifecycle. Moreover, the contextual management of data that needs to correspond with the user's view and constraints has to be taken into account. It requires also an adaptive graphical 2D/3D representation, dynamically connected with data from buildings according to the BIM features. Finally, the most important point is the fact that the framework has to take into account the constant evolution of specific data describing building information and the corresponding connected information defined by the user during the building's lifecycle. We have developed a method that combines IFC and the various requirements related to facility management.

3   Overview of Our Approach

In our study context the requirement of the model extensibility and the model evolution generates others difficulties, such as mapping data between two models. Handling information during the building lifecycle requires a contextual and temporal representation of knowledge. It is important to trace each data evolution at a time and to know how to present data according to the user context [6, 7]. To deal with these requirements, we derived Names Graph [4] in order to complete our framework. Based on the context we developed a system description and operators in an architecture called CDMF that allows dealing with the traceability of the data schema evolution. This innovative approach allows knowing, at any time of the project, the current version of the data schema that defines the facility data.

Our approach considers all requirements at large (temporal management, adaptive view, 2D/3D representation) in order to propose a global solution with a framework based on Semantic Web technologies. To meet these requirements, we have built a complete framework, called CDMF, derived from Semantic Web formalism: RDF, Named Graph, OWL and SWRL. These formalisms constitute the base of our approach. We have extracted from each of them the more adapted features to our problematic. RDF formalism allows data modeling and can be used by operators provided by OWL/SWRL. Finally, Named Graph gives a contextual layer to this unit. To obtain a complete formalism, well adapted to facilities management, we have defined a framework called CDMF which will be presented in the following section.

3.1 The CDMF Architecture

The CDMF architecture proposes to use semantic operators in order to manage data in the context of a facility management environment. The objective of CDMF is to join together the semantics of OWL and SWRL in only one formalism. For that DMF defines a whole system of logical operators allowing the description of classes, properties, constraints and of rules. The principal interest of CDMF is to offer a framework facilitating the description of contextual data. This framework offers a single structure that permit us to define a set of data, all types of contexts and the actions that can be realized on these data. CDMF aims at meeting the various needs evoked; moreover, it achieves for the complete system, due to its structure and its operators, a reduction in volume of the data that represents an information system in a collaborative environment, as well as restricted treatments due to the unicity of information. Thus, we used the formalisms of the semantic Web to create an environment meeting in a single way our various needs.

The operators of DMF allow the modeling of knowledge on 3 levels (Table 1): the model level, where DMF makes it possible to define the concepts of modeling (class, property, etc). The diagram level, where DMF allows defining the description of knowledge. The instance level, which makes it possible to define the objects of the real-world according to the structure of the diagram defined in the higher level of abstraction. For each level a set of triplets forms RDF graphs.

Table 1. The 3 levels of the modeling data of DMF

Model	Schema	Instance
dmf:Class type dmf:Class	:Building type dmf:Class	:b1 type :Building
dmf:Property type	:Storey type dmf:Class	:e1 type :Floor
rdf:Property	:contains type	:e2 type :Floor
	dmf:Property	:b1 :contain :s1
		:b1 :contain :s2

The architecture of CDMF is based on the structure of modeling RDF. This structure RDF makes it possible to represent knowledge with graphs. These graphs are modeled using a set of triplets. A triplet is composed of a subject, a predicate, and an object. The architecture of CDMF is composed of two layers: "DMF" and "C". The "DMF" layer is composed of the model construction operators and the "C" layer is composed of the context manager operator and the handling graph operator.

The CDMF architecture is made of the space system stack, the API and the engine. This environment allows the creation of specific applications that permit to deal with facility management requirements. The Space System is used to configure the system and to allow data access. It is based on an RDF document. This space system contains a set of graphs called SystemGraph. From this point, the CDMF engine checks the declared graphs and responds to queries executed from the API. The API CDMF is a set of methods used to handle the data system. This API proposes to access data with two main classes called `SystemSetGraph` and `SystemGraph`. The first one allows to access the system graph which composes the space system. The second one is made of methods that permit to modify system data. For instance, the method `SystemGraph.create()` provides the list of Class elements and Property elements which can be created. The CDMF engine is the kernel of the architecture. This engine uses a space system to configure and to know the set of systems to use. The engine contains processes which manage methods of the API CDMF. The engine selects the system graphs in the space system, and creates data, deletes data, etc.

3.2 DMF: A Reduced Set of Modeling Operators

This section presents the DMF stack. This stack is made of operators which allow to model information (from simple and monovalued attributes to complex 3D objects) into semantic graphs. This section enables us to show that the formalism that we have defined has a restricted set of operators. We show that these operators can be combined to meet all the needs for semantic modeling defined in the statements. For each operator we give its equivalent in SWRL or OWL.

- `dmf:Class` defines a class. The equivalent operator in OWL is `owl:Class`.
- `dmf:Property` carries out the definition of a property of a Class.
- `dmf:Equal` defines the equality between two variables. This operator makes it possible to test if two resources are equivalent.
- "`dmf:Var`" makes it possible to define variables used in the logical formulas. Its equivalent is defined in SWRL by the operator "`swrl:Variable`".
- "`dmf:Pred1`" makes it possible to define unary predicates. Its equivalent is defined in SWRL by "swrl:ClassAtom".
- "`dmf:Pred2`" makes it possible to define binary predicates. The equivalent operators in SWRL are "`swrl:IndividualPropertyAtom`" and "`swrl:DatavaluedPropertyAtom`". A binary predicate is a property with a subject and an object. To make the correspondence with RDF, the terms of subject and object are used in order to define the first and last element of a triplet RDF.

Fig. 1. Hierarchy of CDMF operators and properties using Protégé

- "dmf:Equiv" makes it possible to define that two classes are equivalent. The set of the elements of the type A is equivalent to the set of the elements of the type B. The equivalent operator in OWL is "owl:equivalentClass".

- etc .

3.3 Context and Mapping Operators

This section presents the operators defined in the stack C of our architecture. These operators are used to handle graphs and to define contexts. With these operators, new graphs can be generated by combination of existing graphs. These operators are commonly used to update the data model definition when a norm in architecture is upgraded. For example, the IFC norm has been updated six times since 2000. The elements defined in this part use the space of name cdmf. For each type of graph we present its definition by using DMF operators, as well as an example of use with the result of the operation carried out on the graphs.

Union Operator. The result of the addition of G1 and G2 is the union of the set of the triplets of G1 and the set of the triplets of G2. Table 2 gives its definition in DMF (Table 2).

Table 2. DMF definition of the union operator

```
Class(AddGraph)
Property(args)
args(?x,?y) → AddGraph(?X) ∧ rdf:Bag(?y)
args(?x,?y) ∧ rdf:li(?y,?Z) → CdmfGraph(?Z)
```

The operator of a union of graphs is defined by the class `cdmf:AddGraph`. It has a property `cdmf:args`. This property is a list of RDF elements (`rdf:Bag`) whose elements are graphs. The definition of these elements allows the union of two or several graphs. Table 3 shows an example of a union of graphs as well as the result of the operation.

Table 3. Script defining the union of two graphs G1 and G2

```
:Ga1 rdf:cdmf        type:AddGraph
:Ga1 cdmf:args :li1
:li1 rdf:Li   :G1
:li1 rdf:Li   :G2
:G1{    :b1 rdf:type :Building
        :e1 rdf:type :Floor}
:G2{    G1:b1 G1:contain     :e1}
```

G1 defines two objects b1 and e1 of the `Building` type and `Floor`. G2 defines a relation `contain` between b1 and e1. The resources b1 and e1 in G1 and G2 are the same resources because their URI is identical. Indeed b1 and e1 are defined in G1, their URI is the concatenation of the URI of G1 with b1. In G2, we define the namespace G1 with the URI of G1, therefore `G1:b1` and `G1:e1` in G2 is the same URI as `:b1` and `:e1` in G1. The result of the calculation of this combination is presented in Table 4.

Table 4. Script resulting from the union of G1 and G2

```
:Ga1 { :b1 rdf:type
:Building
:e1 rdf:type
:Floor
:b1 contain
  :e1}
```

Intersection Operators. The intersection operator can be defined in different manners and can imply a different result according to the type of intersection carried out. The intersection operator is defined by two elements `cdmf:InterGraph` and `cdmf:CompInterGraph`. The first element defines a "traditional" intersection. The second element makes it possible to specify on which elements of a triplet the intersection is carried out.

Traditional Intersection. The result of the intersection between G1 and G2 is the set of the identical triplets in G1 and G2 (Table 5).

Table 5. DMF definition of the traditional intersection operator (cdmf:InterGraph operators)

```
Class(InterGraph)
Property(arg1)
Property(arg2)
arg1(?x,?y) → CdmfGraph(?y)
arg2(?x,?y) → CdmfGraph(?y)
```

This operator has two properties cdmf:arg1 and cdmf:arg2. These two properties are CdmfGraph types representing the two graphs on which the intersection must be computed. Table 6 defines an intersection between the two graphs G1 and G2. The result of this intersection is the empty set, because the set of triplets is disjoint.

Table 6. Script defining the union of two graphs G1 and G2

```
:G1{   :b1 rdf:type :Building
:e1 rdf:type :Floor}
:G2{G1:b1 :contain G1:e1}
:Gi1 rdf:cdmf type:InterGraph
:Gi1 cdmf:arg1     :G1
:Gi1 cdmf:arg2     :G2
```

Composed Intersection. The composed intersection makes it possible to determine which part of the triplet is concerned in the calculation of the intersection. In the case of the "traditional" intersection, one carries out the intersection on the set of triplets of each graph (Table 7). Here we can compose the intersection with the various parts of a triplet (subject, object). Below you will find possible combinations of intersections.

- The intersection on the subject in the two graphs. The result of the intersection between G1 and G2 is the set of the triplets whose subjects are identical in G1 and G2.
- The intersection on the object in the two graphs. The result of the intersection between G1 and G2 is the set of the triplets whose objects are identical in G1 and G2.
- The intersection on the subject of the triplets of a graph with the object of the triplets of the other graph. The result of the intersection between G1 and G2 is the set of the triplets whose subjects of the graph G1 are identical to the objects of the graph G2.
- The intersection on the subject or the object. There is a last combination which is actually the addition of two intersections. The result of the intersection on the subject of G1 and the subject or the object of G2 is equivalent to the sum of the intersections on the subject of G1 and G2, and on the subject of G1 and the object of G2.

Table 7. DMF definition of the composed intersection operator (cdmf:CompInterGraph operators)

```
Class(CompInterGraph)
Property(arg1)
Property(arg2)
Property(on1)
Property(on2)
arg1(?x,?y) → CdmfGraph(?y)
arg2(?x,?y) → CdmfGraph(?y)
on1(?x,?y) → Equal(?y,'Subject') ∧ Equal(?y,'Object')
on2(?x,?y) → Equal(?y,'Subject') ∧ Equal(?y,'Object')
```

The intersection operator cdmf:CompInterGraph has two properties cdmf:arg1 and cdmf:arg2 which are the two graphs on which the intersection is carried out. It has two additional properties cdmf:on1 and cdmf:on2 respectively defining the two parts of the triplets used to carry out the calculation of an intersection. Table 8 defines a composed intersection between the graphs G1 and G2 previously defined (e.g. Table 3).

Table 8. Script defining the composed intersection of two graphs, G1 (on subject part) and G2 (on object part)

```
:Gci2  rdf:cdmf type:CompInterGraph
:Gci2  cdmf:arg1:G2
:Gci2  cdmf:on1 'Object'
:Gci2  cdmf:arg2:G1
:Gci2  cdmf:on2 'Subject'
:Gic2  {        :e1 rdf:type  :Floor
                :b1 :contain  :e1}
```

Difference Operator. The difference between two graphs is indicated by the element cdmf:RemoveGraph. The result of the difference between G1 and G2 is the suppression of the set of the triplets of G2 in G1 (Table 9).

Table 9. DMF definition of the difference operator

```
Class(RemoveGraph)
Property(cdmf:src)
Property(cdmf:rem)
cdmf:src(?x,?y)→      RemoveGraph(?x)      ∧
CdmfGraph(?y)
cdmf:rem(?x,?y)→      RemoveGraph(?x)      ∧
CdmfGraph(?y)
```

The class cdmf:RemoveGraph has two properties cdmf:src and cdmf:rem. The second property constitutes the set of the triplets to be withdrawn from the graph indicated by the first argument.

Table 10. Script defining the difference between two graphs, G1 and G2.

```
:Gr1 rdf:cdmf    type:RemoveGraph
:Gr1 cdmf:src    :G1
:Gr1 cdmf:rem    :G2
:G1{      :b1 rdf:type  :Building
     :e1 rdf:type :Floor
     :b1 :contain :e1}
:G2{      :b1 rdf:type  :Building}
:Gr1{:e1 rdf:type        :Floor
     :b1 :contain:e1}
```

In this operation, only the identical triplets are a removed graph source.

Mapping Operator. The last type of operation on the graphs is the operation of mapping described by the element `cdmf:MapGraph`. A graph of mapping is a transformation of a graph into another graph using mapping rules;

Table 11. DMF definition of the mapping operator

```
Class(MapGraph)
Property(src)
Property(map)
src(?x,?y)→ MapGraph(?x)∧ CdmfGraph(?y)
```
```
map(?x,?y)→ MapGraph(?x)∧ CdmfGraph(?y)
```

The mapping operator has two properties `cdmf:src` and `cdmf:map` indicating the source graph and the target graph. The result of the operation of mapping is the set of the triplets which is defined by the rules of `Gmap`. A rule in `Gmap` is described by an operator of implication. All the triplets of `Gsrc` are transformed into triplets defined by the rules (Table 12 & 13).

Table 12. Script defining the mapping of graph *Gsrc* using the rules defined in a graph

```
:Gsrc{     :b1 rdf:type  :Building
           :e1 rdf:type  :Floor
           :b1 :contain  :e1}
:Gmap{Gsrc:Building(?x) → Gx:Building(?x)
      Gsrc:Floor(?x)→ Gx:BuildingStorey(?x)
      Gsrc:contain(?x,?y)→ Gx:relContains(?x)}
:Gmap1  rdf:cdmf   type:MapGraph
:Gmap1  cdmf:src          :Gsrc
:Gmap1  cdmf:map          :Gmap
```

In this part we have studied five operators which allow to carry out various combinations of graphs. These five operators are the union, the difference, the intersection (traditional and composed) and the mapping. They constitute the first part of the C stack. The second part of the C operators is the definition of a particular graph `SystemGraph`. This element associates various types of information with a graph. This element is used to represent contexts.

Table 13. Script presenting the result of the mapping of the graph G1 previously defined (Table 3)

```
:Gmap1{ Gsrc:b1 rdf:type
        Gmap:Building
          Gsrc:e1 rdf:type
        Gmap:BuildingStorey
          Gsrc:b1 Gx:relContains  Gsrc:e1}
```

3.4   Context Modeling, the Element SystemGraph

The element `cdmf:SystemGraph` uses the mechanism of Named Graphs to define the contexts with the help of the properties. The `SystemGraph` element associates with the graphs presented above all useful information which is needed to respond to the set of problems met in facility management. This element defines the nature of the graph, on which a graph data model is based. The element also defines the context of use and actions that can be realized on this graph.

`SystemGraph` evokes the data model on which the associated graph is built. A protégé description of the SystemGraph is depicted in figure 2.

For instance, the definition of building X is based on a data model that describes the composition of a building. The data model allows to check the data coherence of the associated graph and allows to indicate which kind of data can be generated in the graph. This data model is defined with the help of operators introduced in DMF. In fact, the `SystemGraph` defines actions that can be undertaken on the graph such as reading, writing or deleting. This can be done according to the actions which are authorized on the associated graph. The description of the context in `SystemGraph` is a list of RDF resources. This section presents the definition of `SystemGraph` with its properties: `cdmf:model`, `cdmf:of`, `cdmf:Action`, `cdmf:graph`. The name space cdmf is used to present these elements.

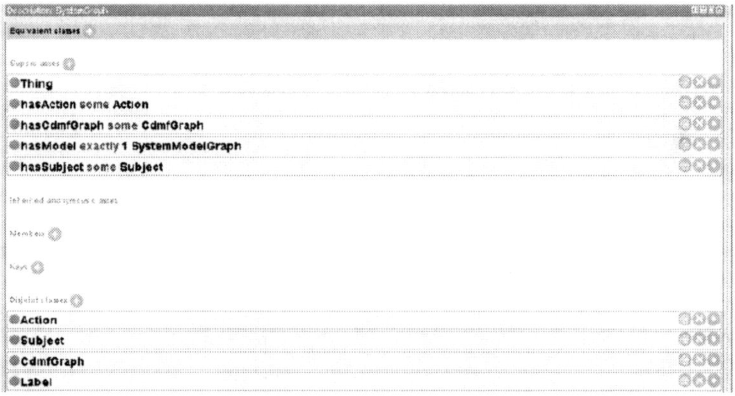

Fig. 2. Description of `SystemGraph` into Protégé

The property `cdmf:model` defines the model on which a `SystemGraph` element is based. The associated model will be used to define the objects and the properties which can be generated in the `SystemGraph` graph. Subsequently, it is possible to check the data coherency by comparing it to the model. `SystemGraph` has a model which is also a `SystemGraph`. CDMF defines a class `cdmf:SystemModel Graph` to represent a specific `SystemGraph`. This type of `SystemGraph` contains definitions of classes, properties and rules defined in the syntax DMF.

The Property `cdmf:of` defines the subject of the `SystemGraph` element. This property defines the context. It associates a set of RDF resources which resume what is described by the `SystemGraph`. For instance, `SystemGraph` can be the description of a data model in the building field. `SystemGraph` can be a data model in a certain version or `SystemGraph` can represent data on a certain date and in a certain language, for a certain user. It can also define the nature of the graph and the conditions that have to be fulfilled in order to be able to access a graph system.

The property `cdmf:Action` determines the actions authorized on the graph. It defines the actions of writing, suppression and modification. If no action is associated to the system, this implies that only the visualization of information is possible.

The element `cdmf:Action` determines which actions are possible, on which part of the data and starting from which model.

An action has one or two properties. If it has only one property add then the addition is allowed. If it has only one property remove then the system allows the deletion of data. If it has the two properties, we can add and remove data in the graph system. An element `cdmf:Add` defines which information we can add (`cdmf:model`) and where it has to be added (`cdmf:addIn`).

The Element `cdmf:Remove` indicates the suppressible data which have to be removed. If it does not have this property, all the data of the graph of the system can be deleted. The property `cdmf:From` binds an element of the `cdmf:From` type. According to the origin of the suppression (`cdmf:graph`), this element defines the action to be realized: either an addition in a `cdmf:RemoveGraph`, or a suppression in the graph `cdmf:graph`.

The property `cdmf:graph` contains the associated graph representing the data. The associated graph is a `cdmf:graph` type. `SystemGraph` has an attribute of the `cdmf:graph` type. Thus, `SystemGraph` can refer to all the types of graphs presented in CDMF.

4 Active3D Facility Server

This section presents the Active3D Facility Server, a web collaborative platform dedicated to the facility management, taking into account all aspects of the building's lifecycle. Due to the lack of space, we will illustrate only our proposal with two examples of use. The first example concerns the initialization of a space system when a facility manager needs to configure the platform. This extension is realized by defining a specific model. This model will be used in the building definition process. The second point illustrates the use of context to display specific information to users.

4.1 Configuration of a SpaceSystem

In facility management, various versions of the building can be managed and presented to different actors in many countries. The representation of a building mixes textual and graphic representations. The first step in facility management consists in creating the data model. A building description will be generated starting from this model. The new data model is created from a new applicative environment. An initial space system is created. The graphical representation is given in Fig. 2.

Following this step, the facility manager can store his data in the graph and has the possibility to create data starting from `SystemGraph 'Space System'`. The creation of `SystemGraph` includes a model, a context (list of resources) and the graph of data. For the model, the facility manager has to choose among the `SystemModelGraphs"` available. A `SytemModelGraph` element is a `SystemGraph` whose characteristic it is to contain models in its associated graph. A `SystemModelGraph` represents only a DMF model. For the context, the list of resources contains only one resource where the representation is 'Building Model'.

For the associated graph, the facility manager creates a new RDF graph which will contain the definition of the model. The result is presented in Fig. 2.For AEC projects, we have based our model definition on the IFC 2X3. This model contains approximately 600 classes [5, 11]. The following snapshot presents a part of the IFC model in the application. This model is created with the tools proposed by the application (creation of classes and properties).

Fig. 3 presents a snapshot of an IFC building. Each IFC object is represented in the Building Model by an operator `dmf:Class`. IFC links are represented by an operator `dmf:Property`. From this `SystemGraph`, we can declare classes, properties, rules, etc. In this example, we have created simply three classes which are `Building`, `Floor` and `Space` and a property `contain`.

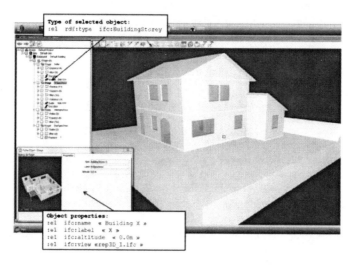

Fig. 3. An example of a 3D view of a building object in a Facility Management view using DMF operators

4.2   Context Representation

From the `SystemGraph` element, the facility manager defines a view on data according to a specific context. This context can be linked to a specific step in the building's lifecycle or it can be linked to a specific type of user (for example plumbers, architects or structure engineers). In the Active3D collaborative platform, this context is used to build user models that define data, operators and interface for a

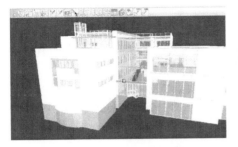 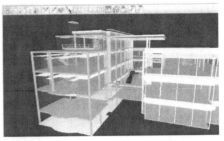

Fig. 4. Architectural view of a building. In this snapshot it is required to display the walls for the architect.

Fig. 5. Structural view of a building. This view is required for structure engineers. The corresponding graph provides all elements needed to make structure calculations.

specific user. Thus, during the identification protocol, when a user tries to connect himself to the platform, a specific graph is built and a view of a building is built according to its context. Figures 4 and 5 show two different views of the same building according to the Architect view and the Structure Engineering view respectively.

5 Conclusions

In this paper we have presented a Semantic Web approach for facility management. This approach allows facility managers to support the building's lifecycle management from the design to the destruction of the building in a collaborative context. Several actors provide and handle building information. This approach is based on a semantic model called CDMF and the IFC 2x3 standard which defines the 3D geometries of the objects of building. CDMF improves data management during the lifecycle of a building. Our proposition, based on graph combinations and the contextual element SystemGraph, addresses the problem of model evolution, of data mapping, of the management of temporal data, and of the adaptation of data according to the use and the user. Our framework facilitates data maintenance (data migration, model evolution) during the building lifecycle and reduces the volume of data. A collaborative Internet platform was developed to support the building's lifecycle. This platform is mainly used to federate all the actions realized on a building during its lifecycle, to merge all information related to these actions in an adaptive hypermedia graph, to extract some trade views of the building by combining information collected during the lifecycle from heterogeneous sources and to handle all these views through a dynamic and adaptive 3D interface. Currently, the Active3D platform supports more than 70 million square meters of building where more than 400 actors from all civil engineering domains collaborate at each step of the building's lifecycle. Semantic management of these millions of object requires some optimizations to reduce the data extraction time from semantic graphs. To meet these new challenges, we are working on a new semantic engine using based technique on the Model Checking. The objective will be the rapid extraction and verification of relevant semantic graphs in different contexts of use.

References

1. Klyne, G., Carroll, J.J.: Resource description Framework (RDF): Concepts and Abstract Syntax (2004), http://www.w3.org/TR/rdf-concepts/
2. McGuinness, D.L., Van Harmelen, F.: OWL Ontology Language: Overview (2004), http://www.w3.org/TR/owl-features/
3. Horrocks, I., Patel-Schneider, P.F., Boley, H., Tabet, S., Grosof, B., Dean, M.: SWRL: A Semantic Web rule Language: Combining OWL and RuleML (2004), http://www.w3.org/Submission/SWRL/
4. Carroll, J.J., Bizer, C., Hayes, P., Stickler, P.: Named Graph. Provenance and Trust (2005), http://www2005.org/cdrom/docs/p613.pdf
5. http://www.iai-international.org (2007)
6. Guha, R. V., Fikes, R.: Contexts for the semantic web. In: McIlraith, S.A., Plexousakis, D., van Harmelen, F. (eds.) ISWC 2004. LNCS, vol. 3298, pp. 32–46. Springer, Heidelberg (2004)
7. Guha, R.V.: Contexts: A Formalization and Some Applications. PhD thesis (1995)
8. McCarthy, P.: Introduction to Jena (2004), http://www-128.ibm.com/developerworks/java/library/j-jena/
9. Prud'hommeaux, E., Seaborne, A.: SPARQL Query Language for RDF (2005), http://www.w3.org/TR/rdf-sparql-query/
10. Bizer, C., Cyganiak, R.: NG4J Named Graph API for Jena (2005), http://sites.wiwiss.fu-berlin.de/suhl/bizer/ng4j/
11. IFC 2x3 Workshop, Boston, USA (March 19, 2007), http://127.0.0.1:4664/redir?url=http%3A%2F%Fbuildingsmart%2E com%2Eau%2F&src=1&schema=2&s=suabHoX9yEfSmitJzdEaD6NuyKQ
12. Cruz, I.F., Xiao, H., Hsu, F.: An Ontology-based Framework for Semantic Interoperability between XML Sources. In: Eighth International Database Engineering & Applications Symposium (July 2004)
13. Klein, M.: Interpreting XML via an RDF schema. In: ECAI workshop on Semantic Authoring, Annotation & Knowledge Markup, Lyon, France (2002)
14. Keith, A., Atkin, B., Bröchnet, J., Haugen, T.: Facilities Management, Innovation and Performance. Taylor and Francis Edition (2004) ISBN 0415321468
15. Barrett, P., Baldry, D.: Facilities Management, Towards Best Practice. Blackwell Publishing (2003) ISBN 0632064455
16. Lee, G., Sacks, R., Eastman Charles, M.: Specifying parametric building object behavior (BOB) for a building information modeling system, Automation in Construction. Knowledge Enabled Information System Applications in Construction, vol. 15(6), pp. 758–776. Elsevier, Amsterdam (2006)
17. NBIMS: National Building Information Modeling Stan-dard Part-1: Overview, Principles and Methodologies, US National Institute of Building Sciences Facilities Information Council, BIM Committee (2007), http://www.facilityinformationcouncil.org/bim/publications. php
18. NBIMS: National BIM Standard Purpose, US National Institute of Building Sciences Facilities Information Council, BIM Committee (2006), http://www.nibs.org/BIM/NBIMS_Purpose.pdf
19. Autodesk White Paper: Building Information Modelling (2002), http://images.autodesk.com/apac_sapac_main/files/4525081_BIM _WP_Rev5.pdf

20. Tolman, F.: Product modelling standards for the building and construction industry: past, present and future, Automation in Construction, 8th edn., pp. 227–235 (1999)
21. NIST CIS2 Web Site, Web Site (Available online at (2007), `http://cic.nist.gov/vrml/cis2.html`
22. Eastman, C., Wang, F., You, S.F., Yang, D.: Deployment of an AEC industry sector product modelo. Computer Aided Design 37(12), 1214–1228 (2005)
23. Zamanian, K.M., Pittman, J.H.: A software industry perspective on AEC information models for distributed collaboration, Automation in Construction, vol. 8(3), pp. 237–248 (1999)
24. SABLE Web Site, Web Site (Available online at (2005), `http://www.blis-project.org/sable/`
25. Cruz, C., Nicolle, C.: Active3D: Vector of Collaboration, Between Sharing and Data Exchange, INFOCOMP. Journal of Computer Science 5(3), 1–8 (2006)
26. Campbell., D.A.: Building Information Modeling: The Web3D Application for AEC. In: ACM Web3D, Perugia, Italy (2007)
27. Vanlande, R., Nicolle, C., Cruz, C.: IFC and Buildings Lifecycle Management. Journal of Automation in Construction (2008)

Service Reliability Assessment in a Composition Environment

Abhishek Srivastava and Paul G. Sorenson

Department of Computing Science, University of Alberta, Edmonton, Canada
{sr16,paul.sorenson}@ualberta.ca

Abstract. A service composition environment is one where a service interacts
with other services to form a composite application. In such an environment, the
reliability of an individual service is influenced by the reliability figures of the services it interacts with. Reliability measuring procedures in the past tend to ignore
this influence and calculate the individual reliabilities of services in isolation. In
this work, we present a technique which allows us to calculate the reliability of
a service incorporating the influence of the interacting services. This is done by
representing the entire service domain as a continuous time Markov chain and
finding the 'failure distance' of each service. The failure distance of a service is
an expression of its reliability. The proposed technique is validated by running
experiments in a simulated environment wherein services are randomly made to
fail and service compositions are formed based on reliability figures of individual
services. It is shown that the compositions formed utilizing the proposed technique are much more reliable than those formed with service reliability being
calculated in isolation.

1 Introduction

The world today is undergoing an economic revolution wherein service dominated
economies are fast replacing product based manufacturing economies [1][2]. Organizations, in such a scenario, are more inclined towards offering functionalities as services
rather than complete end-products, which the clients may harness according to their
customized respective requirements. The extensive penetration of the 'internet' in the
daily lives of people figures prominently in the acceptance and adoption of the service-
oriented model. Service vendors readily make use of this medium, and conveniently
offer their expertise as web-based services.

Services render further flexibility to vendors and customers alike by being formed
into compositions to cater to larger and more complex functionalities. The same service
is combined with various other services in different contexts to form different composite
applications. This effectively enhances reusability of the services and ensures a much
larger degree of choice to the customers with the same resources.

There are several issues however that accompany service composition such as: governance [3], service selection [4], reliability etc. We dwell upon the issue of reliability
in this paper. Ensuring a service composition that maintains a high level of reliability is
non-trivial. The selection of appropriate services for the composition with high values
of individual reliability figures is therefore crucial.

J. Filipe and J. Cordeiro (Eds.): WEBIST 2010, LNBIP 75, pp. 30–45, 2011.

Existing techniques of service composition calculate the reliabilities of the individual services in isolation. Subsequently high reliability value services are combined to form high reliability compositions. Such techniques however assume that the individual reliabilities of services are in no way influenced by the reliability values of the interacting services. This we feel in not an accurate assumption.

In this paper, we propose a novel technique that calculates the reliability of individual services taking into account the influence that the presence of other services in the domain, particularly the services that they directly invoke, have on them. By this, we mean the varying degrees of coupling that services have on each other in an interactive environment lends its influence on the reliability figures of individual services. Suppose for example two services A and B are provided by the same organization and thus A invokes B much more than another service offering the same functionality as B (thus A and B have a high value of coupling). Further suppose that B is a highly unreliable service. As A uses B so often, it would appear to A's parent that A is quite unreliabile. The reliability of services in an environment in which the influence of interacting services is taken into account forms the basis of the technique proposed in this paper. Previous methods tend to ignore this influence and calculate reliability by treating the individual services in isolation [16] [17] [19] [18].

The remainder of this paper is structured as follows. Section 2 is a discussion on relevant related work done in the past. Section 3 is a discussion on how the service domain is represented in our work. Subsequently, the representation of this service domain as a continuous time Markov chain (CTMC) [11](the CTMC representation is a requirement for the proposed technique) is also discussed in the same section. Section 4 comprises a detailed description of the use of the CTMC representation to express how 'close' or 'far' each individual service is from the 'fail' state taking into account its interactions with other services in the domain. Section 5 describes the experiments conducted by us and the results of the same, that validate the technique, and finally Section 6 concludes the paper with pointers at future work.

2   Related Work

Substantial research has been done in the past on the issue of computing the reliability of a composite application on the basis of the individual reliability of its constituent services. The technique discussed by Yu *et al.* is for QoS in general and reliability is one among a number of parameters [16]. Their approach is quite basic. They assume that the reliability values of individual services are given and the reliability of the composite application is simply the product of the reliabilities of individual constituent services. Tsai *et al.* present a method of first calculating the reliability of individual services using a technique called 'group testing' [17]. In this technique, the service in question is put through the same test as a number of other functionally equivalent services of known reliabilities. The other services are assigned appropriate weights on the basis of their reliability values. Depending on how close or far the result of the service in question is from that of the other services, the service is assigned a weight which is an approximate reflection of its reliability. Next, using the reliability of individual services so calculated, the reliability of the composite application is calculated using one of various simple formulae depending upon how the individual services are connected in the application: as a 'sequence', 'choice', 'loop' or 'concurrently'. Zeng *et al.*, in their approach represent the various possible composite applications as a directed acyclic graph (DAG) [18]. In this DAG, they find a 'critical path'. The reliability of the composite application is a product of $e^{rel(s_i)*z_i}$ where $rel(s_i)$ is the reliability of service i and $z_i = 1$ if service i falls in the critical path, and $z_i = 0$ otherwise. The reliabilities of individual services are calculated using historical data as the ratio of successful service delivery to total number of invocations. Wang *et al.* present an interesting technique for calculating the reliability of the service composition [19]. Their method assumes that the transition behaviour of the system from one service to another follows the Markov process [11]. They express a 'reliable' transfer from each service to every other service in the form of a matrix. The reliability of a service composition is expressed by raising this matrix to a power that is equal to the number of transition steps required to move from the initial service to the final service of the composition. Subsequently, the matrix is raised to all possible powers from 0 to ∞, representing all possible service compositions and the summation of this geometric progression gives the reliability of the composition. More recently Epifani *et al.* present a dynamic modeling technique wherein Bayesian estimation techniques are used to dynamically revise the non-functional attributes of the constituent services of a composite application [24]. The posterior distribution of non-functional attributes such as reliability are determined on the basis of prior distribution and a better service composition is achieved.

All these methods, while being relevant suffer from the assumption that the reliability of individual services in a service domain is calculated in isolation. We feel that in an environment like this where services interact in a complementary manner to form composite applications, a certain degree of 'coupling' among services does exist. This coupling may arise out of business relationships, better 'inter usage' capability, or other miscellaneous factors. In our work, we assign a value to the coupling between interacting services. The higher this value, the greater is the coupling. The reliability calculation of individual services is therefore done incorporating these coupling values. Subsequently, the services with the best individual values of reliability, so calculated, collectively contribute to the best reliability value for the composite application.

3   Service Domain Representation

In this work, we look at the service domain as a group of services which are assumed to have been already discovered. A set of services from this domain need to be selected and loosely 'chained' together to form a composite application. A common example of a composite application is a 'trip planner' whose goal is to plan a trip for prospective clients. The constituent services in this case may be: a) a flight reservation service, b) a hotel booking service, c) a payment processing service, etc.

The representation of the service domain in our work has been done as a *multi-tier acyclic graph*, where each tier represents a certain functionality and is populated by the set of simple services that possess the capability to perform the respective functionality. The size of this set is dynamic in nature and is characterized by frequent entry of new service instances, as well as upgrade and departure of existing ones. The left panel of Figure 1 shows a simple representation of this. Services B, C, that are at the same

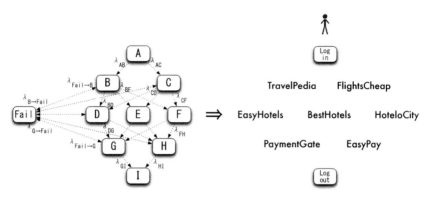

Fig. 1. The service domain

level, represent functionally equivalent services. The same holds for services D, E, F, as well as G, H. The work-flow is from top to bottom, never from bottom to top and hence there are no cycles. Thus a service at a certain level 'invokes' one of the services at the level immediately below it, and subsequently this invoked service invokes one of the services from the next level, and so on. In this way, a composite application gets formed. It should be noted that a service invokes one at the lower level only *after* it has completed executing its own task. An example of this service domain representation (the 'trip-planner' example) is shown on the right panel of Figure 1.

A variable called 'coupling', as mentioned earlier, is assigned between each service at a certain level to each and every service at the next immediate level. The coupling C_{ij}, depends upon factors such as business relationships between the providers of services i, and j, degree of ease in inter usage between the two services, and other miscellaneous factors. A high value of C_{ij} indicates a high degree of coupling between i, and j. For example, assuming the services in our trip-planner example, 'TravelPedia' and 'HoteloCity' are provided by the same parent organization. It is expected therefore that there is a high value of coupling between the two. The value of coupling between services ranges from 1 to ∞. A value of 1 indicates ordinary interaction with no special bonding between the services, whereas higher values indicate better bonding. The coupling values are assigned when a service enters a domain, on the basis of expert judgement after a thorough investigation of its nature and interactions.

For each service in the domain, there is a service completion rate which is the rate at which the respective service completes the requests. The service completion rate of service i, μ_i may be calculated as follows:

$$\mu_i = \frac{no.\ of\ service\ requests\ completed\ by\ service\ i}{total\ time} \qquad (1)$$

Subsequently, a transition rate (λ_{ij}) between a calling service i, and the called service j is calculated as:

$$\lambda_{ij} = C_{ij} \cdot \mu_i \qquad (2)$$

where C_{ij} is the coupling between services i, and j, and μ_i is the service completion rate of service i. The transition rates are indicated by dotted arrows between services in the left panel of Figure 1.

Besides these transition rate values, there is a 'failure rate' ($\lambda_{i \to fail}$) from each service i in the domain to the 'fail' state. The independent failure rate of each service i is expressed as follows:

$$\lambda_{i \to fail} = \frac{no.\ of\ times\ service\ i\ fails}{total\ up\text{-}time} \tag{3}$$

There is correspondingly a 'recovery rate' ($\lambda_{fail \to i}$) from the fail state to each service i in the domain. The recovery rate is calculated as follows:

$$\lambda_{fail \to i} = \frac{no.\ of\ times\ service\ i\ recovers\ from\ failure}{total\ down\text{-}time} \tag{4}$$

The 'invoking' behavior of services at each level in the domain is assumed to be unaffected by the service selections prior to it in the domain, $i.e.$ by the service selections at the function levels above it. The service domain is thus represented as a Continuous Time Markov Chain (CTMC) [11]. This is done by first representing the service domain as a $Stochastic\ Petri\text{-}Net$ [12], and then converting the same to the equivalent CTMC representation. A detailed description of the conversion of the representation of a system to its equivalent CTMC representation is given in [13]. Owing to the simplicity of our service domain representation, there is an almost one-to-one correspondence between our representation and the CTMC representation. Each service in our representation corresponds to a 'state' in the CTMC representation. In addition to the service states, there is a 'fail' state which represents the state of failure of any of the services.

The motive behind representing the service domain as a CTMC is to take advantage of the various analysis procedures meant for the latter, and in effect to come up with useful results regarding the reliability of the system.

The transition rates between states in the CTMC are expressed in the form of a matrix called the $infinitesimal\ generator\ matrix$ (IGM). The value of the ij^{th} element of this matrix is equal to the value of the rate of transition from the ith state to the jth state of the CTMC. The sum of the elements in each row of this matrix is always zero. Therefore the ii^{th} element in each row is the negative of the summation of the other elements in the row.

The transition rates in the case of our service domain are the transition-rate values between services that are calculated using equation (2), and the transition-rate values between the services and the 'fail' state that are calculated using equations (3) and (4). The infinitesimal generator matrix for our trip-planner example whose coupling values between services and service completion rate values are tabulated respectively in Figures 2 (a) and 2 (b) is shown in Figure 3.

For example, the transition rate value from service $BestHotels$ to $EasyPay$ is calculated using equation (2) as follows (shown in bold in the matrix):

$$\lambda = Coupling_{BestHotels\text{-}EasyPay} * Completion\text{-}rate_{BestHotels}$$
$$= 1.9 * 3.2 = 6.08$$

	Log in/out	TravelPedia	FlightsCheap	EasyHotels	BestHotels	HoteloCity	PaymentGate	EasyPay
Log in/out	--	1.0	1.0	--	--	--	--	--
TravelPedia	--	--	--	1.4	1.7	1.5	--	--
FlightsCheap	--	--	--	1.1	2.1	1.9	--	--
EasyHotels	--	--	--	--	--	--	1.4	2.7
BestHotels	--	--	--	--	--	--	2.2	1.9
HoteloCity	--	--	--	--	--	--	1.2	1.7
PaymentGate	1.0	--	--	--	--	--	--	--
EasyPay	1.0	--	--	--	--	--	--	--

	Failure rate	Recovery rate	Completion rate
Log in/Log out	--	--	1.0
TravelPedia	0.2	0.7	1.7
FlightsCheap	0.08	0.5	2.4
EasyHotels	0.05	0.009	1.4
BestHotels	0.3	0.002	3.2
HoteloCity	0.08	1.1	1.8
PaymentGate	0.2	0.06	0.8
EasyPay	0.3	0.7	1.4

(a)   (b)

Fig. 2. (a) Coupling values, (b) Initial failure, recovery, and service completion rate values

$$
IGM = \begin{bmatrix}
-2.0 & 1.0 & 1.0 & 0 & 0 & 0 & 0 & 0 & 0 \\
0 & -8.02 & 0 & 2.38 & 2.89 & 2.55 & 0 & 0 & 0.2 \\
0 & 0 & -12.32 & 2.64 & 5.04 & 4.56 & 0 & 0 & 0.08 \\
0 & 0 & 0 & -5.79 & 0 & 0 & 1.96 & 3.78 & 0.05 \\
0 & 0 & 0 & 0 & -13.42 & 0 & 7.04 & \mathbf{6.08} & 0.3 \\
0 & 0 & 0 & 0 & 0 & -5.3 & 2.16 & 3.06 & 0.08 \\
0.8 & 0 & 0 & 0 & 0 & 0 & -1.0 & 0 & 0.2 \\
1.4 & 0 & 0 & 0 & 0 & 0 & 0 & -1.7 & 0.3 \\
0 & 0.7 & 0.5 & 0.009 & 0.002 & 1.1 & 0.06 & 0.7 & -3.071
\end{bmatrix}
$$

Fig. 3. Infinitesimal Generator Matrix

The last column and row ($9th$ from left and top) of the infinitesimal generator matrix correspond to the fail state, and its elements are simply obtained from the table in Figure 2 (b) as the initial failure and recovery rate values respectively of each service.

A number of analysis techniques require that the transition values between the different states of a CTMC be expressed as a probability. To take advantage of these techniques, an approximate transition probability matrix is obtained from the infinitesimal generator matrix, which is called the *embedded Markov chain matrix*. Each ij^{th} element of this matrix is obtained as the ratio of the corresponding element of the infinitesimal generator matrix to the sum of all the elements except the ii^{th} element in the corresponding row of the infinitesimal generator matrix. The ii^{th} element of the embedded Markov chain matrix is always zero. The embedded Markov chain matrix P for our trip-planner example corresponding to the infinitesimal generator matrix is shown in Figure 4.

As an example, the element in the embedded Markov chain matrix corresponding to the element in bold in the IGM is calculated as follows:

$$
P = \frac{6.08}{7.04 + 6.08 + 0.3} = 0.453
$$

$$P = \begin{bmatrix} 0 & 0.5 & 0.5 & 0 & 0 & 0 & 0 & 0 & 0 \\ 0 & 0 & 0 & 0.297 & 0.36 & 0.318 & 0 & 0 & 0.025 \\ 0 & 0 & 0 & 0.214 & 0.409 & 0.37 & 0 & 0 & 0.007 \\ 0 & 0 & 0 & 0 & 0 & 0 & 0.339 & 0.653 & 0.008 \\ 0 & 0 & 0 & 0 & 0 & 0 & 0.525 & 0.453 & 0.022 \\ 0 & 0 & 0 & 0 & 0 & 0 & 0.408 & 0.577 & 0.015 \\ 0.8 & 0 & 0 & 0 & 0 & 0 & 0 & 0 & 0.2 \\ 0.824 & 0 & 0 & 0 & 0 & 0 & 0 & 0 & 0.176 \\ 0 & 0.228 & 0.163 & 0.003 & 0.001 & 0.357 & 0.02 & 0.228 & 0 \end{bmatrix}$$

Fig. 4. Embedded Markov Chain Matrix

4 Reliability in Terms of 'Failure Distance'

The CTMC representation of the service domain is utilized to calculate the reliability values. More precisely, the CTMC representation is used to find the 'failure distance' of individual services, and this failure distance is regarded as an expression of reliability. The larger the failure distance of a service, the higher is its reliability.

It is worthwhile to mention at this point that the failure distance of a service is measured as the 'number of transitions' that the system needs to go through before converging to the 'fail' state, given that it starts at the service in question. The larger the number of transitions, the larger the failure distance. This is further elaborated upon, in the subsequent portion.

The CTMC representation of the service domain which is used to calculate the failure distance includes the infinitesimal generator matrix (shown in Figure 3 for our example) which consists of the transition rate values between every pair of 'invoking' and 'invoked' services in the domain. Another important component of the CTMC representation is the *probability vector*. The elements in the probability vector correspond to the various states of the CTMC representation. Each element in the vector represents the probability that the system exists in the corresponding state at a certain stage. Thus initially, when number of transitions, $t = 0$, the probability vector may be represented as π_0, where

$$\pi_0 = \{p_1^0, p_2^0, p_3^0, \ldots, p_n^0\} \tag{5}$$

$p_i^0 (i = 1, 2, \ldots, n)$ are the values representing the probability that the system initially is in state i. Furthermore, after the first transition, $t = 1$,

$$\pi_1 = \pi_0 \cdot P \tag{6}$$

where P is the embedded Markov chain matrix (shown in Figure 4 for our example). As mentioned earlier, the embedded Markov chain matrix (P) consists of the transition probability values from each state in the system to every other state. It is analogous to the transition probability matrix of a discrete time Markov chain [11].

Thus, if we continue multiplying the probability vector with the embedded Markov chain matrix P, we eventually arrive at a probability vector, π_s, which remains constant, *i.e.* it does not change with further multiplication with P.

$$\pi_1 = \pi_0 \cdot P \Rightarrow \pi_2 = \pi_1 \cdot P \Rightarrow \cdots \pi_s = \pi_s \cdot P \tag{7}$$

π_s is called the *equilibrium probability vector*. Each element in this vector represents the probability of the system being in the corresponding state at equilibrium.

We now show that the equilibrium probability vector is the same as the left-hand eigenvector of matrix P corresponding to the unit eigenvalue [20]. If e_i^T is the left-hand eigenvector of a matrix P corresponding to the eigenvalue λ_i, then we know that

$$\lambda_i \cdot e_i^T = e_i^T \cdot P \tag{8}$$

when $\lambda_i = 1$, *i.e.* the unit eigenvalue, then

$$e_i^T = e_i^T \cdot P \tag{9}$$

Observing equations (7) and (9) together,

$$e_i^T = e_i^T \cdot P \Leftrightarrow \pi_s = \pi_s \cdot P \Rightarrow e_i^T = \pi_s$$

The equilibrium probability vector is thus easily calculated as the left hand eigenvector (normalized to sum to 1) corresponding to the unit eigenvalue, of the embedded Markov chain matrix of the CTMC representation of any service domain. The equilibrium probability vector for our trip-planner example is shown below:

$$[0.2092, 0.1173, 0.1137, 0.0593, 0.0888, 0.0991, \ldots$$

$$\ldots 0.1083, 0.1488, \mathbf{0.0555}] \tag{10}$$

Of the elements of this equilibrium probability vector, the one corresponding to the 'fail' state (shown in bold) of the CTMC representation, gives the probability of the system being in the fail state at equilibrium. If the probability of the system being in the fail state at equilibrium is high, we conclude that the service that is far from equilibrium is also far from the fail state, and vice-versa. Therefore, if we somehow find a way of calculating the distance of a service from equilibrium, it would also give us an estimate of its distance from failure. Thus the problem of finding the distance of a service from failure is translated to that of finding the distance of the service from equilibrium.

We utilize the method put forward by William J. Stewart to calculate the distance of the service from equilibrium at the various stages of service selection [21]. The method is explained as follows.

Let x_1^0 represent the probability vector that models a system that has a 100% probability of being in state 1 initially when the number of transitions $t = 0$,

$$x_1^0 = \{1, 0, 0, \ldots, 0\} \tag{11}$$

similarly,

$$x_2^0 = \{0, 1, 0, \ldots, 0\} \tag{12}$$

and in general,

$$x_i^0 = \{0, 0, 0, \ldots, 0, 1, 0, \ldots, 0\} \tag{13}$$

Let the left-hand eigenvectors of matrix P be

$$\{e_1^T, e_2^T, \ldots, e_n^T\}$$

corresponding respectively to the eigenvalues,

$$\{\lambda_1, \lambda_2, \ldots, \lambda_n\}$$

Since x_i^0 in equation (13) is a row vector, it may be expressed as a linear combination of other row vectors. Thus,

$$x_i^0 = c_{i1} \cdot e_1^T + c_{i2} \cdot e_2^T + \ldots + c_{in} \cdot e_n^T \tag{14}$$

where $c_{ij}(j = 1, 2, \ldots, n)$ are currently unknown constants whose values and significance will subsequently be discussed.

Just like π_1 was computed in equation (6), x_i^1 which is the probability vector after the first transition $t = 1$ given that the system starts (at $t = 0$) with a 100% probability of being in state i, is also computed as,

$$\text{equation (6): } \pi_1 = \pi_0 \cdot P \Rightarrow x_i^1 = x_i^0 \cdot P$$

Thus, from equation (14), it follows that,

$$x_i^1 = x_i^0 \cdot P = c_{i1} \cdot e_1^T \cdot P + c_{i2} \cdot e_2^T \cdot P + \ldots + c_{in} \cdot e_n^T \cdot P \tag{15}$$

Using equation (8): $\lambda_i \cdot e_i^T = e_i^T \cdot P$, we get,

$$x_i^1 = c_{i1} \cdot \lambda_1 \cdot e_1^T + c_{i2} \cdot \lambda_2 \cdot e_2^T + \ldots + c_{in} \cdot \lambda_n \cdot e_n^T \tag{16}$$

Similarly, we get x_i^2 as,

$$
\begin{aligned}
x_i^2 &= x_i^1 \cdot P \\
&= c_{i1} \cdot \lambda_1 \cdot e_1^T \cdot P + c_{i2} \cdot \lambda_2 \cdot e_2^T \cdot P + \ldots + c_{in} \cdot \lambda_n \cdot e_n^T \cdot P \\
&= c_{i1} \cdot \lambda_1^2 \cdot e_1^T + c_{i2} \cdot \lambda_2^2 \cdot e_2^T + \ldots + c_{in} \cdot \lambda_n^2 \cdot e_n^T
\end{aligned}
$$

Thus, after a certain number of transitions, the vector x_i eventually converges to the equilibrium probability vector. Say after k steps,

$$x_i^k = c_{i1} \cdot \lambda_1^k \cdot e_1^T + c_{i2} \cdot \lambda_2^k \cdot e_2^T + \ldots + c_{in} \cdot \lambda_n^k \cdot e_n^T \tag{17}$$

Now similarly, let x_j^0 represent the probability vector such that the system is 100% surely in state j initially when the number of transitions $t = 0$. Thus,

$$x_j^0 = \{0, 0, 0, \ldots, 0, 1, 0, \ldots, 0\}$$

Just like x_i^0 in equation (14), x_j^0 is also expressed as a linear combination of the left hand eigenvectors of P,

$$x_j^0 = c_{j1} \cdot e_1^T + c_{j2} \cdot e_2^T + \ldots + c_{jn} \cdot e_n^T$$

Similarly,

$$
\begin{aligned}
x_j^1 &= c_{j1} \cdot e_1^T \cdot P + c_{j2} \cdot e_2^T \cdot P + \ldots + c_{jn} \cdot e_n^T \cdot P \\
&= c_{j1} \cdot \lambda_1 \cdot e_1^T + c_{j2} \cdot \lambda_2 \cdot e_2^T + \ldots + c_{jn} \cdot \lambda_n \cdot e_n^T
\end{aligned}
$$

and after k steps,

$$x_j^k = c_{j1} \cdot \lambda_1^k \cdot e_1^T + c_{j2} \cdot \lambda_2^k \cdot e_2^T + \ldots + c_{jn} \cdot \lambda_n^k \cdot e_n^T \tag{18}$$

Observing equations (17) and (18) together, the only difference between the two equations are the constants c_{il}, and c_{jl} where $l = 1, 2, \ldots, n$. In other words, the difference in the state of the system after k transition steps, when the starting state was state i, and when the starting state was state j, is represented by the difference in the values of the constants c_{il}, and c_{jl}, where $l = 1, 2, \ldots, n$. The values of c_{il}, and c_{jl}, $(l = 1, 2, \ldots, n)$ therefore hold the key to finding the difference in the distance (in terms of number of transition steps) of state i, and state j from any other state of the system. Thus, these constants also reflect the difference in distance of the two states from the equilibrium state.

To calculate the values of $c_{1l}, c_{2l}, c_{3l}, \ldots, c_{nl}$, where $l = 1, 2, \ldots, n$, we make the following observations. We know that,

$$x_1^0 = \{1, 0, 0, \ldots, 0\}$$
$$x_2^0 = \{0, 1, 0, \ldots, 0\}$$
$$\vdots$$
$$x_n^0 = \{0, 0, 0, \ldots, 1\}$$

Writing this in matrix form,

$$X = \begin{bmatrix} 1 & 0 & 0 & \ldots & 0 \\ 0 & 1 & 0 & \ldots & 0 \\ 0 & 0 & 1 & \ldots & 0 \\ \vdots & \vdots & \vdots & \ddots & \vdots \\ 0 & 0 & 0 & \ldots & 1 \end{bmatrix} = \text{Identity Matrix} \tag{19}$$

We also know that,

$$x_1^0 = c_{11} \cdot e_1^T + c_{12} \cdot e_2^T + \ldots + c_{1n} \cdot e_n^T$$
$$x_2^0 = c_{21} \cdot e_1^T + c_{22} \cdot e_2^T + \ldots + c_{2n} \cdot e_n^T$$
$$\vdots$$
$$x_n^0 = c_{n1} \cdot e_1^T + c_{n2} \cdot e_2^T + \ldots + c_{nn} \cdot e_n^T$$

Writing this in matrix form as well,

$$\begin{bmatrix} x_1^0 \\ x_2^0 \\ x_3^0 \\ \vdots \\ x_n^0 \end{bmatrix} = \begin{bmatrix} c_{11} & c_{12} & c_{13} & \ldots & c_{1n} \\ c_{21} & c_{22} & c_{23} & \ldots & c_{2n} \\ c_{31} & c_{32} & c_{33} & \ldots & c_{3n} \\ \vdots & \vdots & \vdots & \ddots & \vdots \\ c_{n1} & c_{n2} & c_{n3} & \ldots & c_{nn} \end{bmatrix} \begin{bmatrix} e_1^T \\ e_2^T \\ e_3^T \\ \vdots \\ e_n^T \end{bmatrix} \tag{20}$$

Therefore,

$$X = CE^T$$

From equation (19), we know that X is the identity matrix (I), therefore,

$$I = CE^T \Rightarrow C = \frac{I}{E^T} = (E^T)^{-1}$$

$(E^T)^{-1}$ is the matrix of the right-hand eigenvectors of matrix P. The values of the constants c_{ij}, which are capable of determining the distance of the various states from equilibrium, are thus easily computed as the right-hand eigenvectors of matrix P. Of these right-hand eigenvectors, the sub-dominant eigenvector gives the *best* estimate of the distance of each state from equilibrium [21]. The sub-dominant eigenvector for our trip-planner example is shown below:

$$[0.3749, 0.3566, 0.3606, 0.3513, \mathbf{0.3435}, 0.3476, \ldots$$

$$\ldots 0.3352, 0.3420, 0.1038] \tag{21}$$

Translating these results to the service domain, we are in a position to calculate via the CTMC representation of the domain, the 'distance' of each service from equilibrium.

The important point here, however, is that the distance that needs to be calculated is the failure distance and not necessarily the equilibrium distance. A clear understanding of the relationship between the failure state and the equilibrium state needs to be established. We attempt to do this through a simple example.

Suppose, the failure probability at equilibrium is very high (say 0.9). This means that the probability that the system at equilibrium is in the fail state is 0.9. This is represented by the element corresponding to the fail state in the equilibrium probability vector π_s of equation (7). In such a scenario, the larger the distance of a service from equilibrium, the larger the failure distance and hence higher its reliability. Conversely, suppose the failure probability at equilibrium is a small value (*e.g.* 0.2). In this case, the smaller the distance of a service from equilibrium, higher its reliability. In general, if the failure probability at equilibrium is greater than 0.5, a larger distance from equilibrium reflects higher reliability and vice-versa for a failure probability smaller than 0.5. The failure distance of a service is calculated using the formula in equation (22).

$$Failure\ Distance = \frac{1}{\lambda_{i \to Fail} * c_{i2}^{10 \cdot (0.5 - \pi_s(Fail))}} \tag{22}$$

c_{i2} is the magnitude of the ith element of the subdominant right-hand eigenvector of the embedded Markov chain matrix (P) of the CTMC representation of the service domain. The magnitude of the sub-dominant eigenvector gives the *best* estimate of the distance of the ith state from equilibrium, as mentioned earlier [21]. The larger the value of c_{i2}, the larger the distance of the ith state from equilibrium. Therefore in equation (22), as long as the failure probability is less than 0.5, the factor $c_{i2}^{10 \cdot (0.5 - \pi_s(Fail))}$ is in the denominator of the expression (since $(0.5 - \pi_s(Fail))$ is a positive value). Thus, a larger value of c_{i2} (which expresses a larger distance from equilibrium) results in a smaller value of failure distance. Also, the smaller the value of $\pi_s(Fail)$, the higher the power to which the c_{i2} gets raised and hence the failure distance becomes smaller. The opposite holds whenever $\pi_s(Fail)$ is greater than 0.5. When the failure probability at equilibrium is exactly 0.5, the factor $c_{i2}^{10\cdot(0.5-\pi_s(Fail))}$ becomes equal to 1 and the failure distance depends only on the current value of the factor $\lambda_{i\rightarrow Fail}$. The failure distance values calculated for the services in our trip-planner example are: $TravelPedia \rightarrow$ 489.24 ; $FlightsCheap \rightarrow$ 1163.94 ; $EasyHotels \rightarrow$ 2091.66 ; $BestHotels \rightarrow$ 385.19; $HoteloCity \rightarrow$ 1370.28 ; $PaymentGate \rightarrow$ 644.16 ; and $EasyPay \rightarrow$ 392.76 . The calculation of failure-distance for $BestHotels$ is shown below:

$$Failure\ Distance_{BestHotels} = \frac{1}{0.3 * 0.3435^{10\cdot(0.5-0.0555)}}$$
$$= 385.19$$

The failure distance values so calculated take into account the interactions between the services. This is achieved owing to the fact that the transition rate values between the services in the CTMC representation have been considered in the calculation.

5   Experimental Validation

In this section, we attempt to experimentally validate the technique proposed in this paper to calculate the individual reliabilities of services in a domain taking into account the influence of interacting services. To do this, experiments were conducted on a service domain with 29 services (excluding the first and the last) spread over 6 levels of functionality. Seven different sets of initial fail-rate and coupling values were experimented with. The experimental domain is shown in Figure 5.

Simulations were run on the experimental domain, wherein services were allowed to fail randomly at their respective fail-rate values. 10,000 simulation runs were conducted, where each run comprised a failure being forced at each functionality level. Every time that a service failed, its own fail-rate was increased marginally (we could have recomputed the fail-rate value following equation (3) with the same effect; in the interest of simplicity we increased the fail-rate marginally), and so was the fail-rate of the services in the functionality level immediately above it. The increase in fail-rate of the parent services was proportional to the value of coupling between them and the failing service. Therefore, a service that had a stronger coupling with the failing service suffered a larger increase in its fail rate. This was done in conformance with the general belief that the reliability value of a service influences the reliability of the interacting services, particularly the ones that invoke it.

A number of simulation scenarios were observed. However, only the two main ones have been discussed here. The first simulation scenario was the static scenario, wherein services were allowed to fail, their fail-rates on failing were increased, and they were allowed to fail again. The fail-rate of services were allowed to rise indefinitely. The second scenario was a more dynamic scenario, wherein services were allowed to fail, and their fail-rates were increased on failing as in the static case. However, once the fail-rate of a service exceeded a certain maximum, the service was taken-out for 'repair' and brought in after a few runs with its fail-rate reinstated to its original value.

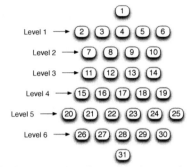

Fig. 5. Service domain used in the experiments

The motive behind this simulation exercise was to get an idea of the possible system behaviour if it were observed for a very long period of time (one in which 10, 000 failures occurred at each functionality level). The number of failures for each service returned by the simulation formed the basis for the validation of our proposed technique against the existing techniques for reliability assessment in an interactive environment.

The proposed technique, described in previous sections, involved the representation of the service domain in its equivalent CTMC form, putting together the 'infinitesimal generator matrix' (shown in Figure 3 for the trip-planner example) of this CTMC, calculating the 'embedded Markov chain matrix' (shown in Figure 4 for the trip-planner example), and subsequently finding the left-hand eigenvector (corresponding to the unit eigenvalue) which is the equilibrium probability vector of the system (shown in equation (10)) and the subdominant right-hand eigenvector of this matrix. Finally the equilibrium probability vector and the subdominant right-hand eigenvector were used to calculate the 'failure distance' of each service in the domain using equation (22). The service selected for composition at each functionality level was the one with the *largest* value of failure distance at that level. This service was considered to be furthest from the 'fail' state and thus the most reliable.

The existing techniques as discussed in the 'related work' section (section 2) are varied. However, in terms of calculating the individual reliabilities of services, all of them are similar in that they all calculated the individual reliabilities of the services in isolation. That is to say that they assume that the reliabilities of individual services in the domain are unaffected by their interaction with other services in the domain. Therefore, to replicate the existing techniques in this domain, the initial fail-rate values of the services were utilized, and at each level the service which had the *smallest* fail-rate value at that level was selected.

The sequence followed in the experiments for the static scenario is now described. The proposed technique and existing techniques were first applied on the experimental domain. These gave the set of services selected at each level. The simulation, was next run for 10, 000 iterations each. Each iteration comprised the occurrence of 1 failure at each functionality level. The failing services on each iteration were compared with the services selected by the two techniques (proposed and existing). If any of the selected services by a selection technique happened to fail in an iteration of the simulation, the

Static scenario			
	Existing techniques		Proposed technique	
	Failures	Reliability	Failures	Reliability
Domain 1	6,050/10,000	39.5%	1,408/10,000	85.92%
Domain 2	8,765/10,000	12.35%	712/10,000	92.88%
Domain 3	9,008/10,000	9.92%	16/10,000	99.84%
Domain 4	9,844/10,000	1.56%	526/10,000	94.74%
Domain 5	9,778/10,000	2.22%	521/10,000	94.79%
Domain 6	6,490/10,000	35.1%	4,236/10,000	57.64%
Domain 7	9,983/10,000	1.7%	170/10,000	98.3%

(a)

Dynamic scenario (repair time: 1 iteration)			
	Existing techniques		Proposed technique	
	Failures	Reliability	Failures	Reliability
Domain 1	8,231/10,000	17.69%	100/10,000	99%
Domain 2	1,168/10,000	88.32%	244/10,000	97.56%
Domain 3	1,969/10,000	80.31%	157/10,000	98.43%
Domain 4	1,420/10,000	85.8%	161/10,000	98.39%
Domain 5	3,705/10,000	62.95%	669/10,000	99.31%
Domain 6	688/10,000	93.12%	181/10,000	98.19%
Domain 7	7,199/10,000	28.01%	4,492/10,000	55.08%

(b)

Fig. 6. (a) Results of experiments in a static scenario (no repair of services), (b) Results of experiments in a dynamic scenario (with repair of services)

selected technique was said to have failed in that iteration. In other words, a selection was said to be a success on a particular iteration if and only if none of the services selected (at any level) was one of the failing services in the iteration.

The experimental procedure for the dynamic scenario was similar with the only difference being that the selection techniques (both proposed and existing) were applied after every simulation run rather than only once in the beginning. This was because, with services being taken out for repair, the complexion of the domain was possibly changing on every run.

Subsequently the reliability of the composite application selected by either selection technique was calculated as shown in equation (23).

$$Reliability = \frac{total\ no.\ of\ iterations - total\ no.\ of\ failures}{total\ no.\ of\ iterations} \tag{23}$$

The results for the two scenarios are shown in the tables in Figures 6 (a), and 6 (b). The results show that in both cases, the proposed technique outperform the existing techniques. The results therefore indicate that the proposed technique does manage to compose a more reliable application in a scenario where the service components are interacting with each other and the reliability of a service that invokes another is affected by that of the one invoked.

6   Conclusions

Ensuring a high value of reliability to service compositions is often a critical requirement. A simple way of doing this is to calculate the reliability of services individually and put together highly reliable services with the hope of forming a reliable composition. This approach is usually not appropriate because the individual reliabilities of services are affected by the presence of interacting services in the domain and their respective reliabilities. The approach proposed in this paper takes into account these interactions and comes up with a reliability measure called failure distance for individual services. Services with a high value of failure distance are subsequently combined to form reliable compositions.

Service composition based on the reliability of individual services is only a part of the model that we are putting together as part of our research. Our service composition model, besides reliability, incorporates the reputation of individual services, their cost to customers, and the time that requests have to wait at the service before being served; in coming up with appropriate compositions. The compositions so formed are not necessarily optimal with respect to each of the mentioned Quality of Service (QoS) attributes but on the whole comprise each of the attributes in good measure.

References

1. Gallouj, F.: Innovation in the service economy: the new wealth of nations. Edward Elgar Publishing (2002)
2. Battilani, P., Fauri, F.: The rise of a service-based economy and its transformation: the case of Rimini. In: Rimini Centre for Economic Analysis. Working Paper Series (2007)
3. Why runtime governance is critical for service-based applications, White Paper, Progress Software Corporation (2009)
4. Yu, T., Lin, K.-J.: Service selection algorithms for web services with end-to-end QoS constraints. Springer, Heidelberg (2005)
5. Ran, S.: A model for web services discovery with QoS. ACM SIGecom Exchanges, 1–10 (2003)
6. Curbera, F., Duftler, M., Khalaf, R., Nagy, W., Mukhi, N., Weerawarana, S.: Unraveling the Web Services Web: An Introduction to SOAP, WSDL, and UDDI. In: IEEE Internet Computing, pp. 86–93 (2002)
7. Gao, Z., Wu, G.: Combining Qos-based service selection with performance prediction. In: IEEE International Conference on e-Business Engineering (ICEBE), pp. 611–614 (2005)
8. Kokash, N.: Web service dicovery with implicit QoS filtering. In: Proceedings of the IBM PhD Student Symposium. In Conjunction with the International Conference on Service Oriented Computing, pp. 61–66 (2005)
9. Deora, V., Shao, J., Shercliff, G., Stockreisser, P.J., Gray, W.A., Fiddian, N.J.: Incorporating qoS specifications in service discovery. In: Bussler, C.J., Hong, S.-k., Jun, W., Kaschek, R., Kinshuk, Krishnaswamy, S., Loke, S.W., Oberle, D., Richards, D., Sharma, A., Sure, Y., Thalheim, B. (eds.) WISE 2004 Workshops. LNCS, vol. 3307, pp. 252–263. Springer, Heidelberg (2004)
10. Ankolekar, A., Burstein, M., Hobbs, J.R., Lassila, O., McDermott, D., Martin, D., McIlraith, S.A., Narayanan, S., Paolucci, M., Payne, T., Sycara, K.: DAML-S: Web service description for the semantic web. In: International Semantic Web Conference (ISWC), pp. 348–363 (2002)
11. Norris, J.R.: Markov Chains. Cambridge University Press, Cambridge (1998)
12. Balbo, G.: Introduction to stochastic petri nets. Lectures on Formal Methods and Performance Analysis: First EEF/Euro Summer School on Trends in Computer Science, 84–155 (2002)
13. Zhovtobryukh, D.: A petri net-based approach for automated goal-driven web service composition. Society for Computer Simulation International 83(1), 33–63 (2007)
14. Kim, K.H.: Toward QoS certification of real-time distributed computing systems. In: Proceedings of the 7th IEEE International Symposium on High Assurance Systems Engineering, HASE 2002 (2002)
15. Yin, G.G., Zhang, Q.: Discrete-time markov chains: Two-time-scale methods and applications. In: Stochastic Modelling and Applied Probability Series. Springer, Heidelberg (2005)

16. Yu, T., Lin, K.-J.: Service selection algorithms for Web services with end-to-end QoS constraints. In: Proceedings of the International Conference on E-Commerce Technology (2004)
17. Tsai, W.T., Zhang, D., Chen, Y., Huang, H., Paul, R., Liao, N.: A Software Reliability Model for Web Services. In: Proceedings on Software Engineering and Applications, SEA (2004)
18. Zeng, L., Benatallah, B., Dumas, M., Kalagnanam, J., Sheng, Q.Z.: Quality driven web services composition. In: Proceedings of the 12th International Conference on World Wide Web (2003)
19. Wang, W.-L., Wu, Y., Chen, M.-H.: An Architecture-Based Software Reliability Model. In: Proceedings of the 12th International Conference on World Wide Web (2003)
20. Greub, W.H.: Linear Algebra. Springer, Heidelberg (1981)
21. Stewart, W.J.: Introduction to the numerical solution of markov chains. CRC press, Boca Raton (1991)
22. Sniedovich, M.: Dynamic Programming. CRC press, Boca Raton (1992)
23. Nelson, B.L. (ed.): Stochastic Modeling. Dover publications, New York (2003)
24. Epifani, I., Ghezzi, C., Mirandola, R.: Model Evolution by Run-Time Parameter Adaptation. In: Proceedings of the International Conference on Software Engineering (2009)

Automatic Web Service Tagging Using Machine Learning and WordNet Synsets*

Zeina Azmeh, Jean-Rémy Falleri, Marianne Huchard, and Chouki Tibermacine

LIRMM, CNRS and Montpellier II University
161, rue Ada, 34392 Montpellier Cedex 5, France
{falleri,azmeh,huchard,tibermacin}@lirmm.fr

Abstract. The importance of Web services comes from the fact that they are an important means to realize SOA applications. Their increasing popularity caused the emergence of a fairly huge number of services. Therefore, finding a particular service among this large service space can be a hard task. User tags have proven to be a useful technique to smooth browsing experience in large document collections. Some service search engines proposes the facility of service tagging. It is usually done manually by the providers and the users of the services, which can be a fairly tedious and error prone task. In this paper we propose an approach for tagging Web services automatically. It adapts techniques from text mining and machine learning to extract tags from WSDL descriptions. Then it enriches these tags by extracting relevant synonyms using WordNet. We validated our approach on a corpus of 146 services extracted from Seekda.

Keywords: Tags, Web services, Text mining, Machine learning.

1 Introduction

Service-oriented architectures (SOA) are achieved by connecting loosely coupled units of functionality. The most common implementation of SOA uses units of functionality invokable though Internet, called Web Services. Using SOA, a developer can quickly build a complex software by using already available Web services. One of the main tasks is therefore to find the relevant Web services to use in the software. With the increasing interest toward SOA, the number of existing Web services is dramatically growing. Finding a particular service among this huge amount of services is becoming a time-consuming task.

Web services are usually described with a standard XML-based language called WSDL. The WSDL format has been designed to be processed automatically by programs, but it includes a documentation part that can be filled with a text indicating to the user what the service do. Unfortunately, this documentation part is often not filled by the creators of the services. In this case, the potential users of the service spend time to understand its functionality and to decide whether or not they will use it. Moreover, it is common that a user has finally selected a service but finds out that in fact this service is irrelevant. When this case occurs, the user might want to easily get a list of services

---

* France Télécom R&D has partially supported this work (contract CPRE 5326).

J. Filipe and J. Cordeiro (Eds.): WEBIST 2010, LNBIP 75, pp. 46–59, 2011.

offering a similar functionality. *Tagging* is a mechanism that has been introduced in search engines and digital libraries to fulfill exactly this objective.

Tagging is the process of describing a resource by assigning some relevant keywords (tags) to it. The tagging process is usually done manually by the users of the resource to be tagged. Tags are useful when browsing large collections of documents. Indeed, unlike with traditional hierarchical categories, documents can be assigned an unlimited number of tags. It allows cross-browsing between the documents. Seekda[1], one of the main service search engines, already allows its users to tag its indexed services. Tags are also useful to have a quick understanding of a particular service. Moreover, since tags are words particularly important for the services, they are a good basis for other important tasks, like service classification or clustering.

In this paper, we present an approach that automatically extract a set of relevant tags from a WSDL service description, documented or not. We use a corpus of user-tagged services to learn how to extract relevant tags from untagged service descriptions. Our approach relies on text mining techniques in order to extract candidate tags out of a description, and machine learning techniques to select relevant tags among these candidates. The extracted set of tags is then enriched with semantically related tags using the WordNet ontology [11]. We have validated this approach on a corpus of 146 user-tagged Web services extracted from Seekda. Results show that this approach is significantly more efficient than the traditional (but fairly efficient) *tfidf* weight (explained in Section 2.1).

The remaining of the paper is organized as follows. Section 2 introduces the context of our work. Then, Section 3 details our tag extraction process. Section 4 presents a validation of this process and discusses the obtained results. Before concluding and presenting the future work, we describe the related work in Section 5.

2 Context of the Work

Our work focuses on extracting tags from service descriptions. In the literature, we found a similar problem: *keyphrase extraction*. Keyphrase extraction aims at extracting important and relevant short phrases from a plain-text document. It is mostly used on journal articles or on scientific papers in order to smooth browsing and indexation of those documents in digital libraries. Before starting our work, we analyzed one assessed approach that performs keyphrase extraction: Kea [12] (Section 2.1). After this analysis, we concluded that a straightforward application of this approach is not possible on service descriptions instead of plain-text documents (Section 2.2).

2.1 Description of Kea

Kea [12] is a keyphrase extractor for plain-text documents. It uses a Bayesian classification approach. Kea has been validated on several corpora [16,17] and has proven to be an efficient approach. It takes a plain-text document as input. From this text, it extracts a list of candidate keyphrases. These candidates are the $\bigcup_{i=1}^{k} k$-grams of the text. For

---

[1] http://www.seekda.com

instance, let us consider the following sample document: "*I am a sample document*". The candidate keyphrases extracted if $k = 2$ are: *(I,am,a,sample,document,I am,am a,a sample,sample document)*. To choose the most adapted value of k for the particular task of extracting tags from WSDL files, we made some measurments and found that 86% of the tags are of length 1. It clearly shows that one word tags are assigned in the vast majority of the cases. Therefore we will fix $k = 1$ in our approach (meaning that we are going to find one word length tags). Nevertheless, our approach, like Kea, is easily generalizable to extract tags of length k.

Kea then computes two features on every candidate keyphrase. First, *distance* is computed, which is the number of words that precede the first observation of the candidate divided by the total number of words of the document. For instance, for the sample document, $distance(am\ a) = \frac{1}{5}$. Second, *tfidf*, a standard weight in the information retrieval field, is computed. It measures how much a given candidate keyphrase of a document is specific to this document. More formally, for a candidate c in a document d, $tfidf(c, d) = tf(c, d) \times idf(c)$. The metric $tf(c, d)$ (*term frequency*) corresponds to the frequency of the term c in d. It is computed with the following formula: $tf(c, d) = \frac{occurences\ of\ c\ in\ d}{size\ of\ d}$. The metric $idf(c)$ (*inverse document frequency*) measure the general importance of the term in a corpus $\mathcal{D}$. $idf(c) = log(\frac{|\mathcal{D}|}{|\{d:\ c\ \in d\}|})$.

Kea uses a naive Bayes classifier to classify the different candidate keyphrases using the two previously described features. The authors showed that this type of classifier is optimal [7] for this kind of classification problem. The two classes in which the candidate keyphrases are classified are: *keyphrase* and *not keyphrase*. Several evaluations on real world data report that Kea achieve good results [16,17]. In the next section, we will describe how WSDL files are structured and highlight why the Kea approach is not directly applicable on this kind of data.

2.2 WSDL Service Descriptions

The documents from which we intend to extract tags are service descriptions in the WSDL format. This format is XML-based and aims at describing the different elements involved in a web service. Those elements are: *services, ports, port types, bindings, types* and *messages*. Their descriptions always come with a name, called *identifier* (example: *MyWeatherService, ComputeExchangeRatePort*). They can optionally come with a plain-text documentation. Figure 3 (left) shows the general outline of a WSDL file.

One simple idea to extract tags from services would be to use Kea on their plain-text documentations. Unfortunately, an analysis of our service corpus (see Section 3.1 for more information about this corpus) shows that about 38% of the services are not documented at all. Using only plain-text documentation of the WSDL to tags service would therefore leaves at least 38% of the services untagged, which is not acceptable. Another important source of information to discover tags are the identifiers contained in the WSDL. For instance *weather* would surely be an interesting tag for a service named *WeatherService*. Unfortunately, identifiers are not easy to work with. Firstly because identifiers are usually a concatenation of different words (remember $MyWeatherService$). Secondly because they can be associated to different kinds of elements (services, ports, types, ...) that have not the same importance in a service

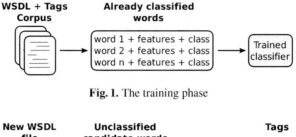

Fig. 1. The training phase

Fig. 2. The tag extraction phase

description. For all of these reasons, extracting candidate tags from WSDL files is not straightforward. Several pre-processing and text-mining techniques are required. Moreover, the previous described feature (*tfidf* and *distance*) are not easy to adapt on words coming from a service descriptions. First because WSDL deals with two categories of words (the one coming from the documentation and the one coming from the identifiers) that are not necessary related. Second because the *distance* feature is meaningless on the identifiers, which are defined in an arbitrary order.

3   Tag Extraction Process

Similarly to Kea, we model the tag extraction problem as the following classification problem: classifying a word into one of the two *tag* and *no tag* classes. Our overall process is divided into two phases: the *training* phase and the *tag extraction* phase.

Figure 1 summarizes the behavior of the training phase. In this phase we dispose of a corpus of WSDL files and associated tags. Since we did not find such a publicly available corpus, we created one by using data from Seekda. The creation of this *training corpus* is described in Section 3.1. From this training corpus, we first extract a list of candidate words by using text-mining techniques. The extraction of these candidates is described in Sections 3.2 and 3.3. Then several *features* are computed on every candidate. A *feature* is a common term in the machine learning field. It can be seen as an attribute that can be computed on the candidates (for instance the frequency of the words in their WSDL file). Finally, since manual tags are assigned to those WSDL files, we use them to classify the candidate words coming from our WSDL files. Using this set of candidate words, computed features and assigned classes, we train a classifier. This trained classifier will then be used to classify words coming from subsequent WSDL files during the *tag extraction* phase.

Figure 2 describes the *tag extraction phase*. First, like in the *training phase*, a list of candidate words is extracted from an untagged WSDL file. The same features as in the training phase are then computed on those words. The only difference with the training phase is that we do not know in advance which of those candidates are true tags. Therefore we use the previously trained classifier to automatically perform this classification. Finally the tags extracted from the WSDL file are the words that have been classified in the *tag* class. It is noteworthy to remark that the *training* phase is only performed once, while the *tag extraction* phase can be applied an unlimited number of times.

3.1   Creation of the Training Corpus

As explained above, our approach requires a training corpus, denoted by $\mathcal{T}$. Since we want to extract tags from WSDL files, $\mathcal{T}$ has to be a set of couples $(wsdl, tags)$, with $wsdl$ a WSDL file, and $tags$ a set of corresponding manually assigned tags. We were not aware of such a publicly available corpus. Therefore we decided to create one using data from Seekda. Indeed, Seekda allows its users to manually assign tags to its indexed services. We created a program that crawls on the Seedka services and extracts the WSDL files together with the user tags. To ensure that the services of our corpus were significantly tagged, we only retain the WSDL files that have at least five tags. Using this program, we extracted 150 WSDL files. Then, we removed from $\mathcal{T}$ the WSDL files that triggered parsing errors. Finally, we dispose of a training corpus containing 146 WSDL files together with their associated tags.

To clean the tags of the training corpus, we performed the three following operations:

- We removed the non alpha numeric characters from the tags (we found several tags like _onsale or :finance),
- We removed a meaningless and highly frequent tag (the _unkown tag),
- We divided the tags with length $n > 1$ into n tags of length 1, in order to have only tags of length 1 (the reason has been explained in section 2.1). The length of a tag is defined as the number of words composing this tag.

Finally, we dispose of a corpus of 146 WSDL files and 1393 tags (average of 9.54 tags per WSDL). An analysis of $\mathcal{T}$ shows that about 35% of the user tags are already contained in the WSDL files. Now that we have this training corpus, we will shortly describe the approach upon which our work is built.

3.2   Pre-processing of the WSDL Files

As we have seen before, a WSDL file contains several element definitions optionally containing a plain-text documentation. The left side of figure 3 shows such a data structure. In order to simplify the WSDL XML representation in a format more suitable to apply text mining techniques, we decided to extract two documents from a WSDL description:

- A set of couples $(type, ident)$ representing the different elements defined in the WSDL. We have $type \in (Service, Port, PortType, Message, Type, Binding)$ the type of the element and $ident$ the identifier of the element. We call this set of couples the *identifier set*.

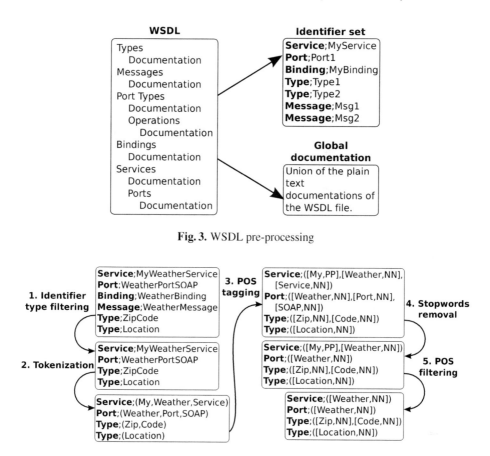

Fig. 3. WSDL pre-processing

Fig. 4. Processing of the identifiers

– A plain text containing the union of the plain-text documentations found in the WSDL file, called the *global documentation*.

This pre-processing operation is summarized in the figure 3.

3.3   Selection of the Candidate Tags

As seen in the previous section, we dispose now of two different sources of information for a given WSDL: an *identifier set* and a *global documentation*. Unfortunately, those data are not yet usable to compute meaningful metrics. Firstly because the identifiers are names of the form *MyWeatherService*, and therefore are very unlikely to be tags. Secondly because this data contains a lot of obvious useless tags (like the *you* pronoun). Therefore, we will now apply several text-mining techniques on the identifier set and the global documentation.

Figure 4 shows how we process the *identifier set*. Here is the complete description of all the performed steps:

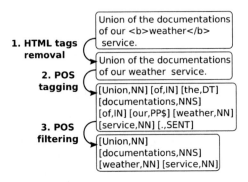

Fig. 5. Processing of the global documentation

1. **Identifier Type Filtering:** during this step, the couples *(type,ident)* where $type \in$ *(PortType,Message,Binding)* are discarded. We applied this filtering because very often, the identifiers of the elements in those categories are duplicated from the identifiers in the others categories.
2. **Tokenization:** during this step, each couple $(type, ident)$ is replaced by a couple $(type, tokens)$. $tokens$ is the set of words appearing in $ident$. For instance, *(Service,MyWeatherService)* would be replaced by *(Service,[My,Weather,Service])*. To split $ident$ into several tokens, we created a tokenizer that uses common clues in software engineering to split the words. Those clues are for instance a case change, or the presence of a non alpha-numeric character.
3. **POS Tagging:** during this step each couple $(type, tokens)$ previously computed is replaced by a couple $(type, ptokens)$. $ptokens$ is a set of couples $(token_i, pos_i)$ derived from $tokens$ where $token_i$ is a token from $tokens$ and pos_i the part-of-speech corresponding to this token. We used the tool *tree tagger* [25] to compute those part-of-speeches. Example: *(Service,[My,Weather,Service])* is replaced by *(Service,[(My,PP),(Weather,NN),(Service,NN)])*. *NN* means noun and *PP* means pronoun.
4. **Stopwords Removal:** during this step, we process each couple $(type, ptokens)$ and remove from $ptokens$ the elements $(token_i, pos_i)$ where $token_i$ is a *stopword* for $type$. A stopword is a word too frequent to be meaningful. We manually established a stopword list for each identifier type. Example: *(Service,[(My,PP),(Weather, NN),(Service,NN)])* is replaced by *(Service,[(My,PP)(Weather,NN)])* because *Service* is a stopword for service identifiers.
5. **POS Filtering:** during this step, we process each couple $(type, ptokens)$ and remove from $ptokens$ the elements $(token_i, pos_i)$ where $pos_i \notin$ *(Noun,Adjective, Verb,Symbol)*. Example: *(Service,[(My,PP),(Weather,NN))* is replaced by *(Service, [(Weather,NN)])* because pronouns are filtered.

Figure 5 shows how we process the *global documentation*. Here is the complete description of all the performed steps:

1. **HTML Tags Removal:** the HTML tags (words begining by ¡ and ending by ¿) are removed from the global documentation.

2. **POS Tagging:** similar to the POS tagging step applied to the identifier set.
3. **POS Filtering:** similar to the POS filtering step applied to the identifier set.

The union of the remaining words in the identifier set and in the global documentation are our candidate tags. When defining those processing operations, we took great care that no correct candidate tags (i.e. a candidate tag that is a real tag) of the training corpus have been discarded. The next section describes how we adapted the Kea features to these candidate tags.

3.4 Computation of the Features

After having applied our text mining techniques on the identifier set and the global documentation, we dispose now of different well separated words. Therefore we can now compute the $tfidf$ feature. But words appearing in documentation or in the identifier names are not the same. We decided (mostly because it turns out to perform better) to separate the $tfidf$ value into a $tfidf_{ident}$ and a $tfidf_{doc}$ which are respectively the $tfidf$ value of a word over the identifier set and over the global documentation. Like in Kea, we used the method in [10] to discretize those two real-valued features.

The $distance$ feature still has no meaning over the identifier set, because the elements of a WSDL description are given in an arbitrary order. Therefore we decided to adapt it by defining five different features: $in\_service$, in_port, in_type, $in\_operation$ and $in\_documentation$. Those features take their values in the $(true, false)$ set. A $true$ value indicates that the word has been seen in an element identifier of the corresponding type. For instance $in\_service(weather) = true$ means that the word $weather$ has been seen in a service identifier. $in\_documentation(weather) = true$ means that the word $weather$ has been seen in the global documentation.

In addition of these features, we compute another feature called pos. We added this feature, not used in Kea, because it significantly improves the results. pos is simply the part-of-speech that has been assigned to the word during the POS tagging step. If several parts-of-speech have been assigned to the same word, we choose the one that has been assigned in the majority of the cases. The different values of pos are: *NN (noun), NNS (plural noun), NP (proper noun), NPS (plural proper noun), JJ (adjective), JJS (plural adjective), VV (verb), VVG (gerundive verb), VVD (preterit verb), SYM (symbol).*

3.5 Training and Using the Classifier

We applied the previously described technique to all the WSDL files of $\mathcal{T}$. In addition to the previously described features, we compute the is_tag feature over the candidates. This feature takes its values in the $(true, false)$ set. $is\_tag(word) = true$ means that $word$ has been assigned as a tag by Seekda users for its service description. We have serialized all those results in an *ARFF* file compatible with the Weka tool [29]. Weka is a machine learning tool that defines a standard format for describing a training corpus and furnish the implementation of many classifiers. One can use Weka in order to train a classifier or compare the performances of different classifiers regarding a given classification problem. Table 1 shows an extract of the ARFF file we produce. In this table, words are displayed for the sake of clarity, but in reality, they are not present in the ARFF file. The ARFF file only contains features.

Table 1. Extract of the ARFF file

Word	$TFIDF_{id}$	$TFIDF_{doc}$	$IN\_SERVICE$	...	IN_DOC	POS	IS_TAG
Weather	[0, 0.01]	]0.01, 0.04]	×			NN	×
Location	]0.03, 0.1]	]0.04, 0.15]			×	JJ	
Code	]0.03, 0.1]	]0.01, 0.04]			×	VV	

With this ARFF file, we used Weka to train a naive Bayes classifier, shown as optimal for our kind of classification task [7]. This trained classifier can now be used in the tag extraction phase. As previously said, the beginning of this phase is the same as the one of the training phase. It means that the WSDL file goes through the previously described operations (pre-processing, candidates selection and features computation). Only this time, the value of the is_tag feature is not available. This value will be automatically computed by the previously trained classifier.

3.6   WordNet for Semantically Related Tags

In our approach, the classifier that we built determines whether a word in a WSDL file is a tag or not. Thus, it extracts the tags appearing inside the WSDL files only. This way, we miss some other interesting tags like associated words or synonyms. In order to solve this issue, we used the WordNet lexical database [11]. In WordNet a word may be associated with many synsets (synonym sets), each corresponding to a different sense of a word.

Our corpus consists of 146 WSDL files, each of which is assigned two sets of tags: user tags and our automatically extracted tags. Our objective is to enrich each set of tags with semantically similar words extracted from WordNet. Thus, for each tag we identify the possible senses and the synonyms set related to each sense. We add the extracted synonyms to the corresponding set of tags, and we perform some experiments to evaluate the obtained tags, as we show in the next section.

4   Validation of the Proposed Work

This section provides a validation of our technique on real world data from Seekda. We conduct experiments in which we assess the precision and recall of our trained classifier.

Methodology. We carried out our experiments on three stages. In the first one, the trained classifier is applied on the training corpus $\mathcal{T}$ and its output is compared with the tags given by Seekda users (obtained as described in Section 3.1).

After having conducted the first experiment, a manual assessment of the tags produced by our approach revealed that many tags not assigned by the user seemed highly relevant. This phenomenon has also been observed in several human evaluations of Kea [16,17], that inspired our approach. It occurs because tags assigned by the users are not the *absolute truth*. Indeed, it is very likely that users have forgotten many relevant tags, even if they were in the service description. To show that the real efficiency of our approach is better than the one computed in the first experiment, we perform a second experiment. In this experiment, we manually augmented the user tags of our corpus with additional tags we found relevant and accurate by analyzing the WSDL descriptions of the services. In the final experiment, we enriched the user tags as well as our automatically extracted tags with semantically related tags using WordNet.

Metrics. In the evaluation, we used precision and recall. First, for each web service $s \in T$, where T is our training corpus, we consider: A the set of tags produced by the trained classifier, M the set of the tags given by Seekda users and W the set of words appearing in the WSDL. Let $I = A \cap M$ be the set of tags assigned by our classifier and Seekda users. Let $E = M \cap W$ be the set of tags assigned by Seekda users present in the WSDL file. Then we define $precision(s) = \frac{|I|}{|A|}$ and $recall(s) = \frac{|I|}{|E|}$, which are aggregated in $precision(T) = \frac{\sum_{s \in T} precision(s)}{|T|}$ and $recall(T) = \frac{\sum_{s \in T} recall(s)}{|T|}$. The recall is therefore computed over the tags assigned by Seekda users that are present in the descriptions of concerned services. We did not compute the recall for the WordNet extracted tags, because these tags may not be present in the WSDL descriptions.

Evaluation. Figure 6 (left) gives results for the first experiment where the output of the classifier is compared with the tags of Seekda users, while in Figure 6 (right), enriched tags of Seekda users are used in the comparison (curated corpus). In this figure, our approach is called *ate (Automatic Tag Extraction)*. To clearly show the concrete benefits of our approach, we decided to include in these experiments a straightforward (but fairly efficient) technique. This technique, called *tfidf* in Figure 6, consists in selecting, after the application of our text-mining techniques, the five candidate tags with the highest *tfidf* weight.

In Figure 6 (left), the precision of *ate* is 0.48. It is a significant improvement compared to the *tfidf* method that achieves only a precision of 0.28. Moreover, there is no significant difference between the recall achieved by the two methods. To show that the precision and recall achieved by *ate* are not biased by the fact that we used the training corpus as a testing corpus, we performed a 10 folds cross-validation. In a 10 folds cross-validation, our training corpus is divided in 10 parts. One is used to train a classifier, and the 9 other parts are used to test this classifier. This operation is done for every part, and then, the average recall and precision are computed. The results achieved by our approach using cross-validation ($precision = 0.44$ and $recall = 0.42$) are very similar to those obtained in the first experiment.

In Figure 6 (right), we see that the precision achieved by *ate* in the second experiment is much better. It reaches 0.8, while the precision achieved by the *tfidf* method increases to 0.41. The recall achieved by the two methods remains similar. The precision achieved by our method in this experiment is good. Only 20% of the tags discovered by *ate* are not correct. Moreover, the efficiency of *ate* is significantly higher than *tfidf*.

Evaluation after using WordNet. We enriched the tags sets with semantically similar words extracted using the WordNet, as described above. We recalculated the precision value, considering these new sets of enriched user tags and automatically extracted tags. The precision value has increased by 9%, reaching the value of 89% of correctness. Thus, using the WordNet has improved the precision value and enriched the services with tags that are not necessarily present in the WSDL descriptions.

Threats to Validity. Our experiments use real world services, obtained from the Seekda service search engine. Our training corpus contains services extracted randomly with

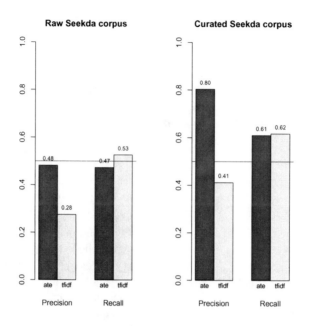

Fig. 6. Results on the original and manually curated Seekda corpus

the constraint that they contain at least 5 user tags. We assumed that Seekda users assign correct tags. Indeed, our method admits some noise but would not work if the majority of the user tags were poorly assigned. In the second experiment, we manually added tags we found relevant by examining the complete description and documentation of the concerned services. Unfortunately, since we are not "real" users of those services, some of the tags we added might not be relevant.

5   Related Work

In this section, we will present the related work according to two fields of research: keyphrase extraction and web service discovery.

5.1   Keyphrase Extraction and Assignment

According to [27], there are two general approaches that are able to supply keyphrases for a document: *keyphrase extraction* and *keyphrase assignment*. Both approaches are using supervised machine learning approaches, with training examples being documents with manually supplied keyphrases.

Keyphrase Assignment. In the *keyphrase assignment* approach, a list of predefined keyphrases is treated as a list of classes in which the different documents are classified. Text categorization techniques are used to learn models for assigning a class (*keyphrase*) to a document. Two main approaches of this category are [9,19].

Keyphrase Extraction. In the *keyphrase extraction* approach, a list of candidate keyphrases are extracted from a document and classified into the classes *keyphrase* and *not keyphrase*. There are two main approaches that fall in this category: one using a genetic algorithm [26] and one using a naive Bayes classifier (Kea [12]).

5.2 Web Service Discovery

Web service discovery is a wide research area with many underlying issues and challenges. A quick overview of some of the works can be acquired from [4,18][2]. Here, we describe a selection of works, classified using their adapted techniques.

Using Machine Learning Techniques. Many approaches adapt techniques from machine learning field, in order to discover and group similar services. In [5,15], service classifiers are defined depending on sets of previously categorized services. Then the resulting classifiers are used to deduce the relevant categories for new given services. In case there were no predefined categories, unsupervised clustering is used. In [21], CPLSA approach is defined that reduces a services set then cluster it into semantically related groups.

Using Service Matching Techniques. In [20], a web service broker is designed relying on approximate signature matching using xml schema matching. It can recommend services to programmers in order to compose them. In [13], a service request and a service are represented as two finite state machines then they are compared using various heuristics to find structural similarities between them. In [8], the Woogle web service search engine is presented, which takes the needed operation as input and searches for all the services that include an operation similar to the requested one. In [3], tags coming from folksonomies are used to discover and compose services.

Using Vector Space Model Techniques. The vector space model is used for service retrieval in several existing works as in [23,28,6]. Terms are extracted from every WSDL file and the vectors are built for each service. A query vector is also built, and similarity is calculated between the service vectors and the query vector. This model is sometimes enhanced by using WordNet, structure matching algorithms to ameliorate the similarity scores as in [28], or by partitioning the space into subspaces to reduce the searching space as in [6].

Using Formal Concept Analysis Techniques. A collection of works [1,22,2], adapt the formal concept analysis method to retrieve web services more efficiently. Contexts obtained from service descriptions are used to classify the services as a concept lattice. This lattice helps in understanding the different relationships between the services, and in discovering service substitutes.

6   Conclusions and Future Work

With the emergence of SOA, it becomes important for developers using this paradigm to retrieve Web services matching their requirements in an efficient way. By using Web

---

[2] The second one is edited by the responsible of Seekda's technical infrastructure.

service search engines, these developers can either search by keywords or navigate by tags. In the second case, it is necessary that the tags characterize accurately this service. Our work contributes in this direction and introduces a novel approach that extracts tags from Web service descriptions and enrich them using the WordNet ontology. This approach combines and adapts text mining as well as machine learning techniques. It has been experimented on a corpus of user-tagged real world Web services. The obtained results demonstrated the efficiency of our automatic tag extraction process, and the enrichment of semantically similar tags. The use of WordNet has improved the precision of the returned tags and enriched the services with tags that are not necessarily present in the WSDL descriptions. The proposed work is useful for many purposes. First, the automatically extracted tags can assist the users who are tagging a given service, or to "bootstrap" tags on untagged services. They are also useful to have a quick understanding of a service without reading the whole description. They can also be used to help in building domain ontologies like in [24] [14], also in tasks such as service clustering (for instance by measuring the similarity of the tags of two given services), or classification (for instance by defining association rules between tags and categories). One of our perspectives is to work on extracting composed tags, which consist of more than one word. A one-word tag is sometimes insufficient to describe some concepts (for example *exchange rate* or *Web 2.0*).

References

1. Aversano, L., Bruno, M., Canfora, G., Penta, M.D., Distante, D.: Using concept lattices to support service selection. International Journal of Web Services Research 3(4), 32–51 (2006)
2. Azmeh, Z., Huchard, M., Tibermacine, C., Urtado, C., Vauttier, S.: Wspab: A tool for automatic classification & selection of web services using formal concept analysis. In: Proceedings of the 6th IEEE European Conference on Web Services (ECOWS 2008), pp. 31–40. IEEE Computer Society Press, Dublin (2008)
3. Bouillet, E., Feblowitz, M., Feng, H., Liu, Z., Ranganathan, A., Riabov, A.: A folksonomy-based model of web services for discovery and automatic composition. In: IEEE International Conference on Services Computing (SCC), pp. 389–396. IEEE Computer Society, Los Alamitos (2008)
4. Brockmans, S., Erdmann, M., Schoch, W.: Service-finder deliverable d4.1. research report about current state of the art of matchmaking algorithms. Tech. rep., Ontoprise, Germany (October 2008)
5. Crasso, M., Zunino, A., Campo, M.: Awsc: An approach to web service classification based on machine learning techniques. Inteligencia Artificial, Revista Iberoamericana de Interligencia Artificial 12(37), 25–36 (2008)
6. Crasso, M., Zunino, A., Campo, M.: Query by example for web services. In: SAC 2008: Proceedings of the ACM symposium on Applied computing. pp. 2376–2380. ACM, New York (2008)
7. Domingos, P., Pazzani, M.J.: On the optimality of the simple bayesian classifier under zero-one loss. Machine Learning 29(2-3), 103–130 (1997)
8. Dong, X., Halevy, A., Madhavan, J., Nemes, E., Zhang, J.: Similarity search for web services. In: VLDB 2004: Proceedings of the Thirtieth International Conference on Very Large Data Bases, pp. 372–383. VLDB Endowment (2004)
9. Dumais, S.T., Platt, J.C., Hecherman, D., Sahami, M.: Inductive learning algorithms and representations for text categorization. In: Gardarin, G., French, J.C., Pissinou, N., Makki, K., Bouganim, L. (eds.) CIKM, pp. 148–155. ACM, New York (1998)

10. Fayyad, U.M., Irani, K.B.: Multi-interval discretization of continuous-valued attributes for classification learning. In: IJCAI, pp. 1022–1029 (1993)
11. Fellbaum, C. (ed.): WordNet: An Electronic Database. MIT Press, Cambridge (1998)
12. Frank, E., Paynter, G.W., Witten, I.H., Gutwin, C., Nevill-Manning, C.G.: Domain-specific keyphrase extraction. In: Dean, T. (ed.) IJCAI, pp. 668–673. Morgan Kaufmann, San Francisco (1999)
13. Günay, A., Yolum, P.: Structural and semantic similarity metrics for web service matchmaking. In: EC-Web, pp. 129–138 (2007)
14. Guo, H., Ivan, A.A., Akkiraju, R., Goodwin, R.: Learning ontologies to improve the quality of automatic web service matching. In: Williamson, C.L., Zurko, M.E., Patel-Schneider, P.F., Shenoy, P.J. (eds.) WWW, pp. 1241–1242. ACM, New York (2007)
15. Heß, A., Kushmerick, N.: Learning to attach semantic metadata to web services. In: International Semantic Web Conference, pp. 258–273 (2003)
16. Jones, S., Paynter, G.W.: Human evaluation of kea, an automatic keyphrasing system. In: JCDL, pp. 148–156. ACM, New York (2001)
17. Jones, S., Paynter, G.W.: Automatic extraction of document keyphrases for use in digital libraries: Evaluation and applications. JASIST 53(8), 653–677 (2002)
18. Lausen, H., Steinmetz, N.: Survey of current means to discover web services. Tech. rep., Semantic Technology Institute (STI) (August 2008)
19. Leung, C.H., Kan, W.K.: A statistical learning approach to automatic indexing of controlled index terms. JASIS 48(1), 55–66 (1997)
20. Lu, J., Yu, Y.: Web service search: Who, when, what, and how. In: Weske, M., Hacid, M.-S., Godart, C. (eds.) WISE Workshops 2007. LNCS, vol. 4832, pp. 284–295. Springer, Heidelberg (2007)
21. Ma, J., Zhang, Y., He, J.: Efficiently finding web services using a clustering semantic approach. In: CSSSIA 2008: Proceedings of the 2008 International Workshop on Context Enabled Source and Service Selection, Integration and Adaptation, pp. 1–8. ACM, New York (2008)
22. Peng, D., Huang, S., Wang, X., Zhou, A.: Management and retrieval of web services based on formal concept analysis. In: Proceedings of the The Fifth International Conference on Computer and Information Technology (CIT 2005), pp. 269–275. IEEE Computer Society, Los Alamitos (2005)
23. Platzer, C., Dustdar, S.: A vector space search engine for web services. In: Third IEEE European Conference on Web Services, ECOWS 2005. pp. 62–71 (2005), http://dx.doi.org/10.1109/ECOWS.2005.5
24. Sabou, M., Wroe, C., Goble, C.A., Mishne, G.: Learning domain ontologies for web service descriptions: an experiment in bioinformatics. In: Ellis, A., Hagino, T. (eds.) WWW, pp. 190–198. ACM, New York (2005)
25. Schmid, H.: Probabilistic part-of-speech tagging using decision trees. In: Proceedings of International Conference on New Methods in Language Processing, Manchester, UK, vol. 12 (1994)
26. Turney, P.D.: Learning algorithms for keyphrase extraction. Inf. Retr. 2(4), 303–336 (2000)
27. Turney, P.D.: Coherent keyphrase extraction via web mining. In: Gottlob, G., Walsh, T. (eds.) IJCAI, pp. 434–442. Morgan Kaufmann, San Francisco (2003)
28. Wang, Y., Stroulia, E.: Semantic structure matching for assessing web-service similarity. In: Orlowska, M.E., Weerawarana, S., Papazoglou, M.P., Yang, J. (eds.) ICSOC 2003. LNCS, vol. 2910, pp. 194–207. Springer, Heidelberg (2003)
29. Witten, I.H., Frank, E.: Data Mining: Practical Machine Learning Tools and Techniques with Java Implementations. Morgan Kaufmann, San Francisco (1999)

Minimal-Footprint Middleware to Leverage Qualified Electronic Signatures

Clemens Orthacker and Martin Centner

Institute for Applied Information Processing and Communications (IAIK)
Graz University of Technology, Graz, Austria
clemens.orthacker@iaik.tugraz.at, mcentner@student.tugraz.at

Abstract. Qualified electronic signatures are recognized as being equivalent to handwritten signatures and are supported by EU legislation. They require a secure signature creation device (SSCD) such as a smart card. This paper presents a novel approach for the integration of smart cards in web applications without the requirement to install dedicated software on the user's computer. The signature creation process is split into two parts: One part is performed on the server side and the other part (requiring access to functions of the secure signature creation device) is deployed and executed as a lightweight component in the user's browser on demand. This significantly facilitates the usage of smart cards for the creation of qualified electronic signatures and therefore counteracts their low market penetration all over Europe. The approach has meanwhile attracted attention in various Member States and proved ideal for the quick integration and deployment of a large number of diverse and rapidly evolving SSCDs.

Keywords: Qualified electronic signatures, e-Government.

1 Introduction

Handwritten signatures play an important role in day-to-day business. They are typically used to authenticate the origin of a document and to give evidence of the intent of the signatory with regard to that document. Electronic signatures may provide an adequate equivalent in electronic business. This is also supported by the EU directive on electronic signatures [3], which defines a legal framework for electronic signatures and has been adopted into national legislation by the EU member states. The required infrastructure is already available in a number of the EU member states and other countries. However, electronic signatures as electronic equivalent to handwritten signatures have not yet reached a wide-spread use beyond specific application areas such as e-government.

In this paper we present an approach that aims at facilitating the further dissemination of Qualified Signatures. In particular we address the issues of integrating the means required for signature creation with Web applications and the deployment of such means.

The proposed minimal-footprint middleware may be deployed with a web application or as a central service and handles the details of signature creation. It enables a

J. Filipe and J. Cordeiro (Eds.): WEBIST 2010, LNBIP 75, pp. 60–68, 2011.
© Springer-Verlag Berlin Heidelberg 2011

user to create Qualified Signatures as defined by the EU directive without requiring dedicated software to be installed by the user. To access a secure signature creation device (SSCD) as required for Qualified Signatures, a lightweight component is on demand deployed and executed in the user's browser.

The minimal-footprint middleware is a technology neutral concept. To study the concept and to provide an open-source implementation the MOCCA project[1] was initiated by the Austrian Federal Chancellery and the Graz University of Technology. Although other web technology would be conceivable, the MOCCA implementation relies on Java Applets and the PC/SC interface to stay as platform and browser independent as possible. Meanwhile MOCCA has been deployed in production for important e-government services in Austria.

In the following this paper will give a short introduction to Qualified Signatures and their requirements in section 2 and to Secure Signature Creation Devices as required for Qualified Signatures in section 3. Section 4 discusses ways of integrating the creation of Qualified Signatures with applications. The minimum-footprint middleware concept and it's reference implementation MOCCA is discussed section 5.

2   Qualified Signatures

The EU directive on electronic signatures [3] defines special requirements for *advanced electronic signatures*, *secure signature creation devices* (SSCD), *qualified certificates* (QC) and certification service providers issuing qualified certificates. The requirements aim at high level of security.

Advanced electronic signatures based on QC and which are created by a SSCD—commonly referred to as *Qualified Signatures*—are required to

> ... (a) satisfy the legal requirements of a signature in relation to data in electronic form in the same manner as a handwritten signature satisfies those requirements in relation to paper-based data; and (b) are admissible as evidence in legal proceedings. [3, Article 5]

Studies by the European Commission (e.g. [2]) show that corresponding legislation and infrastructure is available in a majority of the EU member states. However, Qualified Signatures have not yet found widespread use beyond specific application areas such as e-government.

[9] studies the reasons for the slow adoption ratio of Qualified Signatures. As electronic signatures do not provide much benefit by themselves, their dissemination is largely dependent on availability of corresponding applications. On the other hand, the effort required for integration of electronic signatures with applications must usually be justified considering the potential usage ratio. Hence, the adoption of electronic signatures currently suffers from a chicken-and-egg problem. The problem is intensified by the fact, that currently there is a significant effort required by application providers for integrating and deploying the means required for the creation of qualified signatures.

---

[1] http://Mocca.egovlabs.gv.at

3   Secure Signature Creation Devices

Almost all SSCDs provided for the creation of Qualified Signatures are based on smart-card technology. They are either implemented as chip-cards in credit-card size with an interface according to ISO/IEC 7810 and ISO/IEC 7816, use a contactless interface according to ISO/IEC 14443 or are directly integrated with a corresponding terminal device to be used as USB token. Therefore almost all SSCDs share at least a common low level interface defined by ISO/IEC 7816 parts 3, 4 and 8. In practice however, this just means that communication with an SSCDs is based on the exchange of Application Protocol Data Units (APDUs). To be able to access the functions of an SSCD a lot of additional information is required. Smart cards implementing ISO/IEC 7816 part 15 try to provide this required information in a standardized way. However only a few SSCDs implement ISO/IEC 7815–15 and even if they do, it remains rather impossible to interface SSCDs in a complete generic way. Therefore, either applications have to know how to access a specific SSCD or need layer of abstraction and another component doing so.

PC/SC[2] has become the de facto standard for integration of smart cards and smart-card readers into mainstream operating systems, with other technologies such as CT-API[3] losing importance. PC/SC allows for communication with smart-cards on the basis of APDUs. On the contrary, a number of competing solutions exist for the abstraction and integration of electronic signatures and other cryptographic functions based on smart cards into operating systems and applications. To name just a few, there are operating system dependent solutions like Microsoft's CSP/CNG[4], Keychain Services[5] in Apple OS X and more operating system independent solutions such as PKCS#11[6] All these solutions have in common, that they require a module implementing the specifics for each particular SSCD they are going to support. Of course, these modules look quite different for any of the solutions. Thus it is not surprising, that none of them is currently able to support all or even most of the available SSCDs. In fact, there is also a number of SSCDs for which not any such module is available. Additionally, the installation and update of specific modules can also be a challenging task for end users if this is not performed by the operating system or applications automatically.

The EU directive on electronic signatures requires that SSCDs must ensure that "the signature-creation-data used for signature generation can be reliably protected by the legitimate signatory against the use of others" [3, ANNEX III]. Most SSCDs implement this by requiring the user to provide a secret personal identification number (PIN). Any solution accessing the SSCD must therefore also be able to provide the user with a possibility to enter the PIN to authorize the signature. This might be done by an appropriate user dialog or by activating a PIN-pad on the smart-card terminal if available.

---

[2] http://www.Pcscworkgroup.com/
[3] CardTerminal Application Programming Interface
http://www.Tuvit.de/downloads/Tuev-IT/CTAPI11EN.pdf
[4] Crypto Service Provider / Crypto Next Generation http://msdn2.microsoft.com/en-us/library/aa380256.aspx
[5] http://Developer.apple.com/mac/library/documentation/Security/Conceptual/Security_Overview/Security_Services/Security_Services.html
[6] http://www.Rsa.com/rsalabs/node.asp?id=2133

4   Application Integration

SSCDs implement only basic cryptographic algorithms. Signatures on electronic documents usually require a signature format such as CMS[7] and XMLDSig[8] (or their corresponding formats for Advanced Electronic Signatures, CAdES and XAdES[9]). If applications directly interface SSCDs or access their functions by interfaces discussed in section 3, they also need to implement the processing of the required signature formats. Abstraction of this functionality can be provided by libraries which have to be integrated with the application or can be achieved by the use of a middleware that provides signature creation services.

To enable users to create Qualified Signatures in Web applications, these applications need a way to employ the user's SSCD. There are however no standard means provided by Web browsers for the creation of electronic signatures. Therefore, middleware solutions have been developed that need to be installed on the user's machine and allow to be triggered through a Web browser. The middleware then takes over the task of creation a Qualified Signature with the user's SSCD and returns it back the application. Such solutions are for instance used by the Austrian Citizen Card [4],[6] and the German e-Card-API-Framework [1]. Of course such middleware may also be accessed by local applications on the user's machine.

The EU directive on electronic signatures mandates that "Secure signature-creation devices must not alter the data to be signed or prevent such data from being presented to the signatory prior to the signature process" [3, ANNEX III]. Therefore middleware for the creation of Qualified Signatures usually also provides the possibility to view the to-be signed data.

The traditional middleware approach represents a convenient way to integrate Qualified Signatures with applications and especially with Web applications. However, conventional middleware software needs to be installed on the user's machine as a prerequisite. The minimum-footprint middleware approach eliminates this requirement by providing the required components for accessing the user's SSCD on demand.

5   Minimal-Footprint Middleware

The general concept of the approach is to split the signature creation process into two parts, use a small component executed in the user's browser to perform the part that needs access the functions of the SSCD and deploy this component on demand. Everything that may be performed securely on the server is kept out of this component, to allow for a minimal-footprint on the user's machine. From the application's point of view however, there is just a conventional middleware taking over the task of creating an electronic signature.

---

[7] Cryptographic Message Syntax (CMS) – IETF RFC 3852 http://tools.ietf.org/html/rfc3852

[8] XML Signature Syntax and Processing – W3C Recommendation http://www.w3.org/TR/xmldsig-core/

[9] CMS Advanced Electronic Signatures – ETSI TS 101 733 and XML Advanced Electronic Signatures – ETSI TS 101 903 http://www.etsi.org/WebSite/Technologies/ElectronicSignature.aspx

The Austrian Federal Chancellery and the Graz University of Technology have initiated the project "MOCCA" in 2008 with the aim to provide an open source implementation of a minimal-footprint middleware.

5.1 SSCD Access

In the context of the MOCCA project several technologies for implementation of the browser component and accessing the SSCD have been assessed. The goal was to support the mainstream operating systems (Windows, Mac OS X and Linux) and at least the three most used Web browsers (Internet Explorer, Firefox and Safari). Firefox and Internet Explorer would principally allow access to SSCD functions using scripting technologies such as Java-Script and VB-Script. However, this requires appropriate modules for integration of the SSCD with the operating system (Internet Explorer: CSP) and the browser (Firefox: PKCS#11), respectively. The appropriate modules have to be installed and configured by the user. As an alternative browser plug-in technologies such as Flash, Silverlight and Java Applets where evaluated. A possibility for accessing an SSCD using Flash or Silverlight in the available versions was not found.

Java Applets provide operating system and browser independent access to smart cards via the Java Smart Card I/O API using the PC/SC interface. The targeted operating systems provide out of the box support for PC/SC and for many of the smart-card readers on the market. Therefore, a user only needs to plug a supported smart-card reader and is not required to install additional software.

Statistics show, that more than 50% of internet users are using a browser with a Java-Plugin in the relevant version[10]. For those not having a Java-Plugin installed, Java provides an easy installation procedure that could also be triggered by the middleware directly. As Java is general technology not only required for the creation of electronic signatures and already available on more than the half of the users' machines, the requirement not needing to install dedicated software is considered to be met. Therefore, Java Applets where chosen for the implementation of the browser component of MOCCA.

5.2 Architecture

The architecture of MOCCA is designed to be as technology neutral and open as possible. This should allow for future adaptations if required. It is organized into four different layers as shown in figure 1.

For integration with applications it was chosen to implement the Security-Layer interface (SL) and a transport binding of HTTP(S) as defined by the Austrian Citizen Card specification. SL is an open concept comparable with OASIS-DSS[11] and not restricted to Austrian Citizen Cards. Additional interfaces (such as OASIS-DSS) could easily be implemented by extending or adapting the two uppermost layers.

The Security-Layer interface allows for the creation of CMS and XAdES signatures. Currently, MOCCA only implements the creation of XAdES signatures. The corresponding SL request consists of elements specifying the signature key to be used, the

[10] Source: http://Riastats.com/
[11] OASIS – Digital Signature Service (http://www.oasis-open.org/committees/dss/)

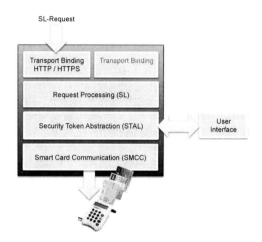

Fig. 1. Layers of MOCCA

data to be signed and the XML document the created signature should finally be embedded in. There is great flexibility in specifying how the middleware should retrieve and transform the data for signing and whether the data should be embedded into the signature or referenced externally.

Transport Binding Layer. A transport binding of HTTP/HTTPS is provided to enable an application to access the middleware through the browser by using simple Web forms carrying an SL request.

Request Processing Layer (SL). performs all the steps required for the creation of an XAdES signature except for the calculation of the signature value.

Security Token Abstraction Layer (STAL). consists of a client and a server part. The server part offers a Web service. The client part is included in the Java Applet. The client connects back to the Web service of the server when the Applet has been started. The Web service is then used to send commands from the server to the client part of the STAL.[12]

Smart Card Communication Layer (SMCC). is also included in the Java Applet and called by the STAL to handle communication with SSCDs and smart-card readers via PC/SC.

All XML processing required for the creation of a XAdES signature is performed in the request processing layer. This allows for very simple STAL commands. Currently, the STAL supports only two basic commands. One for retrieving certificates and other information stored on a SSCD and one for the creation of a signature using the SSCD. Additionally, the STAL may call back to the Request Processing layer for retrieving the

---

[12] A Standard SOAP based Web service with swapped roles of server and client has been chosen in favor of a reversed SOAP (PAOS) binding. This allows for a standard Java client implementation and for non-Java clients (e.g. Java Script, Flash, etc.) to connect to the server. This may become relevant if other technologies would allow SSCD access in the future and should be integrated.

data referenced by the to-be signed signature. This is used to enable the user to retrieve and view the data to-be signed as explained below.

5.3 Security Model

A Java Applet may be signed to ensure it's integrity and to allow the user to verify that it is from a reliable source. If a Java Applet also needs access to local resources it must be signed. The first time a signed Applet is loaded by the Java-Plugin the user needs to give consent for executing it and may choose to always trust the issuer of the Applet.

It was chosen to encapsulate all security relevant parts of the process of creating a Qualified Signature within the signed Java Applet. The Applet may be signed by a trusted third party and different service instances may provide the same signed Applet.[13] For the purpose of creating a Qualified Signature, users therefore only need to trust the issuer of the signed Applet. This is considered to be equivalent with the requirement to trust the issuer of other conventionally installed software used for the creation of Qualified Signatures (e.g. locally installed middleware-software, PKCS#11 modules, etc.).

The entire XML processing is performed outside the Java Applet, to keep it as small and simple as possible. The Applet only receives the *SignedInfo* part of the XAdES signature, which contains the references and hash values of the to-be signed data. However, the Applet allows the user to retrieve and view the to-be signed data. When it retrieves this data it calculates the hash value and compares it with the hash value of the corresponding reference in the *SignedInfo*. That way, the Applet can ensure the data retrieved for viewing is actually the data going to be signed. When the user decides not view the to-be signed data, there is also no need to compare the hash values.

The security relevant communication with smart cards and smart-card readers is handled entirely within the Applet. The Applet is relying on PC/SC communication only. Therefore, it needs to know how to employ the functions of a particular SSCD. To keep the footprint of the Applet to a minimum, it does not rely on additional modules such as PKCS#11 that would need to be deployed with the Applet. The SSCD abstraction is therefore implemented directly by the SMCC layer of the Applet.

5.4 State of Implementation and Findings

Since the start of the MOCCA project it includes support for a variety of private sector issued Austrian Citizen Cards as well as the Austrian health-insurance card ("e-card"), which is issued since 2005 to virtually all Austrian residents. In addition to the creation of Qualified Signatures, MOCCA also supports authentication using the Austrian Citizen Card [7] [6].

MOCCA has been deployed in production for authentication and the creation of Qualified Signatures for a number of e-government services in Austria. This includes, the Austrian online tax declaration service *FinanzOnline*[14], which is the most used e-government service in Austria. Additionally it has been successfully used in the past

---

[13] The Applet provided with the official MOCCA distribution is actually signed by the Secure Information Technology Center – Austria (A-SIT), which is the Austrian confirmation body for electronic signature solutions.

[14] https://finanzonline.bmf.gv.at

student union election, which was the very first lawful election in Austria using remote e-voting facilities.

A number of other SSCDs from different EU countries have been integrated in the context of the "STORK" pan european project on electronic identities[15] This includes the Belgian "BELPIC" and smart-cards form Italy, Portugal, Estonia and Spain. MOCCA is deployed in several other EU Member States on different scales from regional to nationwide. For Switzerland and Liechtenstein, this also necessitated the integration of further SSCD implementations.

Smart-card manufacturers have introduced updates to their card operating systems and new versions of existing cards are issued. Just as with support for entirely new SSCDs, this requires updates to implementations and deployed services. The constantly evolving European SSCD landscape introduces new challenges for the timely provision of their support in existing and new services. Additional difficulties are often caused by card manufacturers keeping interface specifications confidential. Naturally, it is quite difficult to meet non-disclosure requirements while providing an open source implementation. Hence, MOCCA often has to rely on standard compliance and experimentation.

Since the main objectives are a minimal-footprint and no need to install dedicated software, simply relying on existing drivers or libraries (e.g. PKCS#11) provided by card manufactures and third parties is generally not an option. Current work is therefore focused on new scalable means for integration of a large number of different European SSCD implementations and ways to keep them up-to-date.

6   Conclusions

The presented minimal-footprint middleware represents a concept to leverage the use of Qualified Signatures in Web applications. It enables users to create Qualified Signatures without requiring them to install dedicated software as a prerequisite. At the same time it encapsulates the details of the signature creation process and hides them from the application. This allows for an easy integration with applications.

The authors have proven the concept by an open-source implementation "MOCCA", which is now an important building block of Austrian e-government services.

The principle concept is technology neutral. For implementation of MOCCA, Java Applets and the PC/SC interface have been chosen. These two technologies are available across browsers and operating system platforms.

There are other solutions for the creation of electronic signatures available on the market, which also use Java Applet technology. However, to the best of our knowledge, none of these solutions is implemented as middleware. The middleware concept, would yet allow to switch technologies without affecting application integration. If technologies should emerge in the future that would allow for an even better handling of the SSCD integration, it would suffice to adapt just the middleware. The minimal-footprint middleware concept therefore has all the advantages of a conventional middleware without the need to be installed by the user.

---

[15] http://www.Eid-stork.eu/

References

1. Bundesamt fr Sicherheit in der Informationstechnik: BSI - Technische Richtlinie: eCard-API-Framework, BSI TR-03112 (2008), http://www.bsi.bund.de/cln_136/ContentBSI/Publikationen/TechnischeRichtlinien/tr03112/index_htm.html
2. European Commission / European eGovernement services (IDABC): Preliminary Study on Mutual Recognition of eSignatures for eGovernment applications, Report (November 2007), http://ec.europa.eu/idabc/en/document/6485
3. European Parliament and Council: Directive 1999/93/EC of the European Parliament and of the Council of 13 December 1999, on a Community framework for electronic signatures (December 1999), http://eur-lex.europa.eu/LexUriServ/LexUriServ.do?uri=CELEX:31999L0093:EN:HTML
4. Hollosi, A., Karlinger, G.: The Austrian Citizen Card. AG Bürgerkarte (May 2004), http://www.buergerkarte.at/konzept/securitylayer/spezifikation/20040514/introduction/Introduction.en.html
5. Leitold, H., Hollosi, A., Posch, R.: Security architecture of the austrian citizen card concept. In: Proceedings of 18th Annual Computer Security Applications Conference, 2002 , pp. 391–400 (2002)
6. Rössler, T.: Giving an interoperable e-ID solution: Using foreign e-IDs in Austrian e-Government. Computer Law & Security Report 24(5), 447–453 (2008)
7. Rössler, T., Leitold, H.: Identifikationsmodell der österreichischen Bürgerkarte. In: Proceedings of the D-A-CH Security Conference 2005. University of Technology Darmstadt, Germany (2005)
8. Roßnagel, H.: On diffusion and confusion – why electronic signatures have failed. Lecture Notes in Computer Science – Trust and Privacy in Digital Business pp. 71–80 (2006), http://dx.doi.org/10.1007/11824633_8
9. Roßnagel, H.: Mobile qualifizierte elektronische Signaturen. Datenschutz und Datensicherheit (2009)

Structured Collaborative Tagging: Is It Practical for Web Service Discovery?

Maciej Gawinecki[1], Giacomo Cabri[1], Marcin Paprzycki[2], and Maria Ganzha[2,3]

[1] Department of Information Engineering
University of Modena and Reggio Emilia, Modena, Italy
[2] Systems Research Institute, Polish Academy of Sciences, Warsaw, Poland
[3] Institute of Informatics, University of Gdańsk, Gdańsk, Poland
{maciej.gawinecki,giacomo.cabri}@unimore.it
{marcin.paprzycki,maria.ganzha}@ibspan.pl

Abstract. One of the key requirements for the success of Service Oriented Architecture is *discoverability* of Web services. However, public services suffer from the lack of metadata. Current methods to provide such metadata are impractical for the volume of services published on the Web: they are too expensive to be implemented by a service broker, and too difficult to be used for retrieval. We introduce *structured collaborative tagging* to address these issues. Here, user tags not only aspects relevant for her but also suggested ones (input, output and behavior). Cost, performance and usability of the proposed technique obtained during the Semantic Service Selection 2009 contest are reported. Obtained results suggests that there is no "free lunch." While the method is user-friendly and supports effective retrieval, it still involves cost of attracting the community, and is practical only as complementary one. The analysis shows this is due to user's autonomy as to what, when and how to tag.

Keywords: Web service, Discovery, Collaborative tagging.

1 Introduction

For an application developer there are two key benefits of exploitation of public Web services: (i) a high degree of reuse of software building blocks available as readily deployed services, and (ii) access to data, functionalities and resources that would be otherwise not available to her [40]. For a service provider the benefit of exposing her data, functionality or resources as API is a new distribution channel for her business, research or activity in general [27]. To achieve these goals, it is necessary to make Web services *discoverable*. In the traditional Service Oriented Architecture (SOA) vision, service providers register services using a service broker, while service requestors use the same broker to discover them. In this vision, development of the service registry boils down to implementation of the following methods:

- *Adding Service* as a link and an interface description (WSDL) of a service,
- *Adding Metadata* about functionality of added Web service,
- *Service Discovery* using the provided service metadata.

J. Filipe and J. Cordeiro (Eds.): WEBIST 2010, LNBIP 75, pp. 69–84, 2011.

Until January 2006, the role of service brokers was played mainly by the UDDI Business Registries (UBRs), facilitated by Microsoft, SAP and IBM [36]. Afterwards, a large number of services has been published on the Web (in the form of WSDL definitions) and current service brokers, like SeekDa.com, harvest WSDL definitions from the Web and add them to the registry automatically [25,1]. However, there is no longer any "authority" to add/verify/standardize service metadata.

Many current approaches for adding metadata are impractical. They are too expensive to be implemented by the service broker or too difficult to be used for retrieval. The goal of our work is to provide a description method that is *practical*: *affordable* for a service broker, and *usable* for a software developer. The contributions of this chapter toward achieving this goal are as follows:

- We define practical criteria for a description method, illustrate the lack of practicality of current approaches against those criteria and identify challenges to make description method more practical (Section 2).
- We address the identified challenges by defining a practical method for providing metadata (Section 3), type and representation of the metadata (Section 4), and a discovery mechanism operating on those metadata (Section 5). Our method is a variation of *structured collaborative tagging*. The method allows to structure annotation and to explicitly split the functional categorization from the description of the service interface. Specifically, to differentiate between tags describing *input*, *output*, and *behavior* of a service.
- We report evaluation results obtained for those criteria during our participation in the Cross Evaluation track of the Semantic Service Selection 2009 contest [33] (Section 6).

2 Problem Definition

Our goal is to define a method for building a Web service registry where finding a required service is not only effective, but also easy for a user and keeps service broker costs of adding metadata low. This means that besides traditional *performance* criteria for service retrieval, we should stress the *managerial* and the *usability* ones. Specifically, we consider:

Performance Criteria. To evelop a registry that enables effective retrieval we need to consider the following criteria (adopted from the Semantic Service Selection (S3) contest [33]):

1. *Retrieval effectiveness*. This criterion reflects the relevance of returned results by the method.
2. *Query response time*. This criteria reflects the average query response time of a matchmaker for a single request.

Managerial Criteria. To develop a registry that is affordable for a service broker we need to consider the following criteria (adopted from from the related domain of software reuse libraries [29]):

1. *Investment cost.* This criterion reflects the cost of setting up a Web service registry that implements the given method, pro-rated to the size of the registry (tens of thousands of services, e.g in `SeekDa.com`).
2. *Operating cost.* This criterion reflects the cost of operating a Web service registry, pro-rated to the size of the registry.

Usability Criteria. To develop a registry that is usable for a software developer we need to consider the following criteria (again, from [29]):

1. *Difficulty of use.* This criterion accounts for the fact that the various methods provide varying intellectual challenges to their users.
2. *Transparency.* This criterion reflects to what extent the operation of the Web service registry depends on the users understanding of how the retrieval algorithm works.

2.1   Identifying Challenges

The following approaches to service discovery were compared against the proposed criteria:

- *Taxonomy-based Retrieval.* Taxonomies of service categories are used by UDDI Web service registries and specialized Web service portals (e.g. XMethods).
- *WSDL-based Signature Matching* [39,6] . In signature matching the goal is to find a service operation with a matching signature (input/output parameter names and types) or more generally, a whole service (with a matching operation). Matching is based on syntactical or structural similarity and is used, for instance, by the `Merobase.com` software components registry.
- *Ontology-based Service Specification Matching* [17] . Service specification determines the logic-based semantic relation between service preconditions (expected world state in which a service may be invoked) and effects (how world state is changed by service invocation). For instance, a service S may match a request, if the effect of S is more specific than required and preconditions of S are more general than required.

One can observe these approaches are impractical for building Web-scale registry of Web services for the following reasons (challenges).

A. Operating cost scales poorly with for the number of services. in ontology- and taxonomy-based approaches; as they require a person skilled in a given metadata formalism to categorize (annotate) a Web service with respect to an already established taxonomy (ontology) and extend the taxonomy (ontology). In the first case the operation is expensive, if Web services are added automatically from the Web, because the categorization (annotation) cannot be delegated to the provider. In the latter case, if adding new service requires an extension of the taxonomy (ontology), the whole operation can be complex. It might involve reconsidering the complete taxonomy (ontology) and possibly reclassifying (re-annotating) all Web services within the revised taxonomy (ontology).

B. Open-domain Registry Requires Large Investment Cost. As noted, operating cost for ontology- and taxonomy-based approaches is high if the taxonomy (ontology) is not defined carefully. Defining a taxonomy (ontology) for open range of domains in advance is expensive. To limit the cost, public UDDI registries reuse taxonomies proven in business categorization, e.g. UNSPSC [37]. In case of ontology-based approaches finding ontologies that cover sufficient range of domains with sufficient level of details and integrating them together is prohibitively costly.

C. Query Formulation for Formal Description Methods is Difficult. Overly complex encoding schemes are wasteful unless a service requestor is provided computer assistance in formulating equally complex queries [30]. Thus richer expressiveness of complex approaches like ontology-based specification matching might be not justified comparing to less complex (and thus easier to use) taxonomies and operation signatures.

D. Authoritatively Defined Descriptions may be not Transparent. This is often the case that there is a gap between how a user imagines a software component, a Web service in particular, and how it has been described in the registry [9,8]. For instance, the way the taxonomy structure has been defined by the authority, or the service has been classified by a service provider, is very often not obvious for the user [35]. Furthermore, input and output parameter names and types in WSDL definitions are usually assigned by convention or by the preference of the provider [6] that is unfamiliar to a user. Thus, in both cases, using the wrong query keyword(s) may result in failing to find the right service.

E. Supporting Complementary Retrieval Criteria. To achieve high effectiveness of service retrieval it is enough to encode, in service metadata, only information that is relevant to the searcher [30]. However, searchers differ in what information/criteria are relevant to them and it is impossible to envision all of them in advance, for instance situation when user will search for a "free of charge" service. Still, none of considered families of approaches support such *ad hoc* search criteria. On the contrary, it is assumed that searchers share a subset of common criteria: functional equivalence, interface compatibility and functionality scope equivalence [23]. Unfortunately, some methods support only part of them. For instance, signature matching considers only interface compatibility (input and output parameters) and ignores functionality equivalence (service behavior); service categorization with respect to a taxonomy is a way to group services of similar functionality or functionality scope but it does not support interface compatibility search.

F. Support for Interactive Search. User often starts a search for a Web service with an unclear goal in mind and thus needs to interact with the system in subsequent query/results steps to find the right Web service. To support such active interaction, the system needs to return not only relevant results, but also to do it in short time. However, many ontology-based approaches employ computationally expensive matchmaking algorithms with implementations too slow to be useful [32].

G. Limited Available Information about Web Service. To encode information relevant for a searcher (Challenge E) it is necessary to have this information available. A service provider that has developed a service, has all the knowledge available but is rarely the case he documents it completely in a WSDL definition [1]. Still, for Web services harvested automatically from the Web WSDL is the only source of information

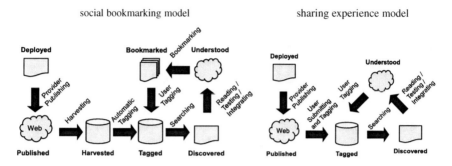

Fig. 1. Two tagging models show changing state of a service and user actions

about the Web service, thus its content might be not sufficient to categorize a service or provide its specification.

3 Architecture of Collaborative Tagging Portal

To face the above identified challenges we propose application of collaborative tagging. The technique has been initially proposed for service annotation by [28] as an alternative to authoritatively defined taxonomies. Collaborative tagging relies on voluntary participation of the community. Thus operating cost of describing is limited by putting the burden of description work on the community (Challenge A). The vocabulary used by taggers is not predefined: the process of vocabulary expansion and tagging object with respect to expanded vocabulary is continuous [35], eliminating thus investment cost (Challenge B) and operating cost of re-categorization (Challenge A). The advantage of tags is they can capture aspects of a service that are important for the community but has not been encoded neither in the WSDL definitions from service providers, nor in the authoritative classification; moreover, they use vocabulary more relevant and intuitive to a developer [10,8]. Therefore, the distance between what the developer wants and how it is described in the registry can be minimized [38] (Challenge D).

We propose to put a Web service registry behind an online portal where the process of collaborative tagging and searching of Web services is tightly intertwined. Marlow et al. [26] and Halpin et al. [15] discuss different elements of generic tagging system architecture. Below we address those architectural elements that are challenging for making tagging of Web services practical.

3.1 Supporting User Motivation

Tagging relies on voluntary participation and thus important incentive must attract a user to participate. The works of [14,24,26,31] discuss the number of motivations to tag and incentives to contribute to collaborative online projects (like open source software or Wikipedia). The following appear relevant for the technical community of software engineers: future retrieval (organizational), communal collaboration, information sharing, reciprocity ("I help you hoping you will help me in the future"), and autonomy

("I decide what to tag"). We propose two alternative tagging models to support realiza-tion of different subsets of those incentives (summarized in Figure 1):

- *Social bookmarking model* (inspired by such social bookmarking systems as del.icio.us). The model supports search task through cooperative organiza-tion of the registry content. A user bookmarks a service during discovery to keep a reference to it for further recall. She tags her collection of bookmarks with key-words to organize it, i.e. to ease the process of re-finding a service. Finally, she shares her bookmarks with the rest of the community, because she cannot describe all services in the registry alone and believes others will share their bookmarks with her.
- *Sharing experience model* (inspired by ProgrammableWeb.com, the community-driven registry of public APIs). In this model tagging is just one of the means a user has to share his experience about a service with the rest of the com-munity. Other content includes: comments, ratings, additional descriptions, code snippets for invoking a service, applications/mash-ups using the service, how-to tutorials etc.

3.2 Supporting Service Understanding

Users tend not too tag Web services if they do not have any comprehension of them, for instance they have not tried them [4]. However, understanding what a service does in most cases is more complex process than understanding an article (for tagging at del.icio.us) or interpretation of a photograph (at Flickr.com). Given that ini-tially WSDL definition is the only available source of information (Challenge G), we identified the following means to ease this process: (1) *names and natural language documentation* of service, provider, operations and their parameters, (2) *external site* of the provider (linked in WSDL), (3) *behavior sampling* to test how a service behaves (possible by generating client stub from the WSDL), and (4) *users experience* obtained from the previous means that can be documented in different form (see, the sharing experience model).

3.3 Tag Bootstrapping

A service needs to discovered before it gets tagged but untagged services cannot be dis-covered if tag-based search is the only search mechanism. This results in a deadlock. It can be prevented by bootstrapping a service with initial tags before it is actually added to the registry. Since services are harvested automatically from the Web, we propose to bootstrap tags using one of tags suggesting algorithms (e.g. [7]). Still, some services can be submitted manually by a user (in experience sharing model), and thus the same user may be encourage to submit also initial tags.

4   Metadata Representation

In our approach a user may describe a service she searches for in terms of interface it exposes—*input, output* query keywords—and the category to which it belongs—*behavior* query keywords (Challenge E). Hence, we model a service request q as a service template: $q = (q\_i, q\_o, q\_b)$, where q_i, q_o, q_b are sets of query terms describing three aspects: *input*, *output* and *behavior*, respectively. For instance let us consider the following service request:

> I'm looking for a service to geocode a given US address. The expected service takes as input a structured US postal address (street, city, zip code) and returns a geographical coordinates: latitude and longitude.

One of possible formulations of the service request in our query language is:

$$q\_i = (\texttt{street\_name}, \texttt{city\_name}, \texttt{state\_code}, \texttt{US}, \texttt{zip\_code})$$
$$q\_o = (\texttt{geocoordinate}, \texttt{latitude}, \texttt{longitude})$$
$$q\_b = (\texttt{geocoding}, \texttt{US\_address}, \texttt{usa})$$

To support such queries, the services in the registry should be annotated in a symmetric way. However, an unstructured annotation does not specify if a given tag describes *input*, *output* or *behavior* of a service. For instance, for a given service, tags find, location and zip are ambiguous. They do not specify whether the service finds a location for a zip code or a zip code for a location.

We address the problem by introducing *structured collaborative tagging*. Here, structured tagging implies: categorization of service functionality (*behavior* tags), description of a service interface (*input* and *output* tags) and identification of additional service characteristics, like the functionality scope (*behavior*, *input* and *output* tags). Note, that experiments of [38] on retrieval effectiveness have shown that tags cannot be used alone for effective retrieval, but only as a complementary mechanism to traditional classification schemes. This might have been caused by the fact that traditional classification schemes focus on predefined aspects, while tagging on those that are actually important for individual users. Structured tagging supports tagging on both types of aspects (Challenge E).

4.1   Metadata: Structured Tagging Model

Formally, we model service functionality utilizing three aspects: *input*, *output*, and *behavior*. We represent each aspect as a folksonomy. A folksonomy F is a set of annotations (a, t, s), posted by an actor a (a user or the system) who tagged a service s with a tag t. In this way we have specified three folksonomies F_i, F_o, F_b for *input*, *output* and *behavior*. Figure 2 shows examples of such folksonomies. For instance, F_b is defined by the following annotations: (bob, geographic, ZipGeocoder), (bob, geocoding, ZipGeocoder), (bob, find, DistanceCalculator), (alice, find, ATM-Locator), (alice, location, ATMLocator), (alice, geographic, ATMLocator), (alice, geocoding, ZipGeocoder). It can be seen that to classify a service aspects, an individual user provides one or more tags. Hence, many users may agree to tag a certain service part with the same tag. As a result the consensus on what a service does, consumes and returns emerges from annotations of the community. Figure 2 shows what consensus the community achieved on the ZipGeocoder service. For instance, two users agreed that a service does geocoding, and one of them classified it also as a geographic service.

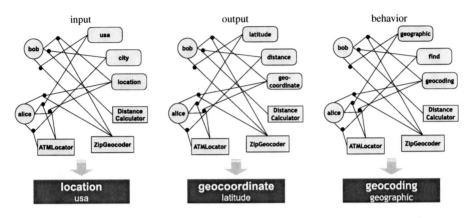

Fig. 2. Example folksonomies for three service parts and descriptions (tag clouds) of the ZipGeocoder service extracted from them. A circle depicts a tagging user, rectangle—a tagged service and rounded box—a tag used. Each black spot defines a single annotation. A tag cloud is a visual depiction of user-generated tags for a given service part. The bigger the tag, the more users provided it.

To manipulate relations F_i, F_o, F_b we use two standard relational algebra operators with set semantics. *Projection* (π_p), projects a relation into a smaller set of attributes p. *Selection* (σ_c), selects tuples from a relation where a certain condition c holds. Hence, π_p is equivalent to the SELECT DISTINCT p clause in SQL, whereas σ_c is equivalent to the WHERE c clause in the SQL.

5   Service Discovery

In service retrieval the community tags play a number of roles: (i) provide a network of links to browse services [28], (ii) facilitate quick understanding about a service, without reading a complex documentation, and (iii) provide metadata for ranking-based search [3,2]. We propose an approach for service discovery that uses tags primary for the latter role. With regard to query formulation our method is easy to use, because it accommodates natural language queries (Challenge C). On the other hand, returned ranking of results may be imperfect (incomplete or irrelevant), thus delegating much of the tedious retrieval/selection/assessment activity to the user. This increases the difficulty of our method. With regard to transparency of our method we assess it as high, because our matchmaking mechanism is straightforward (Challenge D). Firstly, the representations of the query and of the service description are structured in the same way. Secondly, a user in the system can be both searcher and tagger and thus see the mapping between queries and services better. Thirdly, as we shall see, matchmaking and ranking is based on simple concepts of tag overlap and tag popularity.

5.1   Service Matchmaker

The proposed matchmaker, called WSColab, (a) classifies services as either relevant or irrelevant to the service request, and (b) ranks relevant services with respect to their estimated relevance to the service request.

Service Binary Classification. The matchmaker returns services that are either inter-face compatible (there is at least one matching *input* tag and *output* tag) or functionally equivalent (there is at least one matching *behavior* tag). Formally, the set of results of the query q is defined as $r(q, (F_i, F_o, F_b)) = r(q_i, F_i) \cap r(q_o, F_o) \cup r(q_b, F_b)$, where $r(q_b, F_b) = \pi_s(\sigma_{t \in q_b}(F_b))$ and

$$r(q_i, F_i) = \begin{cases} \pi_s(\sigma_{t \in q_i}(F_i)), & q_i \neq \emptyset \\ S, & q_i = \emptyset \end{cases}$$

($r(q_o, F_o)$ is defined analogously to $r(q_i, F_i)$). Empty set of query keywords for a given aspect means that a user does not care about values for this aspect.

Ranking Services. The matchmaker should rank higher those services that are both functionally equivalent and interface compatible to the service request. Interface com-patibility is estimated as the similarity between interface (input and output) tags and interface query keywords. Functionality equivalence is estimated as the similarity be-tween behavior tags and behavior query keywords. Hence, the combination of those two heuristics may be represented as the weighted sum of similarity scores for single aspects: $sim(q_b, \sigma_s(F_b))$, $sim(q_i, \sigma_s(F_i))$ and $sim(q_o, \sigma_s(F_o))$:

$$sim(q, s) = w_b \cdot sim(q_b, \sigma_s(F_b)) + w_i \cdot sim(q_i, \sigma_s(F_i)) + w_o \cdot sim(q_o, \sigma_s(F_o))$$

Our initial experiments have shown that the functionality equivalence heuristics is more sensitive to false positives, because it may classify as relevant those services that have similar scope of functionality (e.g. usa), but are not functionally equivalent. Hence, we give more weight to the *input/ouput* aspects ($w_i = w_o = 0.4$) than to the *behavior* aspect ($w_b = 0.2$). To estimate similarity between the query keywords and the tags we borrowed a standard cosine similarity measure with TF/IDF weighting model [34] from information retrieval[1] For instance, for the input query keywords q_i and the input tags $\sigma_s(F_i)$ of the service s we define the similarity as:

$$sim(q_i, \sigma_s(F_i)) = \frac{\sum_{t \in q_i} w_s, t}{W_s},$$

$$w_s, t = tf_s, t \cdot idf_t, \quad W_s = \sqrt{\sum_{t \in q_i} w_s, t^2}, \quad tf_s, t = \frac{n_s, t}{N_t}, \quad idf_t = \log\frac{|S|}{1 + |S_t|}$$

where n_s, t is the number of actors that annotated an input of the service s with the tag t ($|\pi_u(\sigma_s, t(F_i))|$) and N is the number of annotations all actors made for the input of the service s ($|\pi_u(\sigma_s(F_i))|$). $|S|$ is the number of all registered services and $|S_t|$ is the number of services having input annotated with the tag t ($|\pi_s(\sigma_t(F_i))|$). As a result, service s_1 is ranked higher than s_2 in a single ranking if: (a) s_1 shares more tags with the query than the s_2 does, (b) shared tags of the s_1 have higher relevance weights (more users proposed them) than those of the s_2, and (c) shared tags of the s_1 are more specific (less common among tagged services) than those of the s_2. We also assumed that more people agree on major features than on minor ones and thus the criterion (b) is introduced to avoid assigning high rank to services that share some

---

[1] We evaluated also other similarity measures but they performed worse [12].

minor features (e.g. usa), but not major ones (e.g. location). The criterion (c) is to prevent services with very common tags from domination in the ranking. Usage of ranking method well known in information retrieval gave us the chance to implement the mechanism using the fast query evaluation algorithms based on (in-memory) inverted files [42] (Challenge F).

6   Evaluation

The goal of the evaluation was to empirically validate whether structured collaborative tagging can be a practical solution for Web service description. Specifically, we evaluated our method against three types of criteria (defined in Section 2): managerial, performance, and usability.

6.1   Assessing Managerial Criteria

Here, the goal was to estimate what are the investment and the operating cost for our solution and how they are to scale for large Web service repositories.

Procedure. To assess those costs we simulated the process of Web service tagging in terms of the social bookmarking cycle (see Section 3.1). We used the collection of data-centric Web services from the Jena Geography Dataset (JGD) [21]. The 50 services have been annotated by the community using our structured collaborative tagging model. System tags were generated manually by the organizers of the S3 contest (see [13] for details). To collect community tags we developed a collaborative tagging portal [11], where incoming users were given one of ten prepared software engineering tasks. For each service in the portal each user has been asked to: (a) tag its *behavior*, *input* and *output*, and (b) classify it as either relevant for the task (potentially useful in the context of the task) or irrelevant. The only source of information about service functionality was documentation and parameter names extracted from the WSDL definitions and other people's tags. Note, that the authors of the JGD test collection had saved the taggers's cognition effort by documenting all missing but relevant information in original WSDL definitions (for this goal they used instruments described in Section 3.2). The tagging process has been completed in the open (non-laboratory) environment, where users could come to the portal any number of times, at any time. We invited to participate our colleagues, with either industrial or academic experience in Web services, SOA or software engineering in general. Furthermore, we have sent invitations to the open community, through several public forums and Usenet groups concerned with related topics. The annotation portal was open for 12 days between September 16 and 27, 2009. Total of 27 users provided 2716 annotations. The contribution of users was significant: 46% to 61% (depending on a service aspect) of tags were new (not system).

Results. The only investment cost stemmed from approximately 40 man-hours spent to develop the annotation portal (Challenge B). The operating cost included almost 5 man-hours spent to invite taggers and promote the portal and about 3 man-hours on maintenance of the portal during the annotation process (fixing bugs) and answering to taggers' questions. This shows there is no free manpower in collaborative tagging: remaining operating cost was due to marketing actions required to attract the community

(Challenge A). If operating cost is acceptable, a question remains whether such invest-ment grants retrieval effectiveness. In case of tag-based search effectiveness depends on whether someone has described a service that a user searches for in a way she would describe it [35]. Figure 3a shows that people are very selective on which services to tag. Thus, for larger service catalogs, tags are likely to be distributed among services with respect to a power law, like in Web-scale tagging systems for other domains. Particu-larly, unpopular services may be found in a very long tail of little-tagged and untagged services and thus remain difficult to discover.

6.2   Assessing Retrieval Performance

An experimental evaluation has been performed during the Cross-Evaluation track of the Semantic Service Selection 2009 contest [33]. By participation in the contest we wanted to validate: (1) whether less formal descriptions do not result in worse perfor-mance than methods using Semantic Web Services, and (2) whether additional oper-ating cost spent on attracting the community is justified by performance improvement with respect to methods with no operating cost (i.e. methods automatically describing services). We briefly report the experimental setup of the contest and results. The com-plete experimental setup and detailed results analysis are reported in [22,13].

Competing Matchmakers. WSColab has been compared with five other matchmakers tested over the same collection of services and service requests. The competitors with more formal descriptions included: *SAWSDL-MX1* [18], *SAWSDL-MX2* [19], *SAWSDL-iMatcher3/1* [41], and *IRS-III* [5]. The family of methods based on automatically de-scribed services was represented by the *Themis-S* [20].

Test Data. All participants were given services and service requests from the Jena Ge-ography Dataset [21] to encode in their formalisms. For services we reused service tags collected previously (see Section 6.1). The nine service requests have been annotated in the following way. Each service request was a *natural language* (NL) *query* that needed to be translated into a *system query*. We collected query formulations from as many users as possible and the performance of our matchmaker has been further aver-aged over all query formulations. To avoid participation of persons who already have seen service descriptions, the collection process has been performed in a more con-trolled environment than tagging of services. We extended our annotation portal with a functionality of presenting service requests and collecting system queries from users. User could see neither services in the registry, nor results of her queries. The only infor-mation shared was the vocabulary used to describe services during the tagging phase. It was presented as: (1) query suggestions (through query autocompletion technique), and (2) three tag clouds, one for each aspect of the annotation. No information has been given about which service has been described by which tags.

Relevance Judgments. The relevance of Web service responses has been checked against *binary* relevance judgments and *graded* relevance judgments [23]. Both types of judgments considered functional equivalence, functional scope and interface-compati-bility of the answer. Due to limited space we report only the results for graded relevance judgments. Note, however, that the results were stable—the position of WSColab in the ranking of compared matchmakers did not change with respect to the binary relevance judgments.

Performance Metrics. The retrieval effectiveness against the graded relevance judgments has been measured using the $nDCG\_i$—a normalized Discount Cumulative Gain at the rank (cut-off level) i [16]. Let G_i be a gain value that the i-th returned service gains for relevance. We define

$$DCG\_i = \begin{cases} G\_1 & , i = 1 \\ DCG\_i - 1 + G\_i/log\_2(i+1) & , i \geq 2 \end{cases}$$

The Discount Cumulative Gain (DCG) realistically rewards relevant answers in the top of the ranking more than those in the bottom of the ranking. Calculated DCG_i is then normalized by the ideal possible DCG_i to make the comparison between different matchmakers possible. The discount factor of $log\_2(i+1)$ is relatively high, to model an impatient user who gets bored when she cannot find a relevant answer in the top of the ranking. We also plot the $nDCG$ curve, where the X-axis represents a rank, and the Y-axis represents a $nDCG$ value for a given rank. An ideal matchmaker has a horizontal curve with a high $nDCG$ value; the vertical distance between the ideal $nDCG$ curve and the actual $nDCG$ curve corresponds to the effort a user wastes on less than perfect documents delivered by a particular matchmaker. The efficiency of matchmakers has been measured in terms of average query response time on an Intel Core2 Duo T9600 (2.8GHz) machine with 4GB RAM running Windows XP 32bit.

Results. All the results reported here are courtesy of the S3 contest organizers. Figure 3b shows the $nDCG$ curves for the compared systems. The performance of the WSColab is the closest to the performance of an ideal one (with respect to the $nDCG$ measure). It has a relative performance of 65-80% over most of the ranks while (except for the first two ranks) the remaining systems have a relative performance less than 55-70%. Here, the intuition is that a user needs to spend less effort to find relevant service with WSColab than using other matchmakers. This not only justifies the operating cost of our description method, but also shows that our matchmaker can be competitive to matchmakers working with more formal service descriptions. Detailed results analysis (found in [13]) reveals the possible cause: authors of formal approaches have encoded only information about major features of the service. Encoding minor features (e.g. `miles`) would require spending additional effort on expending existing domain ontologies (Challenge A). Collaborative tagging does not require any additional effort when extending vocabulary and thus minor features have been encoded (Challenge E).

With regard to retrieval efficiency, the average query response time of the WSColab is below 1 millisecond. The second top-efficient matchmaker is the SAWSDL-iMatcher3/1 with 170 milliseconds of average query response time (Challenge F).

6.3 Assessing Usability Criteria

We asked how well our solution resolved usability-related challenges (C and D). For this goal we analyzed retrieval effectiveness of each query formulating user. Only one

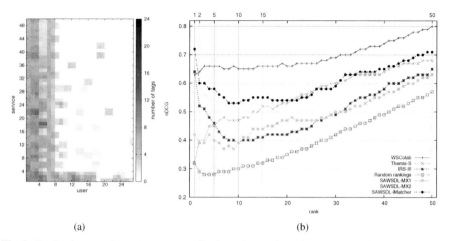

(a)   (b)

Fig. 3. Evaluation results: (a) user contributions in tagging the same services (darker area represents more tags provided by a given user for a given service); (b) the nDCG curves for the six different matchmakers averaged over 4 different graded relevance judgments. Shown courtesy of the S3 contest organizers.

of the five users have used query language improperly by constantly putting the keywords related to the input and keywords related to output in the input field. He received the worst retrieval effectiveness (averaged over queries) among all users. This may suggest the we should make search interface more supportive in understanding the query language (Challenge C). With regard to the description transparency (Challenge D), we observed that users found non-system tags very valuable for describing service requests—the query keywords were system tags, for only 22% for the behavior aspect, 26% for the input, and 34% for the output. This shows that most descriptions are transparent for a user. Still, in a few cases performance of users suffered from vocabulary and structure gaps: someone had described a searched service in a different way that the searcher would (e.g. used altitude instead of height, or put information about output in the behavior field).

7   Concluding Remarks

To be discoverable a service needs to be described. We asked whether structured collaborative tagging can be a practical approach for describing Web services based only on available WSDL information harvested automatically from the Web. Our work provides several suggestions in this direction. Structured collaborative tagging offers competitive retrieval performance with respect to more expensive (in terms of description) methods based on semantic annotation. It is easy to use and relatively transparent, thus usable for a searcher. However, it does not allow to eliminate operating cost completely. Participation in collaborative tagging is voluntary, and hence certain amount of time and resources must be spent on marketing to attract and to develop a community of developers around the portal. Most importantly, collaborative tagging suffers from the lack of *controllability*. Controlling the annotation process is necessary to get services with insufficient descriptions described but it cannot be reconciled with one of the major motivations of a user to participate: her *autonomy* as to what, when and how to tag [24]. Consequently, many services will not described at all, thus remaining non-discoverable. This suggests that structured collaborative tagging should be implemented by the service broker only as a description method complementary to traditional ones.

Acknowledgements. We would like to thank to: Ulrich Küster (for the organization of the Cross-Evaluation track), Patrick Kapahnke and Matthias Klusch (for their general support and organization of the S3 contest), Holger Lausen and Michal Zaremba (for providing SeekDa data), M. Brian Blake, Elton Domnori, Grzegorz Frackowiak, Giorgio Villani and Federica Mandreoli (for the discussion). Finally, we would like to thank voluntary participants of our experiment for their enthusiasm.

References

1. Al-Masri, E., Mahmoud, Q.H.: Discovering Web Services in Search Engines. IEEE Internet Computing 12(3) (2008)
2. Bouillet, E., Feblowitz, M., Feng, H., Liu, Z., Ranganathan, A., Riabov, A.: A Folksonomy-Based Model of Web Services for Discovery and Automatic Composition. In: IEEE SCC, pp. 389–396 (2008)
3. Chukmol, U., Benharkat, A.-N., Amghar, Y.: Enhancing Web Service Discovery by Using Collaborative Tagging System. In: NWESP, pp. 54–59 (2008)
4. Cuel, R., Oksana, T.: SeekDa Case. Tech. rep., Insemtives Project (2010)
5. Dietze, S., Benn, N., Domingue, J., Conconi, A., Cattaneo, F.: Two-fold service matchmaking – applying ontology mapping for semantic web service discovery. In: Gómez-Pérez, A., Yu, Y., Ding, Y. (eds.) ASWC 2009. LNCS, vol. 5926, pp. 246–260. Springer, Heidelberg (2009)
6. Dong, X., Halevy, A.Y., Madhavan, J., Nemes, E., Zhang, J.: Similarity Search for Web Services. In: VLDB (2004)
7. Falleri, J.R., Azmeh, Z., Huchard, M., Tibermacine, C.: Automatic Tag Identification In Web Service Descriptions. In: WEBIST (2010)
8. Fernández, A., Hayes, C., Loutas, N., Peristeras, V., Polleres, A., Tarabanis, K.A.: Closing the Service Discovery Gap by Collaborative Tagging and Clustering Techniques. In: SMRR (2008)
9. Furnas, G.W., Landauer, T.K., Gomez, L.M., Dumais, S.T.: The vocabulary problem in human-system communication. Commun. ACM 30(11) (1987)
10. Furnas, G.W., Fake, C., Ahn, Von Ahn, L., Schachter, J., Golder, S., Fox, K., Davis, M., Marlow, C., Naaman, M.: Why do tagging systems work? In: CHI (2006)
11. Gawinecki, M.: WSColab Portal (2009), http://mars.ing.unimo.it/wscolab/
12. Gawinecki, M., Cabri, G., Paprzycki, M., Ganzha, M.: Trade-off between Complexity of Structured Tagging and Effectiveness of Web Service Retrieval. In: Daniel, F., Facca, F.M. (eds.) ICWE 2010. LNCS, vol. 6385, pp. 289–300. Springer, Heidelberg (2010)
13. Gawinecki, M., Cabri, G., Paprzycki, M., Ganzha, M.: Evaluation of structured collaborative tagging for Web service matchmaking.In: Semantic Services: Advancement through Evaluation (2011) (to appear)

14. Golder, S.A., Huberman, B.A.: Usage patterns of collaborative tagging systems. Journal of Information Science 32(2), 198–208 (2006)
15. Halpin, H., Robu, V., Shepherd, H.: The complex dynamics of collaborative tagging. In: WWW, pp. 211–220 (2007)
16. Järvelin, K., Kekäläinen, J.: Cumulated gain-based evaluation of IR techniques. ACM Trans. Inf. Syst. 20(4), 422–446 (2002)
17. Klusch, M.: Semantic web service coordination. In: CASCOM: Intelligent Service Coordination in the Semantic Web, ch. 4, pp. 59–104 (2008)
18. Klusch, M., Kapahnke, P.: Semantic Web Service Selection with SAWSDL-MX. In: SMRR, vol. 416 (2008)
19. Klusch, M., Kapahnke, P., Zinnikus, I.: SAWSDL-MX2: A Machine-Learning Approach for Integrating Semantic Web Service Matchmaking Variants. In: ICWS, pp. 335–342 (2009)
20. Knackstedt, R., Kuropka, D., Müller, O., Polyvyanyy, A.: An Ontology-based Service Discovery Approach for the Provisioning of Product-Service Bundles. In: ECIS (2008)
21. Küster, U.: Jena Geography Dataset (2009), http://fusion.cs.uni-jena.de/professur/jgd
22. Küster, U.: JGDEval at S3 Contest 2009 - Results (2010), http://fusion.cs.uni-jena.de/professur/jgdeval/jgdeval-at-s3-contest-2009-results
23. Küster, U., König-Ries, B.: Relevance Judgments for Web Services Retrieval - A Methodology and Test Collection for SWS Discovery Evaluation. In: ECOWS (2009)
24. Kuznetsov, S.: Motivations of contributors to wikipedia. SIGCAS Comput. Soc. 36(2), 1 (2006)
25. Lausen, H., Haselwanter, T.: Finding Web Services. In: ESTC (June 2007)
26. Marlow, C., Naaman, M., Boyd, D., Davis, M.: HT06, tagging paper, taxonomy, Flickr, academic article, to read. In: HYPERTEXT, pp. 31–40. ACM, New York (2006)
27. Mashery: Selling beyond your site: Five key api strategies for retailers, business white paper (2010), http://www.mashery.com
28. Meyer, H., Weske, M.: Light-weight semantic service annotations through tagging. In: Dan, A., Lamersdorf, W. (eds.) ICSOC 2006. LNCS, vol. 4294, pp. 465–470. Springer, Heidelberg (2006)
29. Mili, A., Mili, R., Mittermeir, R.T.: A survey of software reuse libraries. Ann. Softw. Eng. 5, 349–414 (1998)
30. Mili, H., Mili, F., Mili, A.: Reusing Software: Issues and Research Directions. IEEE Trans. Softw. Eng. 21(6), 528–562 (1995)
31. Preece, J.: Sociability and usability in online communities: determining and measuring success. Behaviour & Information Technology 20(5), 347–356 (2001)
32. Semantic Service Selection contest—Summary Report (2008), http://www-ags.dfki.uni-sb.de/~klusch/s3/s3c-2008.pdf
33. Semantic Service Selection contest (2009), http://www-ags.dfki.uni-sb.de/~klusch/s3/html/2009.html
34. Salton, G., Buckley, C.: Term-Weighting Approaches in Automatic Text Retrieval. Inf. Process. Manage. 24(5), 513–523 (1988)
35. Shirky, C.: Ontology is Overrated: Categories, Links, and Tags (2005), http://www.shirky.com/writings/ontology_overrated.html
36. SOA World Magazine: Microsoft, IBM, SAP To Discontinue UDDI Web Services Registry Effort (2009), http://soa.sys-con.com/node/164624

37. United Nations Standard Products and Services Code (2009),
    http://www.unspsc.org
38. Vanderlei, T.A., Durao, F.A., Martins, A.C., Garcia, V.C., Almeida, E.S., de Lemos Meira,
    S.R.: A cooperative classification mechanism for search and retrieval software components.
    In: SAC, pp. 866–871. ACM, New York (2007)
39. Wang, Y., Stroulia, E.: Semantic structure matching for assessing web-service similarity. In:
    Orlowska, M.E., Weerawarana, S., Papazoglou, M.P., Yang, J. (eds.) ICSOC 2003. LNCS,
    vol. 2910, pp. 194–207. Springer, Heidelberg (2003)
40. Weerawarana, S., Curbera, F., Leymann, F., Storey, T., Ferguson, D.F.: Web Services Plat-
    form Architecture: SOAP, WSDL, WS-Policy, WS-Addressing, WS-BPEL, WS-Reliable
    Messaging and More. Prentice Hall PTR, Upper Saddle River (2005)
41. Wei, D., Wang, T., Wang, J., Chen, Y.: Extracting semantic constraint from description text
    for semantic web service discovery. In: ISWC, pp. 146–161 (2008)
42. Zobel, J., Moffat, A.: Inverted files for text search engines. ACM Comput. Surv. 38(2), 6
    (2006)

In-Context Annotations for Refinding and Sharing

Ricardo Kawase, Eelco Herder, George Papadakis, and Wolfgang Nejdl

L3S Research Center, Leibniz Universität Hannover
Appelstr. 4, 30167 Hannover, Germany
{kawase,herder,papadakis,nejdl}@L3S.de

Abstract. Annotations support understanding, interpretation, sensemaking and scannability. As valuable as in paper-based contexts, digital online annotations provide several benefits for annotators and collaborators. To further explore the real benefits of online annotations, we implemented a simple Web Annotation tool, SpreadCrumbs, to support our studies. The tool provides a simple annotation mechanism, simulating real-world paper-based annotations. In addition, the tool supports search, sharing capabilities and social navigation. We conducted a series of user studies that empirically demonstrates the benefits of "in-context" annotations for refinding and sharing.

Keywords: Annotation, In-context, Trail, Social media, Social network, Online collaboration, User interface, SpreadCrumbs.

1 Introduction

The World Wide Web is arguably the biggest source of information nowadays. Whereas the exchange of ideas on the Web was predominantly one-way, the Web 2.0 now offers a new means of interactions and has shifted more power and influence to users. However, there are still a number of features missing that are essential for supporting information classification, retrieval, processing and understanding. Most of these issues have been reported already during the early inception of the Web, mainly from the hypertext community [1] [2]. In particular, frequently mentioned are: the lack of typed or annotated links; the absence of hypertrails; limited browser history mechanisms; and the lack of support for annotations.

In order to bring these missing features into the Web, a common workaround is to create applications that enhance the Web usability, such as search engines, tagging systems, annotation systems, social networks and others. The competitive character within the Web 2.0 has arguably led to a more powerful reincarnation of the rich features that once were part of the classic hypertext systems [3]; albeit as a collection of diverse, disconnected applications, interoperating on top of a common Web platform. Surprisingly, despite the prevalence of interactive applications and social networking, thus far Web annotation systems haven't seen a significant take-up [4].

Given the absence of any dominant mature annotation system, it appears that there is still no generally accepted, concrete method for straightforward online annotation. This is surprising, given the abundance of literature showing the importance of annotations for comprehension and their benefits for reading and writing proposes [5].

J. Filipe and J. Cordeiro (Eds.): WEBIST 2010, LNBIP 75, pp. 85–100, 2011.

Similar to the paper-based environment, digital annotations are expected to be useful for supporting comprehension and interpretation [6]. Moreover, comments and references are known to stimulate associative thinking, which can be even better reproduced digitally, by what we call "hypertrails". For this reason, our research goal is to understand users' annotation behaviors and identify the benefits and drawbacks of online annotations and trails.

Based on insights gained from earlier work and an analysis of the reasons that hampered wide-spread adoption of earlier annotation systems, we created SpreadCrumbs [7, 8]. SpreadCrumbs is an online annotation tool that allows the users to place annotations within Web resources, either for themselves or for other users. In this work we introduce the application, its main functionalities and present a system evaluation.

The rest of this work is structured as follows: In section 2, we discuss related work in the field of annotations and annotations systems, followed by the description of Spreadcrumbs in section 3. In section 4 we present a preparative study on annotations for the experiments and studies, of which the setup is described in section 5. The results are presented in section 6, followed by our conclusions in section 7.

2   Related Work

2.1   Paper Annotations

We adopt the definition of annotations as set forth by MacMullen [9] and Marshall [10]: *An annotation is any additional content that is directly attached to a resource and that adds some implicit or explicit information in many different forms.*

Annotations may serve different purposes, such as:
signaling a foreshadow, aiding memory and interpretation or triggering reflection. Additionally, annotations may occur in many different forms; for example: by highlighting, encircling or underlining text, we emphasize the importance of a certain part of the document; a strikethrough indicates that something is wrong, misplaced or not relevant; arrows signal relations between two or more elements.

In [3], the authors draw a comparison between the early Hypertext pioneers visions and the present-day Web applications, commonly known as Web 2.0. The results of their analysis show that most of these systems support both private and public annotations and provide support for collaboration. Even though these features are identical with the first ideas of the Hypertext, the annotations are limited, because they reside exclusively bound to individual Web 2.0 services providers and they are not "in-context" – More specifically, they are not visualized together and associated with the annotated content (the topic of interest), which the benefits will be exposed later.

2.2   Digital Annotation Systems

The Fluid Annotations projects [11] introduce an online annotation system that supports in-context annotation in an extension of the open hypermedia Arakne Environment [12]. Their studies focused on evaluations and the presentation of the annotations in terms of visual cues, interactions, accommodation and animated transactions. Their main approach to in-context notes uses between-lines annotations. Their evaluations give valuable insights into the usability and manipulation of annotations. Nevertheless, we believe disrupting the original layout of the annotated content may be more confusing and disruptive than beneficial.

Another annotation system is MADCOW [13, 14] a digital annotation system organized in a client-server architecture, where the client is a plug-in for a standard web browser allowing users to annotate Web resources. Although MADCOW supports different representations for annotations, previous work comparing paper-based and digital annotations [15] suggests that paper-based annotations should not be mimicked by similar representations but by providing the means to achieve the same goals. In addition, the placeholders of the annotations are inserted between the HTML content which can be disruptive, distractive and may lead to the problem of orphan annotations. Finally, usage complexity will impact the dissemination of any new technology, and in particular, will always be an obstacle for the non engaged users. The annotation interface in their work has not been evaluated.

A more full-fledged annotation tool is Diigo . Using the Diigo toolbar, users can highlight text or attach 'inline sticky notes' to Web pages. Despite the wealth of features, Diigo cannot boast a big user population. According to online user comments, this is due to both usability issues and the fact that all annotations are public by default. We understand that sharing annotations is one of the main possible advantages of digital annotations systems; however in light of Diigo, we believe that a 'shared' annotation must not be mistaken for a 'public' one. The benefits of reliable collaborators are not fully applicable in the 'public' scenario; we elaborate, further on this point in sub-section 2.3.

In summary, there are numerous and similar annotations systems - most of them are discontinued works which have neither developed further nor been presented in further studies.

2.3 Social Navigation

Social navigation support (SNS) describes techniques for guiding users through specific chosen resources [16]. In AnnotatEd [17] the authors introduce two types of SNS: traffic-based and annotation-based. Our model more is related to the annotation-based style, in that every annotated page becomes a step in a trail.

Annotation-based social navigation support has been shown to be more proficient and reliable than traditional footprint-based social navigation support [18]. When the annotated resource reflects the interest of the annotator, it appends more value to the SNS. Annotation based SNS assists users in gathering information by making it easier to re-access the information and by showing the collective wisdom of the collaborators.

Allowing users to "attach" their personal insights to a resource increases the reliability of annotation-based navigation support. Previous study of annotation-based SNS shows that users are particularly interested in being informed about resources annotated by others. Annotated resources are significantly more likely to be visited by users, specifically after being annotated [18].

3 SpreadCrumbs

SpreadCrumbs is an in-context Web annotation system, which has been implemented as an extension of the Mozilla Firefox Web browser. The underlying assumption of SpreadCrumbs is that users can annotate Web resources with keywords or sentences and create hypertrails through a set of annotations. These annotations can not only be used for one's own reference, but can also be shared within a social network. The design of SpreadCrumbs has deliberately been kept minimalistic. Following the approaches seen in related work, we chose the basic visual metaphor for the annotations: Post-it notes.

The Post-it representation has an optimized approach to simulate the most common paper based annotations forms namely underlining, highlighting and notation in margins. The idea is not to mimic different representations but to provide a way to achieve the same goals: signalling for future attention, comprehension and summarization. In addition post-it notes are extremely efficient as "in-context" landmarks which are the main purpose of the research.

Furthermore, by bringing the annotation behaviour to the digital online environment we also add valuable features that are not applicable in the paper-based scenarios. The most prominent are the re-finding and the social sharing possibilities. The content of an annotation is easily searchable within the tool and shareable with other users.

3.1 The Browser Add-On

The SpreadCrumbs Browser add-on is a Javascript implementation based on AJAX principles. We used the AJAX and Javascript library from Yahoo, The Yahoo! User Interface Library (YUI). The library provides functionalities for drag & drop and other manipulations used in SpreadCrumbs. A simple client server architecture stores all the data on the server providing the user the possibility to access her data anytime from any computer where the client application is installed.

Once the client add-on is installed to the browser the user can access the sidebar. Through the sidebar the users have access to straightforward ordinary actions like creating account, profile management, login and logout. Additionally, the user has direct access to a contact managing webpage and a tabbed annotation-browser-window. From the right-click context menu an option is available to annotate the page, the same as from a small annotation button near the address bar.

3.2 Networking

As a non-mandatory step, new users may add their social network contacts to become collaborators in SpreadCrumbs. From the sidebar the users have access to the 'contact manager' webpage, from which they can import their contacts from their Facebook Network using Facebook Connect technology. Once the contacts are imported they become part of the user's SpreadCrumbs network and the user is able to share annotations with her contacts. If at some point these contacts join SpreadCrumbs and grant permission to Facebook Connect; their accounts will be synchronised and all the annotations previously shared by some other user will be retrieved.

3.3 Annotating

Annotations (which we will refer to as 'crumbs') are added via the right-click context menu by the option "Add Crumb", which results in the opening of a pop-up window that contains three fields: the receivers of the annotations, a topic and the content. By default, annotations are private. An auto-completion drop-box helps the user in adding receivers from her contact list.

Once the annotation is created, a post-it note appears in the screen, originally on the clicked spot but easily relocated by drag & drop (Fig. 1). When any of the involved users in the annotation accesses the annotated website, post-it note will be displayed. Additionally, if the user keeps her connection to Facebook through SpreadCrumbs, the receivers of the annotation will get a notification on Facebook and a notifying e-mail about the new annotation.

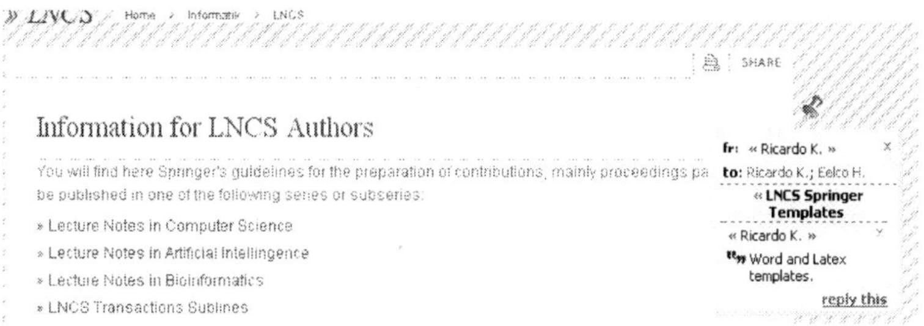

Fig. 1. Page annotated with SpreadCrumbs

3.4 Reacting

Each annotation is an entity in a thread (a crumb in a trail) and diverse actions can be taken over it. When visualizing an annotation, any of the involved users has the ability to interact with it: moving it around, closing it, following trails and replying.

Connect and Disconnect. Each user has her individual status in the context of one annotation. The status "Connected" is the normal status to visualize the annotations; "Disconnected" means that she will not visualize the annotation anymore once she comes back to the website; and "Stand by" means that she will not visualize the annotation again until some modification has occurred in the annotation thread.

Replying. The reply link on an annotation brings up the same window pop-up as adding an annotation offering to the user just the content field to be filled. Once confirmed, the reply is attached to the first post-it note and the same notifications actions are triggered. Any user involved in the annotation is able to add a reply to the running thread, which is visible to all participants. This action simulates a micro in-context forum on each annotated web page.

Following Trails (SNS). What makes SpreadCrumbs unique is that the annotated pages are not simply a loose collection, but the resources become interconnected. Each annotation is associated with links that can be followed from the crumb: the user trail and the topic trail. Near the name of each user who annotated the page and near the topic text there are two small linked arrows indicating the path to the previous and to next annotation in the hypertrail. Following the previous/next link next to the name of a user will redirect the current user to the next/previous annotated page where both users share another annotation.

Following the topic trail will lead the user to web pages on which the user has annotations with the same topic description. A simple illustrative example: one user privately annotates five different pages with the topic "Conference" adding specific content for each annotation. Once it is done, each conference page annotated has a link connecting to each other. A temporal defined (and connected) collection of web resources was created and at any time the user is able to remove, edit or add new stop points in this trail. The final output is a simulation of the Memex idea where the resources are now annotated and associated in accordance with the user's preferable organization.

Providing sharing capabilities of these trails, SpreadCrumbs grants Social Navigation Support in a very concrete and defined manner. Differently from others SNS systems, the resources are not only a collection of links but they have a well-defined temporal order, each resource becomes interconnected and they hold in-context insights from the annotation authors.

3.5 Browsing Annotations

The SpreadCrumbs' sidebar contains a browser pane with three different tabs that shows the three facets of the organizational dimensions of a trail: topics, pages, people. Additionally, a small pane in the bottom shows detailed information on the selected trail.

The tab 'topics' shows the trails grouped by topic description. The user visualizes distinct items that represent the different trail-topics she created. From this pane, the user is able to access the annotated page, edit the topic description and change her status in the topic. By clicking or selecting one of the topic-trails the bottom pane loads and displays all the crumbs belonging to this trail assembled by page. In this pane the user has the same possibilities to directly access the annotated page, to edit the crumb and to reply it.

The second tab, page, shows the trails grouped by the resource annotated. The visualization has the title extracted from the Webpage and the trail last modified date as well. The user has the possibility to edit the name of the page, if she wants to. It is important to notice that although trails mainly contain the same page title in this facet they will not be grouped together since the grouping is based on the URL location of the annotation. By clicking or selecting one of the page-trails the bottom pane loads and displays all the crumbs belonging to this trail assembled by the different topics existing on the selected page with same management capabilities.

Finally, the people tab shows items that represent the trails from the user's contacts. The item visualization shows the name of the contact and her last activity on the trail. It also indicates whether the contact is already connected to SpreadCrumbs' network or not (due to the fact that is possible to share annotations to imported contacts that are not subscribed to SpreadCrumbs). By clicking or selecting one of the people-trails, the bottom pane works in the way as the topics tab previously described.

4 Understanding Annotations

The first step in our studies is to fully comprehend the desired annotation features needed on the web. In order to understand the real use of annotations and Web annotations we conducted a field-study examining the paper-based annotations of 22 PhDs students and pos-Docs in their own work environment [15]. For each participant, we looked at the last 3 research papers or articles that they have printed and read. In total we have collected 66 articles, covering a total of 591 pages of text. This is a mere preparative step to the incoming experiments presented on Section 5.

We found 1778 annotations and an average of 3.08 annotations per page. **Table 1** below shows the average of each type of annotation based on Marshall's proposed classification [10] by forms and functions.

Although most of the annotations consist of highlighting activities, we identified in our previous study that it does not imply that mimicking this feature is the most appropriate approach to be followed. We identified that paper-based highlights are used for signalling and attributing different levels of importance and to help memorization during the reading activity. However, digital highlight is usually a non-persistent activity to help focusing on the text and re-finding – users highlight the text with the mouse cursor while reading. Excessive amounts of digital highlighting turns out to be more distractive than helpful. The conclusion of this work led us to the consideration that annotation systems should emphasize re-finding, visual overviews, grouping, sharing and collaborating rather than to try and mimic the 'old-fashioned' paper-based annotation.

Table 1. Collected annotations classified by type

Annotation types		
Highlighting/Mark sections headings	153	8.6%
Highlighting/Mark text	1297	73%
Problem solving	2	0.1%
General notes (Notes in the margins)	326	18.3%

5 Web Annotations in Practice

The next step after understanding annotations is to observe and analyze Web annotations in practice. To evaluate the usability and performance of Web annotations, we ran a series of laboratory experiments and processed the usage logs. The aim of our experiment was threefold: 1) examine the possible benefits of annotations over bookmarks for personal information management, and 2) evaluate social navigation support in an arbitrary scenario. In this section we describe the experiments.

5.1 Annotations vs. Bookmarks

The goal of our first study was to quantitatively estimate the efficiency and ease-of-use of annotations as a means for personal information management and refinding. As a reference point, we compared Annotations with (Social) Bookmarks. Our participant pool consisted of 24 males and 10 females, with an average age of 28. The participants were randomly and equally split into two groups: the first group created annotations using the Delicious social bookmarking service, the second group made use of SpreadCrumbs.

After a short introduction to the basic features of the tool (either SpreadCrumbs or Delicious), each individual session was conducted. We asked the participant to find answers for ten random questions. This task was presented as 'just' an exercise in order to get used to the system. In reality this first task was a preparational step for the second round of the experiment. All questions were specific information-finding tasks that could be solved by a brief internet search with any popular search engine. We ensured that the questions were sufficiently obscure, to minimize the chance of participants knowing the answers themselves.

Five months after the initial round of the studies, the participants were invited to participate again. This time, their task was to relocate the answers that they had previously found during the first task. The long time interval ensured that the participants remembered neither the answers they had provided nor the resources they had used to find the answers. In total, 30 out of the initial 34 participants were involved in this phase of our study (21 males and 9 females, average age 28 years).

The participants were divided into three equivalent groups of 10 people, each one corresponding to a specific refinding methodology and corresponding tool. As a base line, the first group used a search engine in their efforts to carry out their tasks (in other words, they had to search again for the same information). The second group used bookmarks to refind the information. This group consisted of those subjects that used Delicious in the previous session and had the URLs of the visited resources at their disposal. The third group consisted of the SpreadCrumbs users. The members of this group had the in-context annotations at their disposal.

We ensured that all participants accomplished all of their tasks under the same conditions and that their performance is compared on an equal basis. After the appropriate Web resource was found, thus completing the 'searching stage', the participant had to locate the answer in the page and highlight it using the mouse – the browsing stage. There were no instructions or restrictions on how to proceed at this stage: the participants were allowed to perform this task the way they would in a non-controlled environment. The necessary data for estimating and evaluating the average and overall browsing time per individual were collected using screen capture and data-logging software that recorded all participants' actions.

5.2 Shared Annotations

To evaluate the usability and benefits of annotations we asked the same 34 participants from the previous study to play a role in a scenario on collaborative decision making. The participants were asked to plan a trip to London, by reviewing the options, as collected by their 'partner' (the experimenter). Via either SpreadCrumbs or Del.icio.us, the participant received a number of annotations/bookmarks on suitable hotels, restaurants, museums and musicals in London. The participants evaluated the given options – by visiting the bookmarked sites and/or by reading the annotations – and finally decided for one option in each category.

Upon completion of all tasks, the subjects were asked to fill out two questionnaires, one regarding the information refinding experience and another one investigating their opinion on the tool they used.

6 Results

From the refinding task we collected a total of 297 successful activities, evenly distributed across the conditions. With this data we extend our analysis [19], investigating further aspects that may have contributed to the results. First, the most appropriate metric for expressing the overall performance of each group is arguably the *average time* taken to complete the *browsing phase* – therewith ignoring the time it took participants to locate the page in the *searching phase*. In our case, the available sample of 99 browsing times produces the following mean values: 46s for Search Engine, 38s for Bookmark, and 21s for Annotation. It turns out therefore that the performances of the first two groups differ slightly, whereas the performance of Annotation is substantially better, corresponding to a time that is almost the half of the other two groups. This suggests that in-context annotation boosts refinding to a great extent.

This fact is also advocated by the outcomes of the corresponding independent two-tailed t-tests between groups Search Engine and Annotation (Table 2B) as well as between Bookmark and Annotation (Table 2C). Both tests produce a significant result ($p < 0,01$) with a medium effect size r.

By contrast, when comparing the performance of the first two groups, the value resulting from t-test is well above the threshold (Table 2A). This result does not match our initial expectation that Bookmark would outperform Search Engine due to the wealth of cues associated with them - the comments that were attached to bookmarks as well as the keywords of the tags that were drawn from the questions or even the answers. However, this equivalence can partially be explained by the *theory of context-dependency* [20]. This theory states that all context knowledge acquired in the refinding process, including even the non-semantically related elements located within the target information, serves as relevant cues for refinding information. According to the theory, search engine users acquired a comprehensive enough context while searching and browsing the search results, which assisted them in the browsing stage, whereas the bookmark users had to acquire the context during the browsing stage itself. It should be stressed that the performance of the search group would have been significantly worse if we also took into account the searching stage, which is minimized for bookmarks' users.

Table 2. Results of t-test between Search Engine and Bookmark (A), between Search Engine and Annotation (B) and between groups Bookmark and Annotation (C)

	A		B		C	
	Search Engine	Bookmark	Search Engine	Annotation	Bookmark	Annotation
Mean	46:30.9	37:45.5	46:30.9	20:41.2	37:45.5	20:41.2
Variance	02:19.5	00:57.8	02:19.5	00:17.4	00:57.8	00:17.4
Observations	99	99	99	99	99	99
df	98		98		98	
t(98)	1,21		4,07		3,88	
p	0,11		< 0,01		< 0,01	
r	0,12		0,38		0,36	

The increase in performance of annotation users is also verified by the distributions of the browsing times of each group, which are presented below in Fig. 2A. This diagram depicts a well formed normal distribution corresponding to Annotation that has its mean close to the beginning of the x axis. On the other hand, Search Engine and Bookmark exhibit two almost coinciding distributions that are positively skewed and have their means located further away from the y axis. The skew shows that annotations have particularly been useful for some specific questions – for the majority of questions the browsing time is more or less similar.

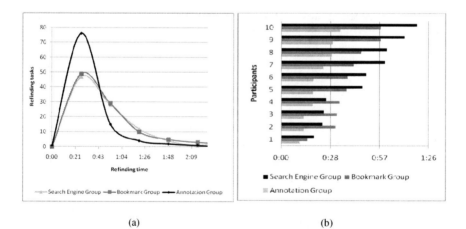

(a)   (b)

Fig. 2. Distribution of refinding tasks by time (A). Average browsing time (x-axis) per participant in ascending order (B).

Finally, in Fig. 2B. we illustrate the average browsing time of each participant for each one of the three groups. Participants are actually presented in ascending order, starting from the one with the shortest time and ending with the least efficient one.

This diagram makes clear the fact that the poor performance of Search Engine and Bookmark is not caused by a few, slow performing participants. Conversely, the majority of them had large average browsing times, in contrast to the users of SpreadCrumbs that in general relocated the required information quite quickly.

Thus far we have focused on the effect of the diverse tools on users' efficiency, thus ignoring other important factors, like the size of the visited pages as well as the use of browsers' "find" functionality. Due to their significance, we have devoted the following two subsections to their analysis.

6.1 CTRL+F

As it has already been mentioned, the browsers' "find" (CTRL+F) functionality plays a major role in relocating a specific piece of information within a web page. In order to quantify its degree of use, we measured the percentage of tasks of each group that were carried out with its help and present the outcomes in Fig. 3A. As expected, it is evident that CTRL+F has been extensively used by the subjects of Search Engine and Bookmark, whereas participants of Annotation resort to it to a lesser extent. They actually use it solely in the cases of modified web pages that result in misplaced or orphan annotations, as in these cases the annotations are of little help and the user has to resort to other means for pinpointing the desired information.

Judging from the wide use of the CTRL+F strategy, it is reasonable to assume that "find" helps participants to perform better in refinding information. To verify this assumption, we estimated the average browsing time that corresponds to subjects using it and compared against that of those that did not use it. This comparisons were made in the context of all three groups, and their outcomes, presented in Fig. 3B., suggest the opposite: participants that took advantage of this functionality needed *significantly* more time in completing their tasks than those that did not. Hence, although this functionality is supposed to constitute a quite handy tool for locating information, in practice there is no evidence supporting its beneficial contribution to re-visitation efficiency. A likely explanation, which we investigate further in the next subsection, is that CTRL+F is mainly used when users encounter pages that do not allow for quick visual scanning due to their length.

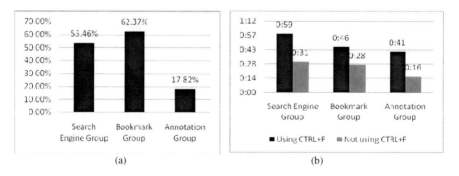

(a)   (b)

Fig. 3. Percentages of usage (y-axis) of the browser's "find" functionality of each group (A). Average times (y-axis) of each group distinguishing tasks where the browser's "find" functionality was used (B).

In the following table (Table 3), we briefly present the results of an independent t-test that show the significant differences in the performance between the subjects that do and those that do not use the "find" functionality. A more detailed investigation of the correlation between this functionality and the size of the web pages follows in the next subsection.

Table 3. Results of t-test between the tasks which had and hadn't the assistance of the "find" functionality for each group

Search Engine Group	$t(94)=2.54$, $p<0.01$, $r=0.25$
Bookmark Group	$t(84)=2.54$, $p<0.01$, $r=0.27$
Annotation Group	$t(18)=3.08$, $p<0.01$, $r=0.59$

6.2 Page Content Size

As mentioned in the previous subsection, there is likely to be a correlation between the length of web pages and the usage of CTRL+F as a means for refinding. To investigate this correlation, we divided the participants of each group into two subgroups; one that used CTRL+F, and one that did not. For each of these subgroups we estimated the average size of the accessed web pages in terms of number of words and calculated the average browsing time – see Fig. 4. The figure shows that – in particular in the Bookmark and Annotation groups – there is no interdependency between page size and the usage of CTRL+F. However, it shows that the browsing time is significantly higher in the CTRL+F condition, which suggests that the find functionality does *not* sufficiently leverage the detrimental effect of long and possibly unstructured pages.

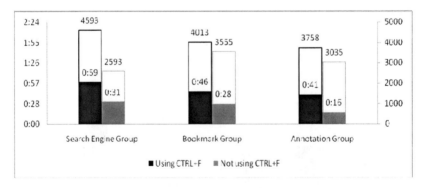

Fig. 4. Average times (y-axis left) of each group and average Web page sizes (number of words) (y-axis right) distinguishing tasks where the browser's "find" functionality was used

In order to examine the effect of page size on browsing time, we clustered the pages that were used by our subjects according to their number of words and estimated the average time related to each cluster. In Fig. 5 we present the performances associated with each application and page cluster. It is obvious that no trend can be identified for Search Engine and Bookmark, as they depict a high variance, whereas Annotation has a more stable but still volatile behavior. By manually observing the structure of the visited web pages, we came to the conclusion that the size of the page has no significant influence on the browsing stage, as opposed to the web page structure. This is in line with our qualitative analyses, presented below, whose outcomes indicate that, in the absence of in-context annotations, a well structured content together with an elegant layout, and a nice organization that is rich in anchors; substantially assist users in refinding information.

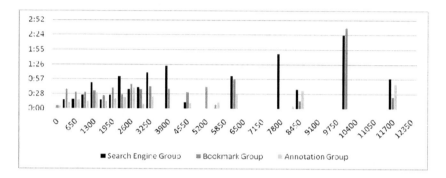

Fig. 5. Average times (x-axis) of each group by Web page size (y-axis)

6.3 Shared Trails and Annotations

In the second part of the studies (described in Section 5.2), 50% of the users who received the suggestions from their 'partner' via Delicious did not read or even did not notice the additional comments on each bookmark, which were displayed just below the page title and the URL. One participant explicitly told us that she noticed them only in the middle of the task. Another participant said that she noticed the comments, but did not read all of them because she thought they were irrelevant.

By contrast, all the participants who received the suggestions via SpreadCrumbs indeed noticed and read the comments, which were displayed as post-it notes. They all accessed the bookmarked pages and read the shared comments in the context. During the interview after the task, some of them confirmed that their choices were influenced by those comments.

The results show that if annotations are meant to provide additional information and to influence the receiver's opinion or choices, they should be presented as such, in the context. A text snippet below the title, as provided by many social bookmarking sites, is clearly not sufficient to catch the receiver's attention and may be overlooked during a collaborative knowledge building process.

6.4 User Feedback

After completing the set of tasks, each participant was asked to fill out a questionnaire, with the aim of distilling opinions on the tool used as well as the experiments in general. The answers were given by selecting the appropriate value on a 7 point Likert scale. The user experience survey consisted of 13 questions, taken from established surveys on user satisfaction, frustration and disorientation. The Crombach a of 0,762 indicated a good reliability and the results were grouped nicely into the three factors.

Participants from the Bookmarking and the Annotating group reported less frustration than participants from the Search group. Further, the participants from the Annotation group reported a marginally significant lower value of difficulties in finding the right information. Whereas most other questions did not result in significant differences in answers, the overall trend indicated positive effect of bookmarking - and of annotation in particular - on the subjective user experience.

It is also worth mentioning that five participants of the annotation group marked the same page, a page that had been changed during the time interval between the first and the second session of the study. As a result, the annotations they had posted were misplaced in all the five cases, which caused a slight delay in the refinding task. Two of them suggested a more intuitive way of attaching annotations that involved arrows. Even though this way could well solve the issue of misplaced annotations, it will still be of no help for orphaned ones, which is in the cases where the annotated information has been completely removed. This issue is actually considered as one of the most complicated and challenging problems of the in-context annotation approach [21, 22].

7 Conclusions

In this work, we presented the SpreadCrumbs Web annotation tool and demonstrate how it is able to overcome the limitations of previously existing annotation mechanisms. With SpreadCrumbs, users can place Post-it-like notes at any location of a Web page. From our user studies and a literature survey we identified that user needs for making annotations in the Web environment do not differ significantly from their needs in the paper environment [23]. In addition, Spreadcrumbs supports different user tasks, not only private annotations, but also personal reminders, refinding enhancement, and social bookmarking with extensive support for social navigation and collaboration.

We also presented empirical results that show the important role of annotations in the digital environment, the outperformance of in-context annotations over bookmarks in terms of supporting information refinding, the analysis and the impact of in-context annotations on social and collaborative scenarios and finally the usability and users' opinion feedback.

Although we have seen the importance and benefits of annotations, no annotation system is widely adopted. This implies that there are still several issues to be studied and solved. The main challenge for annotation systems is on the user interface level. It is necessary to balance the classic tension between full-fledged features and ease of use. Particular attention should be paid to the question to what extent annotation systems should provide and emphasize social bookmarking features.

References

1. Halasz, F.G.: Seven issues: Revisited. Closing plenary address. In: Proceedings of ACM Hypertext Conference, San Antonio, Texas, (December 18,1991)
2. Vitali, F., Bieber, M.: Hypermedia on the web: What will it take? ACM Computing Surveys 31(4es) Article No. 31 (1999)
3. Millard, D.E., Ross, M.: Web 2.0: hypertext by any other name? In: Proceedings of the Seventeenth Conference on Hypertext and Hypermedia, HYPERTEXT 2006, Odense, Denmark, August 22 - 25 (2006)
4. Karger, D., Katz, B., Lin, J., Quann, D.: Stickey notes for the semantic web. In: Proc. Intelligent User Interfaces (2003)
5. O'Hara, K., Sellen, A.: A Comparison of Reading Paper and On-Line Documents. In: Proceedings of the ACM Conference on Human Factors in Computing Systems, CHI 1997 (1997)
6. Marshall, C.: Toward an Ecology of Hypertext Annotation. In: Proceedings of the Ninth ACM Conference on Hypertext and Hypermedia, Hypertext 1998 (1998)
7. Kawase, R., Nejdl, W.: A Straightforward Approach for Online Annotations: SpreadCrumbs - Enhancing and Simplifying Online Collaboration. In: WEBIST, pp. 407–410. INSTICC Press (2009)
8. Kawase, R., Herder, E., Nejdl, W.: Annotations and Hypertrails with SpreadCrumbs: An Easy Way to Annotate, Refind and Share. In: WEBIST 2010: Proceedings of the 6th International Conference on Web Information Systems and Technologies (2010)
9. MacMullen, W.J.: Annotation as Process, Thing, and Knowledge: Multi-domain studies of structured data annotation. SILS Technical Report TR-2005-02. UNC School of Information and Library Science (2005)
10. Marshall, C.: Annotation: From Paper Books to the Digital Library. In: Proceedings of the ACM International Conference on Digital Libraries, DL 1997 (1997)
11. Zellweger, P., Mangen, A., Newman, P.: Authoring fluid narrative hypertexts using treetable visualizations. In: Proceedings of ACM Hypertext (2002)
12. Bouvin, N.O.: Unifying strategies for Web augmentation. In: Proceedings of ACM Hypertext 1999, pp. 91–100 (1999)
13. Bottoni, P., Civica, R., Levialdi, S., Orso, L., Panizzi, E., Trinchese, R.: MADCOW: a multimedia digital annotation system. In: Proceedings of the Working Conference on Advanced Visual interfaces, AVI 2004, Gallipoli, Italy, May 25 - 28 (2004)
14. Bottoni, P., Levialdi, S., Labella, A., Panizzi, E., Trinchese, R., Gigli, L.: MADCOW: a visual interface for annotating web pages. In: Proceedings of the Working Conference on Advanced Visual interfaces, Venezia, Italy, May 23 - 26 (2006)
15. Kawase, R., Herder, E., Nejdl, W.: A comparison of paper-based and online annotations in the workplace. In: Cress, U., Dimitrova, V., Specht, M. (eds.) EC-TEL 2009. LNCS, vol. 5794, pp. 240–253. Springer, Heidelberg (2009)
16. Brusilovsky, P.: Adaptive hypermedia. User Modeling and User Adapted Interaction 11 (1/2), 87-110 (2001); Claypool, M., Le, P., Wased, M., and Brown, D Implicit interest indicators. In: Claypool, M., Le, P., Wased, M., Brown, D. (eds.) Proceedings of 6th International Conference on Intelligent User Interfaces, pp. 33–40 (2002)
17. Farzan, R., Brusilovsky, P.: AnnotatEd: A Social Navigation and Annotation Service for Web-based Educational Resources. In: Proc. of E-Learn 2006, AACE, Honolulu, HI, USA, October 13-17, pp. 2794–2802 (2006)

18. Farzan, R., Brusilovsky, P.: Social navigation support through annotation-based group modeling. In: Proceedings of 10th International User Modeling Conference, pp. 463–472 (2005)
19. Kawase, R., Papadakis, G., Herder, E., Nejdl, W.: The impact of bookmarks and annotations on refinding information. In: Proceedings of the 21st ACM Conference on Hypertext and Hypermedia, HT 2010, Toronto, Ontario, June 13 - 16 (2010)
20. Pitkow, J.E., Kehoe, C.M.: Emerging trends in the WWW user population. Commun. ACM 39(6), 106–108 (1996)
21. Cockburn, A., McKenzie, B.: What do Web users do? An empirical analysis of Web use. Int. J. of Human-Computer Studies 54(6), 903–922 (2001)
22. Wang, S.: Annotation Persistence Over Dynamic Documents. Doctoral Thesis. Massachusetts Institute of Technology (2005)
23. Fu, X., Ciszek, T., Marchionini, G.M., Solomon, P.: Annotating the web: An exploratory study of web users needs for personal annotation tools. In: The 68th Annual Meeting of the American Society for Information Science & Technology (ASIS&T), Charlotte, NC, USA (2005)

Concept Signatures and Semantic Drift

Jon Atle Gulla[1], Geir Solskinnsbakk[1], Per Myrseth[2]
Veronika Haderlein[2], and Olga Cerrato[2]

[1] Norwegian University of Science and Technology, 7491 Trondheim, Norway
[2] Det Norske Veritas, 1363 Høvik, Oslo, Norway
{jag,geirs}@idi.ntnu.no
{Per.Myrseth,Veronika.Haderlein,Olga.Cerrato}@dnv.com

Abstract. Ontology evolution is the process of incrementally and consistently adapting an existing ontology to changes in the relevant domain. Semantic drift refers to how ontology concepts' intentions gradually change as the domain evolves. Normally, a semantic drift captures small domain changes that are hard to detect with traditional ontology management tools or ontology learning methods, but may be important to the maintenance of the ontology. This paper discusses a new approach to detecting semantic drift that makes use of concept signatures reflecting the textual references to concepts over time. Comparing how signatures change over time, we see how concepts' semantic content evolves and how their relationships to other concepts gradually reflect these changes. An experiment with the DNV's business sector ontology from 2004 and 2008 demonstrates the value of this approach to ontology evolution.

Keywords: Semantic web, Ontology, Evolution, Concept signatures, Text mining.

1 Introduction

Ontologies have in recent years become increasingly important in enterprises' pursuit of more efficient IT architectures. The ontologies define standardized vocabularies for application integration and enable more integrated operations inside and across enterprises. Also, new ontology-supported applications now range from intelligent information retrieval solutions to service composition and intelligent agents.

Ontology evolution is the timely adaptation of ontology structures to changes in the domain. The underlying requirement to all ontologies is that their content is consistent with the way important phenomena are understood and referred to in the domain. Their classes, individuals and properties must correspond to people's terminologies for categorizing and characterizing domain aspects. When the perception of the domain changes, this has to be reflected in the ontology as well.

Unfortunately, developing and maintaining ontologies is still a tedious and expensive undertaking. As opposed to data models in traditional transaction systems, ontologies' large scope necessitates the involvement of domain experts of different backgrounds and different roles. As models of real world phenomena they are also intrinsically complex and hard to validate. On top of this the formal notation of many ontologies makes it difficult to maintain the models unless ontology experts are available.

J. Filipe and J. Cordeiro (Eds.): WEBIST 2010, LNBIP 75, pp. 101–113, 2011.
© Springer-Verlag Berlin Heidelberg 2011

Since ontologies need to be updated and evaluated at regular intervals, the maintenance costs tend to grow unacceptably high if appropriate tool support is not available.

Most ontologies today are maintained manually by dedicated teams of domain experts and ontology modelers. Traditional modeling techniques are applied, which requires long face-to-face sessions with modeling, discussion, and evaluation. Formal procedures for suggesting and approving ontology changes are enforced to ensure the necessary quality of these changes. For smaller updates, though, it should be possible to employ more cost-effective approaches with less human involvement. Most of the concepts and structures are already there, and the task is to verify whether anything has to be changed, added or deleted. Ontology evolution, thus, should lend itself better to tool support than full-fledged ontology engineering projects.

In this paper we present a new approach to ontology evolution that makes use of concept representations – signatures – that capture small semantic changes to concepts over time. Since these signatures are constructed automatically from textual descriptions of existing concepts, they are geared towards updating existing structures rather than developing new ontologies.

In section 2 we discuss the problem of semantic drift in ontologies. Section 3 is devoted to concept signatures, whereas Section 4 demonstrates how these signatures are generated to analyze evolutionary changes to a real industrial ontology. A discussion of results is given in Section 5, followed by related work in Section 6 and conclusions in Section 7.

2   Semantic Drift

An ontology is formally defined as an *"explicit specification of a conceptualization"* [1]. It has a formal foundation that supports taxonomic relationships and some degree of reasoning. Moreover, the ontology provides an abstract simplified view of the world that is shared by a community and prepared for a particular purpose.

An ontology language like OWL represents this conceptualization in terms of classes, individuals, properties and various constraints and operators. Even though other languages choose other primitives, they tend to categorize phenomena along the same line to accommodate a sound logical foundation. For this paper, though, it suffices to assume that ontologies consist of concepts that are related – taxonomically and non-taxonomically – to each other.

2.1   Evolutionary Changes

Stojanovic et al [2] define ontology evolution as a cyclic process consisting of *change capturing, change representation, semantics of change, change implementation, change propagation* and *change validation*. Whereas ontology management and versioning systems deal with the representation, implementation and propagation of changes, the more difficult part of change capturing has been left to manual effort and some limited ontology learning support.

The captured ontology changes fall into two distinct categories:

- *Existential Changes.* Existing ontology concepts may be deemed irrelevant, and new concepts may need to be added to the ontology. An ontology of computers, for example, may not need to include floppy disks any more, as these are not used by modern computers. Similarly, GPS receivers are now a natural part of a mobile phone ontology, even though it had nothing to do with phones 10 years ago.
- *Relational Changes.* Both taxonomic and non-taxonomic relationships between concepts may change over time. In the example above, GPS receivers may now be modeled as a part of a smart phone, and computers now are more closely related to games and entertainment than a few years ago.

In principle, changes may be imposed to the ontology from three kinds of analyses: *Structure-driven* changes are motivated from structural properties of the existing ontology itself. *Usage-driven* changes reflect changes in users' behavior over time, while *data-driven* changes stem from a modification of the underlying knowledge such as text documents [2].

Our approach combines the usage-driven and the data-driven approach to ontology evolution. The object of our analysis is a collection of text documents, though the documents are assumed to be allocated to the correct ontology concepts by the users. This allocation indicates the users' understanding of the concept at a particular point of time.

2.2 Semantic Drift in Ontologies

A concept's semantic value – i.e. our understanding of the concept – may change over time in response to general changes to the domain or our own insight. Our perception of computers, for example, is very different from what people associated with computers when the first PCs were introduced. We say that the meaning of computers has drifted as the technology developed and computers got ever more powerful.

We may define the notion of *semantic drift* as

> the gradual change of a concept's semantic value as understood by the relevant community

Moreover, we distinguish between *intrinsic* and *extrinsic* semantic drift of concepts.

Intrinsic drift means that a concept's semantic value is changed with respect to other concepts in the ontology. This will typically be reflected in changes to the relationships in the ontology, though the concepts may still be the same. Extrinsic drift happens when a concept's semantic value is changed with respect to the phenomena it describes in the real world. In the case of mobile phones, we may say that there has been an extrinsic change over the last 20 years as our phones today are vastly different from what we had 20 years ago. In the ontology an extrinsic drift may cause all kinds of changes and updates.

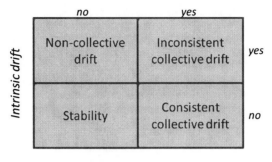

Fig. 1. Types of semantic drift

Figure 1 sums up the nature of semantic changes associated with intrinsic and extrinsic drift. If a concept is exposed to extrinsic, but no intrinsic drift, it means that the whole ontology is undergoing a collective consistent drift that may not necessitate any changes to the ontology. On the other hand, no extrinsic drift and substantial intrinsic drift means that a concept's relationships to other concepts in the ontology may no longer be correct, even though the concept itself has not changed its meaning. We say that the concept is floating with respect to other concepts. In cases of both extrinsic and intrinsic drift we are dealing with inconsistent collective drift of concepts in an ontology that is no longer valid.

3 Concept Signatures

An ontology consists of inter-related concepts and normally has a sound logical foundation that allows some reasoning and verification checks. The meaning of an individual concept is however not entirely clear. Providing a taxonomic structure and adding associations between concepts give us some semantic clues, though it is not sufficient to recognize the concept in the real world. Logically, we assume the existence of an interpretation that maps for example the concept *Computer* to the set of all computers in the world, though for all practical purposes these interpretations are not available and machine-processable to us.

Most ontologies, thus, provide informal textual descriptions that try to help us understand how the concept is to be interpreted. In the petroleum ontology for ISO15926 there is a concept *Christmas tree* that is modeled as an artefact and decomposed into a number of specialized Christmas trees [3]. These structures do not help us recognize Christmas trees in the petroleum business, though a simple natural language comment linked to the concept may give us an impression of what it is: *"An artefact that is an assembly of pipes and piping parts, with valves and associated control equipment that is connected to the top of a wellhead and is intended for control of fluid from a well."*

3.1 Definition

For our purposes it is more useful to link concepts to our linguistic world than to an imaginary interpretation function that points to real world phenomena. The textual description of Christmas tree above is not accurate, but is available and can be analyzed linguistically and statistically. As long as languages are used fairly consistently, the analysis of linguistic expressions can tell us how a community deals with a concept at particular points in time. This is captured by means of word structures called concept signatures.

We define a concept signature as follows:

A concept signature $S_{c,t}$ is a materialization of the concept C through linguistic forms at some time t.

The signature is not a semantic representation of the concept. It merely shows how words and linguistic expressions are used to refer to and discuss the concept. The signature thus can be used to relate concepts at a linguistic level without being forced to formalize a mapping to real-world phenomena.

A concept signature is represented as a vector

$$S_{c,t} = (u_1,.., u_n),$$

where u_i is the weight of linguistic unit i. Linguistic units may be individual words, phrases, argument structures, or any other linguistic structure that can be systematically extracted from text.

Examples of concept signatures from our DNV study are given in Figure 3. The linguistic units in this case are individual nouns and noun phrases, and their weights indicate their relative importance in understanding the concept. For *Consulting* in 2004, the top-ranked phrases *process industry* and *advanced cross-disciplinary competence* tell us that consulting was considered a cross-disciplinary activity with a primary focus on the process industry. The bottom-ranked phrase *environmental performance* reveals that DNV only rarely thought of consulting as related to environmental issues. These linguistic units are not synonyms that point to the same concept, like in WordNet's synsets, but terms that content-wise has something to do with the concept.

4 Concept Signature Construction

Det Norske Veritas (DNV) is an international company specializing in risk management and certification. As an industrial conglomerate DNV is involved in a number of business segments that each constitute a subdomain within risk management and certification. Their web site mirrors their business activities and forms a taxonomy of DNV's business activities. Each web page at their site represents a concept in this taxonomy, and the text of the web page is our source for understanding this concept.

In 2004 this taxonomy counted 227 concepts (web pages) that on the average were described by texts of a few hundred words each. As their business domain evolved, their taxonomy was expanded into 369 concepts in 2008.

Constructing concept signatures for all their concepts in 2004 and 2008, we followed the procedure below for each concept:

- *Preprocessing stages*: After collecting the text describing the concept, the text was tagged using the Penn treebank tag set. Irrelevant stop words were removed, and the resulting text was stemmed.

- *Selection of linguistic units*: Two lists were generated from the stemmed text above: (1) List of noun phrases, and (2) list of individual nouns only.

- *Signature construction:* For every element of the two lists, the tf.idf score was computed. The tf.idf score of term t for concept C is given as

$$tf_{i,c} * idf_{i,c},$$

$tf_{i,c} = f_{i,c}/max_j(f_{j,c})$ and $idf_i = log(N/n_i)$. The variable $f_{i,c}$ is the frequency of term i in concept C's text, $f_{j,c}$ is the maximum frequency of any term in this text, N is the number of concepts, and n_i is the number of concepts, whose text descriptions contain term i.

The two lists of elements with tf.idf scores are then merged into a vector representing the signature of that concept.

The whole procedure is illustrated in Figure 2, and examples of signatures generated are found in Figure 3. *Consulting* in DNV in 2004, as illustrated by the signature in Figure 3(a), was best understood as part of the process industry and international affairs. In 2008 the consulting concept had more to do with EFTA, performance issues and risk management.

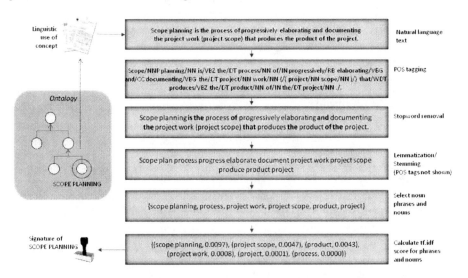

Fig. 2. Generating concept signature for SCOPE PLANNING

5 Using Concept Signatures to Detect Drift

The concept signatures tell us how concepts are referred to in the linguistic communities. Our understanding of the totality of these terms is our implicit understanding of the concept. Since the concept signatures are formally represented as vectors, they can also be compared using standard information retrieval calculations

Phrasal terms		Single terms	
process industry	4.63	firm	1.95
advanced cross-disciplinary	4.63	compet	1.72
competence	2.66	cross	1.69
international clients	2.66	matur	1.35
effective risk handling	2.66	strong	1.30
fast-moving world	2.66	advanc	1.13
strong business orientation	2.66	enhanc	0.92
international experience	2.66	dividend	0.92
improved health	2.66	differ	0.84
firm base	2.66	foundat	0.84
genuine industry knowledge	2.66	experienc	0.78
worldwide network	2.66	usa	0.78
strong technological competencies	2.66	save	0.78
enhanced public confidence	2.66	manag	0.75
direct savings	2.66	technolog	0.75
unique independence	2.66	perform	0.74
technology competencies	2.66	base	0.74
better safety management	2.66	genuin	0.74
full access	2.31	provinc	0.74
experienced consultants	2.11	fast	0.74
environmental performance			

(a)

Phrasal terms		Single terms	
efta inspection	5.91	efta	1.23
real performance	5.91	risk	0.57
industry best practices	5.21	softwar	0.55
risk management services	4.81	consult	0.55
right questions	4.81	knowledg	0.55
business functions	4.52	smart	0.51
operational excellence	4.30	inspect	0.50
knowledge management	3.71	busi	0.48
improvement opportunities	3.20	function	0.48
friday last week	2.95	manag	0.42
ict systems	2.95	abil	0.42
new premises	2.95	object	0.40
norwegian competition authorities	2.95	real	0.38
høvik	2.95	uncertainti	0.35
efta surveillance authority	2.95	question	0.34
efta team	2.95	technolog	0.33
other asset	2.95	complex	0.31
onboard dnv navigator	2.95	â	0.31
management control	2.95	km	0.31
smart ways	2.95	columbia	0.31
telecoms contract	2.95	copyright	0.31
columbia shipmanagement	2.95	improv	0.29
clients she threats	2.95	surveil	0.28
systems functionality	2.95	privaci	0.28
significant risk factor	2.95		
environment risk management	2.95		
in-depth industry insight	2.95		
smart organizations	2.95		

(b)

Fig. 3. (a) Signature of 'consulting' from 2004. (b) Signature of consulting from 2008.

like cosine similarity and euclidian distance. This enables us to run some automatic tests on possible semantic drift in ontologies.

We have so far defined three different tests for semantic drift: individual concepts, non-taxonomic relationships, and taxonomic relationships. Each of them is explained in the following.

5.1 Individual Concepts

A concept exposed to extrinsic change will have significantly different signatures at different points of time. This means that the cosine similarity of signatures at times t_1 and t_2 will be below a certain threshold α:

$$Sim(S_{C,t1}, S_{C,t2}) < \alpha$$

where

$$Sim(X,Y) = \sum_{i=1}^{n}(x_i * y_i)/(\sqrt{\sum_{i=1}^{n}x_i^2} * \sqrt{\sum_{i=1}^{n}y_i^2})$$

The constant α depends on a number of factors and defines what counts as significant in this context. For our analysis of DNV, *Consulting* in 2004 and 2008 had a cosine similarity of 0.27. Other tests with consulting indicate that this is a fairly small similarity that reflects a genuine change of meaning over the years. The concept *Seaskill*, on the other hand, had a larger cosine similarity of 0.45 and seems not to be drifting significantly.

A low similarity score is an indication that the concept has undergone substantial extrinsic changes. To what extent that should be reflected in changes to the ontology depends on the possible changes to related concepts.

5.2 Non-taxonomic Relationships

Non-taxonomic relationships constitute semantic associations between concepts. Important permanent relationships tend to be modeled explicitly in the ontology, whereas less obvious or fluctuating ones are often left out of the model. If the importance or stability of a relationship changes over time, a reconsideration of which relationships to include will be needed.

Let us define the Concept Relation vector for concept C at time t as follows:

$$R_{C,t} = (r_{C,L1}, ..., r_{C,Lm})$$

Where $r_{C,Li} = Sim(S_C, S_{Li}) \geq \beta$

The concept relation vector for concept C provides a ranked list of concepts that are semantically related to C. The relation score, which is between 0 and 1, reveals the relative strength of the relationships compared to all other concepts related to C. The constant β gives a lower bound for when two concepts are to be regarded as related.

Normally, you would like to concentrate on high-level concept relationships first to make sure that ontology relationships are defined and kept at the highest possible level. This keeps the ontology more general and prevents unnecessary duplications from being introduced at lower levels in the ontology.

Figure 4 shows the top-level concept relation vector for *Consulting* in 2004. Only top-level concepts are included, and all related subconcepts are incorporated into the top-level concept's relationship to consulting. That is, the relation score for each top-level concept like *Process_industry* and *Asset_operation* are average scores of all their subconcepts related to consulting.

Figure 5 shows how a high-level temporal analysis is conducted by means of concept relation vectors. In addition to using top-level concept relation vectors for 2004 and 2008, we have also recorded the number of subclasses supporting each top-level concept's relation score.

Concepts most similar to Consulting in 2004	
process_industry	0,313683
asset_operation	0,233114
energy	0,225704
qualification_verification	0,122025
transportation	0,102305
classification	0,086659
organisation	0,082843
technologyservices	0,075651
careers	0,072296
certification	0,067242
publications	0,066085
press	0,04665
maritime	0,045062
location	0,044662

Fig. 4. Concept relation vector for Consulting

For every top level concept related to *Consulting*, there is one bullet for 2004 and one for 2008 in the figure. The strength of these relationships – the relation score – is indicated along the vertical axis, whereas the number of subclasses underlying every top-level concept is reflected by the size of the bullets. For example, consulting's relationship to careers has not changed much over the years with a relation score of about 0.06-0.07. However, in 2004 the relationship was limited to only one subclass of careers, while in 2008 there were relationships between consulting and 13 subclasses of careers. In the diagram this is shown by the much larger size of the bullet for 2008.

As seen from the results, the nature of consulting in DNV has shifted from maritime and process-oriented industries to ICT, software and risk management. This suggests significant intrinsic changes to the consulting concept that should impose changes to the ontology.

More generally, a substantial change of relation score to another concept necessitates an evaluation of whether this relationship should exist in the ontology or not. A small bullet means that the relationship is only relevant for a few subclasses and may therefore not be represented as a relationship to the top-level concept in the ontology. A large bullet, like for maritime in Figure 5, implies that many subclasses are related to the concept, indicating that the relationship in the ontology should be linked to the top-level concept rather than directly to its subclasses.

5.3 Taxonomic Relationships

Concept signatures may also be used to analyze the hierarchical structures of the ontology. In Figure 6 we have calculated the similarity between *Consulting* and all its specializations and parts for 2004 and 2008, filtered out those below a certain threshold β and ranked them according to similarity scores. A high similarity score means that the specialization is central to the core understanding of the superclass.

It is however not obvious how such a ranked list of specializations should be interpreted. Other experiments with concept signatures reveal that we should not expect a very high similarity between super and subordinate concepts, though there should always be some minimum similarity for the properties they share [4].

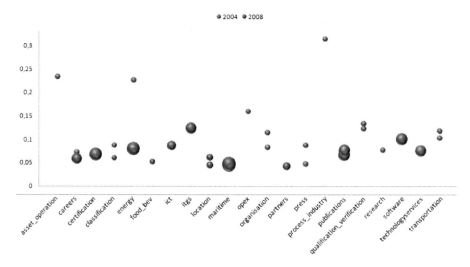

Fig. 5. Consulting's non-taxonomic relationships to other major concepts in 2004 and 2008

As seen from the figure, the composition of *Consulting* has been fairly stable over these years. Specializations like *Process, General industries, Safety health environment* and *Enterprise Management* are equally central in 2008 as in 2004. A few interesting changes should be noted, though. *Asset operations* and *Project management* (PM) were seen as core activities of consulting in 2008, but were rather distant in 2004. We also see that DNV terminated its software consulting activities between 2004 and 2008.

6 Discussion

We have in this paper shown how the notion of concept signatures helps us analyze the evolutionary aspects of ontologies. The method uncovers semantic drift among concepts in the ontology, both with respect to real-world phenomena and the concepts' relationships to other concepts in the ontology.

Our technique relies on good text fragments that describe or define the existing concepts in the ontology. Because it makes use of the existing ontology, it does not suffer from the noise that has hampered traditional ontology learning approaches. Only real concepts are subjected to the analysis, and we can concentrate fully on verifying the quality of these concepts as they are currently modeled. Since the analysis is geared towards the temporal development of the concepts, we need not to worry about the exact relationship between text and concepts, as long as we can assume that this relationship is unchanged over time. Unfortunately, this also means that the method will not detect any missing concepts in the ontology.

In a temporal perspective there will always be some semantic drift. Our understanding of concepts change as the domain change, and many concepts reflect more technological level or state of the art than fixed and permanent terminologies. This does not mean, though, that ontologies should be updated whenever a noticeable

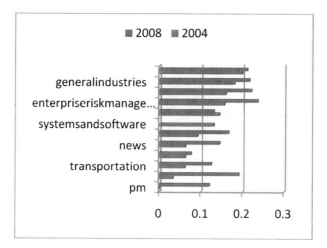

Fig. 6. Specializations of *Consulting*

semantic drift is detected. Before updating the ontology, we need to understand both the nature of semantic drift and the extent of semantic drift among all the ontology concepts.

This also means that the method will not detect any missing concepts in the ontology.

In a temporal perspective there will always be some semantic drift. Our understanding of concepts change as the domain change, and many concepts reflect more technological level or state of the art than fixed and permanent terminologies. This does not mean, though, that ontologies should be updated whenever a noticeable semantic drift is detected. Before updating the ontology, we need to understand both the nature of semantic drift and the extent of semantic drift among all the ontology concepts.

A fundamental problem of our current approach is the generation of concept signatures. Since we depend on texts attached to every single concept, these texts tend to be rather short and shallow. Our statistical approach would benefit from longer texts, from which more reliable statistical data can be extracted.

7 Related Work

Our approach to detecting semantic drift draws on research on ontology learning and evolution [2, 5]. However, standard data-driven ontology learning methods tend to use uncategorized text both to extract concepts and describe their properties (e.g. [6]). This makes it difficult to take into account the existing ontology and any manual additions to it. Ontology learning has proven useful in extracting entirely new concepts and concept structures, though the nature of the text mining techniques used in ontology learning makes them less useful when the concepts are already known beforehand.

Some recent work on belief change theory [7, 8] and collaborative environments [9] provide alternative approaches to ontology evolution, though neither addresses the way concepts are materialized through language.

Enkhsaikhan et al. [10] describe a method for building term clusters that describe existing top-level concepts like *Politics* and *Economy*. This enables an analysis of temporal concept development similar to ours, though their approach does not use vectors or linguistic characterizations of concepts. They have a simpler way of describing the concepts that does not support our fine-grained analaysis of concept development.

Our focus on individual concepts' evolution rather than the ontology as a whole is similar to work done in logic and conceptual structures [11, 12].

The idea of concept signatures is inspired by the concept vectors used in Su's ontology mapping approach [13], though her vectors did not try to capture any temporal development of concepts. The vectors contained both definitional and non-definitional terms and were merely used to recognize product similarities across product catalogs.

8 Conclusions

This paper has presented a new approach to detecting semantic drift in ontologies over time. The notion of concept signatures is introduced and used to capture deeper linguistic characterizations of concepts. These signatures reflect the use of concepts in people's everyday language and provide a bridg between the conceptual and linguistic world.

The approach has been applied to an informal ontology maintained by a large enterprise in Norway. Data about the ontology from 2004 and 2008 were used to generate concept signatures and analyze the way the terminology has developed. The analysis shows that the method is able to capture small semantic changes to concepts that are hard to detect manually or by means of traditional ontology learning techniques. Primarily, these are changes to the concepts' relation to reality, but the method also uncovers secondary changes to the relationships among concepts in the ontology. The detected semantic changes shed light on why and how the ontology had been updated between 2004 and 2008.

Our current approach makes use of standard statistical methods for constructing concept signatures. If the textual descriptions of concepts are short, the statistical data is too limited to produce signatures of the necessary quality. Our future research, thus, will look into the use of more sophisticated linguistic techniques in the signature generation process. This includes both deeper grammatical analysis of sentences and utilization of semantic lexica.

Acknowledgements. We would like to thank the LongRec project, funded by the Research Council of Norway under project number 176818/I40, for supporting this research.

References

1. Gruber, T.: A Translation Approach to Portable Ontology Specifications. Knowledge Acquisition 5(2), 199–220 (1993)
2. Stojanovic, L.: Methods and Tools for Ontology Evolution. PhD thesis. University of Karlsruhe (2004)

3. Gulla, J.A.: Experiences with Industrial Ontology Engineering. In: Filipe, J., Cordeiro, J. (eds.) Enterprise Information Systems. LNBIP, vol. 19, Springer, Heidelberg (2009)
4. Solskinnsbakk, G., Gulla, J.A., Haderlein, V., Myrseth, P., Cerrato, O.: Quality of Subsumption Hierarchies in Ontologies. Accepted for publication at NLDB 2009: 14th International Conference on Applications of Natural Language to Information Systems, June 24-26, 24–26. Saarland University, Saarbrücken (2009)
5. Haase, P., Sure, Y.: D3.1.1.b State of the Art on Ontology Evolution. SEKT Deliverable (2004)
6. Gulla, J.A., Sugumaran, V.: An Interactive Ontology Learning Workbench for Non-Experts. In: Proceedings of the 2nd International Workshop on Ontologies and Information Systems for the Semantic Web (ONISW 2008), Napa Valley, pp. 971–978. ACM Press, New York (2008) ISBN 978-1-60558-225-9
7. Flouris, G., Plexousakis, D., Antoniou, G.: A Classifiation of Ontology Change. In: Proceedings of the 3rd Italian Semantic Web Workshop, Semantic Web Applications and Perspectives, SWAP (2006)
8. Lee, K., Meyer, T.: A Classification of Ontology Modification. In: Proceedings of the 17th Australian Joint Conference on Artificial Intelligence (2004)
9. Noy, N., Chugh, A., Liu, W., Musen, M.: A framework for ontology evolution in collaborative environments. In: Cruz, I., Decker, S., Allemang, D., Preist, C., Schwabe, D., Mika, P., Uschold, M., Aroyo, L.M. (eds.) ISWC 2006. LNCS, vol. 4273, Springer, Heidelberg (2006)
10. Enkhsaikhan, M., Wong, W., Liu, W., Reynolds, M.: Measuring Data-Driven Ontology Changes using Text Mining. In: Proceedings of the Sixth Australiasian Conference on Data Mining and Analytics, pp. 39–46 (2007)
11. Foo, N.: Ontology Revision. In: Ellis, G., Rich, W., Levinson, R., Sowa, J.F. (eds.) ICCS 1995. LNCS, vol. 954, pp. 16–31. Springer, Heidelberg (1995)
12. Wassermann, R.: Revising Concepts. In: Proceedings of the 5th Workshop on Logic, Language, Information and Communication, WoLLIC 1998 (1998)
13. Su, X., Gulla, J.A.: An Information Retrieval Approach to Ontology Mapping. Data & Knowledge Engineering 58(1), 47–69 (2006)

TagMe!: Enhancing Social Tagging with Spatial Context

Fabian Abel, Nicola Henze, Ricardo Kawase, Daniel Krause, and Patrick Siehndel

IVS – Semantic Web Group & L3S Research Center, Leibniz University, Hannover, Germany
{abel,henze,kawase,krause,siehndel}@L3S.de

Abstract. TagMe! is a tagging and exploration front-end for Flickr images, which enables users to annotate specific areas of an image, i.e. users can attach tag assignments to a specific area within an image and further categorize the tag assignments. Additionally, TagMe! automatically maps tags and categories to DBpedia URIs to clearly define the meaning. In this work we discuss the differences between tags and categories and show how both facets can be applied to learn semantic relations between concepts referenced by tags and categories. We also expose the benefits of the visual (spatial) context of the tag assignments, with respect to ranking algorithms for search and retrieval of relevant items. We do so by analyzing metrics of size and position of the annotated areas. Finally, in our experiments we compare different strategies to realize semantic mappings and show that already lightweight approaches map tags and categories with high precisions (86.85% and 93.77% respectively). The TagMe! system is currently available at http://tagme.groupme.org.

1 Introduction

Tagging systems like Flickr[1] or Delicious[2] enable people to organize and search large item collections by utilizing the Web 2.0 phenomena: Users attach tags to resources and thereby create so-called tag assignments which are valuable metadata. However, imprecise or ambiguous tag assignments can decrease the performance of tagging systems regarding search and retrieval of relevant items.

For example a tag assignment, alloted to an image may only describe a small part of an image and hence cannot be used to derive the overall topic of the image correctly. Some tag assignments are valid for a user-specific point of view, e.g., a tourist would tag an image of a landmark in a different way than a geologist. And finally tag assignments suffer from ambiguity in natural languages.

For disambiguation, approaches like MOAT [1] exist, which support users to attach URIs describing the meaning of a tag to a particular tag assignment analogously to semantic tagging in Faviki[3]. A more sophisticated approach, which exploits Wikipedia and WordNet[4] to detect the meaning of tags, is presented in [2].

---

[1] http://Flickr.com
[2] http://Delicious.com
[3] http://Faviki.com
[4] http://Wordnet.princeton.edu/

J. Filipe and J. Cordeiro (Eds.): WEBIST 2010, LNBIP 75, pp. 114–128, 2011.
© Springer-Verlag Berlin Heidelberg 2011

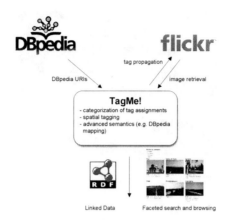

Fig. 1. Conceptual architecture of TagMe!

In this paper, we extend the common folksonomy model by flexible, contextual tagging facets. We present the TagMe! system that introduces novel tagging facets: Tag assignments are enriched with a DBpedia URI [3] to disambiguate the meaning of a tag. So-called *area tags* enable users to annotate a specific part of an image (spatial tagging). Furthermore, a *category* dimension is offered to categorize tag assignments.

In the evaluation we show that users appreciate the new tagging features. We present and examine different strategies to automatically map tags and categories to meaningful URIs. Further, we illustrate how the different context facets can be exploited to improve search and learn semantics among tags and categories. For example, we show that the introduced tagging facets are beneficial to identify similar tags and to learn semantic relations between semantic concepts referenced by the tags and DBpedia URIs.

The paper is structured as follows: In Section 2 we introduce the TagMe! system and outline how to integrate tagging facets in the user interface of a tagging system and explain how to extend traditional tagging models to offer additional tagging facets. The benefits of the additional contextual information are evaluated in Section 3. In Section 4 we discuss TagMe! with respect to related tagging systems. Finally, Section 5 summarizes the advantages of the multi-faceted tagging and gives an outlook on future work.

2 TagMe! System

TagMe! [4] is an online image tagging system where users can assign tags to pictures available in Flickr. Figure 1 outlines the conceptual architecture of TagMe!, which can basically be considered as an advanced tagging and search interface on top of Flickr. Users can directly import pictures from their own Flickr account or utilize the search interface to retrieve Flickr pictures. If users tag their own images in TagMe! then the tags are propagated to Flickr as well. Moreover, TagMe! maps DBpedia URIs to tag and category assignments by exploiting the DBpedia lookup service[5] (cf. Section 2.1).

---

[5] http://Lookup.dbpedia.org

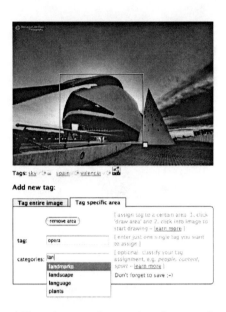

Fig. 2. User tags an area within an image and categorizes the tag assignment with support of the TagMe! system

Hence, all tags and categories have well-defined semantics so that applications, which operate on TagMe! data, can clearly understand the meaning of the tag and category assignments. The (meta)data created in TagMe! is made available according to the principles of Linked Data [5] using the MOAT ontology[6] and Tag ontology[7] as primary schemata.

TagMe! extends the Flickr tagging functionality in two further facets, specifically *categories* and *area tags*. For each tag assignment the user can enter one or more categories that classify the annotation. While typing in a category, the users get auto-completion suggestions from the pre-existing categories of the user community (see bottom in Figure 2). TagMe! users can immediately benefit from the categories as TagMe! provides a faceted search interface that allows to refine tag-based search activities by category (and vice versa). Additionally, users are enabled to perform *spatial tag assignments*, i.e. use tags to annotate a specific areas of an image, which they can draw within the picture (see rectangle within the photo in Figure 2) similarly to *notes* in Flickr or annotations in LabelMe [6]. When tagging, people usually only tag the main content of the picture, giving less or almost none importance to supplementary scenery images.

Area tags motivate the users to do so adding significant semantic value to each annotated image. Moreover, each spatial tag assignment has a globally unique URI and is therewith linkable, which allows users to share the link with others so that they can point their friends and other users directly to a specific part of an image. For example,

---

[6] http://Moat-project.org/ns

[7] http://www.Holygoat.co.uk/projects/tags

if users follow the link of the spatial tag assignment "opera"[8], shown in Figure 2 then they are directed to a page where the corresponding area is highlighted, which might be especially useful in situation where users discuss about specific things within a picture. While the area tags add an enjoyable visible feature for highlighting specific areas of an image and sharing the link to such areas with friends, we consider them as highly valuable to improve search by detecting tag correlations or to enhance the identification of similar tags (see Section 3).

2.1 Mapping to DBpedia URIs

For realizing the feature of mapping tags and categories to DBpedia [3] URIs we first compared the following two strategies.

DBpedia Lookup. The naive lookup strategy invokes the DBpedia lookup service with the tag/category that should be mapped to a URI as search query. DBpedia ranks the returned URIs similarly to PageRank [7] and our naive mapping strategy simply assigns the top-ranked URI to the tag/category in order to define its meaning.

DBpedia Lookup + Feedback. The advanced mapping strategy is able to consider feedback while selecting an appropriate DBpedia URI. Whenever a tag/category is assigned, for which already a correctly validated DBpedia URI exists in the TagMe! database then that URI is selected. Otherwise the strategy falls back the naive DBpedia Lookup.

Figure 3 shows the accuracy of both strategies. The mappings of the naive approach result in a precision of 79.92% for mapping tags to DBpedia URIs and 84.94% for mapping categories. The consideration of feedback improves the precisions of the naive DBpedia Lookup clearly to 86.85% and 93.77% respectively, which corresponds to an improvement of 8.7% and 10.4%. As the mapping accuracy for categories is higher than the one for tags, it seems that the identification of meaningful URIs for categories is easier than for tags. In summary, the results of the DBpedia mapping are very encouraging. Moreover, the precision of the category mappings, which are determined by the strategy that incorporates feedback, will further improve, because—fostered by TagMe!'s category suggestion feature—the number of distinct categories seems to converge (cf. Figure 5). Further, the mapping strategies can be enhanced by also considering the context of the tag/category that should be mapped. For example, for mapping a tag assignment one could select the DBpedia URI, which best fits to the DBpedia URI of the category that is associated to the tag assignment. Implementation of such advanced mapping strategies is part of our future work. In the current TagMe! implementation we thus apply the *DBpedia Lookup + Feedback* strategy and manually correct wrong URI mappings.

2.2 Faceted Tagging

To express the introduced enhancements of the TagMe! tagging system in a formal way, current folksonomy models need to be extended. Formal folksonomy models are e.g. presented in [8,9]. They are based on bindings between users, tags, and resources. According to [10] a folksonomy is defined as follows:

---

[8] http://Tagme.groupme.org/TagMe/resource/403/tas/1439

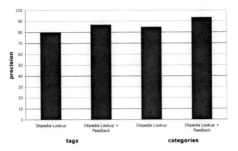

Fig. 3. Precision of mapping tags and categories to DBpedia URI

Definition 1 (Folksonomy). A *folksonomy* is a quadruple $\mathbb{F} := (U, T, R, Y)$, where:

- U, T, R, are finite sets of instances of *users*, *tags*, and *resources*, respectively, and
- Y defines a relation, the *tag assignment*, between these sets, that is, $Y \subseteq U \times T \times R$.

However, this simple folksonomy model is not sufficient to describe the tag assignments in more detail, i.e. assign context information to a tag assignment. To allow users to create these different facets of a tag assignment, we extend the given folksonomy:

Definition 2 (Faceted Folksonomy). A *faceted folksonomy* is a tuple $\mathbb{F} := (U, T, R, Y, C, Z)$, where:

- U, T, R, C are finite sets of instances of *users*, *tags*, *resources*, and *context-information* respectively,
- Y defines a relation, the *tag assignment* that is, $Y \subseteq U \times T \times R$ and
- Z defines a relation, the *context assignment* that is $Z \subseteq Y \times C$

In the TagMe! system, the *context information* can be a) an area, b) a DBpedia URI or c) a category. All context information are assigned to a tag assignment by a relation Z.

By utilizing the additional information, tag assignments become more connected to each other (see Figure 4). For example, two tags assigned to the same area within an image or having the same DBpedia concept can be considered as synonyms, while two tags that are assigned to different areas in an image are possibly not that strongly related to each other.

3   Analysis and Benefits of TagMe!

An analysis of the TagMe! data set reveals that the users appreciate the multi-faceted tagging in TagMe! as 874 of the 1295 tag assignments, which were performed within the three weeks after the launch of the system, were categorized and 645 times the users assigned a tag to a specific area within a picture. Given this initial data set, we analyzed the following questions.

- How are categories used in comparison to tags and what are the benefits of categorizing tag assignments?
- What are the benefits of assigning tags to specific areas within an image (spatial tag assignments)?

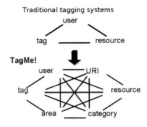

Fig. 4. The Faceted Folksonomy in the TagMe! system

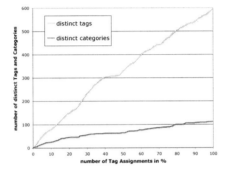

Fig. 5. Growth of number of distinct tags in comparison to distinct categories

3.1 Analysis of Category and DBPedia Context

Figure 5 shows the evolution of the number of distinct tags and categories: Although categories can be entered freely like tags, they grow much less than tags. Further, only 31 of the 79 distinct categories (e.g., "car" or "sea") have also been used as tags, which means that users seem to use different kinds of concepts for categories and tags respectively.

The TagMe! system supports users in assigning categories by means of auto-completion (see Figure 2). During our evaluation we divided the users into two groups: 50% of the users (*group A*) got only those categories as suggestion, which they themselves used before, while the other 50% of the users (*group B*) got categories as suggestions, which were created by themselves or by another user within their group. This small difference in the functionality had a big impact on the alignment of the categories. The number of distinct categories in group A was growing 61.94% stronger than in group B. Hence, the vocabulary of the categories can be aligned much better if categories, which have been applied by other users, are provided as suggestions as well.

Categories also enable to identify similar and related tags, which can, for example, be used for tag recommendations or query expansion. The identification of related tags is often based on tag co-occurrence analysis [11], i.e. two tags are related if they are often assigned to the same resource.

Table 1 lists tags related to the tag "clouds". As we can see, the *tag-based* co-occurrence strategy does not perform that well as it also ranks tags such as "horse" or "field" within as the top five most related tags. The *category-based* strategy

Table 1. Identifying tags related to "clouds"

Rank	Tag-based	Category-based	Area-based
1	horse	sky	sky
2	sky	field	sun
3	tower	river	cloud
4	field	snow	cross
5	trees	water	sunset

promotes basically those tags to the top of the ranking that share the most categories with "clouds". For example, "sky" and "clouds" share categories such as "nature" or "landscape". In general, the category-based strategy for detecting related tags seems to work better. However, in the given example, it still ranks the rather unrelated tag "field" very high. In our experiments, the best results are produced by the *area-based* strategy, which refines the category-based approach: It ranks those tags higher that occur in spatial tag assignments, whose areas overlap with the areas of the given tag. As shown in Table 1, it also produces—in comparison to the other strategies—the most reasonable ranking of tags related to "clouds". Four of the top five tags are apparently related ("cross" seems to be the only exception).

From our initial experiments on identifying similar tags, we draw the conclusion that tags, which share the same category and are often assigned to similar areas within an image (cf. *area-based*), are closer related than tags that often co-occur at same resource. In our future work we will further investigate whether our conclusion holds, especially in larger datasets where categories might introduce noise as they increase the overall connectivity of the folksonomy graph (cf. Figure 4).

DBpedia URIs introduce well-defined semantics to the TagMe! folksonomy. For example, some syntactically different tags or categories like "car" and "automobile" refer to the same semantic concept, which causes problems for tag-based search, e.g. when searching for "car" images that are tagged with "automobile" are possibly not returned. Here, DBpedia URIs can have a positive impact on the recall when executing tag-based search: as both tag assignments, i.e. "car" and "automobile", are mapped to "http://dbpedia.org/resource/Automobile", TagMe! can simply search via the DBpedia URI whenever users search via "car" or "auto" to increase recall of the tag-based search operations. Overall, the DBpedia URI mapping reduces the number of distinct concepts within TagMe! by 14.1% and 20.9% for tags and categories respectively.

3.2   Analysis of Spatial Annotations

In this section we analyze the nature of spatial annotations. We characterize the positions as well as the size of area annotations and identify usage patterns. Given these characteristics one can build algorithms that exploit area annotations for improving search or learning semantics from tags [12].

Position of Annotations. Figure 6 shows that, in general, area annotations are uniformly distributed on the images. As one would expect, in the center of an image there

Fig. 6. Density map of all area annotations: the brighter the color the more annotations have been assigned to the corresponding part of an image

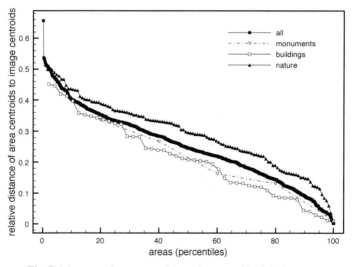

Fig. 7. Distance of area centroids to the centroid of the images

are more annotations done than at the border of the images. In particular, area annotations that are categorized as "people" or "friends" often occur in the center of an image (see Figure 8(i)). Further, categories can be differentiated according to their usage in combination with area annotations. For example, some categories have never or very seldomly been used when a specific area of an image was tagged (e.g., "time", "location", or "art") while others have been applied almost only for tagging a specific area (e.g., "people", "animals", or "things").

A numerical analysis of the dataset, using a simple heuristic as the Euclidean distance of an annotated area to the center of the image, also shows distinct usage patterns

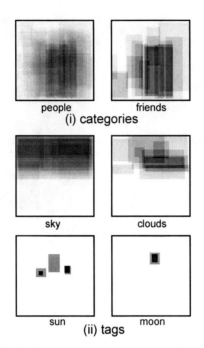

Fig. 8. Annotated areas: the darker the color the more annotations have been assigned to the corresponding part of an image

for some categories. Figure 7 plots the distances for all area annotations and compares them with area annotations of specific categories. We found, in average, that the distance from the center of all annotated areas to the center of the images is 0.25, ranging from 0 (image center) to $\sqrt{1/2}$ (image border)[9] . In addition, after computing the averages for each category, we identified that, for example, annotated areas in the category *nature* are in average farther from the center of the image (0.29) in contrast to the ones in the category *monuments* (0.18) or *buildings* (0.21) which tend to be closer to the center point as depicted in Figure 7. This exposes the idea that the *distance* feature indeed provides unique characteristics of the spatial tag assignments that can be further explored.

Area annotations can moreover be used to learn relations among categories and tags. Figure 8 shows (i) the areas that have been annotated whenever the categories "people" and "friends" have been used (the darker an area the more tags have been assigned to that area). As the areas that have been tagged in both categories strongly correlate and as category "people" was used more often than category "friends" one can deduce that "friends" is possibly a *sub-category* of "people" even if both categories would never co-occur at the same resource. Relations between tags can also deduced by analyzing the tagged areas. Figure 8 shows (ii) the areas that were tagged with "sky", "clouds",

[9] The distance between the center (coordinates $x_c=1/2$, $y_c=1/2$) and a farthest point, for example coordinates $x=0, y=0$ is given by the formula $\sqrt{(x-x_c)^2+(y-y_c)^2}=\sqrt{1/2}$.

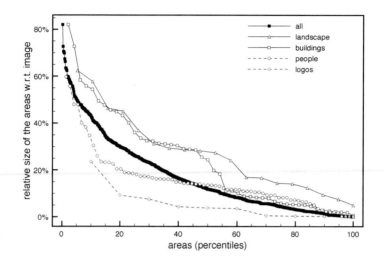

Fig. 9. Size of areas: the size of the area is specified with respect to the size of the tagged images, i.e. which parts of the images are covered by the area tag. The general distribution (*all*) differs from the distribution in context of specific categories (e.g., *landscape* or *logo*).

"sun", and "moon"[10] and via the size and position of the area it is possible to learn that an entity *is part of* or *contained in* another entity (e.g., "sun, moon, and clouds are contained in sky"). The learned relations among tags and categories can moreover be used to learn and refine relations between URIs (ontology concepts) as TagMe! maps tags and categories to DBpedia URIs (see Section 2.1).

Size of Annotations. As the position and overlap of annotated areas provides a new form of deriving relations among tags, the individual analysis of the size of areas also provides valuable and discrete information about tags and categories assignments.

For example, Figure 9 shows the distribution of the size of the areas for the overall categories in the dataset and four selected categories to be analyzed, namely: landscape, buildings, people and logos. We can clear identify a difference among these categories regarding the size of the annotated area. Additionally, comparing to the average distribution of area izes of all categories, areas in the categories of *people* or *logos* are, in majority, smaller while areas in the categories *landscapes* or *buildings* are mostly larger.

Intuitively, regarding ranking algorithms for search and retrieval of relevant items, one basic assumption that we expect is that the bigger is the annotated area of a tag or category, the bigger is its relevance. This assumption indeed stands and has been empirically demonstrated in our previous work [12]. However, the observation of individual characteristics of areas for each category (and tag) has not been taking in account, therefore leaving place for possible improvements. The assumption *"the bigger the more important"* shall then be improved to *"the bigger, with respect to the average size of areas in the same category, the more important"*.

---

[10] The visualizations are based on 25 ("sky"), 10 ("clouds"), 6 ("sun"), and 2 ("moon") tag assignments respectively.

3.3 Synopsis

The two tagging facets, categories and areas, which are applied in TagMe! also have a positive impact on the retrieval of folksonomy entities such as searching for resources or receiving tag recommendations as those facets can be applied to detect correlations between the entities. For example, tag recommendations are usually based on tag co-occurrence, e.g. if different tags are often assigned to same resources then they can be considered as *tag pair* and whenever one of the tags occurs at some resource it is likely that the other tag is relevant for that resource as well. By exploiting the category facet, TagMe! can increase the number of such tag pairs by 367%. Further, the category dimension has potential to compute the similarity of two tags more precisely, e.g. in addition to the (relative) number of times two tags occur at same resources one can consider the (relative) number of times these tags have been used in the same category. The areas of tag assignments can be exploited similarly to refine the correlations between tags. The analysis of the size, position, and overlap of areas moreover promises to improve the quality of search and ranking.

The results of our analyses can be summarized as follows.

- The usage of categories differs from the usage of tags: Even for those users, who did not receive the category suggestions, the number of distinct categories is growing slower than the number of distinct tags.
- Categories are used to further describe and classify tag assignments, and allow the user to solve the problem of ambiguous tags.
- Categories and area tags enhance the connectivity of the folksonomy and provide big potential to improve search or recommender applications (e.g., categories in TagMe! increase the co-occurrence rate of tags by 367%).
- The DBpedia mapping reduces the number of distinct tags and categories and can therewith be used to improve recall of tag-based search.
- For identifying related tags, tag assignments enriched with category and area facets are a more valuable source of information than traditional tag assignments: Tags, which share the same categories and are often assigned to similar areas within an image, are closer related than tags that simply co-occur at same resources.
- The spatial tag assignments can be used to learn typed relations among tags and categories such as *sub-category*, *sub-tag*, *part-of*, or *contained-in* relations. As tags and category assignments are mapped to meaningful URIs (ontological concepts), it is possible to propagate the learned relations to ontologies.
- The spatial annotations implicitly add valuable metadata to the tag assignments that can improve search rankings and recommendations. The usefulness of the spatial annotation feature is derived from the interpretation of size and position metrics of the annotations, for example, the bigger is the annotated area of a tag, the bigger is its relevance.

These findings motivate to exploit the different facets embedded in *faceted folksonomies* (cf. Definition 2.2) such as the TagMe! folksonomy. In our future work we will analyze the impact of those facets on search and ranking.

4   Related Work

The analyses in the previous section revealed several technical advantages of the tagging facets available in the TagMe! system. In this section we compare the tagging and tag-based exploration features of TagMe! from the perspective of the end-users with other tagging systems: Flickr, Delicious, Faviki [13] and LabelMe [6]. Our comparison among the systems is partially based on the dimensions of the *tagging system design taxonomy* proposed by Marlow et al. [14]. For example, we compare the (i) "Tagging rights", (ii) "Tagging support" and (iii) "Aggregation model" of those systems. These characteristics define respectively (i) who can tag, (ii) if the user gets assistance from the system during the tagging process and (iii) whether the system allows users to assign the same tag more than once to a particular resource (aggregation model = bag) or not (aggregation model = set).

We extend the tagging design taxonomy with the following additional dimensions related to tagging.

Semantic Tagging. We consider tagging as semantic tagging whenever the meaning of a tag is clearly defined, for example, by attaching a URI explaining the meaning of the tag [1].

Spatial Tagging. The practice of annotating a specific piece of a resource, e.g., parts of an image or paragraphs in a text.

Tag Categorization. A method enabling users to categorize or classify the tags and tag assignments.

Further, we introduce two dimensions that characterize to which degree users can exploit the tags to retrieve resources within the system.

Tag-based Navigation. Not all systems that provide tagging functionality also allow their users to explore and browse content based on tags, e.g. initiating search by clicking on a tag.

Faceted Navigation. By faceted navigation, we mean the feature of filtering resources based on the different dimensions of a tag assignment, i.e. by user, tag, or resource, category, or area (cf. Folksonomy model, Section 2.2). For example, in Delicious people can navigate through bookmarks annotated with specific tags (tag dimension) by a specific user (user dimension).

Table 2 summarizes the characteristics of TagMe! and similar tagging systems according to the taxonomy explained above.

The social bookmarking system Faviki and TagMe! are the only systems listed in Table 2 that allow for semantic tagging. Both systems primarily map tag assignments to DBpedia URIs [7]. Faviki requests the end-users to explicitly select the appropriate URIs while TagMe! is doing the mapping automatically. A fundamental restriction of Faviki is that only those tags, which correspond to a meaningful URI, can be assigned to a bookmark. Faviki supports users with a list of URI suggestions from which the users have to select one URI. Delicious and TagMe! provide tagging support by means

Table 2. TagMe! system characteristics in comparison to other social tagging and annotating systems

Dimension/System	*Flickr*	*Delicious*	*Faviki*	*LabelMe*	*TagMe!*
Semantic tagging	no	no	yes	no	yes
Spatial tagging	no	no	no	yes	yes
Tag categorization	no	tag bundles	no	no	tas categorization
Tagging support	viewable	suggested	suggested	viewable	suggested
Tagging rights	permission-based	free-for-all	free-for-all	free-for-all	free-for-all
Aggregation model	set	bag	bag	bag	bag
Tag-based navigation	yes	yes	yes	no	yes
Faceted navigation	yes (user, group)	yes (user)	yes (user)	no	yes (user, category)

of auto-completion. Flickr and LabelMe, which is an online annotation tool for images, do not provide tag suggestions but tags already assigned to a resource are *viewable* when adding new tags. In Flickr, users are not allowed to assign the same tag more than once to a particular resource (aggregation model = set) and moreover the owner of a picture has to grant others the permission to tag the picture (tagging rights: permission-based) which results in so-called *narrow folksonomies* [15]. In contrast, the other systems listed in Table 2 do not impose these restrictions which allows for *broad folksonomies*.

TagMe! provides two tagging features that are currently not sufficiently implemented in other systems: spatial tagging and tag categorization. Flickr and also MediaWiki[11] platforms enable users to add notes or comments to specific areas within pictures. However, similarly to LabelMe, which allows users to attach keywords to arbitrarily formed shapes within an image, these systems do not provide means for tag-based navigation based on such spatial annotations, i.e. users cannot click on a spatial tag assignment to navigate to other resources that are related to the corresponding tag (and possibly to the area). TagMe! offers tag-based navigation, which is common in tagging systems such as Flickr and Delicious, also for spatial tag assignments. A further innovation of TagMe! is the tag categorization that is performed on the level of tag assignments (*tas categorization*) and can therewith be used to disambiguate the meaning of a particular tag assignment (cf. Section 3). Delicious, on the contrary, only supports grouping of tags in so-called *tag bundles*. These tag bundles enable users to organize tags but do not help them to disambiguate specific tag assignments. They are moreover seldomly used: Tonkin reports that approx. 10% of the Delicious users have more than five tag bundles [16].

The structure of folksonomies (see Section 2.2) can be exploited to navigate through the resource corpus of a tagging system with respect to different facets. For example, when clicking on a tag in Flickr to explore related pictures, users can filter the results to narrow down the results to pictures of a specific *user* or pictures that occur in a specific *group* of pictures. In addition to the feature of browsing resources in context of specific users—as possible in Flickr, Delicious, and Faviki—TagMe! allows such tag-based faceted navigation by applying the categories of tag assignments as filters.

---

[11] http://www.Mediawiki.org

5   Conclusions

In this paper we discussed multi-faceted tagging in the TagMe! system. TagMe! is a tagging and exploration interface for Flickr and enables users to (1) categorize their tag assignments and (2) attach tag assignments to a specific area within an image. Moreover, all tag assignments are mapped to DBpedia URIs that describe the meaning of the tag. Our analyses reveal that strategies, which exploit categories and spatial tag assignments, provide better results in detecting similar or related tags than naive tag-based co-occurrence strategies. Further, both facets can be exploited to automatically learn new relations among tags and categories (e.g., *contained-in* or *sub-tag*) and therewith also among the corresponding DBpedia URIs. Our feedback-based mapping strategy is able to map tag and category assignments with a precision of more than 85% and 90% respectively to the correct URIs. The DBpedia mapping itself has the potential to increase the precision and recall of search in tagging systems as it solves the problem of ambiguous as well as synonymous tags. The new tagging facets give the users new means to navigate through images and further allow for advanced search and ranking algorithms. Additionally we exposed that spatial annotations have valuable embedded information that has not been fully explored in the literature. The simple analyses of the data demonstrated that the spatial tag assignments have individual characteristics of size and position, thus could be exploited to improve different functionalities such as search and recommendations. In our future work we will examine whether it is possible to learn more fine-grained relations by connecting the semantic tags and categories in TagMe! with external domain ontologies. For example, if two objects within the same image are tagged with *person* or *friend* (spatial tagging) one could assume that there is a *foaf:knows* relation between both persons. Further, we will analyze the impact of spatial tagging on search and try to answer whether the size of a tagged area matter or whether the proximity of the tagged area is relevant to the midpoint of the picture. To explore these research questions on larger data sets, we would like to integrate the TagMe! tagging features into an other photo sharing platforms such as Arsmeteo (http://www.arsmeteo.org).

References

1. Passant, A., Laublet, P.: Meaning Of A Tag: A collaborative approach to bridge the gap between tagging and Linked Data. In: Proceedings of the WWW 2008 Workshop Linked Data on the Web (LDOW 2008), Beijing, China (2008)
2. Marchetti, A., Tesconi, M., Ronzano, F., Rosella, M., Minutoli, S.: SemKey: A Semantic Collaborative Tagging System. In: Workshop on Tagging and Metadata for Social Information Organization at WWW 2007, Banff, Canada, May 8-12 (2007)
3. Auer, S., Bizer, C., Kobilarov, G., Lehmann, J., Cyganiak, R., Ives, Z.G.: DBpedia: A nucleus for a web of open data. In: Aberer, K., Choi, K.-S., Noy, N., Allemang, D., Lee, K.-I., Nixon, L.J.B., Golbeck, J., Mika, P., Maynard, D., Mizoguchi, R., Schreiber, G., Cudré-Mauroux, P. (eds.) ASWC 2007 and ISWC 2007. LNCS, vol. 4825, pp. 722–735. Springer, Heidelberg (2007)
4. Abel, F., Kawase, R., Krause, D., Siehndel, P.: Multi-faceted Tagging in TagMe! In: Bernstein, A., Karger, D.R., Heath, T., Feigenbaum, L., Maynard, D., Motta, E., Thirunarayan, K. (eds.) ISWC 2009. LNCS, vol. 5823, Springer, Heidelberg (2009)

5. Berners-Lee, T.: Linked Data - design issues. Technical report, W3C (2007),
   `http://www.w3.org/DesignIssues/LinkedData.html`
6. Russell, B.C., Torralba, A.B., Murphy, K.P., Freeman, W.T.: LabelMe: A Database and Web-based tool for Image Annotation. International Journal of Computer Vision 77, 157–173 (2008)
7. Bizer, C., Lehmann, J., Kobilarov, G., Auer, S., Becker, C., Cyganiak, R., Hellmann, S.: Dbpedia - a crystallization point for the web of data. Web Semantics: Science, Services and Agents on the World Wide Web (2009)
8. Halpin, H., Robu, V., Shepherd, H.: The Complex Dynamics of Collaborative Tagging. In: Proc. of 16th Int. World Wide Web Conference (WWW 2007), pp. 211–220. ACM Press, New York (2007)
9. Mika, P.: Ontologies are us: A unified model of social networks and semantics. In: Gil, Y., Motta, E., Benjamins, V.R., Musen, M.A. (eds.) ISWC 2005. LNCS, vol. 3729, pp. 522–536. Springer, Heidelberg (2005)
10. Hotho, A., Jäschke, R., Schmitz, C., Stumme, G.: Information retrieval in folksonomies: Search and ranking. In: Sure, Y., Domingue, J. (eds.) ESWC 2006. LNCS, vol. 4011, pp. 411–426. Springer, Heidelberg (2006)
11. Sigurbjörnsson, B., van Zwol, R.: Flickr tag recommendation based on collective knowledge. In: Proc. of 17th Int. World Wide Web Conference (WWW 2008), pp. 327–336. ACM Press, New York (2008)
12. Abel, F., Henze, N., Kawase, R., Krause, D.: The impact of multifaceted tagging on learning tag relations and search. In: Aroyo, L., Antoniou, G., Hyvönen, E., ten Teije, A., Stuckenschmidt, H., Cabral, L., Tudorache, T. (eds.) ESWC 2010. LNCS, vol. 6089, pp. 90–105. Springer, Heidelberg (2010)
13. Milicic, V.: Case study: Semantic tags. W3C Semantic Web Case Studies and Use Cases (2008), `http://www.w3.org/2001/sw/sweo/public/UseCases/Faviki/`
14. Marlow, C., Naaman, M., Boyd, D., Davis, M.: HT06, tagging paper, taxonomy, flickr, academic article, to read. In: Proc. of the 17th Conf. on Hypertext and Hypermedia, pp. 31–40. ACM Press, New York (2006)
15. Vander Wal, T.: Explaining and showing broad and narrow folksonomies (2005),
    `http://www.personalinfocloud.com/2005/02/explaining_and_.html`
16. Tonkin, E.: Searching the long tail: Hidden structure in social tagging. In: Proceedings of the 17th SIG Classification Research Workshop (2006)

Personalized Information Search and Retrieval through a Desktop Application

M. Elena Renda

Istituto di Informatica e Telematica del CNR
Via G. Moruzzi,1, I-56124 Pisa (PI), Italy
elena.renda@iit.cnr.it

Abstract. An important aspect of current Search Engines is that they answer queries crudely rather than learning the long-term requirements specific to a given user or, more precisely, to a specific information seeking task. If the same query is submitted by different users to a typical search engine, it will probably return the *same* result, regardless of *who* submitted the query. In our opinion, *smart* searching is definitely the next level of search technology. In this paper we present a *Personalized Information Search Assistant*, $P\mathcal{I}SA$, an environment where the user will not only be able to search/retrieve/be informed about documents *relevant* to her interests, but she will also be provided with highly personalized tools for organizing documents and information into a personal workspace. The major novelty of $P\mathcal{I}SA$ is that it combines all the characteristics of an on-line metasearch system with working space organization features in a *desktop application*, providing the user with a *single user point of view* personalized search environment.

1   Introduction

A common characteristic of most of the traditional search and retrieval services is that they are oriented towards a generic user and answer queries crudely rather than learning the short- and/or long-term requirements specific to a given user or, more in general, to a specific information seeking task. Consider, for instance, a farmer and a computer scientist, and the query "apple production": while the farmer may be interested in documents dealing with the fruit production, the computer scientist may want documents related to Apple Computers. Now suppose that users wish to perform searches about the same topic in different moments, to find relevant documents that have appeared, for instance, since the last time a search was performed. What often happens is that users' effort in searching documents is forgotten and lost. Without any "help", the user is required to repeat over and over the manual labour in searching and browsing the Web to find relevant documents just like the last time. With such a simple search facility users frustration increases as their demands become more complex and as the volume of information to look for -and published- increases.

On the other side, the available *Information Resources* differ in the kind, quantity and quality of information and services they provide, and in what kind of users they are supposed to be addressed to. They may also be extremely heterogeneous with respect to the *metadata schema* they use to describe the provided information. The alternative to individually query each resource has been offered by *Metasearch Systems* [4,27] which

J. Filipe and J. Cordeiro (Eds.): WEBIST 2010, LNBIP 75, pp. 129–146, 2011.
© Springer-Verlag Berlin Heidelberg 2011

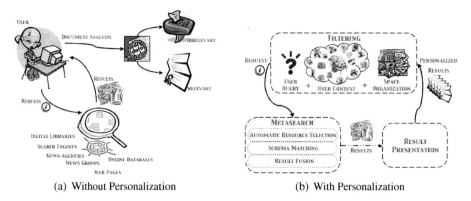

(a) Without Personalization   (b) With Personalization

Fig. 1. Web Search Scenario

provide a unified interface for simultaneously searching over multiple and heterogeneous resources, giving users the impression of querying one coherent, homogeneous resource.

Summarizing, in order to satisfy her information needs, a user has to (i) select the most promising information resources from the heterogeneous set available over the Web (a search engine, a digital library, and so on); (ii) submit the request to one or more of the selected resources available, from which she will receive a list of results; and (iii) select and collect the most relevant information (Fig. 1(a)). This sequence has to be repeated over and over, each time the user submits a query, even if it could be related to, or even the same of, the previous. New emerging services are necessary to prevent users from being drowned by the flood of available on-line information. In our opinion, *smart* and *personalized* searching is definitely the next level of search technology.

A system for searching and browsing the Web tailored and customized "ad-hoc" to the user should "know":

- *where to search*, by selecting a subset of *relevant* resources among all those that can be accessed (*Automatic Resource Selection*);
- *how to query* different resources, by matching the query language used by each of the selected resource (*Schema Matching*);
- *how to combine* the retrieved information from diverse resources (*Rank Fusion*);
- *how to present* the results according to user's preferences (*Result Presentation*).

The issue of learning the user's preferences may be addressed by mean of "profiles" (*User Profiling* [20,36]). This profile can be then used by the assistant for selecting a subset of *relevant* resources among all those that can be accessed (*Automatic Resource Selection* [21,30]), and finding matchings against content profiles for retrieving relevant information and filtering out the irrelevant ones (*Information Filtering* or *Content-based Filtering* [6]).

For helping users in finding actual relevant information while searching the Web, we modeled and designed P$\mathcal{I}$SA, a *Personalized Information Search Assistant* which supports the users in the task of organizing the information space they are accessing to, according to *their own subjective perspective*, and helps them in retrieving *actual* relevant information from the Web with minimum cost, in terms of effort and time. The *Personalized Information Search Assistant* (in the following called *assistant*) is a desktop application that (i) allows the user to organize her personal information space based on her own perspective, thus realizing her personalized folder hierarchy; (ii) automatically learns the long term interests of the user, by looking at her behavior in using the system; (iii) automatically learns the best information resources (w.r.t. the user information needs) where to search for information; (iv) fetches (either automatically or on a user-demand fashion) the relevant information from the preferred information resources; (v) filters and delivers the results to the user according to her delivery preferences. Figure 1 summarizes how such a personalized approach (Fig. 1(b)) may improve the Web information search scenario without personalization (Fig. 1(a)).

The major novelty of P$\mathcal{I}$SA is that it combines all the characteristics of an on-line metasearch system with working space organization features in a *desktop application*, providing the user with a *single user point of view* personalized search environment. User evaluation and experimental results are very promising, showing that the personalized search environment P$\mathcal{I}$SA provides considerably increases effectiveness and user satisfaction in the searching process.

The paper is organized as follows: the next section provides an overview of personalized systems presented in the literature which may compete with P$\mathcal{I}$SA; Sect. 3 introduces P$\mathcal{I}$SA, describing in detail its functionality, its architecture and the user interface; in Sect. 4, the evaluation methodology is described and the experimental results are reported; finally, Sect. 5 concludes.

2   Related Work

Personalization can be classified into two main approaches: *User-driven Personalization* and *System-driven Personalization*.

User-driven Personalization involves a user directly supporting the personalization process by providing explicit input. Many commercial information filtering systems use the approach of user-defined profiles to personalize search results. Within these systems, the user explicitly initiates actions (like setting configuration values) and provides sample information in order to control the personalization process [29,40].

System-driven Personalization reflects the desire to place most of the burden of constructing the user profile on the system, rather than on the user: the system observes user activities and behaviors, and dynamically creates a profile of the user to be used to automatically filter out, recommend and match users with other users, information and services, leaving the user with less control over the personalization process [1,2,5].

The requirement for personalization is also well known in the context of Digital Libraries (DLs). Some DLs provide simple personalized search functionality, such as providing the so-called *alerting services* (see, *e.g.*, [18,10]), *i.e.*, services that notify a user (typically by sending an e-mail) with a list of references to new documents deemed relevant to some of the user topic of interest (manually specified). Other DLs, for instance, give users the possibility to organize their personal information space (see, *e.g.*, [19]), and collaborate within community of users with similar interests (see, *e.g.*, [33]).

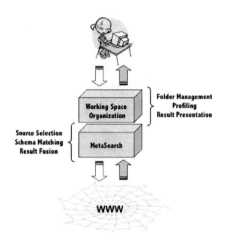

Fig. 2. Logical view of P$\mathcal{I}$SA functionality

In [39], the authors present a system for personalizing search via client-side automated analysis of user's interests and activities, re-ranking the final results according to different ways of representing the user, the corpus and the documents. Similarly, P$\mathcal{I}$SA is a desktop application, thus it is always available on the machine the user is using, and provides user profiling and document filtering. On the other hand, P$\mathcal{I}$SA also provides automatic source selection, rank fusion, different search mechanisms, and the working space organization feature. Furthermore, P$\mathcal{I}$SA is a working prototype with a fully featured user interface.

Several -supposed- P$\mathcal{I}$SA competitors can be found in searching the web for "personalized information", "assistant" or "profiling systems". Nevertheless, none of them are desktop applications tailored ad-hoc to the user needs, but on-line personalized services, which often provide only part of the features P$\mathcal{I}$SA has, or require collaborative filtering among the users of similar groups(*Collaborative Filtering* [22]). Differently, the *Personalized Information Search Assistant* we will present in this paper is *personalized* from a single user point of view. To the best of our knowledge, there is no desktop application presented in the literature providing information space organization, profiling, filtering and metasearch features as the P$\mathcal{I}$SA desktop application presented here.

3   P$\mathcal{I}$SA - The Assistant

The main principle underlying the personalized environment we propose here is based on the folder paradigm. That is, the user can organize the information space into her own folder hierachy, using as many folders as she wants, named as she wants, similarly to what happens, *e.g.*, with folders in e-mail programs. In our system, a folder is a holder of documents relevant to the user and, tipically, contains semantically related documents. This means that the content of a folder implicitly determines the topic of the folder. For this reason, we associate to each folder a profile, a compact representation of what the folder is about. Thus, *folder profiles*, which depend on the documents the corresponding folder currently contains, determine the documents that will be retrieved

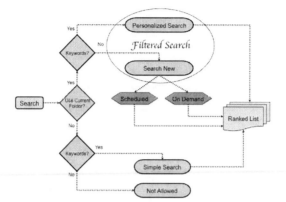

Fig. 3. P$\mathcal{I}$SA search mechanisms

for that folder. The user's set of folder profiles represents the collection of topics the user is interested in; consequently, the *user profile* consists of the collection of profiles related to the folders she owns.

P$\mathcal{I}$SA functionality can be logically organized into two main categories (Fig. 2): *working space organization*, and *metasearch*.

The working space organization functionality allows the user to login to the system, manage folders and documents, update profiles, and set up her personal data and system preferences; on the other hand, the assistant, based on the user behaviors, tries to "understand" her interests and automatically generates a "profile" representing the user (the user profile), and a set of profiles representing her interests (the folder profiles). These profiles, along with the user preferences, are then used as filters over the results obtained for the specific user request, in order to deliver only the "right" information, and present the personalized result list in the way that is more suitable for the user. Folder profiles and the user profile are updated from time to time (*Scheduled Profile Updating*). When a user has considerably changed the content of a folder, she may also request an immediate update (*On-demand Profile Updating*) of the profile.

The metasearch functionality allows the user to decide what kind of search she wants to perform over the Web. The search mechanisms (Fig. 3) provided by P$\mathcal{I}$SA are essentially of two types:

1. *Filtered Search*: the user is interested in finding new documents *not yet* retrieved for the current folder and she is:
   - looking for new documents (*Search New*) -relevant to the folder- published on the resources after the last search was performed (information maintained, for each folder, by storing the SEARCHTIMESTAMP); or
   - looking for new documents related to the folder by providing one or more keywords (*Personalized Search*).
2. *Simple Search*: the user does not associate any folder to the keywords she looks for, *i.e.*, she issues a "simple query" like through Web search engines.

The *Search New* mechanism can be performed *On-Demand* for a specific folder at user request, or for all the folders the user owns at a scheduled time (*Scheduled Search New*), according to the settings the user configured in her system preferences.

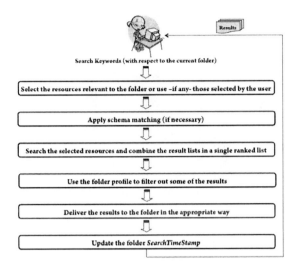

Fig. 4. *Personalized Search*: search keywords on user demand w.r.t. the current folder

Filtered Searches may be accomplished in at least two ways: (i) through query expansions techniques [8,15], *i.e.*, by expanding the query with significant terms of the folder profile and then submitting the expanded query; or (ii) issuing the query, and then filtering the result list w.r.t. the folder profile [11,31]. The latter approach is used in *Personalized Search*, where the profile is used as a post-filter, *i.e.*, after the results have been retrieved, while in *Search New* the folder profile is used as a pre-filter, by selecting some of the significant terms of the profile and using them as the query (recall that in this case the user does not provide any keyword).

Another important difference between these search mechanisms is the folder-query association: while in the *Filtered Searches* the user explicitly declares to use the folder profile as a filter, and the folder will be the final repository of the results, in the *Simple Search* only the user profile can be used, if possible, for filtering the retrieved documents and the repository of the results will be the user HOME folder (folder created by default together with the TRASH folder). It is worth noting that there is always a current folder: if no folder is selected, the current folder is the HOME folder.

Within the metasearch functionality, the assistant can perform in background a certain number of actions, including automatic resource selection, schema matching, profile management, document fusion, and document filtering. Thus, when a search is started, either on-demand or at a scheduled time, the assistant automatically selects the information resources to query, applies schema matching (if necessary), queries the selected resources, combines the results in a single result list and filters the results, either by means of the folder profile -if the query is associated with a given folder, or by means of the user profile otherwise. As an example, Fig. 4 shows the flow diagram for the *Personalized Search* mechanism, when the user selects a folder and wants to search for documents relevant to that folder containing the KEYWORDS she provides.

P$\mathcal{I}$SA architecture consists of the *Graphical User Interface*; the *User Database*, for storing user, folders, documents, preferences and profiles data; the *Profiler*; the *Source*

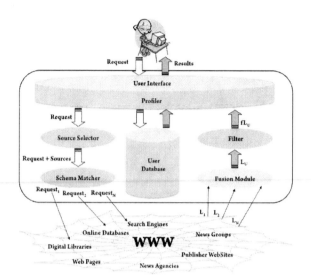

Fig. 5. P$\mathcal{IS}$A architecture

Selector; the *Schema Matcher*; the *Fusion Module*; and the *Filter* (Fig. 5). The proto-type has been entirely developed using the Java Programming language, to guarantee the portability of the application across different platforms. Furthermore, in develop-ing the prototype we took care of its modularity: each component can be easily modi-fied/enriched or substituted with minimal effort. In particular, the prototype is based on the following development environment and libraries:

- Java Platform, Standard Edition, and the Java Development Kit, version 6.0 [24];
- MySQL version 5.0.51 and the MySQL Connector/JDBC version 3.1.8 [28];
- Apache Lucene library version 2.2 [3].

In the following we describe each P$\mathcal{IS}$A component and corresponding functionality in detail.

3.1 Graphical User Interface

From the user's perspective, P$\mathcal{IS}$A Graphical User Interface (GUI) consists of a main menu and a set of windows and actions allowing the user to personalize the system step by step, via the folder and document management, the filters and the set of pref-erences she can modify. The application has a main pull down menu, with each entry of the menu corresponding to a user action. Every action can be also invoked through keyboard shortcuts.

Each component in P$\mathcal{IS}$A has a tooltip text, which comes out by moving the mouse over it, for providing instant help to the user.

Login Window. The first window the user is presented with P$\mathcal{IS}$A is the login window. After logging in, the user will be presented with the main user interface window and she can use the system, until she decides to quit. The first time the user accesses the assistant, P$\mathcal{IS}$A automatically creates the HOME and TRASH folders.

Fig. 6. P$\mathcal{I}$SA Graphical User Interface: main application window. The folder listing panel (on the left), the document listing panel (on the right), and the search panel (at the bottom), with the WHAT tab selected.

Main Window. The main window is composed of three parts: the folder listing panel, the document listing panel, and the search panel (Fig. 6).

The folder listing panel is a tree representing the user hierarchical folder structure. By selecting one folder, the user can: (i) have a view of the documents the folder contains; (ii) rename the selected folder[1]; (iv) delete the selected folder[1]; (iii) create a new folder as a child of the selected one[2]; (v) empty the selected folder; (vi) empty the TRASH folder; (vii) move a folder from an existing parent folder to a new parent folder[1] (by simply moving the folder in the folder tree - drag&drop).

The document listing panel includes a table representing the documents contained in the folder. The table has several columns, each one describing an attribute of the document: the NAME, *i.e.*, the title of the document retrieved, the URL, the RESOURCE from which the document has been retrieved, the SCORE of the document within the result list, the DATE of delivery, and the QUERY the user performed for retrieving that document. Since the documents are not created via user operations, but delivered by the system after a search session, the user cannot modify any of the document attributes. By selecting one of the rows of the document table, the content of that document will be displayed in the bottom side of the document panel. Furthermore, the user can delete the document(s), and cut and paste one or more documents from one folder to another.

---

[1] Forbidden for HOME and TRASH folders.

[2] Forbidden for TRASH folder.

In the bottom side of the main window there is the search panel, a tabbed pane with two tabs: WHAT and WHERE. Figure 6 shows, as an example, the main application window with the WHAT tab selected.

In the WHAT tab the user can choose to search documents with the provided GLOBAL SCHEMA, *i.e.*, search one or more keywords within one or more of the given attributes; alternatively, the user can initiate a search without any schema, *i.e.*, search one or more keywords irrespective of the attribute where they are located in the target schema of the queried resource(s). The GLOBAL SCHEMA P$\mathcal{I}$SA provides is composed of three attributes: TITLE, AUTHOR, and DESCRIPTION.

In the WHERE tab the user can chose one or more resources to query if she has some preferences; alternatively, automatic resource selection is performed if the user has not selected any resource.

In the search panel the user can also choose the maximum number of documents to be returned in the result list.

Finally, the user clicks on the SEARCH button for performing a *Simple Search*, or on the FILTERED SEARCH button for performing a *Filtered Search*. If the user does not type any keyword and clicks on the FILTERED SEARCH button she issues a *Search New* search w.r.t. the currently selected folder, while if she clicks on the SEARCH button, she will be warned of the action inadmissibility (recall Fig. 3).

Personal Settings Window. In this window, the user can fill in a form with her first name and last name, the country, the gender, the birth-date, and the email. Note that none of these data is mandatory, but they can be used for personalization too if available (think, for instance, at the Country when looking for information strictly bounded with the geographic location of the user).

Preferences Window. In this window the user can explicitly define some action the system performs. In particular, the user can set:

- when the system periodically updates the user profile;
- when the system periodically updates the folder profiles;
- when the system periodically search for new documents for each folder owned by the user;
- how the system notifies new documents (the options are: a pop-up window, a sound, or nothing; the default setting is: *no event*);
- how the system ranks the new documents found (the options are: by score, by date, by resource, or no preference; the default setting is *by score*).

Both the Preferences and the Personal Settings windows can be accessed by the user both via the pull down menu on the main window or via the corresponding keyboard shortcut.

Warning Windows. These windows are used by the system to warn the user on an invalid -or unsuccessful- operation.

Confirm Windows. These windows are used by the system to ask the user to confirm some actions, like, *e.g.*, quitting the application.

Acknowledgment Windows. These windows are used by the system to acknowledge the user of the outcome of an action she started.

3.2 User Database

For each user, $P\mathcal{I}SA$ locally creates and maintains a database with several tables, and provides methods for creating, reading and updating them. The USER DATABASE has been realized with the MySQL open source database [28]. The connection and interactions with the database has been realized with the MySQL Connector/J, a native Java driver that converts JDBC (Java Database Connectivity) calls into the network protocol used by the MySQL database.

When the user first register herself to $P\mathcal{I}SA$, the system automatically creates (i) the *Preferences Table*, for storing the system preferences (set by the user or provided by default by the system); (ii) the *Settings Table*, for storing the personal information provided by the user; (iii) the *Folders Table*, for storing all the information related to the folders owned by the user; (iv) the *Documents Table*, for storing all the information related to the documents already retrieved for the user; and (v) the *Profiles Table*, for storing the user profile and the folder profile of each folder owned by the user.

3.3 Profiler

The Profiler's task is to create user and folder profiles, and update them either on-demand or at a scheduled time. In the following we will describe how to build and maintain these profiles by adopting the approach proposed in [33].

Let's denote by t_k, d_j, and F_i a text term, a document, and a folder, respectively. Following the well-known vector space model, each document d_j in a folder F_i is represented as a vector of *weights*, $d_j = \langle w_{j1}, \ldots, w_{jm} \rangle$, where $0 \leq w_{jk} \leq 1$ corresponds to the "importance value" of term t_k in document d_j, and m is the total number of terms occurring in at least one document saved in the folder [35]. For each folder F_i the folder profile $f_i = \frac{1}{|F_i|} \cdot \sum_{d_j \in F_i} d_j$, i.e., f_i is computed as the *centroid* (average) of the documents belonging to F_i. This means that the profile of F_i may be seen as a data item itself [6] and, thus, is represented as a vector of weighted terms as well: $f_i =< w_{i1}, \ldots, w_{im} >$, where $w_{ik} = \frac{1}{|F_i|} \cdot \sum_{d_j \in F_i} w_{jk}$.

The profile p_u of the user u is built as the centroid of the user's folder profiles of user u, i.e., if $\mathcal{F}_u$ is the set of folders belonging to the user u, $p_u = \frac{1}{|\mathcal{F}_u|} \cdot \sum_{F_i \in \mathcal{F}_u} f_i$. As for folder profiles, p_u is represented as a vector of weighted terms as well: $p_u =< w_{u1}, \ldots, w_{un} >$.

Besides the folder and user profiles, the Profiler is also responsible for the personal data the user provided (if any) and the system preferences she set.

3.4 Source Selector

Automatic Resource Selection is based on the assumption of having a significant set of documents available from each information resource (see, *e.g.*, [12]). Usually, these documents are obtained by issuing random queries to the resource (*information resource sampling*, see, *e.g.*, [13]). This allows to compute an *approximation of the content* of each information resource, *i.e.*, a representation of what an information resource is about (*information resource topic* or *language model* of the information resource).

As a result, a *sample* set of documents for each information resource is gathered. This set is the *resource description* or *approximation* of the information resource. This data is then used in the next step to compute the *resource score* for each information resource, *i.e.*, a measure of the relevance of a given resource to a given query. In the following we describe how P$\mathcal{I}$SA computes the *resource goodness* for automatic resource selection by using an adapted version of the CORI resource selection method [12,14].

Consider query $q = \{v_1, ..., v_q\}$. For each resource $\mathcal{R}_i \in \mathcal{R}$, we associate the *resource score*, or simply the *goodness*, $G(q, \mathcal{R}_i)$, which indicates the relevance of resource $\mathcal{R}_i$ to the query q. Informally, a resource is more relevant if its approximation, computed by query-based sampling, contains many terms related to the original query. However, if a query term occurs in many resources, this term is not a good one to discriminate between relevant and not relevant resources. The weighting scheme is:

$$G(q, \mathcal{R}_i) = \frac{\sum_{v_k \in q} p(v_k | \mathcal{R}_i)}{|q|} , \qquad (1)$$

where the *belief* $p(v_k | \mathcal{R}_i)$ in $\mathcal{R}_i$, for value $v_k \in q$, is computed using the CORI algorithm [12,14], *i.e.*, $p(v_k | \mathcal{R}_i) = T_{i,k} \cdot I_k \cdot w_k$, and $|q|$ is the number of terms in q. In $p(v_k | \mathcal{R}_i)$ equation w_k is the weight of the term v_k in q, $T_{i,k}$ indicates the number of documents that contain the term v_k in the resource $\mathcal{R}_i$, and I_k represents the *inverse resource frequency*. The belief $p(v_k | \mathcal{R}_i)$ combines these two measures. $T_{i,k}$ and I_k are defined as:

$$T_{i,k} = \frac{df_{i,k}}{df_{i,k} + 50 + 150 \cdot \frac{cw_i}{\overline{cw}}} \quad (2) \qquad\qquad I_k = \frac{\log\left(\frac{|\mathcal{R}|+0.5}{cf_k}\right)}{\log\left(|\mathcal{R}| + 1.0\right)} \quad (3)$$

where:

$df_{i,k}$ is the number of documents in the approximation of $\mathcal{R}_i$ with value v_k;
cw_i is the number of values in the approximation of $\mathcal{R}_i$;
$\overline{cw}$ is the mean value of all the cw_i;
cf_k is the number of approximated resources containing value v_k;
$|\mathcal{R}|$ is the number of the resources.

In Equation 3, cf_k denotes the *resource frequency*, *i.e.*, the number of resources in which the term v_k occurs. Note that the higher cf_k the smaller I_k, reflecting the intuition that the more a term occurs among the resources the less it is a discriminating term. Finally, given the query q, all information resources $\mathcal{R}_i \in \mathcal{R}$ are ranked according to their resource relevance value $G(q, \mathcal{R}_i)$, and the top-n are selected as the most relevant ones.

3.5   Schema Matching

Given a user query $q = \{A_1 = v_1, \dots, A_q = v_q\}$, written with a schema T (*target* or *global schema*), and a resource R with its own schema S (*source schema*), the *Schema Matching* problem [7,17] can be defined as the problem of transforming each attribute $A_T \in T$ of the query in the correct attribute $A_S \in S$, in order to submit the query to R.

P$\mathcal{I}$SA relies on a simple and effective method to automatically learn schema mappings proposed in [34]. It is based on a reformulation of the CORI resource selection framework presented in the previous Section. Renda and Straccia [34, page 1079] state that "similarly to the resource selection problem, where we have to automatically identify the most relevant libraries w.r.t. a given query, in the schema matching problem we have to identify, for each target attribute, the most relevant source attribute w.r.t. a given structured query". Given a resource S and its metadata schema with attributes $S_1, ..., S_n$, the resource selection task can be reformulated in the schema matching problem as follows: given an attribute-value pair $A_i = v_i$, with A_i being an attribute of the target schema T, select among all the attributes S_j those which are most relevant to the attribute A_i given its value v_i, and map A_i to the most relevant attribute.

Let $\mathcal{R}_k \in \mathscr{R}$ be a selected resource. The problem is to find out how to match the attribute-value pairs $A_i = v_i \in q$ (over the target schema) into one or more attribute-value pairs $A_{k_j} = v_i$, where A_{k_j} is an attribute of the (source) schema of the selected resource $\mathcal{R}_k$. Now consider the resource $\mathcal{R}_k$ and the documents $r_1, \ldots, r_l$ of the approximation of $\mathcal{R}_k$ $Approx(\mathcal{R}_k)$ (computed by query-based sampling). Each document $r_s \in Approx(\mathcal{R}_k)$ is a set of attribute-value pairs $r_s = \{A_{k_1} = v_{k_1}, \ldots, A_{k_q} = v_{k_q}\}$.

From $Approx(\mathcal{R}_k)$, we make a projection on each attribute, *i.e.*, for each attribute A_{k_j} of the source schema we build a new set of documents:

$$C_{k,j} = \bigcup_{r_s \in Approx(\mathcal{R}_k)} \{r \mid r := \{A_{k_j} = v_{k_j}\}, A_{k_j} = v_{k_j} \in r_s\}. \quad (4)$$

The idea proposed in [34] is that each projection $C_{k,1}, \ldots, C_{k,k_q}$ can be seen as a new library, and CORI can be applied to select which of these new resources is the most relevant for each attribute-value pairs $A_i = v_i$ of the query q (see [34] for more details).

3.6   Rank Fusion

In P$\mathcal{I}$SA, we adopted the rank-based method called *CombMNZ*, considered as the best ranking fusion method (see [32] and references therein). *CombMNZ* combination function heavily weights common documents among the rankings, based on the fact that different search engines return similar sets of relevant documents but retrieve different sets of non-relevant documents.

Given a set of n rankings $R = \{\tau_1, \ldots, \tau_n\}$, denote with $\hat{\tau}$ the *fused ranking* (or *fused rank list*), which is the result of a rank fusion method applied to the rank lists in R. To determine $\hat{\tau}$, it is necessary to determine the *fused score* $s^{\hat{\tau}}(i)$ for each item $i \in U$, being $U = \bigcup_{\tau \in R, i \in \tau} \{i\}$, and order $\hat{\tau}$ according to decreasing values of $s^{\hat{\tau}}$. In *linear combination ranking fusion methods*, the fused score $s^{\hat{\tau}}(i)$ of an item $i \in U$ is defined as: $s^{\hat{\tau}}(i) = h(i, R)^y \cdot \sum_{\tau \in R} \alpha_\tau \cdot w^\tau(i)$, where (i) all the rank lists $\tau \in R$ have been normalised according to the same normalization method; (ii) $y \in \{0, 1\}$ indicates whether hits are counted or not; and (iii) $\sum_{\tau \in R} \alpha_\tau = 1$ where $\alpha_\tau \geq 0$ indicates the priority of the ranking τ. In [32] the authors report experimental results on comparing several *rank-based* and *score-based* fusion methods. According to the results reported in that paper, in P$\mathcal{I}$SA: (i) each rank list $\tau \in R$ has been normalized and the *normalised weight* $w^\tau(i)$ of an item $i \in \tau$ has been computed according to the *rank normalization method*: $w^\tau(i) = 1 - \frac{\tau(i)-1}{|\tau|}$; (ii) $y = 0$, *i.e.*, hits have not been counted; (iii) $\alpha_\tau = 1/|R|$, *i.e.*, all rank lists have the same priority.

Table 1. The document matrix

	t_1	...	t_k	...	t_m
d_1	w_{11}	...	w_{1k}	...	w_{1m}
d_2	w_{21}	...	w_{2k}	...	w_{2m}
...	...	...	...	...	...
d_n	w_{n1}	...	w_{nk}	...	w_{nm}

Table 2. The folder profile matrix

	t_1	...	t_k	...	t_m
f_1	w_{11}	...	w_{1k}	...	w_{1m}
f_2	w_{21}	...	w_{2k}	...	w_{2m}
...	...	...	...	...	...
f_v	w_{v1}	...	w_{vk}	...	w_{vm}

3.7 Filter

When the ranked results are available, the Filter role is to filter out some of the results. In particular, if the search issued was the *Personalized Search*, the Filter has to compare each document w.r.t. the folder profile. Recall that each document d_j is represented as a vector of *weights* $d_j = \langle w_{j1}, \ldots, w_{jm} \rangle$, where $0 \leq w_{jk} \leq 1$ corresponds to the "importance value" of term t_k in document d_j (Table 1), and that each profile is represented as a vector of weighted terms as well, *i.e.*, $f_i = [w_{i1}, \ldots, w_{im}]$ (Table 2).

In order to compute the content similarity sim_{ij} between the folder profile f_i and the document d_j, we compute the well-know cosine metric, *i.e.*, the scalar product between two row vectors, and select only those documents with $sim_{ij} > 0$.

Furthermore, the Filter will deliver up to the maximum number of documents, as requested by the user, and visualize them according to the user settings, as set in the System Preferences Window.

4 User Evaluation

In order to provide a preliminary evaluation of $\mathcal{PISA}$ usability, we asked 10 users, after a short presentation of the functionality, to use the system and test the GUI. After this preliminary evaluation, 5 more users joined the group of $\mathcal{PISA}$ evaluators.

To evaluate $\mathcal{PISA}$ effectiveness in providing personalized services, we asked the users to create a certain number of folders, populate them with "pertinent" documents, update the correspondent profiles, and issue a number of queries ranging from 1 to 10 for each profile. The maximum number of returned query results has been set to 10. We asked them to report for each query the total number of documents retrieved, and for each result the precision (which, we recall, is defined as the ratio of the number of relevant documents to the total number of retrieved documents). Furthermore, to understand the precision trend with the use of filtered searches, we asked each user to repeat 2 randomly chosen queries a certain number of times.

The total number of different profiles created is 40, for which the users issued a total number of 220 queries. The returned results have been scrutinized and classified by the users as either relevant or irrelevant for the corresponding profile, and the precision performance metric has been evaluated. In order to evaluate the benefits of $\mathcal{PISA}$ personalized search mechanisms, we asked each user to run the same set of queries without a profile, when they first accessed the system, with empty HOME folder and issuing a simple query (*i.e.*, with no profile, no automatic source selection, no filtering).

Data sets. On-line web information resources periodically modify their interfaces, so that the wrappers to their result pages have to be maintained constantly up-to-date.

In order to avoid spending time in such a tedious activity and concentrate on the personalization evaluation, we decided to download the content of some resources and implement a "static" interface to these local resources. For this purpose, we implemented an indexing engine for locally storing a certain number of information resources.

The INDEXER has been implemented taking advantage of the Lucene libraries [3], which provide Java-based indexing and search technology, as well as spellchecking, hit highlighting and advanced analysis/tokenization capabilities. In the indexing process, we have analyzed the individual documents and their content, split into terms, applied stemming, and eliminated stopwords. In the retrieval phase, Lucene libraries allow us to get back statistical information on the resources, such as the frequencies of the individual terms at the field level and at the document level, and the resource size.

We have locally downloaded and indexed 8 resources for a total of about 45, 000 searchable documents:

1. BIBDB, containing more than 5000 BibTeX entries about information retrieval and related areas;
2. DUBibDB, containing almost 3463 documents with bibliographic data from the Uni Duisburg University BibDB;
3. HCI, containing 26381 documents with bibliographic data from the Human-Computer Interaction (HCI) Bibliography;
4. DC, containing 6276 OAI documents in `Dublin Core` format;
5. ETDMS, containing 200 OAI electronic theses;
6. RFC1807, containing 467 OAI documents in `RFC1807` format;
7. WGA, containing 265 documents from the european Web Gallery of Art [3];
8. NGA, containing 864 documents from the american National Gallery of Art [4], Washington, DC.

Part of these resource collections have been provided by INEX - Initiative for the Evaluation of XML Retrieval [23]. In particular, DUBibDB and HCI collections are part of the INEX Heterogenous Collection Track 2006.

For the profiling and filtering tasks, we computed term weights of the documents by applying the well known $tf \cdot idf$ term weighting model (first introduced in [38]). The *term frequency* tf_{ij} of term t_i in document d_j is defined as: $tf_{ij} = \frac{n_{ij}}{\sum_k n_{kj}}$, where n_{ij} is the number of occurrences of the considered term t_i in document d_j, and the denominator is the sum of the number of occurrences of all terms in document d_j. The *inverse document frequency* idf_i is a measure of the general importance of the term t_i in the corpus of documents D and is defined as: $idf_i = log\frac{|D|}{df_i}$, where $|D|$ is the total number of documents in the corpus, and the denominator is the *document frequency* of term t_i, *i.e.*, the number of documents where the term t_i occurs: $df_i = |\{d \in D : t_i \in d\}|$. A high weight in $tf \cdot idf$ is reached by terms with a high term frequency in the given document and a low document frequency in the whole collection of documents. Thus this model is a good discriminant of common terms.

Result Precision. The average and variance of precision for the sets of queries submitted are reported in Table 3. As seen from the Table, $P\mathcal{I}SA$ is very effective in improving

---

[3] http://www.wga.hu
[4] http://www.nga.gov

Table 3. P$\mathcal{I}$SA experimental results

	Precision		No. of Documents	
	With Profile	Without Profile	With Profile	Without Profile
Average	0.75	0.36	8.01	9.65
Variance	0.10	0.05	7.73	0.41

precision, which is doubled w.r.t. the case of no personalization. In particular, P$\mathcal{I}$SA resulted very effective in: (i) filtering out irrelevant results; and (ii) delivering relevant results in presence of very general queries. The effectiveness of P$\mathcal{I}$SA in discarding irrelevant results can be deduced by Table 3, which reports the average and variance of the number of returned documents in case of personalized and non-personalized queries (we recall that the maximum number of returned documents was set to 10 in both cases). As seen from the Table, the average number of returned documents dropped from 9.65 without personalization to 8.01 with personalization, with higher variance in the latter case. As for (ii), we mention a specific query a user highlighted (several similar queries displayed the same behavior): the query "model" (an intendedly very general query) had precision improved from 0 to 0.7 when executed in the "database" folder, w.r.t. the case of no personalization.

User Satisfaction. All the users highlighted that such a personalized system is safer to use locally, in terms of privacy [37], as they did not like the idea of being profiled on the server side or by on-line services.

All the users reported that P$\mathcal{I}$SA resemblance with a common email program helped them to quickly understand how several GUI components work. The GUI has been classified as intuitive and robust.

Figure 7 shows the precision trend of the 30 queries executed repeatedly as the number of relevant documents in the correspondent folder increases. The queries issued

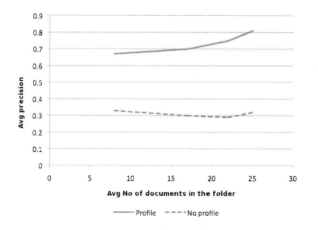

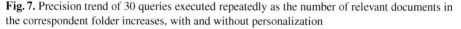

Fig. 7. Precision trend of 30 queries executed repeatedly as the number of relevant documents in the correspondent folder increases, with and without personalization

as personalized searches (straight line) clearly show an increasing trend with respect to the ones issued as simple searches (dotted line), *i.e.*, without personalization, thus improving user satisfaction in the searching process.

5   Conclusions

In this paper we presented P*I*SA - *Personalized Information Search Assistant*, a desktop application which provides the user with a highly personalized information space where she can create, manage and organize folders, search the Web with the different search mechanisms P*I*SA provides, manage documents retrieved by the system into her folders to best fit her needs, and personalize the result delivery and visualization. The assistant learns user and folder profiles from user's choices and preferences, and these profiles are then used to improve retrieval effectiveness in searching, by selecting the relevant resources to query and filtering the results accordingly. User evaluation and experimental results are very promising, showing that the personalized search environment P*I*SA provides considerably increases effectiveness and user satisfaction in the searching process.

P*I*SA prototype has been developed pursuing the goal of realizing modularity, so that each component can be easily modified or substituted with minimal effort. We are currently working to extend P*I*SA (i) by adopting different ways of modeling the users (as proposed in [36,39] and references therein), in order to further improve search effectiveness; and (ii) by including more sophisticated result presentation techniques. Concerning (ii), suppose the documents retrieved are considered not relevant by the user, it could be useful not to entirely download the documents. The *assistant* could highlight important passages within the documents, presenting the user only with the "best" document passage (*Passage Retrieval*) [25,26], or summarize the documents, presenting the user only with the *document summary* (*Summarization*) [9,16]. After analyzing the passages or the summaries, the user can decide whether it is worth downloading the documents and save it in her information space.

Acknowledgements. We really wish to thank all the people who volunteered to test, debug and evaluate P*I*SA. A special acknowledgment to J. C., a great professor to work with, and to P. S., whose suggestions and inestimable support helping us to further improve this work.

References

1. Albayrak, S., Wollny, S., Varone, N., Lommatzsch, A., Milosevic, D.: Agent technology for personalized information filtering: the pia-system. In: Proc. of the 20th Annual ACM Symposium on Applied Computing, pp. 54–59. ACM, New Mexico (2005)
2. Amazon.com: Amazon.com Home Page, http://www.amazon.com
3. Apache Lucene: Apache Lucene Project Home Page, http://lucene.apache.org/
4. Aslam, J. A., Pavlu, V., Yilmaz, E.: Measure-based metasearch. In: Proc. of the 28th Annual International ACM SIGIR Conference on Research and Development in Information Retrieval. Salvador, Brazil (2005)

5. Baillie, M., Crestani, F., Landoni, M.: Peng: integrated search of distributed news archives. In: Proc. of the 29th Annual International ACM SIGIR Conference on Research and Development in Information Retrieval, pp. 607–608. ACM, USA (2006)
6. Belkin, N., Croft, B.W.: Information filtering and information retrieval: Two sides of the same coin? Communications of the ACM 35(12), 29–38 (1992)
7. Bilke, A., Neumann, F.: Schema matching using duplicates. In: Proc. of the 21st International Conference on Data Engineering, pp. 69–80. IEEE Computer Society, Los Alamitos (2005)
8. Billerbeck, B., Zobel, J.: Efficient query expansion with auxiliary data structures. Inf. Syst. 31(7), 573–584 (2006)
9. Boydell, O., Smyth, B.: Social summarization in collaborative web search. Journal of Information Processing and Management: Special Issue on Collaborative Information retrieval 46(6), 782–798 (2010)
10. Buchanan, G., Hinze, A.: A generic alerting service for digital libraries. In: Proc. of the 5th ACM/IEEE-CS Joint Conference on Digital libraries, pp. 131–140. ACM, New York (2005)
11. Callan, J.: Learning while filtering documents. In: Proc. of the 21st Annual International ACM SIGIR Conference on Research and Development in Information Retrieval, Melbourne, Australia, pp. 224–231 (1998)
12. Callan, J.: Distributed information retrieval. In: Croft, W. (ed.) Advances in Information Retrieval, pp. 127–150. Kluwer Academic Publishers, Hingham (2000)
13. Callan, J., Connell, M.: Query-based sampling of text databases. ACM Transactions on Information Systems 19(2), 97–130 (2001)
14. Callan, J., Lu, Z., Croft, B.W.: Searching distributed collections with inference networks. In: Proc. of the 18th Annual International ACM SIGIR Conference on Research and Development in Information Retrieval, Seattle, WA, USA, pp. 21–28 (1995)
15. Carpineto, C., De Mori, R., Romano, G., Bigi, B.: An information-theoretic approach to automatic query expansion. ACM Transactions on Information Systems 19(1), 1–27 (2001)
16. Chen, L., Chue, W.L.: Using web structure and summarisation techniques for web content mining. Information Processing and Management 41(5), 1225–1242 (2005)
17. Dhamankar, R., Lee, Y., Doan, A., Halevy, A., Domingos, P.: iMAP: discovering complex semantic matches between database schemas. In: Proc. of the ACM SIGMOD International Conference on Management of Data, pp. 383–394. ACM Press, New York (2004)
18. Faensen, D., Faulstich, L., Schweppe, H., Hinze, A., Steidinger, A.: Hermes: a notification service for digital libraries. In: Joint Conference on Digital Libraries, pp. 373–380 (2001)
19. Fernandez, L., Sanchez, J., Garcia, A.: MiBiblio: personal spaces in a digital library universe. In: ACM DL, pp. 232–233 (2000)
20. Godoy, D., Amandi, A.: User profiling for web page filtering. IEEE Internet Computing 9(4), 56–64 (2005)
21. Gu, Q., de la Chica, S., Ahmad, F., Khan, H., Sumner, T., Martin, J., Butcher, K.: Personalizing the selection of digital library resources to support intentional learning. In: Christensen-Dalsgaard, B., Castelli, D., Ammitzbøll Jurik, B., Lippincott, J. (eds.) ECDL 2008. LNCS, vol. 5173, pp. 244–255. Springer, Heidelberg (2008)
22. Harpale, A.S., Yang, Y.: Personalized active learning for collaborative filtering. In: Proc. of the 3st Annual International ACM SIGIR Conference on Research and Development in Information Retrieval, pp. 91–98. ACM, New York (2008)
23. INEX: INitiative for the Evaluation of XML Retrieval, http://inex.is.informatik.uni-duisburg.de
24. JAVA: Developer Resources for Java Technology, http://java.sun.com/
25. Jiang, J., Zhai, C.: Extraction of coherent relevant passages using hidden markov models. ACM Transactions on Information Systems 24(3), 295–319 (2006)

26. Liu, X., Croft, W.: Passage retrieval based on language models. In: Proc. of the 11th International Conference on Information and Knowledge Management, pp. 375–382. ACM, New York (2002)
27. Meng, W., Wu, Z., Yu, C., Li, Z.: A higly scalable and effective method for metasearch. ACM Transaction on Information Systems 19(3), 310–335 (2001)
28. MySQL: My SQL Home Page, http://www.mysql.com/
29. MyYahoo: MyYahoo Home Page, http://my.yahoo.com/
30. Nottelmann, H., Fuhr, N.: Evaluating different methods of estimating retrieval quality for resource selection. In: Proc. of the 26th Annual International ACM SIGIR Conference on Research and Development in Information Retrieval (2003)
31. Pazzani, M.J., Billsus, D.: Content-based recommendation systems. The adaptive web: methods and strategies of web personalization, 325–341 (2007)
32. Renda, M.E., Straccia, U.: Web metasearch: Rank vs. score based rank aggregation methods. In: Proc. of the 18th Annual ACM Symposium on Applied Computing, pp. 841–846. ACM, Melbourne (2003)
33. Renda, M.E., Straccia, U.: A personalized collaborative digital library environment: a model and an application. Information Processing & Management 41(1), 5–21 (2005)
34. Renda, M.E., Straccia, U.: Automatic structured query transformation over distributed digital libraries. In: Proc. of the 21st Annual ACM Symposium on Applied Computing, Dijon, France, pp. 1078–1083 (2006)
35. Salton, G., McGill, J.M.: Introduction to Modern Information Retrieval. Addison Wesley Publ. Co., Massachussetts (1983)
36. Schiaffino, S., Amandi, A.: Intelligent user profiling. Artificial intelligence: an international perspective 5640, 193–216 (2009)
37. Smyth, B.: Adaptive information access: Personalization and privacy. IJPRAI 21(2), 183–205 (2007)
38. Sparck Jones, K.: A statistical interpretation of term specificity and its application in retrieval. Journal of Documentation 28, 11–21 (1972)
39. Teevan, J., Dumais, S.T., Horvitz, E.: Personalizing search via automated analysis of interests and activities. In: Proc. of the 28th Annual International ACM SIGIR Conference on Research and Development in Information Retrieval, pp. 449–456. ACM, New York (2005)
40. Wang, Y., Aroyo, L., Stash, N., Rutledge, L.: Interactive user modeling for personalized access to museum collections: The rijksmuseum case study. In: Conati, C., McCoy, K., Paliouras, G. (eds.) UM 2007. LNCS (LNAI), vol. 4511, pp. 385–389. Springer, Heidelberg (2007)

Web Information Systems Portfolios: A Contribution to Pragmatics

Klaus-Dieter Schewe[1] and Bernhard Thalheim[2]

[1] Software Competence Center Hagenberg, Hagenberg, Austria
kdschewe@acm.org
[2] Christian-Albrechts-University Kiel, Institute of Computer Science, Kiel, Germany
thalheim@is.informatik.uni-kiel.de

Abstract. On a high level of abstraction the storyboard of a Web Information System (WIS) specifies who will be using the system, in which way and for which goals. Storyboard pragmatics deals with the question what the storyboard means for its users. One part of pragmatics is concerned with usage analysis by means of life cases, user models and contexts. In this paper we address another part of pragmatics that complements usage analysis by WIS portfolios. These comprise two parts: the *information portfolio* and the *utilisation portfolio*. The former one is concerned with information consumed and produced by the WIS users, which leads to content chunks. The latter one captures functionality requirements, which depend on the specific category the WIS belongs to. Here we concentrate on information services and community WISs.

Keywords: Pragmatics, Web information system, Information portfolio, Utilisation portfolio, Information services, Community systems.

1 Introduction

A Web Information System (WIS) is an information system that can be accessed through the world-wide-web. So far, many approaches to WIS conceptual modelling have been developed, e.g. [2,3,6,8,15,16], most of which are centered around content and naviga-tion modelling, occasionally coupled with specific requirements models.

In [16] we characterised a WIS by strategic characteristics such as purpose, mission, intentions and ambience (more details in [10]), usage characteristics such as tasks, users and stories, content and functionality characteristics, context, and presentation, which leads to an abstraction layer model for WIS development. Central to this approach to WIS development is the method of storyboarding, which on a high level of abstraction specifies who will be using the system, in which way and for which goals. In a nutshell, a storyboard consists of three parts:

- a set of *tasks* that are associated with goals the users may have,
- a set of *actors*, i.e. abstractions of user groups defined by roles that determine obli-gations and rights, and user profiles determining preferences, and
- a *story space*, which itself consists of a hierarchy of scenarios describing scenes and actions, and is accompanied by a *plot* describing the action scheme.

J. Filipe and J. Cordeiro (Eds.): WEBIST 2010, LNBIP 75, pp. 147–161, 2011.

Syntax and semantics of storyboarding including customisation to preferences have been well elaborated in [16,17,19]. However, in order to link storyboarding to the systems requirements and to provide guidelines and means to derive the complex storyboards from informal ideas about a WIS without any technical bias, this has to be complemented by pragmatics, which according to [20] is the "balance between principles and practical usage".

In [18] we addressed the pragmatics of storyboarding focusing on usage analysis. Based on intentions we investigaed *life cases*, *user models* and *contexts*. Life cases capture observations of user behaviour in reality, and can be used in a pragmatic way to specify the story space. Life cases have already been envisioned in [1] and integrated into the entire software engineering process in [5]. They generalise business use cases as in [14]. User models are specified by user and actor profiles, and actor portfolios. They are used to get a better understanding of the tasks associated with the WIS, and the goals of users. Goals have been identified as a crucial component of requirements engineering in [4]. Task descriptions are also used in participatory design, e.g. in [1,7,12]. Contexts characterise the situation, in which a user finds himself at a certain time in a particular location. For WISs we must handle different kinds of contexts and analyse the way they impact on life cases, user models and the storyboard.

In this paper we extend our work on WIS pragmatics focusing on WIS portfolios, which address the pragmatics associated with content and functionality. We distinguish between *information* as processed by humans and *data* as its carrier that is perceived or noticed, selected and organized by its receiver. Content is complex and ready-to-use data, and may be enhanced by concepts that specify the semantic meaning of content objects, and topics that specify the pragmatic understanding of users.

Thus, information is directed towards pragmatics, whereas content may be considered to highlight the syntactical dimension. If content is enhanced by concepts and topics, then users are able to capture the meaning and the utilisation of the data they receive. Analogously, functionality refers to functions offered by the system, thus highlists the dynamic aspects of the syntactic dimension, whereas *utilisation* is linked to the stories supporting users' life cases, thus is directed towards pragmatics. This distinction is illustrated in Figure 1.

Accordingly, a WIS portfolio consists of two parts: the *information portfolio* and the *utilisation portfolio*. The former one is concerned with information consumed and produced by the WIS users, which leads to content chunks. We will elaborate on this in Section 2. The latter one captures functionality requirements. We will elaborate on this in Section 3 focusing on utilisation portfolios for information services and community WISs.

2   Information Portfolios

A WIS portfolio consists of an *information portfolio* and a *utilisation portfolio*. They are mapped to content and functionality specifications, respectively. In doing so we distinguish between *content* provided by the WIS and *information*, which is related to an actor or user.

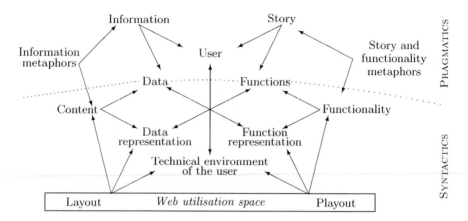

Fig. 1. The Web Utilization Space Based On the Characteristics of WIS

2.1   A Formalised Concept of Persona

The information demand is used to derive the information consumption of each user. This is related to the definition and meaning of information for the user based on received/requested data, which has to be organized, interpreted, understood, and integrated into his/her knowledge. In general, this would require to model the user, the specific request of the user, the ability to understand the data, and the skills, which is infeasible. However, as the information demand of actors is a subset of the one of users represented by the actor, we can use prototypes of individuals called *personae* to determine the information demand. In this way we formalise the concept of persona known from [13]. In addition, we model a task-oriented life case of these individuals, and derive the information demand, data requirement, and the specific utilisation requirements.

A *persona* is characterized by an expressive name, profession, intents, technical equipment, behaviour, skills and profile, disabilities, and specific properties such as hobbies and habits. A persona is a typical individual created to describe the typical user based on the life cases, the context, the portfolio, and the profile. User models characterize profiles for education, work, and personality. This characterization can be extended by

– identity with name, pictures, etc.,
– personal characteristics such as age, gender, location, and socio-economic status,
– characterization of reaction to possible user errors,
– specific observed behaviour including skill sets, behavioural pattern, expertise and background, and
– specific relationships, requirements, and expectations.

Example 1. Let us consider an information service of a city and focus on business people. For these we develop the following specific portfolio:

User Profile. Jack-of-all-trades is a business man. He intends to visit the city through a short-term visit. He is interested in culture and history. He likes short distances and

4-star or better hotels. He is usually in a hurry. He likes good dining and talking. Additionally, he is familiar with technology.

Intention and Information Demand. Jack-of-all-trades visits the information site for business trip preparation. His information demand includes hotel information, spare time information for the evenings, and information on the central traffic.

Content Requirements. The information demand may be mapped to general city information, information on restaurants, traffic, culture, business clubs, and good dining addresses. Therefore, the information consumption of Jack-of-all-trades must be supported by the corresponding databases. At the same time, Jack-of-all-trades requires a handy booking service.

Life Case. The life case we envision includes a brief survey on the city including places to see, the selection of a convenient hotel, a survey of events of interest, the booking procedure for events, a search for good dining places, and some information what else to see and whom to talk to.

Specific Utilisation. The collection of data is similar to a basket collection. Jack-of-all-trades prefers shallow navigation and fast search. He is also interested in highlights for the period he is considering.

Jack-of-all-trades can be exemplified to be a specific persona:

Personal. name: Bernhard Karlowics, age: 48, male, married, lives in northern Germany, profession: business assistant, income: around €50.000 per year

Robustness. errors are not taken as own errors, download time is critical

Kind of User. kind but pretentious, makes quick decisions, interested in history, culture, classical musics, usually in a hurry

Specific Behaviour. resumes story also after hours

Specific Interactivity. works alone, with interruptions, no time for concentrated reading, final results expected

Profile. middle level manager, Masters degree in business and computer engineering, workoholic (around 60 hours per week)

Portfolio. collection of travel details with confirmation and payment, prefers hotels with four-stars or higher, checking through direct connection to booking services

Life case. preparing for travel, single use of the system, email confirmation necessary, spare time information, events of interest, dining places, business clubs

Context. business environment, typically client-server computers at workplace, occasionally mobile phone for contact while on the move

The explicit specification of personae has several benefits. They provide communication means within the development team, focus on a specific target set of actors, and help to make assumptions about the target audience. Thus, personae may augment the WIS portfolio specification, but should not be overused.

2.2 Content Chunks

In order to model the information portfolio we collect the information demand of all actors we would like to support. In addition, we can include some specific information demand of users matching with the groups of users. This information demand can be combined into a single content chunk that is demanded by all actors of similar steps in the life case. This information demand can later be modelled within a database model.

This combination turns around the viewpoint we have taken so far. We try to envision which content is necessary for which actors or users. We may start with the intention why an actor may demand a given content. The content-centered view allows us to derive a specification of steps in which a certain chunk of content is requested.

The content-centered analysis is used during brainstorming sessions in which we try to derive scenarios, intentions, and the information need of users. At the same time we can derive the service kind, utilisation, actors, presentation, content, and functions supporting this content. We can also derive directly the intersection among the content chunks, which provides a basis for the development of queries to extract the content demanded from the WIS.

Content chunks are arranged within *content-extended scenarios*, in which each scene is associated with a content chunk. This content chunk combines the consumption of actors, auxiliary content that is provided for the support of users, and the content that is additionally provided due to the intentions of the WIS provider and the context of the current scene. We further enhance this scenario by data that is produced by the actor or that stems from the environment.

Example 2. Let us continue Example 1 and consider the booking scene. If the actor has decided to choose a particular hotel, then we may associate with the choice action the selection of an identification for the hotel, which extends the booking scene with the content that provides information to the actor on hotels. With the choice of a hotel the actor leaves this scene and produces the selection data. In the next scene the actor can be asked about the payment.

The same scene can also be used in a different scenario, in which the actor first collects all choices in a basket and later confirms those choices, which are the most appropriate.

The information portfolio is also enhanced by information that depends on the WIS context. This can define content associated with control, which normally is internal to the WIS and not accessible by applications, content that is used to determine the transitions and to control the WIS context, e.g. for the pre- and post-scene conditions, transition conditions depending on the databases used, or assignment for collaborating actors, etc., content that might be useful as reference, e.g. meta-information on time, responsibility, and links to other WISs, or application-specific data that is not accessible by the WIS.

The content set required for each step in a life case may become too large. So we must prioritise the development of content chunks. There are two perspectives for prioritising:

- In the usability perspective we evaluate the impact the content has for the the WIS portfolio. The impact is based on the occurrence the content has in steps and activities and on the number of actors requiring this content. The impact is high if the majority of users need it frequently or cannot continue their work if the content is missing.
- In the economic perspective we evaluate the cost/benefit relation. Since projects have limited budget, contract commitments, resource restrictions, technological

constraints, marketplace pressures, and deadlines we must limit the efforts. We may classify those content chunks which have high impact into strategic, high value, targeted and luxuries.

Example 3. The www.cottbus.de WIS provides information on hotels, booking services, etc. For the decision, which information should be provided we may use a classification along usability and economic perspective. We can then assign final decisions to the evaluation such as approved ($\sqrt{}$), under review ($\diamond$), and rejected ($\not\diamond$). In a similar way we may evaluate all content chunks we discovered. The evaluation is used for deciding which content is to be developed and to which extent.

Content chunks are often composed only of data, i.e. they relate to media objects on the conceptual model [16]. The description of the data is based on media types, viewpoints, and adaptation facilities. Content is also based on semantics, i.e. associated concepts capturing basic pieces of knowledge or their annotations, and restricted by pre- and postconditions. Content must also be annotated using a commonly agreed vocabulary or a dictionary. This agreement is bound to actors or communities. We denote items of dictionaries by topics. The pragmatics also reflects the context of potential usage. As content is often used in a form that combines content chunks with other content chunks we also specify related content chunks.

2.3   Content Chunks for the Entry Scene

The entry scene is associated with a specific content chunk that will give rise to the home page of the WIS. Therefore, it must be developed with greatest care. It must contain all essential information of the WIS on the setting, the environment, the characterisation, the main intentions, activities that can be played with, etc. Therefore, we must balance the list of supported tasks in such a way that they become displayable.

The entry scene concerns the initial situation, the emotional environment, and the main intentions a user may have while visiting the WIS. At the same time, the actor must understand what s/he has to expect when entering the WIS. Objectives of the entry page are to introduce the context and essential actions of the WIS, provide information on collaborating actors, show the theme of the WIS, define the kind of scenario to be played, and support an easy match with the information demand of a user or actor.

The attraction of users requires suspense in the opening, as the first impression decides whether a casual user continues within the WIS. Branding, navigation, content and usage must be balanced. Rules for the entry scene must be based on the characteristics of WIS, i.e. on intentions, especially objectives, aims and the target audience, on specifics of supported life cases such as need in guidance, feedback, explanation, specific content, and functionality, on complexity of content, which directly leads to the need to support surveyability, ease of use, and decomposition of content chunks, on variety of functions that must already be provided by the entry scene, on adaptation to user and actor profiles, which requires a rough separation of actors according to their education, work, personality of security profiles, on properties of portfolio such as complexity of problems, need in collaboration, and support for workspace and workplace, and on integration of context, and adaptation of content, functionality, and scenario to the context.

These rules permit the derivation of the general atmosphere and the main intention of the entry scene. Typical examples are categories such as "traditional and serious" for business and work pages, and "energetic" or "vital" providing a flavour of progression and innovation.

Example 4. The entry page must accommodate the large variety of visitors and their information needs, for which we can identify a number of content items that must be provided:

- Immediately and clearly communicate the purpose to the visitor: Each visitor must be supported by descriptive wording and images that are easy and quickly to understand independent from whether the visit is the first or a repeated one. The values of the WIS must be easily detectable. Visitors' positive impressions depend on the trustworthiness and the values of the WIS.
- Creating an identity of the WIS (branding): Users need to quickly capture whether a WIS holds a valuable promise, whether they can trust it, and what content is offered.
- Attract by content: A visitor judges a WIS within seconds of entering it. Therefore, content must be attractive, well-organised, easy to browse, and summarized.
- Personalization of content: The WIS should be tailored to the portfolio and profiles of their visitors. In this case, the system does not require users to learn and memorize its facilities.
- Provide an orientation to the visitor: Navigation must be easy to use and may be based on an exploration metaphor. Users should quickly comprehend how to get around, should be not be forced to guess what can be done next.
- Balanced content and functionality: The trade-off between space used for content or functionality can be resolved by developing patterns that support fast detection of items the user is seeking for, by focusing on the tasks of the user, and by branding in a constricted form.
- Establishing a cohesive and logical layout: The most important information chunks must be immediately identifiable and located. For this the reading and recognition culture of the users must be taken into account.

The pages of a WIS, especially the home page are often designed by graphics experts who tend to use a large number of multimedia features. However, layout and playout have to be in accordance with the rules developed above, which leads to the request to apply screenography [9,11]. This is, however, beyond the scope of this article.

Finally, the entry scene must be considered as one of the main advertisement instruments of the WIS. For this reason, a clear statement of the values of the WIS is the basis for deriving content that conveys these values with the users' first impressions. Typical value properties are

- reliability, availability, actuality, speed, responsiveness, alternatives, ease of use, managing complexity, (filtering) levels, completeness, links, flexibility, support, export, privacy, and guidance for information services, or
- user adaptation, learning styles and preferences, simplicity, support, flexibility, guidance, accessibility, consistency, motivating, clear goals, and responsiveness, or

– portability, speed, shared resources, previewing, alertness, awareness, versioning, mail management, multi-threading, report generation, feedback, mentoring, distribution, flexibility, security, and safety for community sites.

These values of the entry page are a part of the brand of the WIS and must match with the aims and objects that have already been specified for the entire WIS while capturing intentions [18].

3   Utilisation Portfolios

The second constituent of the WIS portfolio is the *utilisation portfolio*, which can be considered to be a collection of requirements for functionality and WIS utilisation in general. It describes the intentions of the users, their goals, their context, and their specific requirements, and as such is based on the life cases that were modelled before, and the profiles and the portfolio of the users and actors. Furthermore, the actor context must be taken into account. Therefore, we first discuss the utilisation portfolio and then derive its impact on the functionality required by the user.

The utilisation portfolio combines the actor or user perspective to the WIS. We already know intentions of users, their profiles, and their life cases. Users are grouped to actors for which portfolios have already been developed. Based on the portfolio and the context specification life cases were extended.

The WIS utilisation portfolio cannot be described in general for all different categories of WIS such as e-business, learning and edutainment, communities, etc., though these categories are mixed in real applications. The separation into categories eases, however, the description of the WIS utilisation portfolio. In the following we will describe the development of the WIS utilisation portfolio for information servives and community WISs.

3.1   Portfolios for Information Services

Information services aim at the delivery of information to customers depending on their information needs. Typical providers are government, news companies, institutions, and individuals. The goods delivered are data, news, and messages. The customer can be an individual, government, or everybody. Typical activities are read, become informed, understand, and become attracted. Information scenarios are based on the word field ^{inform} or more specifically ^{ask} and ^{search}. Therefore, we specialise the brand pattern $\mathcal{P}^W 2\mathcal{U}^A$ to the more specific brand $B^{\mathcal{I}}2V^{\text{inform}}$, $A^{\mathcal{I}}2V^{\text{inform}}$, $C^{\mathcal{I}}2V^{\text{inform}}$.

Within our projects we developed information-intensive sites which need a sophisticated database support and which are based on a variety of various stories of their use. For instance, the $(A,G)^{\mathcal{I}}2(V,C,A,B)^{\text{inform}}$-scenario is a typical for city information WIS. Information services are usually based on a broadband portfolio and are targeted to almost everybody. For this reason they must be robust, flexible, and adaptable.

Example 5.   The *Cottbus interaktive* project is an information service that provides media data such as TV and radio programmes, electronic program guides (EPG), video streams, video text, and also internet data based on cable nets and set-top boxes. The project showed how different media can be combined into one melted and combined service. TV viewers also obtain video stream on their request, EPG information they need, and internet data depending on their selection. The set-top box has a ruler-based navigation and interaction. Therefore, the viewer must be profiled according to the chosen interest and information need. The profile is adapted during the utilisation history. The users history is thus recorded and used for lazy adaptation of their internet profiles.

The TV viewer is interested in TV/Radio-on-main-interest, EPG-on-profile, Video-on-request, Cinema-on-demand, Greeting-and-messages-upon-request, Internet-on-interest, and Internet-on-profile. The utilisation space of the information services is therefore also based on profiles and portfolio of interested and informed users. It also reflects the technical environment such as channel capacity, communication protocols, and demands of supporting competitors. Such kind of information challenges current technology. The service that is currently in use is based on powerful servers, powerful delivery channels, thin request channels, and browser-based set-top boxes.

Life Cases.   The life cases are either specified based on natural language or based on semi-formal specification templates we can use word fields for representation of basic units. We consider two different kinds of word fields for information services:

- Substantive word fields are mapped to content chunks which are containers for content or media object suites. These word fields result in a large variety of requirements for content.
- Verb word fields are mapped to functionality requirements. These functionality requirements are typically based on a small set of typical word fields.

We can distinguish typically five main word fields for information services:

Inform.   The main aim of an information service is to inform the visitor according to his/her information demand and according to the profile and portfolio. Data are received and understood by visitors and reduces the recipient's uncertainty. They are classically a collection of facts from which conclusions may be drawn or knowledge acquired through study or experience or instruction.

Guide and Direct.   Information services steer and direct the visitor through their service. The visitor is proactive according to the data that is provided. Guiding includes also helping the visitor whenever help is appropriate.

Provide.   Information services supply data to the visitor depending on what the visitor desires or needs. Therefore, the service must determine what the visitor needs and demands.

Search.   Searching is a very complex word field which we discuss in the next chapter in detail. Visitors look into or over carefully or thoroughly in an effort to find or discover something within their demands or interests. They examine and check the content provided.

Lead.   Information services take somebody somewhere. This leadership results in a change of the information stage or level of the visitor. This change must also be taken into consideration during later visits. The leadership may cause to undertake a certain action.

Information services are often supporting *infotainment* of visitors. Additional word fields we use for the description of scenarios are:

Advise. The information service recommends visitors. They give information or notice to information. The visitor consults the service for his/her information demand.

Attract. The services causes to approach or adhere the visitor. The visitors need to be fascinated and enchanted and so compelled to a response.

Browse. Information services are consumed by the visitors. Visitors look over casually or through media objects casually especially in search of something of interest.

Offer. Services present data for acceptance or rejection in order to satisfy an information demand. They propose, suggest and make available data.

Weave and Network. Content provided by the information service is united in a coherent whole. Visitors produce their own understanding by elaborately combining elements, by intertwining, or by interlacing. transitive senses

Zapping. Some visitors propel suddenly or speedily through the service. They avoid watching or reading by changing services especially with a address controller or by fast-forwarding an address directory.

Derivation of Functionality. We can use these word fields for derivation of requirements to functionality of the information service:

Information, Communication and Transaction Functions. These functions support visitors in their work, their information demand, and within their intensions. Additionally, all other actors of the system are supported within their portfolio.

Feedback Functions. Feedback functions allow the visitor to give a feedback which is going to answered by the addressee. Therefore, feedback functions are supported by a logistics system for answering and reacting.

Import and Export Functions. Visitors often want to print or integrate the data they got into their personal workspace. Export functions are a must for any information service. Some information services also support business or community scenarios. Therefore, import of data must be supported in a very flexible way.

Combination Functions. Users often want to combine the information they obtain without opening a number of additional browser windows. They can be supported by combination functions whenever data is carried to a basket or to the users workplace or workspace. Typical life cases already require such functionality.

Orientation Functions. Due to the large variety of data visitors need a guidance and an orientation facility beyond navigation bars. Orientation functions allow the visitor to track where they are, how they came, what they can do, and which path they can use for their demand.

Search and Retrieval Functions. Search and retrieval functionality is the basis functionality beside the data presentation and navigation in information services. We distinguish a variety of search functions:

Search and Retrieval based on Meta-properties. Components of media objects are of different importance for queries and especially for search. Some of them are crucial. Some of them are auxiliary. Distinguished components are considered to be meta-properties.

Retrieval on Main Properties. Retrieval is often based on main properties or associations represented in media objects. The meta-properties can be used for retrieval. Association-based retrieval follows associated types. Fuzzy retrieval allows the visitor to ask a question that is transferred or translated to a correct question. Retrieval can be also based on similarity functions such as functions for phonetic matching like soundex functions. Retrieval can also be based on special functions.

Search function can be combined with orientation functions.

Supporting Functions. Visitors and actors working with of for the information service require a large number of functions which are typically the same as for most software systems.

Context-sensitive Help. The visitor often needs help beside the general purpose help or the FAQ lists. Session objects allow to trace the reason for the help request and can support the user.

Privacy Functions. Visitors often do not like to be tracked and monitored. For this reason, a clear statement which privacy policy is applied and privacy functions must be provided.

Tools. Information services development, evolution and maintenance is a complex task that must be supported by a variety of tools for content management, for link control, for maintenance of the site, for adaptation to new technology, for backups, security, mirroring, versioning, for site observation and diagnostics, for site extension and restructuring, for integration of foreign content and functionality, for mediators, and for wrappers.

Tours and Trailers. Novel or casual visitors want to know what is the service providing, what facilities they can use, how they can navigate through the service etc. Trailers and guided tours provide an impression on the service.

Content Chunks. Information services provide content. The utilisation scenarios are thus content-driven. Content and organisation are the critical success factors for information services. Context must be given explicitly. Privacy is often another success factor. Utilisation depends on the portfolio and profile of the users. We may distinguish a variety of utilisation:

- Intention-based utilisation is driven by the intentions of users. They use the information service for recherche, for leisure, study, travel, spare time contacts, get together, etc.
- Life-case-based utilisation is based on assembling supporting material. Information services provide support for life cases and guide the visitor within their life case. Typically, users also need answers to FAQ's.
- Portfolio-based utilisation extend the previous kinds by a workspace, a workplace, a solution space and/or instruments for the solution of tasks. These information services support the tasks of user by appropriate content. This kind of utilisation is often combined with community services or collaboration facilities.
- Profile-based utilisation follows either the educational or personality profile of the user.

3.2 Community Portfolios

Communities and leisure groups are gathering places for registered members, who form an interacting community of various actors with common location, intentions, and time. They are based on shared experience, interests or conviction, and voluntary interaction among members towards common goals. In the case of work communities they deal with issues affecting the legal profession, and are concerned with furthering the best interests of their members. Communities often employ leadership and hosting. Membership requirements and obligations, resources and amenities, member characteristics, community policies, and activity style and pattern create a large variety of community/group WISs.

The utilisation portfolio is based on the community or group member profiles. The general brand $\mathcal{PW}2\mathcal{U}^{\mathcal{A}}$ must also be specialized for community and group services. The provider and the users may coincide for community WIS.

The actions depend on the kind of the community or group. The life cases of these communities and groups vary very much. Nevertheless, we can identify several types of typical scenarios. Active scenarios (^{act}) are activities by the receiving actor(s). Information scenarios (^{inform}) or more specifically ^{ask} and ^{search} are mainly governed by the provider. Participation scenarios (^{attend}) request the interaction of receiving actors. Community and group WIS are mainly following the Group2Group^{act} or the Group2Visitor$^{\text{inform,act}}$ brand.

Discussions are another kind of action. We may distinguish *chat-oriented, collaboration -based*, and *topic-centered* discussion groups. The first group does not limit contributions. Main actions are initiate, respond, inform, summarise, and close. Collaboration-based discussions follow a collaboration pattern and preserve a collaboration style agreed in advance. The main metaphor used is the "meeting". Main actions are open, close, propose agenda, issue discussion, contribute, and inform. Topic-centered discussion groups are based on a topic and preserve dialogue acts. Actors may be authors, responders, organisers, or supporters. Authors are typically classified and have a number of privileges, while responders respond to some data and use a response pattern and preserve a response style. Tokens are a convenient vehicle for support of topic-centered discussions often generalising communication protocols.

Example 6. The process for finding a group decision is typical example for topic-centered discussions. For instance, members of a program committee of a conference collaborate during decision making, whether a paper is to be accepted or rejected. They act either as reviewers or as ordinary members of the program committee. Reviewers of one paper may revise their review, comment on the reviews of other members, and exchange messages within the subgroup of the program committee comprising the reviewers. An ordinary member of the program committee may comment on the reviews and request a change of evaluation.

All members will make a common decision that depends on the other discussion topics, i.e. on the decisions for all papers. Opinions may be stated with a certain confidence. Opinions may be distributed to all or selected members of the program committee. Authors of papers are excluded from all discussions on their papers. The actions of a member of the PC may be mandatory, optional or not permitted. So, we specify these obligations and rights using deontic constraints.

Web2.0 sites provide other examples of enhanced community or group WISs that are even more user-driven. Examples are `GoogleActSense`, `Wikipedia`, `Flickr`, etc. Communities may share their opinion or beliefs or partial knowledge (e.g. `Wikipedia`), their diary or visits (e.g. `del.icio.us`), their intentions of internet utilisation (e.g. `43thing.com`), and more. While these communities are currently more or less leisure communities, they will evolve into large bodies requiring lead enhanced utilisation portfolios for communities.

In particular, support for collaboration and participation will be needed. This gives rise to *collaboration utilisation portfolios*. Collaboration means to work together towards a common goal, i.e. it combines of three aspects:

Cooperation. takes parts of actions into account that jointly define a group action.

Coordination. of actions of individual actors is necessary to achieve the desired result in a cooperative action.

Communication. between actors involved in the same group action is indispensable for coordination. It appears in a variety of facets, e.g. as an act or instance of transmitting a verbal or written message, a process by which information is exchanged between individuals through a common system of symbols, or as a technique for expressing ideas effectively (as in speech) using the technology of the transmission of information (as by print or telecommunication).

So, the main word fields associated for the utilisation portfolio are the following ones:

Contribute. A member of a community gives or supplies a document to the community and shares it with the community subject to certain obligations and responsibilities. Obligations include modification obligations such as updating and removing the document. The member of the community becomes an author and has a role as owner. The community, however, obtains or possesses the contribution. Responsibilities of the author include quality obligations for the contribution.

Join. Users may join a community and thus obtain a role of a member of the community. The membership requires the commitment to the coordination style and coordination pattern of the community. This commitment implies a certain behaviour and collaboration with the members of the community. For instance, members agree on regular occurrence or logical relations. The membership may be public or hidden to visitors.

Meet. Members of a community come together at a particular time or place, entering into conference, argument, or personal dealings with other members of the community or the general auditory. During the meeting they receive or greet in an official capacity of the community. Members may form coalitions before, during and after meetings.

Organize. Becoming a member of a community brings rights and obligations. The member may be permitted to develop a unit within the community and has a function during this development. In this case the member becomes a coherent functioning whole, and contributes with own profile and portfolio. Organisations often require to arrange by systematic planning and united effort.

Publish. The author makes his/her contributions generally known. The community decides, whether the contribution can be disseminated to the public based on the rules of the community. The contribution is then produced or released for distribution.

Subscribe. Communities often have their own publication lines. A member subscribes to some of them according to the rules of the community. The subscribed services are (periodically and regularly) received by the actor. The member of the community agrees to purchase and pay for securities. The subscription can also be extended to new offerings.

Withdraw. The members of a community should have the right to cancel the membership of the community or part of the subscriptions. In this case the user may loose the ownership of contributions s/he made. The withdrawal may require particular official procedures.

4   Conclusions

In this paper we extended our previous work on pragmatics of Web Information Systems. We introduced WIS portfolios, which are composed of an information portfolio and a utilisation portfolio. The information portfolio captures information consumption and production by users in the scenes of the story space. This is linked to the information needed by a user to understand the task and the information demand to perform the appropriate action. Modelling information demand of all potential users is infeasible, but the concept of *persona* permits to deal with prototypical users instead. The integration of information demands leads to content chunks.

Likewise, the utilisation portfolio consists of tasks users might wish to accomplish within the system, and goals they want to achieve by this. It can be considered as the necessary means for collecting functionality requirements. Different from the information portfolio the utilisation portfolio depends on the application category. Here we focused on the categories of information services and community WISs.

WIS portfolios complete the research on WIS pragmatics, which is an independing connector element between systems requirements and conceptual models.

References

1. Carroll, J.M.: Participatory design of community information systems - the designer as bard. In: COOP, pp. 1–6 (2004)
2. Ceri, S., Fraternali, P., Bongio, A., Brambilla, M., Comai, S., Matera, M.: Designing Data-Intensive Web Applications. Morgan Kaufmann, San Francisco (2003)
3. De Troyer, O., Leune, C.: WSDM: A user-centered design method for web sites. In: Computer Networks and ISDN Systems – Proc. 7th Intern. WWW Conference, pp. 85–94. Elsevier, Amsterdam (1998)
4. Giorgini, P., Mylopoulos, J., Nicchiarelli, E., Sebastiani, R.: Reasoning with goal models. In: Spaccapietra, S., March, S.T., Kambayashi, Y. (eds.) ER 2002. LNCS, vol. 2503, pp. 167–181. Springer, Heidelberg (2002)
5. Harel, D., Marelly, R.: Come, Let's play: Scenario-based programming using LSCs and the play-engine. Springer, Berlin (2003)
6. Houben, G.-J., Barna, P., Frasincar, F., Vdovjak, R.: HERA: Development of semantic web information systems. In Third International Conference on Web Engineering – ICWE 2003. In: Cueva Lovelle, J.M., Rodríguez, B.M.G., Gayo, J.E.L., Ruiz, M. (eds.) ICWE 2003. LNCS, vol. 2722, pp. 529–538. Springer, Heidelberg (2003)

 7. Kensing, F., Blomberg, J.: Participatory design: Issues and concerns. Computer Supported Cooperative Work 7(3/4), 167–185 (1998)
 8. Lowe, D.G., Henderson-Sellers, B., Gu, A.: Web Extensions to UML: Using the MVC Triad. In: Spaccapietra, S., March, S.T., Kambayashi, Y. (eds.) ER 2002. LNCS, vol. 2503, pp. 105–119. Springer, Heidelberg (2002)
 9. Moritz, T., Noack, R., Schewe, K.-D., Thalheim, B.: Intention-driven screenography. In: Mayr, H.C., Karagiannis, D. (eds.) Information Systems Technology and its Applications – Proc. ISTA 2007. LNI, vol. P-107, pp. 128–139. GI (2007)
10. Moritz, T., Schewe, K.-D., Thalheim, B.: Strategic modelling of web information systems. International Journal on Web Information Systems 1(4), 77–94 (2005)
11. Noack, R., Thalheim, B.: Patterns for screenography. In: Kaschek, R., Kop, C., Steinberger, C., Fliedl, G. (eds.) Information Systems and e-Business Technologies, Proc. UNISCON 2008. LNBIP, vol. 5, pp. 484–495. Springer, Heidelberg (2008)
12. O'Neill, E., Johnson, P.: Participatory task modelling: users and developers modelling users' tasks and domains. In: TAMODIA, pp. 67–74 (2004)
13. Pruitt, J., Adlin, T.: The Persona Lifecycle. Morgan Kaufmann, San Francisco (2006)
14. Robertson, J., Robertson, S.: Requirements-Led Project Process. Addison-Wesley, Reading (2006)
15. Rossi, G., Schwabe, D., Lyardet, F.: Web application models are more than conceptual models. In P. Chen et al., editors, Advances in Conceptual Modeling. In: Kouloumdjian, J., Roddick, J., Chen, P.P., Embley, D.W., Liddle, S.W. (eds.) ER Workshops 1999. LNCS, vol. 1727, pp. 239–252. Springer, Heidelberg (1999)
16. Schewe, K.-D., Thalheim, B.: Conceptual modelling of web information systems. Data and Knowledge Engineering 54(2), 147–188 (2005)
17. Schewe, K.-D., Thalheim, B.: Personalisation of web information systems - a term rewriting approach. Data and Knowledge Engineering 62(1), 101–117 (2007)
18. Schewe, K.-D., Thalheim, B.: Pragmatics of storyboarding for web information systems: Usage analysis. International Journal of Web and Grid Services 3(2), 128–169 (2007)
19. Schewe, K.-D., Thalheim, B., Wang, Q.: Customising web information systems according to user preferences. World Wide Web 12(1), 27–50 (2009)
20. Webster. Webster's ninth new collegiate dictionary (1991)

Efficient Literature Research Based on Semantic Tagnets: Implemented and Evaluated for a German Text-Corpus

Uta Christoph, Daniel Götten, Karl-Heinz Krempels, and Christoph Terwelp

RWTH Aachen University, Ahornstr. 55, 52074 Aachen, Germany
{uta.christoph,daniel.goetten,karl-heinz.krempels,
christoph.terwelp}@rwth-aachen.de

Abstract. In this paper we present an approach that is capable to automatically generate semantic tagnets for given sets of german tags (keywords) and an arbitrary text corpus using three different analysis methods. The resulting tagnets are used to estimate similarities between texts that are manually tagged with the keywords from the given tagset. Basically, this approach can be used in digital libraries to provide an efficient and intuitive interface for literature research. Although it is mainly optimized for the german language the proposed methods can easily be enhanced to generate tagnets for a given set of english keywords.

Keywords: Semantic networks, Literature research, Text corpus, Text analysis.

1 Introduction

Due to the large amount of data available in the world wide web data structuring is an important topic today. One famous approach is the *semantic web* as proposed by Tim Berners-Lee [2]. The idea is to structure the available data by its semantic meaning to provide much better access methods and possibilities for automatic analysis. Since no suitable semantic wordnets are available for the german language the idea is to build a system that allows to estimate semantic relations for a given set of german words. In the following an approach will be presented that structures *keywords (tags)* and documents by their semantic information and similarities.

Normally, no semantic information is available for information stored in digital libraries and solely simple search interfaces are provided that allow to search for documents by its title or author names. Apparently, research of similar documents is hard and time-consuming in such cases. One approach to solve this problem is to avail keywords that are used to describe the content of single documents and enable the search for documents by their tags.

Although tags allow to categorize documents they do not completely solve the problem described above as illustrated by the following example. Given two similar documents d_1 and d_2 annotated by tags from two disjunct sets S_1 and S_2. It might not be possible to recognize the similarities between d_1 and d_2, if no information about semantic relations between the tags of both sets is given. Especially for a large set of available similar tags to describe each document this problem may occur quite frequently.

J. Filipe and J. Cordeiro (Eds.): WEBIST 2010, LNBIP 75, pp. 162–172, 2011.

The presented approach is based on similarity analysis of documents annotated manually with tags. These document similarities are estimated by automatically extracting semantic relations between the tags of the given set. Both the given tags and the extracted relations form a network called *tagnet*. The derived network of documents is called *similarity net*. Apparently, both networks can be used to make literature research more efficient, by visualizing them in a suitable way. The resulting system provides a quite intuitive interface that enables non-technical users to research literature by surfing through the similarity net.

At first we discuss in Section 2 relevant problems that may occur during automatic text analysis. We show that these problems mainly result from morphological special cases of the german language. As possible solutions the approaches of lemmatization and stemming will be discussed. Afterwards, the idea of the implemented system (the *tagnet builder*) that builds the described networks is introduced in Section 3. Finally, the results are evaluated in Section 4.

2   Problems

Automatic approaches of text analysis are quite error-prone without adaptation to a given scenario. Especially in the case of automatic text analysis of german[1] texts problems occur due to the morphological special cases in the german language. Concerning statistical approaches in text analysis three problems have to be taken into account:

1. multilingualism
2. morphologicial special cases
3. understanding of texts

Since the considered corpus solely consists of german texts we do not consider multilingualism for the moment. For this reason only the problems (2) and (3) have to be discussed.

2.1   Morphological Special Cases

The main objective of the tagnet builder is the extraction of semantic information from keywords based on statistical frequency analysis on the considered text corpus. These frequencies have to be as accurate as possible, so a reliable mapping of all given keywords to unique stems is required. Furthermore, numbers and stop words can be deleted, since they are not relevant for the analysis.

Stemming. *Stemming* is an algorithmical approach for the estimation of unambiguous stems for words of a given language. A famous approach is the *porter stemmer* [7]. An implementation for german words based on this approach is available in terms of *Snowball*[2].

Unfortunately, stemming algorithms do not generate real stems, but unique pseudo stems by suffix stripping based on predefined rules without consideration of grammatical characteristics. Especially for the case of german words two different words might

---

[1] Or other inflectional complex languages.

[2] http://snowball.tartarus.org

be mapped to one stem although there exists no semantic similarity. Thus, this simple stemming approach may deteriorate the quality of the semantic tagnet generated by the tagnet builder.

Lemmatization. To provide mappings to real stems *lemmatization* has to be used. This lemmatization is often based on fullform lexicons that have to be defined in prior. Unfortunately, no complete fullform lexicons are available for the german language due to the possibility of compound words. This problem can be solved with the help of a learning lemmatizer as it has been proposed by P. Perera and R. Witté [6]. Basically, this lemmatizer processes words in three phases.

At first it checks if the current word already is part of the existing fullform lexicon to lemmatize it immediately by its corresponding stem. If the current word is not part of the existing lexicon, it will be classified with respect to its POS-Tags[3]. Then suitable rules for suffix stripping will be applied to get candidate stems that are returned and inserted into the lexicon[4].

2.2   Understanding of Texts

Automatic understanding of texts is a complex problem and still a research topic today. Especially if frequency analysis is used, problems may occur that are referable to words with different meanings in subject to the context.

The approach proposed in this paper will assume that the tagnet builder is solely used for texts of one topic. Thus, the described problem normally will not occur in this scenario, but has to be addressed if texts of different topics should be analysed.

3   Approach

Given an unstructured list of tags, the described system is able to find semantic relations between these tags and store them in a suitable database. Based on this semantic tagnet text similarities can be calculated for a corpus of tagged texts.

3.1   Tagnet Builder

The tagnet builder uses three different approaches to gain as much information about semantic relations between the given tags as possible. These three approaches are:

1. rule-based extraction of semantic relations
2. lexicon-based extraction of semantic relations
3. statistical estimation of semantic relations based on occurrences in a given set of documents

In the following the approaches will be described in detail.

Rule-based Approach. The problem of compound words has been mentioned in the sections above. Nevertheless, analysis of such compounds can be utilized as a first

---

[3] Part-of-speech tagging basically denotes the tagging of words with its grammatical characteristics.

[4] The lexicon may contain intermediately wrong stems, that will be corrected over time.

approach to recognize semantic relations between two words. As an example, *Fach-sprache* (terminology) and *Sprache* (language) can be considered. Obviously, *Sprache* is a suffix and *hypernym*[5] of *Fachsprache*.

A suffix matching based on regular expressions is used to recognize such hypernym relations between different tags. Analogously, semantic specification relations, i.e. *Fach* (subject) specifies *Fachtext* (specialized text) can be recognized by such an approach. In this case prefix matching instead of suffix matching has to be used. Nevertheless, this simple matching approach results in so many wrong matches, that it is not applicable.

Example. Given the two tags *Text* and *Kontext* (context). The simple approach will recognize a hypernym relation between these two tags although this is an incorrect matching since no hypernym relation exists in this case.

As a first solution a minimal string length δ of the string before the suffix is demanded. Recalling the example no semantic relation between *Text*, *Kontext* or other similar tags will be detected for $\delta > 3$. Since, $\delta > 4$ proved not to be useful, $\delta = 4$ is assumed in the following. Nevertheless, some correct matchings cannot be recognized due to this restriction, but estimations show that the number of not recognized existing relations is rather small.

As a result the regular expression for the suffix matching for a given alphabet Σ and a suffix s_1 can be denoted as follows:

$$r_s = (\,(\,(\,(\Sigma+)-)+\Sigma^4\Sigma*)+(\Sigma+\ \Sigma+)\,)\,s_1\,(\varepsilon\,|\,en\,|\,e)$$

If $w_1 \in L(r_s)$ for a given tag s_1 then a hypernym relation between s_1 and w_1 exists. Note that this regular expression has already been adapted to several special cases that occured in the given text-corpus. Furthermore, possible inflective suffixes have been removed from s_1 in prior to match as much inflective forms of the word w_1 as possible. Since this is an exclusively rule-based approach, semantic relations cannot be recognized for morphological special cases. If such words should also be recognized a reliable lemmatizer like the learning lemmatizer described above is needed.

In contrast to this suffix matching, the identification of specification relations is much more complex. This mainly results from two facts:

1. inflectional suffixes
2. erroneous splitting of compounds

In german verbs, nouns and adjectives can be used to create compounds or specify other words. Often inflectional suffixes are removed in those cases. As an example *lesen* (read) and *Lesestrategie* (reading strategy) can be considered. Here, the suffix *n* is removed before composing the two words *lesen* and *Strategie* (strategy). Obviously, most of those semantic relations should be recognized by the tagnet builder.

Additionally, specification relations may be recognized wrongly because of equivocal compounds that are mainly determined by the context. One example is *Texterkennung* that can be decomposed to *Text-erkennung* (text recognition) or *Texter-kennung* (writer identification). In this case only the specification relation between *Text* and

---
[5] Or generic term.

Erkennung is correct, but also the relation between *Texter* and *Kennung* will be recognized. Unfortunately, this problem can solely be solved by manually defined blacklists. Nevertheless, a filter can be defined that filters wrongly detected relations, i.e. between *Text* and *textualisieren* (textualize). This filter checks if for a candidate match the remaining suffix is a known tag or word from a given lexicons. Here, *ualisieren* is not contained in the given lexicon and the relation will be discarded correctly.

Finally, the regular expression can be denoted as follows, where again inflective suffixes are removed from s_1 and the expression is adapted to some special cases:

$$r_p = (\Sigma^4 \Sigma * -) * s_1 (ung \mid en \mid e \mid n \mid \varepsilon)(s \mid - \mid \varepsilon) \Sigma^3 \Sigma *$$

If $w_1 \in L(r_p)$ for a given tag s_1, than a candidate specification relation between s_1 and w_1 exists that has to be filtered using the described filter afterwards.

Lexicon-based Approach. The rule-base approach is solely capable to recognizing hypernym and specification relations. Nevertheless, semantic relations of other types should be identified as well by the tagnet builder, i.e. *schreiben* (write) and *lesen* (read). For this reason a lexicon-based approach is presented, where *Wikipedia*[6] is used as the test lexicon. It is assumed that the given lexicon entries have been normalized by the methods of stop word elimination and stemming described above.

The idea of the lexicon-based approach is to extract lexicon entries for each tag of the given set and perform a frequency analysis for all other tags on these entries. Again, suffixes and prefixes have to be considered during this analysis, but the general approach will be described first.

The main aspect of the lexicon-based approach is to determine the strength of a semantic relation between tags. This significance is estimated based on relative frequencies of tags in the given lexicon entries. The relative frequency γ'_{s_1,s_2} of a tag s_2 in the lexicon entry l_{s_1} for a given tag s_1 is defined as,

$$\gamma'_{s_1,s_2} = \frac{n'_{s_2}}{N} \tag{1}$$

where n'_{s_2} denotes the absolute frequency of the current tag s_2 in the lexicon entry. The relative frequency is then derived by dividing n'_{s_2} by the total number of words N in l_{s_1}. In this simple approach n'_{s_2} is calculated as the frequency of all direct occurrences of s_2 in l_{s_1}.

A further improvement can be achieved by splitting the lexicon entries in headlines and text blocks and giving occurrences in the headlines a higher significance than the ones in the text blocks. This is done by a weight factor $\delta_1 \in [0,1]$. The resulting enhanced relative frequency γ_{s_1,s_2} is denoted as,

$$\gamma_{s_1,s_2} = \delta_1 * \frac{n_{t,s_2}}{N_t} + \frac{n_{h,s_2}}{N_h} \tag{2}$$

where n_{t,s_2} is the absolute frequency of s_2 in the text blocks of l_{s_1}. Analogously, n_{h,s_2} is the absolute frequency of s_2 in the headlines, N_t denotes the number of words in the text blocks, and N_h the number of words in the headlines.

---

[6] http://de.wikipedia.org/

Much more information can be gained by considering occurrences of s_2 in l_{s_1} as prefixe or suffix as well. But occurrences as prefix generally not as relevant as direct or suffix occurrences, since prefixes normally just specify other words in the german language. For this reason the enhanced approach is extended by a weight function which rates the different occurrences in the text blocks by additional parameters δ_2 and δ_3. This distinction is only applied to text blocks in the tagnet builder.

Thus, the enhanced relative frequency within the text blocks n_{t,s_2} is calculated by,

$$n_{t,s_2} = n_{t,s_2}^{direct} + \delta_2 * n_{t,s_2}^{prefix} + \delta_3 * n_{t,s_2}^{suffix} \tag{3}$$

where δ_2 and δ_3 are weight parameters for the absolute frequencies as prefix and suffix, respectively. This allows a much better estimation of semantic relations between tags than the simple approach, since language specific characteristics are taken into account.

Statistical Estimation. In contrast to the approaches described above it is also possible to estimate semantic relations between tags by frequency analysis on texts of a given corpus. Unfortunately, a large text corpus is needed for such statistical approaches in general. Hence, in Section 4.3 it was evaluated how the approach described below works on a corpus of only 200 texts.

Our approach is composed of two estimation steps.

1. estimation of the absolute tag frequencies in the texts
2. estimation of possible semantic relations based on these absolute frequencies

For step (1) basically the approaches described above can be used, so that this step will be skipped here. In the following it is assumed that for the given set of tags S and all texts t_i ($i \in \mathbb{N}$)

$$n_{t_i}(s_j) \forall s_j \in S$$

denotes the absolute tag frequency for tag s_j in the text t_i with $j \in \{1 \ldots |S|\}$. Based on these absolute values it is possible to calculate relative tag frequencies for all tags s_j in the text t_i by

$$n'_{t_i}(s_j) = \frac{n_{t_i}(s_j)}{N_{t_i}} \tag{4}$$

where $N_{t_i} = max(n_{t_i}(s_1), \ldots, n_{t_i}(s_{|S|}))$. These are used to statistically estimate the significance of possibly existing semantic relations between single tags.

Estimation of possible semantic relations. For all texts t_i and a pair of tags (s_1, s_2) with $s_1, s_2 \in S$ it is checked, if $n_t(s_1) > 0$ and $n_t(s_2) > 0$ holds . The set of all such texts is denoted as T. The strength of the statistical relations between these two tags δ_{s_1,s_2} is calculated recursively for all texts $t_i \in T$ ($i \in \{1 \ldots |T|\}$) by

$$\delta_{s_1,s_2}^{(k)} = \frac{\delta_{s_1,s_2}^{(k-1)} * k + n'_{t_k}(s_1) * n'_{t_k}(s_2)}{k+1} \tag{5}$$

where $\delta_{s_1,s_2}^{(0)} = 0$, and $0 \leq k \leq |T|$. The strength of a possible semantic relation between to tags s_1 and s_2 is than given by $\delta_{s_1,s_2} = \delta_{s_1,s_2}^{(|T|)}$.

This results in an histogram of all calculated pairwise statistical relations.

Result Combination. Finally, the tagnet builder combines the three resulting relation sets into one set containing the most relevant relations of all three approaches. Since the quality of this final set mainly depends on the quality of all three sets, it is once again necessary to introduce weight factors that allow to control the influence of a base set on the final set. In case of relation duplicates occuring in two different base sets the average of both weighted qualities is calculated and stored as the new relation quality in the final set.

3.2 Similarity Analysis

In contrast to other approaches which estimate text similarities [5] our approach is based on an uncertainty relation on tagsets S_1 and S_2 of two texts t_1 and t_2 This solves the problem of disjunct tagsets of similar texts and allows to estimate similarity values in such cases. To realize the main objective of our approach the simple estimation is discussed first.

$$\delta'_{t_1,t_2} = \frac{|S_1 \cap S_2|}{|S_1 \cup S_2|} \tag{6}$$

Obviously, no similarity can be calculated for disjunct tagsets.

As a solution the tagsets S_1 and S_2 can be extended by information gained from the generated semantic tagnet. These new sets S'_1 and S'_2 are generated recursively for a fixed number of recursion steps $n_{max} \in \mathbb{N}$. In each recursion step the neighbours of each tag in S_i ($i \in \{1,2\}$) are added to the sets S'_i. In our findings it proved that $n_{max} > 4$ is not useful. Thus, $n_{max} < 4$ is assumed in the following.

Although this idea already allows to calculate similarities between two texts t_1 and t_2 with $S'_1 \cap S'_2 = \emptyset$ it not yet satisfying, since no distinctions are made between the tags in the two sets S'_1 and S'_2. For this reason tag significances $p_{i,j}$ were introduced which depend on the current recursion step n and manually defined significances γ_r for all considered relation types r. The similarity of two texts t_1 and t_2 then can be estimated as

$$\delta_{t_1,t_2} = \frac{1}{2M} * \sum_{i=1}^{N} (p_{1,i} + p_{2,i}) \tag{7}$$

where $N = |S'_1 \cap S'_2|$ and $M = |S'_1 \cup S'_2|$. For a given threshold τ and a text t_1 all texts with $\delta t_1, t_i >= \tau$ ($i \in \{1, \cdots, |T|\}, t_i \neq t_1$) can be queried.

4 Evaluation

The described system has been implemented in Java and evaluated on four different tagsets.

ipTS. This set contains 3087 tags that mainly are part of the topic of text production and writing research which are part of the ipTS[7] research project. Note that this tagset has been preprocessed in terms of removing wrong tags and adjusting flectional suffixes. Thus, the results were somewhat better than the results of the three other tagsets.

---

[7] http://www.ipts.rwth-aachen.de/

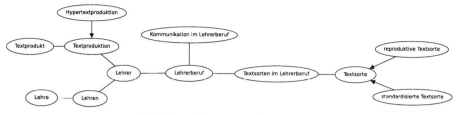

Fig. 1. Part of the extracted semantic net

II. This set contains 2748 tags from the topic of informatics[8].

IDS. This set contains the 1769 most basic german words[9].

AMSÖ. This set contains more than 10 000 occupational qualifications of different topics and thus is the most comprehensive tagset in this evaluation[10].

The evaluation was made by applying the implemented system to these four tagsets. Subsequently the generated semantic tagnets were checked for wrongly recognized semantic relations. Since manual preprocessing is unwanted, the ipTS tagset was the only preprocessed set in this evaluation.

Fig. 1 depicts a part of a semantic tagnet visualization [4] which was generated by the tagnet builder from the ipTS tagset. The semantic tagnet was embedded into the ipTS[11] project website to simplify the literature research task for domain experts. The arrows represent hyperonym relations between keywords, while the undirected edges express generic semantic relations.

4.1 Rule-Based Approach

In the first evaluation step exclusively the rule-based approach was considered. Table 1 contains the evaluation results of the rule-based approach on all four tagsets. Obviously, the rule-based approach works quite well for all given tagsets, since the accuracy is smaller than 1% for most of the sets.

Only for the AMSÖ tagset 1,5% semantic relations were recognized wrongly, due to the tags of different topics. Note that this accuracy does not consider existing semantic relations between tags that are not recognized. However, on average semantic relations between 33% of the given tags were recognized. This is shown in Table 2.

In the first evaluation step exclusively the rule-based approach is considered. Table 1 contains the evaluation results of the rule-based approach on all four tagsets. Obviously, the rule-based approach works quite well for all given tagsets, since the accuracy is smaller than 1% for most of the sets.

The results illustrate the benefit of such a pattern-based approach which estimates the possible semantic relations between the tags in different sets in short time. As an example the semantic relations for the ipTS tagset were estimated in less than 20 seconds on

---

[8] http://is.uni-sb.de/vibi/

[9] http://www.ids-mannheim.de/oea/

[10] http://www.ams.or.at/bis/

[11] http://www.ipts.rwth-aachen.de/

Table 1. Semantic relations extracted by rule-based approach

Tagset	Entries	Relations	Error Rate
ipTS	3807	1287	0,8 %
II	2748	1656	0,6 %
IDS	1769	502	0,4 %
AMSÖ	10 245	1760	1,5 %

Table 2. Number of linked tags

Tagset	Linked tags
ipTS	30,4 % (1160)
II	51,6 % (1419)
IDS	29,5 % (522)
AMSÖ	20,7 % (2122)

the testing machine, while the estimation on the AMSÖ set only took 88 seconds. For a synthetic generated tagset the rule-based approach shows an almost linear growth in runtime for large sets with more than 20 000 entries

4.2 Lexicon-Based Approach

In contrast to this fast rule-based approach the lexicon-based approach needs much more calculation time (more than four hours). For all smaller sets the calculation takes less than one hour. Although the calculation time is much longer than in the rule-based approach, the lexicon-based approach allows to recognize semantic relations between tags that cannot be recognized by the plain rule-based approach as described in Section 3.1.

Table 3 shows the numbers of extracted relations for the given tagsets. In comparison to the rule-based approach many more relations are extracted especially for the AMSÖ tagset.

Table 3. Semantic relations extracted by lexicon-based approach

Tagset	Entries	Relations	Error rate
ipTS	3807	2853	2,8 %
II	2748	3337	5,1 %
IDS	1769	1600	4,7 %
AMSÖ	10 245	5494	3,4 %

This mainly results from the type of the contained tags in this set since there is a wide range of words or concepts that describe similar processes or are somehow related to each other. Consequently, the total number of alike tags is higher for this lexicon-based approach compared to the results of the rule-based approach as shown in Table 4.

Table 4. Number of linked tags

Tagset	Linked tags
ipTS	31,5 % (1198)
II	50,0 % (1376)
IDS	44,7 % (791)
AMSÖ	32,1 % (3286)

4.3 Statistical Approach

The statistical approach has solely been evaluated for the ipTS set due to the lack of a suitable text corpus for the other three tagsets. As expected a very large number of candidate semantic relations were extracted, but mostly with very small semantic strengths. For a proper threshold only 3455 of more than 400 000 candidate relations remained. Unfortunately the number of wrongly recognized semantic relations still were quite high (12%). However it was possible to reduce the error rate to 4,7% by blacklisting problematic tags. It is assumed that the result of the described statistical approach can be improved by a larger text corpus.

5   Conclusions and Outlook

An approach has been described that allows to efficiently generate semantic tagnets for given unstructured lists of tags and an arbitrary text corpus. This semantic tagnet can be used to estimate text similarities for tagged texts in digital libraries to provide a more intuitive way of literature research adapted to the user's cognitive model. In addition to this the generated semantic tagnet could be used to define ontologies or allow users to enhance the network using a suitable interface similar to the idea of *user feedback* as proposed in [3].

In a future version the tagnet builder may be enhanced by some components that allow to extract synonym relations, too. One idea of a rule-based approach has been proposed in [1] for english words. This enhancement would allow to store relations between tags in different languages to create a multilingual semantic net that can be used for a digital library that stores texts in different languages.

Acknowledgements. This research was funded in part by the DFG Cluster of Excellence on Ultra-high Speed Information and Communication (UMIC), German Research Foundation grant DFG EXC 89, and by the German Research Foundation grant for the Project *Interdisciplinary Text Production and Writing (ipTS[12])*.

References

1. Ananthanarayanan, R., Chenthamarakshan, V., Deshpande, P.M., Krishnapuram, R.: Rule based synonyms for entity extraction from noisy text. In: AND 2008: Proceedings of the Second Workshop on Analytics for Noisy Unstructured Text Data, pp. 31–38. ACM Press, New York (2008)

---

[12] http://www.ipts.rwth-aachen.de/

2. Berners-Lee, T., Hendler, J., Lassila, O.: The semantic web - a new form of web content that is meaningful to computers will unleash a revolution of new possibilities (May 2001)
3. Doan, A., McCann, R.: Building data integration systems: A mass collaboration approach. In: IIWeb, pp. 183–188 (2003), http://www.informatik.unitrier.deley/db/conf/ijcai/ijcai2003iiweb.html#DoanM03
4. Götten, D.: Semantische Schlagwortnetze zur effizienten Literaturrecherche. Master's thesis, RWTH Aachen University (2009)
5. Lee, M.D., Pincombe, B., Welsh, M.: An empirical evaluation of models of text document similarity. In: Proceedings of the 27th Annual Conference of the Cognitive Science Society, pp. 1254–1259. Lawrence Erlbaum, Mahwah (2005)
6. Perera, P., Witte, R.: A self-learning context-aware lemmatizer for german. In: Proceedings of Human Language Technology Conference and Conference on Empirical Methods in Natural Language Processing, pp. 636–643. Association for Computational Linguistics, Vancouver (2005), http://www.semanticsoftware.info/durm-german-lemmatizer
7. Porter, M.F.: An algorithm for suffix stripping. Program 14(3), 130–137 (1980)

Personalized e-Government Services: Tourism Recommender System Framework

Malak Al-hassan, Haiyan Lu, and Jie Lu

Quantum Computation and Intelligent Systems Centre,
Faculty of Engineering and Information Technology, University of Technology,
P.O. Box 123 Broadway, NSW 2007, Sydney, Australia
{malak,helenlu,jielu}@it.uts.edu.au
http://www.feit.uts.edu.au/

Abstract. Most governments around the globe use the internet and information technologies to deliver information and services for citizens and businesses. One of the main directions in the current e-government (e-Gov) development strategy is to provide better online services to citizens such that the required information can be located by citizens with less time and effort. Tourism is one of the main focused areas of e-Gov development strategy because it is one of the major profitable industries. Significant efforts have been devoted by governments to improve tourism services. However, the current e-Gov tourism services are limited to simple online presentation; intelligent e-Gov tourism services are highly desirable. Personalization techniques, particularly recommendation systems, are the most promising techniques to deliver personalized e-Gov (Pe-Gov) tourism services. This study proposes ontology-based personalized e-Gov tourism recommender system framework, which would enable tourism information seekers to locate the most interesting destinations and find the most preferable attractions and activities with less time and effort. The main components of the proposed framework and some outstanding features are presented along with a detailed description of a scenario.

Keywords: e-Government, Personalization, Online tourism services, Ontology, Recommendation systems, Framework.

1 Introduction

In the last few years, e-government initiatives have been launched by most of the governments around the globe. E-government uses innovative systems made possible by nformation and communication technologies to achieve better e-services to citizens or business, as well as to enhance process and management of public sector [4]. Significant research efforts devoted in different countries reveal that the e-Gov forms one of the most important parts of government strategies. E-government services along with e-democracy and e-administration are the main focused fields of e-government initiatives [1] [2]. This study focuses on e-Gov services within the tourism domain.

It can be seen from the literature that intelligent e-Gov services with personalization is a clear direction in the development stages of e-Gov services. The current e-Gov development is by large at the stage of the implementation of transaction services. An

J. Filipe and J. Cordeiro (Eds.): WEBIST 2010, LNBIP 75, pp. 173–187, 2011.

exception to this is the development in Singapore and Canada [3] [4] [5], which have offered their citizens simple personalized services through their official portal websites. Intelligent personalized e-Gov service systems are highly desirable.

Since tourism is one of the major profitable industries, many governments around the world have devoted significant effort to promote tourism industry as non-profit services. In the domain of tourism, governments provide information about tourism services including attractions, activities and events that can be visited at different destinations. E-Gov tourism services have the potential for providing better governmental tourism services to citizens and overseas tourists, improving the quality of the provided services and the access to information (24 hours a day, 7 days a week). Nearly all the leading countries that adopt e-Gov initiatives offer online tourism services [5]. The current e-Gov tourism service is mainly about presenting tourism information online, not providing personalized services. Every user who uses the system will be presented with the same set of information and s/he has to find the interesting attractions and suitable activities and this usually takes quite long time.

In order to make e-Gov tourism services more attractive to users, it has been realized that the e-Gov tourism services must be delivered in a user-centric manner, in which e-Gov could improve the delivery of its services to users on a personalized basis to ensure that the heterogeneous users' needs and interests are met without excessive data input from users [7]. Therefore, developing personalized techniques such as recommendation system are promising direction for developing intelligent personalized e-Gov tourism services.

Based on our previous work [6], this study proposes a specific framework for developing personalized e-Gov tourism service systems from user-centric approach. This framework employs advanced recommendation system (RS) techniques and ontology with semantic reasoning. It dynamically updates users' profiles based on a probability technique. Additionally, the proposed framework does not merely use the opinion/rating of tourism services by users to generate recommendations; it enables the semantic representation of the tourism services in the user interface component and this empowers users to find the most favorable attractions and the most suitable activities at a specific destination with least efforts.

The rest of this work is organized as follows: Section 2 reviews some of existing work related to personalization in e-Gov and online tourism service systems. Section 3 presents the proposed framework in details. Section 4 illustrates how the framework works using detailed description of a scenario example. Finally, the conclusion and the future work are given in section 5.

2   Related Work

2.1   Personalization in e-Gov Services

In the context of web, personalized online service is considered as a process of getting web users' information online and using these information to tailor services (e.g. content, webpages, service or product recommendations, etc) to users' needs and preferences [8]. It demonstrated the potential of meeting the user's needs more effectively and efficiently, making online interactions with user faster and easier and increasing online user satisfaction. On the other hand, personalization of e-Gov services can be seen as the adaptation of a particular online service to a single user based on user-related information of that particular user [3]. There are some efforts have been devoted to personalization in e-Gov services as briefed below. Watson and Mundy (2001) suggested that governments have to implement customization that has the potential to improve interaction between governments and citizens. Adopting customization enables governments to make a one-to-one relationship with their citizens and make interaction with users easier. European Commission (2007) proposed a model for the development of e-Gov services. According to this model, personalization is considered the last phase in the development phases of e-Gov services [4].

A few leading countries in e-Gov service developments, such as Singapore and Canada, have offered their citizens simple personalization services through their official portal websites. For example, the e-Gov websites in Singapore and Canada allow their citizens to create their own customized page according to their own individual needs and interests [10]. The customized page can be adjusted to each citizen's preferences and needs in terms of structure and presentation of the website manually or semi-automatically. However, these personalized services are static customization and very limited and far from achieving citizen-centric e-Gov services. More advanced and intelligent e-Gov systems are highly desirable. We recently proposed a new conceptual framework of personalized e-Gov services from citizen-centric approach [6]. This framework can be used in a specific government domain to offer users Pe-Gov services based on their interests/preferences, characteristics and personal needs with least input from users. This study proposes a new framework of Pe-Gov services for tourism domain based on the framework of Pe-Gov services proposed in [6].

2.2   Online Tourism Services

Providing travel-related information and services through web-based technology has revolutionized travel and tourism industry. Nowadays, numerous travel-related websites government and non-government agencies offer different services to users.

The current commercial tourism service systems (i.e. websites) offer tourism services to users through using either search tools or content browsing. Several popular online travel websites have emerged, such as Expedia, Travelocity and ebookers. The offered services through tourism and travel websites could include destinations to visit, airlines and hotels reservation, tour operators, travel planning and many more [15].

Even though the existing travel-related websites can help users find interesting tourism information and services, it seems these websites are relatively poor in aiding users to plan their trips, which includes the determination of where, when and how to go for a trip and what to do at a certain destination from massive amounts of information available. Users may spend significant amount of time and efforts in finding what they really want. This could lead users to waste much more time or effort until they find their request [12]. Additionally, tourists demand tourism products tailored to their actual preferences. On the other hand, they often have complex and multi-interests and their travel desires change rapidly and usually require the tourism products with shorter life cycles [13]. All these make recommendation of suitable tourism products to tourists become one of the most challenging tasks. Therefore, an intelligence system with recommender system is highly desirable in assisting users in choosing their preferred tourism services [11] [12] [13].

Recently, commercial travel and tourism applications have started adopting intelligent techniques, such as RS techniques to assist users in choosing their preferred tourism services [12] [13]. TripleHop's TripMatcher (used by www.skieurope.com) and VacationCoach's expert advice platform (used by travelocity.com) have been developed to offer recommendations to users by suggesting a list of destinations to visit [14]. Dietorecs RS, on the other hand, has developed to provide users with personalized recommendations of complex tourist products including destinations, accommodations and activities [15].

Most of the existed online travel and tourism recommendation systems just used single recommendation technique and therefore lack of intelligent and effective support to users. For Example, TripleHop's TripMatcher and "VacationCoach's Me-Print" use simply one technique (i.e. content-based technique). Similarly, the project Dietorecs uses the case-based reasoning technique [15]. Recently, an expert software agent, named "Traveller" was proposed in [16], this agent offers tourism services by helping users (tourists) in planning their travels. A hybrid technique was used to build this agent, which includes two RS techniques, the collaborative filtering and the content-based recommendation techniques. Both of these techniques use the demographic information about customers to suggest holiday and tour packages to users [16]. Furthermore, in [11] an intelligent personalized RS for tourist attractions in a specific city is developed. This system is built using applying ontology theory, bayesian network, analytic hierarchy process and spatial web service technology [11].

In addition to these systems, some other systems adopted using ontology with different intelligent techniques to enhance delivery of tourism and travel services and information. Such these systems use ontology as iJADE FreeWalker, ontology-based tourist guiding system [17]. It integrates the mobile agent technology (to increase the system's efficiently and scalability), GPS technology (to support location awareness which makes the system has high flexibility and mobility) and ontology (to retrieve the relevant tourist information and further filter the irrelevant information). The authors in [18] proposed intelligent recommendation system based on Jeju travel ontology. It can recommend tourist related travel information using properties and relationship in travel ontology, and help them to expect confusion of roads attractions.

3   Framework of Pe-Gov Tourism Services

The current direction of e-Gov development strategy aims to better serve citizens and deliver the right information to the right citizen with less time and effort. Thus, we propose a conceptual framework for personalized tourism e-Gov services based on our proposed framework in [6], as depicted in Fig. 1. This framework is comprised of four main components: Customized User Interface (CUI), Knowledge Base Repository (KBR), Intelligent Recommendation Engine (IRE) and User Data Collector (UDC). Using this framework, users can request the required services in a simple interaction through a navigation of the hierarchical representation of all available services. Once the required service is selected by a given user, the system will retrieve recommendations to the given user based on the selected service.

The following subsections will illustrate a detailed description of each component with focus on the conceptual functionality of each component rather than technical details.

3.1   Customized User Interface

A user needs to register with the system before he/she can login to the system to get recommendations on the tourism e-Gov services. The user interface of the system consists of two units: Registration or login unit, and the customized user interface (CUI) unit. The CUI unit is the interactive interface between the system and the active user. It contains the tourism items presented in a tree-like catalogue and "MyInterstAlbum". The CUI is generated based on the user's information, including user's demographic information, personal interests and preferences within the tourism e-Gov domain. Each registered user has a "MyInterestAlbum" in his/her own customized page.

"MyInterestAlbum" is used to facilitate users interactive with the system efficiently and friendly. It contains all selected tourism items that the user planning to visit or already visited, rating to the tourism items that have already been visited and a feedback to the selected tourism items. Each time a user enters the system, he or she will be asked to give a feedback and rating for any outstanding tourism item in the "MyInterestAlbum", which has been visited or conducted by the user but not rated yet. The new feedbacks and ratings that are provided by the user will be collected and stored in the user profile DB by the UDC component. The feedbacks would be used for further improvements of the system whereas the ratings would be used by IRE component for further processing.

3.2   User Data Collector Model

The user data collector component is responsible for collecting user related information to the e-Gov tourism services, including the demographic information, personal interests and preferences and the user's tourism e-Gov service usage history. This component performs two tasks. Firstly, it collects user related data from the system through user registration, rating experienced items and feedbacks. Implicit and explicit acquisitions can be used for collecting user related data for web personalization [19] [20]. The implicit acquisition will be used to collect data about citizens' preferences or interests implicitly. It can be collected via tracing a user's navigation sequences when he/she navigates the hierarchical tourism e-Gov service catalogue. While the explicit acquisition will be used during registration and interaction between the user and the system to capture users personal information, including users' demographic data, their interests and preferences through pre-defined forms, as well as to collect users' ratings of tourism items and feedbacks in "MyInterestAlbum". Secondly, UDC updates the user profile DB regularly by recording the captured data from the CUI component into the KBR component.

3.3   Knowledge Base Repository

Knowledge Base Repository (KBR) component contains relevant knowledge of the tourism e-Gov domain. It contains tourism e-Gov ontology, users profile database (DB) and dynamic data controller model, more details of the stored knowledge in KBR is described below.

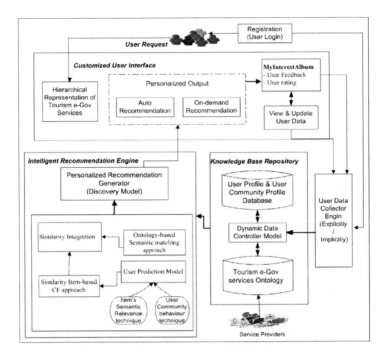

Fig. 1. Framework of Pe-Gov Tourism Service System

Tourism e-Gov Ontology. Tourism ontology O describes the fundamental concepts/ classes (C) that compose the tourism e-Gov domain; relationships among these concepts and properties a concept can have or share. For this study, the Australian online information of tourism services is the source of knowledge to create concepts and associated relationships in the e-Gov tourism ontology. The related Australian government tourism websites have been visited to collect the required knowledge to create the ontology. Actually, collecting related knowledge of e-Gov tourism ontology relies on the purpose that the ontology is used for. The developed ontology, in this study, mainly aims to recommend users with tourism services that may involve attractions to visit and activities to do or events to attend at a specific destination.

Typically, developing domain ontology starts with the design of the ontology schema and finishes with populating of ontology data [21]. The ontology schema contains the definition of the various classes, properties and relationships that represent a specific domain world. Whereas in the populating ontology, the instances for each class in the ontology schema are to be created.

Figure 2 depicts a diagram of part of e-Gov tourism ontology schema. This ontology shows the hierarchal representation of knowledge for e-Gov tourism ontology. It is composed of concepts and properties that identified the interconnections between concepts. It is implemented using Protégé OWL 3.4.4 editor tool. Protégé OWL is a free, open-source platform that provides a growing user community with a suite of tools to construct domain models and knowledge-based applications with ontologies. OWL (Ontology Web Language) is a mark-up language for publishing and sharing data using

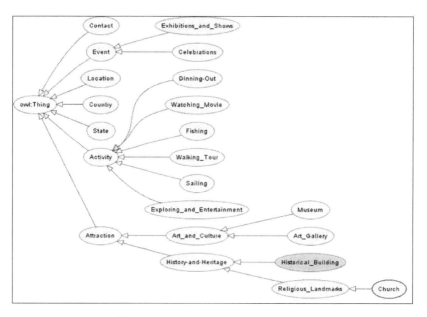

Fig. 2. E-Gov Tourism Ontology Diagram

ontologies on the internet, it also enables users to build ontologies for the Semantic Web (http://protege.stanford.edu/).

Concepts in OWL ontology are described by a set of features and attributes, called properties. OWL has two main types of properties, object properties and data type properties. Object properties link a concept to a concept in ontology. For example, the object property "hasActivity" is defined in e-Gov tourism ontology, it connects attraction concept with activity concept. In the other hand, data type properties are used to describe concepts themselves, the value of this type of properties is a literal (i.e. data values). Attraction name and attraction facilities are examples of data type properties.

Ontology schema can show the semantic relevance among e-Gov tourism concepts at different level of hierarchy (as taxonomies), therefore, it can guide the hierarchical representation of available e-Gov tourism items in the CUI component and can be used as a means of locating and accessing services. It can also be used by the IRE component to facilitate the semantic rule reasoning to find the matching between users' requests and the available tourism items, which could enhance the retrieval of the appropriate content for each user.

User Profile Database. The user profile DB contains all the data that related to users, including users' demographic data and the online tourism items that used by users. The user-related data is stored in the DB as two parts: static and dynamic parts. The static data part is about users' demographic data, including name, age, residential status, favourite type of attractions and general interests related to tourism. This data can be collected explicitly through the tourist account registration when a user visits the system for a first time. In contrast, dynamic data includes the preferences and interests of users that can be extracted from the interaction between users and tourism websites.

In our framework, dynamic data could be the visited attractions and the activities/events that are preferred by users and their opinions (ratings) about the tourism items. This data can be attained implicitly or explicitly. Implicit data can be attained via exploring a user's web-navigation patterns (i.e. click streams) to infer the user's preferences and interests while the explicit data can be attained from "MyInterestAlbum", in which the tourism items that a user prefers and user's rating for these items are available. The user profile is a crucial part for generating recommendations. It forms one of the main sources of information that will be used to accomplish the recommendation process in the IRE component.

Dynamic Data Controller (DDC) Model. This model controls the data that comes into KBR by UDC and interchange data between user profile DB and e-Gov tourism ontology. DDC performs two main tasks. Firstly, DDC adds data that collected by UDC either to user-profile DB or to e-Gov tourism ontology. Secondly, DDC manages data that will be shared between ontology and user profile DB. For instance, user profile DB has a table called user tourism attractions. This table has users and all attractions that stored in the ontology. Accordingly, DDC will manage the access to the ontology, obtaining the attractions and store them in the intended table.

3.4   Intelligent Recommendation Engine

This component is responsible for generating valuable recommendations to users to help them find the most suitable destination with the top N most interesting attractions and activities that meet their preferences.

IRE component uses a new hybrid methodology in order to overcome the limitations of the existing RS techniques and to enhance the recommendations. The typical RS techniques, such as the Content Based (CB) and the Collaborative Filtering (CF), suffer from a set of limitations which may hinder them from being directly applied to e-Gov tourism domain. For instance, the CB technique would recommend highly similar tourism items that belong to the same group or category of the given item. Hence, they ignore the items that belong to other groups but might have interest to the target user. Such technique would not be suitable for e-Gov tourism services as most of users would like to see new tourism items (heterogeneous needs) that may belong to other categories. Furthermore, the rating method used by the CF techniques seems not directly applicable to the e-Gov tourism domain, because it may be hard to use a single rating value to infer a person's taste as people can give the same rating to an item for vastly different reasons [22]. The CF techniques also suffers from data sparsity problem which occurs when the attained ratings are few compared to the number of the available items, and the cold-start problem which occurs when a new user or a new item enters to the system.

A combination of recommendation techniques, termed as hybrid approach, has been used in the literature to overcome the drawbacks of the existing RS techniques and to improve the recommendation performance for a particular application. Different hybrid approaches have been developed in the literature which combine CF with CB and some other techniques in different ways [23]. The new hybrid approach, in our framework, combines the probability technique, item-based CF, and ontology-based semantic similarity to tackle the major problems in tourism services, such as the variety in the e-Gov tourism items, the multi-interest of users, and data saving and retrieving of e-Gov tourism data.

Semantic similarity measure "tries to find clues to deduce that two different data items correspond to the same information" [24]. Data items can be ontology classes, properties, instances or any other information representation entities. Semantic similarity is used differently according to the application domain where it is adopted [25]. It is widely used for semantic information retrieval and information integration, as well as for semantic web service discovery and matching [27]. In the context of ontology field, mostly the semantic similarity is employed to find ontology mapping [28] [29] and to asses the matching between concepts in ontology [34]. A few semantic similarity measures are proposed to compute similarity among instances within ontology. In this study, an ontology-based semantic similarity approach is to be used to find similarity among instances within ontology. The conceptual position in the hierarchical structure of the concepts in ontology and the common information that shared between concepts will be considered to find semantic similarity.

In this study the new hybrid approach consists of the follwing four main steps:

Step 1. Develop a user prediction model to find implicitly the rating of items. A User prediction model will be used to find implicitly the rating of unrated attractions (i.e. items). This model consists of the following two stages:

- Cluster users into a number of groups, called communities. Each community includes a group of users who share common interests. User communities can help IRE to solve the new user problem. The system will recommend proper tourism items to a new user based on his or her user community profile. Clustering techniques such as K-mean and hierarchical clustering [30] [31] are to be used to accomplish this task.
- A probability technique is applied to predict implicitly the rating values of unrated-attractions for users in each community. Three factors are to be used to compute the prediction values of unrated tourism items for a given user, including: (i) the given user's behaviour (ii) users' behaviours in a same community for the given user, (iii) semantic relationship between the given user's profile (interest tourism attractions) and the e-Gov tourism ontology.

The behaviour of a given user, particularly the rated items, can be used in the probability technique to compute the prediction of the preference (i.e. rating value) of a particular unrated item for the given user.

Furthermore, the users' behaviors of a given community are used to predict unrated items for a particular user in that community. Users' behaviors composed of the preferences (rating values) of items that are unrated by a particular user.

Finally, semantic relevance among concepts in domain ontology is to be used to predict a rating value of unrated items for different users. The unrated items belong to those concepts (general preferences of users' profiles) that are not experienced by users yet.

In tourism domain, it is difficult to attain explicit rating for all the tourism items, such as destinations, attraction and activities. This technique can find implicit ratings for un-rated items of a particular user. Hence, the sparsity problem associated with the item-based CF can be alleviated.

Step 2. Find similarity among e-Gov tourism items using CF item-based.

In this step, the obtained implicit ratings of items from step 1 and the explicit ratings of items that rated by users will be used to compute similarities among all instances of tourism e-Gov ontology concepts. One of the popular CF algorithms, the item-based CF algorithm will be utilized for the similarity calculations [32]. Item-based CF algorithm has shown better results than user-based CF one in terms of enhancing the performance and the quality of recommendation [33].

Step 3. Develop ontology-based semantic matching approach to compute similarity among the available instances of concepts (tourism items) in the tourism e-Gov ontology.

Ontology can be used to support find the matching (or similarity) of objects that are conceptually close but not identical. A few methods have been proposed to assess similarities among instances within ontology. Ehrig and his colleagues (2005) presented a comprehensive framework for measuring semantic similarity within and between ontologies. The framework identified three main levels on which the similarity between two entities (concepts or instances) can be measured: data layer, ontology layer, and context layer, which deal with the data representation, ontology meaning, and the usage of these entities, respectively [34]. To find similarities among instances of tourism e-Gov ontology, semantic matching will take into account the structural comparison between two instances in terms of their classes, and the comparison between their attributes and their relations. The involved attributes and relations in comparison of different instances will be determined based on the context of the tourism e-Gov ontology.

Step 4. Generate recommendations by integrating the similarities.

The obtained similarities from steps 2 and 3 will be combined linearly together for each tourism item and the combined similarity will be stored in KBR component as a matrix. This combined similarity will be used to build a discovery model. This model can be used to predict the most relevant items among the available tourism items that a particular user might be interested in. Examples of prediction models that have been used in recommendation systems include *weightedsum* and *regression* models [33]. Additionally, discovery model is responsible for generating offline recommendations that will be added to "MyInterestAlbum" for each user, an example of this type of recommendations is explained in the scenario example of section 4.

A combination of the ontology-based semantic matching and the similarity from the item-based CF would improve the quality of recommendations and the prediction of new tourism items from different categories that could be preferred by a specific user. The main reason for this combination is that the generated recommendations do not merely depend on the opinions of users to the preferred items, but also on the semantic matching of these items based on their underneath hierarchal structure and their attributes and relationships that could be affected by the application context. Additionally, considering semantic matching in this integration could eliminate the sparsity problem if the item-based CF similarity algorithm.

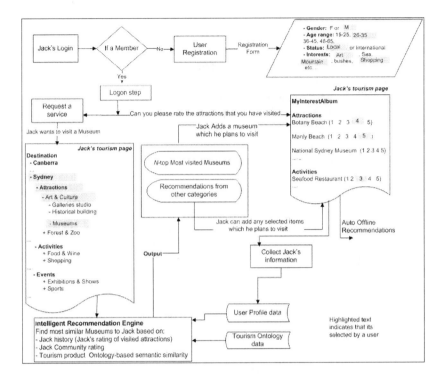

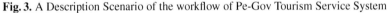

Fig. 3. A Description Scenario of the workflow of Pe-Gov Tourism Service System

4   Workflow of Pe-Gov Tourism Services System

Under the proposed framework, the e-Gov tourism service systems allow users to get specific information about "where to go" or "what to do/see" at a specific destination. Figure 3 illustrates a workflow example of the system.

A Scenario Example. Jack is a local user in Australia; he wants to visit a Museum (as an attraction) at a specific destination (e.g. Sydney). How the proposed framework can help?

Jack is a registered member in the system, so he needs to login to the system using his own user name and password, as depicted in Fig. 3. After login to the system, he can see his own page. A catalogue of all available tourism items (destinations and its attractions and associated activities) presented in a style of directory tree as categories. He can browse the catalogue tree staring from select "Sydney" under the destination category. Then, browse tourism attractions related to Sydney until he finds the Museum attraction node, and select this node. This selection will automatically trigger the IRE component to generate the most interested museums attraction items to Jack.

The discovery model in IRE component is responsible of generating recommendations. To accomplish that, both of Jack's profile (including his rating record) and the combined similarity matrix (that obtained from the item-based CF similarity and the semantic-based similarity, as described in section 3.4, particularly, the one related to the museum category) will be uploaded to the memory. Then the discovery model will use, for example, a weighted sum model to predict the most interested museum items in Sydney. To perform the prediction, the weighted sum model works as follow: Firstly, it finds for each unrated museum item by Jack the most similar museums using the combined similarity matrix; Secondly, it computes for each given unrated item the intersection set between the most similar museums items to the given one and the already rated museums items by Jack; Finally, the gained intersection set will be used to compute the prediction value for this unrated item. The prediction value for each unrated museum item of Jack can be computed as a ratio of summation of the ratings given by Jack on the museums items similar to the given unrated one. Each rating will be weighted by the corresponding similarity between the given unrated item and those ones in the intersection set. Based on the computed prediction values for unrated museums items of Jack, the system will generate the top-N most interested items (higher predicted items) as an ordered list of recommendation in the GUI component.

After that Jack can browse the retrieved museum items list until he chooses a specific museum attraction item. The system, subsequently, will present for each selected museum item the most similar museums. That can be carried out according to the combined similarity matrix that explained in step 4, in section 3.4. Beside that, the system also will ask him whether he is planning to visit this selected Museum. If the answer is positive, the system will ask Jack to add this attraction to his own "MyInterestAlbum". Generating a few most relevant museums items (top-N) for Jack will save his significant amount of time and effort, and will bring his pleasant searching experience.

The recommendation that generated upon Jack's request is called on-demand recommendation. The on-demand recommendation could be homogenous or heterogeneous recommendation. Homogenous recommendation includes recommendations to tourism items that belong to the same category of the requested item, as in the above case, where an ordered list of Museums is generated upon Jack's request. While heterogeneous recommendation involves recommendations to tourism items from different categories that are similar to the requested item. Heterogeneous recommendation can be generated based on the given user's similar neighbours (with similar community or behaviour) and semantic similarity among tourism items. The recommendation will be presented to users in UI component as an ordered list of recommendation by category. Figure 3 depicts that Jack can receive also recommendations from other categories that are similar to the Museum, e.g., items from Galleries Studio category.

Furthermore, the intelligent Pe-Gov tourism service system can present new recommendations to users each time they login to the system. For instance, the system will recognize Jack each time he visits the system and regularly will update the content of his page automatically, a new suggestions for tourism items can be presented. These auto recommendations can be generated dynamically offline to users depending on users profile, their community and the changes that might be occurred to any tourism items. For example, new events of a specific attraction can be recommended for users who are interested in or visited that attraction. Interestingly, the system would be more effective for regular users who visit the system frequently. Irregular users would also be offered recommendations but limited to their available information.

5   Conclusions and Future Work

Intelligent personalization has become a clear direction in the development of delivering e-Gov services by different government agencies. This study proposes a new conceptual framework for delivering Pe-Gov tourism services using RS techniques and semantic ontology. The proposed framework can help users find, efficiently and friendly, the most interesting tourism attractions with the most appropriate activities/events according to their interests, needs and the behaviour/experience of other similar users. The main components of the framework were described. The potential of the proposed framework of offering better tourism services to users has been illustrated by a scenario example. The future work regarding this study would be to develop a working system/prototype based on the proposed framework to verify the proposed approach and methods.

References

1. Millard, J., Havlícek, J., Tichá, I., Hron, J.: Strategies for the future eGovernment. In: The International Conference Agrarian Perspectives XII, CAB Abstracts (2004)
2. Ndou, V.: E-government for Developing Countries: Opportunities and Challenges. The Electronic Journal on Information Systems in Developing Countries 18, 1–24 (2004)
3. Van der Geest, T. M., Van Dijk, J., Pieterson, W. J.: Alter ego: state of the art on user profiling. An overview of the most relevant organisational and behavioural aspects regarding user profiling (2005)
4. Wauters, P., Nijskens, M., Tiebout, J.: The user challenge, benchmarking the supply of online public services. European Commission (2007)
5. Accenture: eGovernment Leadership: high performance, maximum value. In: Fifth Annual Accenture eGovernment study (2004)
6. Al-Hassan, M., Lu, H., Lu, J.: A Framework for Delivering Personalized e-Government Services from a Citizen-Centric Approach. In: The 11th International Conference on Information Integration and Web-based Applications and Services, Kuala Lumpur, Malaysia (2009)
7. Undheim, T. A., Blakemore, M.: A Handbook for Citizen-centric eGovernment. European Commission, Information Society (2007)
8. Lu, J., Ruan, D., Zhang, G. (eds.): E-Service Intelligence: Methodologies, Technologies and Applications, vol. 37. Springer, Heidelberg (2007)
9. Watson, R.T., Mundy, B.: A Strategic Perspective of Electronic Democracy. Communications of the ACM 44, 27–30 (2001)
10. Accenture: Leadership in Customer Service: Delivering on the Promise. Executive Summary (2007), http://nstore.accenture.com/acn_com/PDF
11. Huang, Y., Bian, L.: A Bayesian network and analytic hierarchy process based personalized recommendations for tourist attractions over the Internet. Expert Systems with Applications: An International Journal 36, 933–943 (2009)
12. Fesenmaier, D.R.: Introduction: Recommendation Systems in Tourism. In: Fesenmaier, D.R., Wober, K.W., Werthner, H. (eds.) Destination Recommendation Systems: Behavioral Foundations and Applications, CABI Publishing (2006)
13. Berka, T., Plößnig, M.: Designing Recommender Systems for Tourism. In: Proceedings of ENTER, Cairo (2004)

14. Staab, S., Werthner, H., Ricci, F., Zipf, A., Gretzel, U., Fesenmaier, D.R., Paris, C., Knoblock, C.: Intelligent Systems for Tourism. IEEE Intelligent Systems 17, 53–64 (2002)
15. Ricci, F., Fesenmaier, D.R., Mirzadeh, N., Rumetshofer, H., Schaumlechner, E., Venturini, A., Wober, K.W., Zins, A.H.: DieToRecs: A case-based travel advisory system. In: Fesenmaier, D.R., Wober, K.W., Werthner, H. (eds.) Destination Recommendation Systems: Behavioral Foundations and Applications, CABI Publishing (2006)
16. Schiaffino, S., Amandi, A.: Building an expert travel agent as a software agent. Expert Systems with Applications 36, 1291–1299 (2009)
17. Lam, T.H.W., Lee, R.S.T.: iJADE FreeWalker: an ontology-based tourist guiding system. In: Lee, R.S.T., Loia, V. (eds.) Computational Intelligence for Agent-based Systems, vol. 72, pp. 103–125. Springer, Heidelberg (2007)
18. Choi, C., Cho, M., Choi, J., Hwang, M., Park, J., Kim, P.: Travel Ontology for Intelligent Recommendation System. In: Third Asia International Conference on Modelling and Simulation, pp. 637–642. IEEE, Los Alamitos (2009)
19. Eirinaki, M., Vazirgiannis, M.: Web mining for web personalization. ACM Transactions on Internet Technology 3, 1–27 (2003)
20. Markellou, P., Mousourouli, I., Sirmakessis, S., Tsakalidis, A.: Personalized E-commerce Recommendations. In: Proceedings of the 2005 IEEE International Conference on e-Business Engineering, pp. 245–252. IEEE Computer Society, Los Alamitos (2005)
21. Noy, N., McGuinness, D.: Ontology development 101: A guide to creating your first ontology. Stanford Knowledge Systems Laboratory Technical Report KSL-01-05 and Stanford Medical Informatics Technical Report (2001)
22. Schafer, J.B., Frankowski, D., Herlocker, J., Sen, S.: Collaborative Filtering Recommender Systems. In: Brusilovsky, P., Kobsa, A., Nejdl, W. (eds.) Adaptive Web 2007. LNCS, vol. 4321, pp. 291–324. Springer, Heidelberg (2007)
23. Adomavicius, G., Tuzhilin, A.: Toward the Next Generation of Recommender Systems: A Survey of the State-of-the-Art and Possible Extensions. IEEE Transactions on Knowledge and Data Engineering 17, 734–749 (2005)
24. Tous, R., Delgado, J.: A Vector Space Model for Semantic Similarity Calculation and OWL Ontology Alignment. In: Bressan, S., Küng, J., Wagner, R. (eds.) DEXA 2006. LNCS, vol. 4080, pp. 307–316. Springer, Heidelberg (2006)
25. Albertoni, R., De Martino, M.: Asymmetric and Context-Dependent Semantic Similarity among Ontology Instances. In: Spaccapietra, S. (ed.) Journal on Data Semantics X. LNCS, vol. 4900, pp. 1–30. Springer, Heidelberg (2008)
26. Schwering, A.: Hybrid Model for Semantic Similarity Measurement. In: Chung, S. (ed.) OTM 2005. LNCS, vol. 3761, pp. 1449–1465. Springer, Heidelberg (2005)
27. Wang, X., Hauswirth, M., Vitvar, T., Zaremba, M.: Semantic web services selection improved by application ontology with multiple concept relations. In: Proceedings of the 2008 ACM Symposium on Applied Computing, pp. 1538–1542. ACM, New York (2008)
28. Alasoud, A., Haarslev, V., Shiri, N.: An empirical comparison of ontology matching techniques. Journal of Information Science 35, 379–397 (2009)
29. Giunchiglia, F., Yatskevich, M., Shvaiko, P.: Semantic matching: Algorithms and implementation. In: Spaccapietra, S., Atzeni, P., Fages, F., Hacid, M.-S., Kifer, M., Mylopoulos, J., Pernici, B., Shvaiko, P., Trujillo, J., Zaihrayeu, I. (eds.) Journal on Data Semantics IX. LNCS, vol. 4601, pp. 1–38. Springer, Heidelberg (2007)
30. Kim, B.M., Li, Q., Park, C.S., Kim, S.G., Kim, J.Y.: A new approach for combining content-based and collaborative filters. Journal of Intelligent Information Systems 27, 79–91 (2006)

31. Trujillo, M., Millan, M., Ortiz, E.: A Recommender System Based on Multi-features. In: Gervasi, O., Gavrilova, M.L. (eds.) ICCSA 2007, Part II. LNCS, vol. 4706, pp. 370–382. Springer, Heidelberg (2007)
32. Adomavicius, G., Tuzhilin, A.: Toward the Next Generation of Recommender Systems: A Survey of the State-of-the-Art and Possible Extensions. IEEE Transactions on Knowledge and Data Engineering 17, 734–749 (2005)
33. Sarwar, B., Karypis, G., Konstan, J., Reidl, J.: Item-based collaborative filtering recommendation algorithms. In: 10th International Conference on World Wide Web, pp. 285–295. ACM, New York (2001)
34. Ehrig, M., Haase, P., Stojanovic, N., Hefke, M.: Similarity for ontologies - a comprehensive framework. In: 13th European Conference on Information Systems (2005)

Building a Community Information System for Supporting Disabled Bus Riders and Local Businesses

Akira Kawaguchi[1], Andrew Nagel[1], Chiu Chan[1], and Neville A. Parker[2]

[1] Department of Computer Science, The City College of New York, New York 10031, U.S.A.
[2] CUNY Institute for Transportation Systems, New York, NY 10031, U.S.A.
akira@cs.ccny.cuny.edu, anagel@gc.cuny.edu
chiuchn@gmail.com, parker@utrc2.org

Abstract. This paper discusses the implementation of one type of information system for the New York City bus transit service, as a case study to provide value-added transportation services for people with impaired mobility. Information technology is a key tool for finding flexible transportation services, especially for disabled people. Useful information supplies psychological reassurance to these vulnerable people to make them feel more safe and secure. Residents in metropolitan areas increasingly rely on the convenience of public transportation, and they are becoming used to exchanging information relevant to their regional community in on-line settings. The improvement to transit accessibility needs the exact same type of the cooperation between transportation companies, local business, and residents. The widespread use of mobile wheelchairs has a socioeconomic impact. The significance of this research for the longer-term goals lies in its implications for adaptation of this kind of intelligent model into future welfare or assistive activities.

Keywords: Disability support, Assistive technology, Transportation service, Information system, Accessibility improvement, Bus transit service.

1 Introduction

The number of people who are mobility impaired by age or disability is increasing at a dramatic rate. It is no longer an insignificant or silent part of the society. The 2007 report published by the Department of Economic and Social Affairs, Population Division, of the United Nations estimates the percentage of aged people, those over 60 years old, will grow from the current 11% of the world population to 15% in 2025 and to 22% by the year 2050. When considering developed nations only, the report projects this group will constitute nearly a third of the population [29]. Moreover, the 2007 fact sheet published by the International Day of Disabled Persons reports that around 10% of the world's population today is living with some disability. This means that by the year 2025, it is likely that around 1/5 of the world's total population will need economic and social benefits as well as some kind of artificial perambulatory assistance in their daily lives.

The United States will certainly face challenges as people live longer and in better health. Projections by the U.S. Census Bureau estimate the number of persons ages 65

J. Filipe and J. Cordeiro (Eds.): WEBIST 2010, LNBIP 75, pp. 188–201, 2011.

and over will grow to almost 40 million by the year 2010 [10]. Today, more than 4 million people in the United States are over the age of 85 and about 60,000 topped age 100. By 2020, the Census Bureau further estimates that 7 million to 8 million people will be over age 85 and 214,000 will be over age 100. As life expectancy rises and modern medical technology improves, there is a growing interest in building more advanced support structures for society. In particular, a desire to enhance quality of life with advanced wheelchair designs is a steadily growing phenomenon [8]. A strong demand for a less restrictive environment is also on the rise, such as barrier-free accesses, safer and more convenient route selections, more transportation alternatives, and so on.

The motivation for this research is to address a fundamental question in the handling of these challenging problems. Today's transportation infrastructure is missing a piece in the context of wheelchair mobility. Imagine a great influx of people in wheelchairs having to navigate through crowded aisles and streets. Sidewalks can be harmful or even impassible by those wheelchairs. Correcting these issues universally may require reconsideration of many issues, including roadway traffic, parking space, and accident handling, from both engineering and even legal perspectives. In our view, however, today's information systems can be easily, quickly, and cheaply expanded to enable a dramatic improvement in transportation accessibility by incorporating a community supported web service so users can objectively evaluate whether or not the public transportation services available address their individual needs. The focus of our study here is to call for wide-scale community support towards the deployment of an information system that enables a more future oriented view of this class of services.

Specifically, this paper presents one case study of such a deployment as a means of promoting grassroots activities supporting handicapped people. We discuss the development of one type of on-line database system based on the New York City bus transit service. This is to demonstrate key roles of the information technology and community service, not only in guiding travel route, but also in understanding physical situations in the movement and actual environment of the wheelchair. The government offices and private sectors in the New York metropolitan area are continuously making systemic reforms to ensure that services and supports for people with disabilities are available in the most integrated setting [5]. The priorities are set for assisting with access to health care, benefits, employment, housing, and education [17]. For instance, NYHousingSearch.gov provides a free on-line public service to allow disabled people to locate available housing that meets their individual and family needs at a rent they can afford [7,23,1]. This effort has been supported by grants to promote effective and enduring improvements in community-based long-term care and support systems for seniors and people with disabilities. The question that needs to be answered is the efficacy of the same approach in transportation issues.

Information resources for the disabled need improvement. The government usually requires transportation service providers, such as taxis, limousines and shuttle services, to purchase accessible vehicles or otherwise ensure that they have the capacity to serve people with disabilities [21]. Yet limited awareness of these services or lack of confidence in their reliability may discourage use. So limited availability of accessible transportation services remains a major barrier faced by individuals with disabilities throughout the state, often leading to unemployment, the inability to access medical care, and isolation from friends, family, and full community participation [5]. For the proposed system, it is vital that the people who accept cooperation and evolution openly share with the living community by providing useful information. As more information becomes available and uploaded to the database, the scale and magnitude of support will grow. We will describe ideas on how to involve activities at the local level in this regard. Non-handicapped people need to make a greater effort to educate themselves about disability issues or risk being unprepared for the coming increase in the mobility impaired population. This community can play an important role in providing a respectful environment for the discussion and exploration of these issues. Paired with the primary motive of making it easier for the disabled to access reliable transportation, this system stands to benefit all segments of society.

Paper Organization. The rest of this paper is organized as follows: Section 2 explains our motivation for this research and scope of our work. Section 3 discusses our case study of the implementation of the NYC bus transit service for disabled riders, and Section 4 summarizes our approach for extending this system to incorporate community-support and business incentives. Section 5 discusses related work, and Section 6 concludes our work presented in this paper.

2   Why Do We Need Community Support?

The demand for wheelchairs and other mobility devices in the U.S. is projected to increase 5.0% per year through 2010 to over $3 billion [27]. According to the 2005 Survey of Income and Program Participation report [3], 27.4 million people of age 15 and older (11.9% of U.S. population) had difficulty with ambulatory activities of the lower body, thus required mobility assistance. About 22.6 million people (9.8%) had difficulty walking a quarter of a mile, and 12.7 million were not able to perform this activity. About 21.8 million people (9.4%) had difficulty climbing a flight of stairs, and 7.4 million of them were not able to do it at all. Roughly 3.3 million people (1.4 %) used a wheelchair or similar device, and 10.2 million (4.4 %) used a cane, crutches, or walker to assist with mobility.

Advances in electronic controls, latter-generation secondary batteries, light-weight construction materials and other areas are also stimulating the growth in both the wheelchair- and non-wheelchair-related segments of the personal mobility device industry. Technology for the computerized aid, care, and support of people in mobile wheelchairs is evolving rapidly. Although it is in a branch that spans autonomous process control, intelligent engineering systems, and information management, there exists no widely accepted practice or reference model that leads to the integration of these technical elements into mass transportation systems [19]. This research aims to explore several key issues in implementing assistive infrastructures and surrounding information systems that host macro control for the smooth and safe navigation of mobile wheelchairs in the public transportation environment [11,12,13,14].

Today's physical infrastructure shows a significant transformation that makes it more accessible to wheelchair users. This transformation has been initiated by legislative reform and longstanding social momentum to include people with disabilities as more active participants in the society [9]. Despite these efforts, many aspects remain uncertain as to how to best address these issues in both private organizations and the local community. For the last several years, the metropolitan community in the U.S. has become increasingly aware of the need to get more involved in supporting vulnerable people. Noticeable changes are visible in many cities and parts of the world, such as the installation of elevators, transit lifts, and wheelchair ramps in public areas. These improvements are increasingly legally required for access to public areas such as city streets, public buildings, and restrooms, thus allowing people in wheelchairs and with other mobility impairments to use public sidewalks and public transit more easily and safely. The efforts presented in this paper share the same spirit of this ongoing change and intelligent design movement.

The importance of community support will inevitably grow, which will in turn stimulate the development and deployment of an information product and a practice including a wide range of activities spanning design, instrumentation, computer integration, process and device control, and manufacturing [11,12]. The successful implementation mandates not only interdisciplinary effort across the industrial and academic research spectrum, but also participation and cooperation of wheelchair users, transportation companies, disability advocates, and voluntary experts in public. Overall, it is a continuous process in which users in all parties participate actively from the preliminary study stage to the post evaluation stage, so that the knowledge and experience obtained from them can be applied to the next level of innovation [15].

Information technology is a key for providing flexible transportation services and increased choice for the users (see Figure 1). In addition, useful information supplies psychological reassurance to vulnerable people to make them feel more safe and secure. A federal civil rights procurement law in the U.S. requires electronic and information technology to be accessible to people with disabilities. Flexible services are brought by a wide variety of innovative information services now in use increasingly in many countries. For instance, the presence of ubiquitous network technology that consists of IC tags, wireless tags, RFID tags, and other communication equipment such as portable information terminals makes it possible for elderly people and handicapped people to move freely and independently. The use of more economical PHS communication network generally available in Asian countries can afford precise tracking of wheelchairs moving in and around dense urban areas like hospitals, libraries, and museums. GIS technology that allows conversion of geographical information into electronic form also facilitates the wide-scale integration of navigation assistance and tracking capability into various telecare information systems.

Up-to-date information services such as availability, route guidance, cost, efficiency, and safety must be always available to improve the overall level of public transportation including railroad, bus, airline, and shipping. Traffic-aware routing based on portable GIS device is a new area in vehicle industries. At the same time, traditional internet-based software that can handle scheduling, dispatching and reservation, such as Ecolane DRT, PASS and NaviTrans, plays an important role to implement demand-responsive transportation schemes or flexible door-to-door paratransit service for wheelchair users.

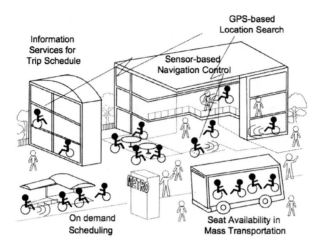

Fig. 1. A vision of mobile wheelchair support in the coming age [11]

3   Bus Transit Services for Wheelchair Riders

The New York City Transit in the Metropolitan Transportation Authority network operates the world's largest fleet of buses (4,373 public buses), serving over 666 million people per year for New York City to sustain its economy and support projected growth [18]. These buses are equipped with wheelchair lifts in either the front or back entrance of the vehicle, and have a "kneeling" feature that lowers the front entrance to within inches of the ground for easy access by any customer with mobility impairments or difficulty using the front steps. The Tokyo Metropolitan Bus Systems in Japan, by comparison, maintain the second largest scale of fleet, but do not run this level of service with lift-equipped vehicles (see Table 1 for the projected improvement from Japanese government standpoint).

The bus system covers routes not served by the city subway system and outlying areas, and stops every 2 blocks on a nearly 24 hour schedule. The bus system is becoming the primary mode of transportation for wheelchair users living in the city. The city convention and visitors bureaus are offering guides that list wheelchair-accessible facilities. However, these brochures are rarely detailed enough to rely on and cannot contribute to a full-scale mechatronics support for barrier-free accesses.

An on-line database system to facilitate the exchange of useful information among disabled bus riders and accessibility supporters in New York City is being built by our efforts. The system has a Web interface to find out the bus routing information on a trip from one point to another point in Manhattan. The capability beyond the "Trip Planner" web system [28] implemented by the Metropolitan Transit Authority is to respond using a map with appropriate paths (sequences of bus rides) to be taken to reach the destination along with the roadside information of toilet options, coffee shops and restaurants accommodating wheelchairs, quick repair services for motor trouble and battery replacement, and purchases of wheelchair equipments, etc., on the selected route. The system works with the Google Maps API to create the visual interface, thereby giving a quick way to narrow down the user choice of accessible sporting and cultural events.

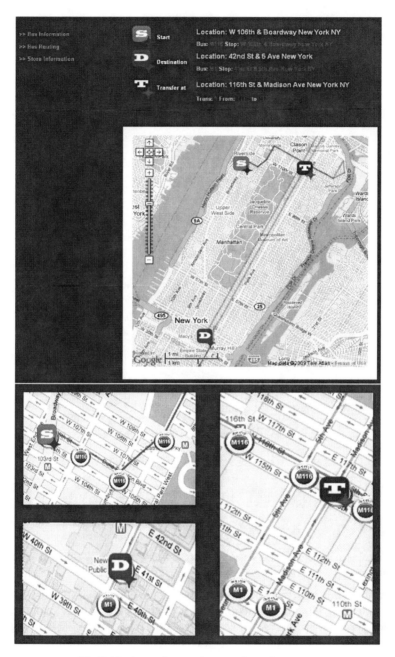

Fig. 2. Manhattan bus routing search service system

3.1 Implementing a Prototype Search Service Application

A prototype system runs on a typical LAMP (Linux-Apache-MySQL-PHP) solution stack. The current release covers the major stopping points and transfer points of the

Table 1. Preset goals for the barrier-free implementations of Japanese public transportation [15]

Transportation Media	2003	2010
Railway cars	24%	30%
Non-step buses	9%	20–25%
Passenger ships	4%	50%
Airplanes	32%	40%

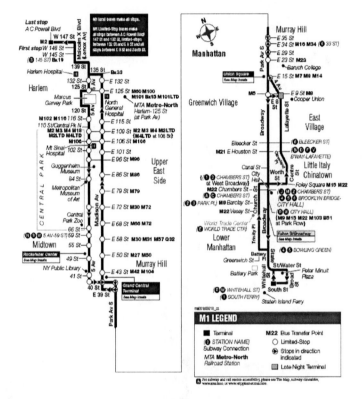

Fig. 3. Manhattan Bus Line Map (duplicated from MTA NYC Transit official site)

MTA bus lines whose services are bound in areas of Manhattan (thus the search capability is limited within Manhattan). The information of such traffic points is hand-populated based on the bus schedules published by the MTA NYC (see Figure 3). Figure 2 shows a view of the system's interface—our periodic build can be accessed at http://134.74.112.41/BusSystem.

A traffic point is a geographical location consisting of latitude and longitude. The point collection is structured as a directed graph in the database. As shown in Table 2, `buspoints` table holds latitude and longitude (double type) of the bus running points. Its ID field (smallint type) has a unique point number for a particular line (char(8) type). Some of the points are of the type (set type) of terminal, transfer, or both. The tag

Table 2. MySQL tables representing bus services

buspoints table							busroute table				
Line	ID	Ptype	Lat	Lng	Tag		LineFr	IDFr	LineTo	IDTo	Bound
M1	1	terminal,transfer	40.822	-73.938	W 147St & ...		M1	1	M2	null	null
M1	2	terminal	40.821	-73.936	W 146St & ...		M1	2	M1	3	south
M1	...	...	...	...	...		M1	...	...	...	...
M1	33	transfer	40.731	-73.992	E 8th & ...		M1	34	M1	null	south
M1	34	terminal,transfer	40.730	-73.991	E 8th & ...		M1	34	M8	null	null

field (varchar(60) type) is for the text address. Another `busroutes` table holds route information or a topological sequence such that one point leads to another point in each bus line. There can be multiple directions per line such as South and North, and East and West bounds, which can be expressed by a bound indicator (enum type). A transfer point is expressed using the name of the line for transfer.

A query transaction computes acyclic paths between start location and destination. The reachability set of a directed graph is a maximal set representing reachability from given starting points to other points in that graph. Notice that there can be combinations of starting points and ending points, each of which establishes a valid route in close proximity. This is because the user's inquiry is usually based on the addresses of the starting and ending points of a trip, not precise initial bus points. Therefore, the bus points approximating the trip must be found within a range of distance (choice of 1/2, 1/4, and 1/8 mile) from the specified addresses. Geocoder public service (http://geocoder.us) is used to find the latitude and longitude of the specified address. Accordingly, the bus points in the `buspoints` table within the requested distance can be found.

Our implementation of on-the-fly travel path computation is based on a *semi-naive evaluation* [2] employed in the recursive, bottom-up evaluation of logic programs (the algorithm can be realized by an iterative execution of SQLs). The problem to address is preventing explosive growth of the graph traversals. There can be multiple ways to complete the trip by hopping around different bus lines. Thus, various heuristic reductions of search space are devised, in particular, the elimination of moves ineffectual to reach the destination (e.g., south-bound transfer from north-bound trip).

The additional task is finding points of interest (eateries, drugstores, etc.) along each possible course of travel. See Figure 4 for the scheme of the computation. The points of interest are found within the excess (1/2, 1/4, and 1/8) of a mile outside the bounding box made out of each leg of bus movement. In Figure 4, two bus stops (line A and B) are found, and the areas enclosed by their neighboring bus stops can also be identified. All the found points are shown together with the bus route on the generated map. The entire procedure to process a user request is processed within a read-uncommitted transaction so as to minimize database overhead. The response time observed so far using a single quad-core based mid-range data server is less than a few seconds, and is quite satisfactory. Figure 5 shows a travel path computed with all the interesting points captured from thousands of hypothetical data populated in the database for test.

4   Community Support for Vulnerable People

For those aging or disabled people whose condition makes them unable to walk, advanced mobile wheelchairs provide many benefits, such as maintaining mobility,

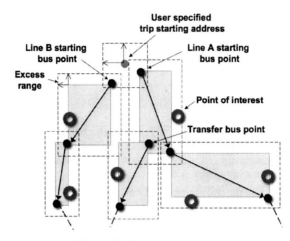

Fig. 4. Finding points of interest

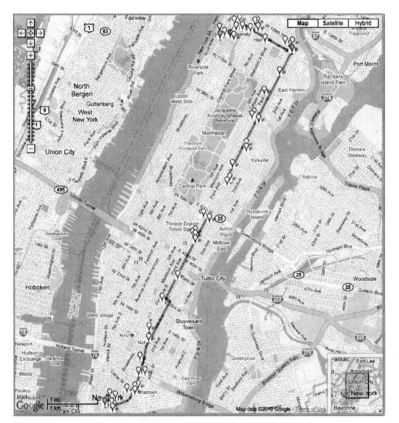

Fig. 5. On-the-fly point capturing

continuing or broadening community and social activities, conserving strength and energy, and enhancing their general quality of life. Particularly residents in metropolitan areas are increasingly utilizing the convenience of public transportation. Separately, they are becoming used to exchanging information relevant to their community in on-line settings. The accessibility improvement needs the exact same type of the coopera-tion between transportation companies, regional and local industry, and local residents: transportation companies, private business, public places, and any points of interest for residents such as restaurants, shopping centers, movie theaters, etc., must supply the accessibility information to a public database system, which in turn provides immedi-ate retrieval for transportation and route selection, thereby giving great aids to realize macro-level control in wheelchair movement.

The Web interface of our system has this additional capability to accumulate com-munity information in the form of a point of interest and/or assistive ability. The peo-ple in the metropolitan areas can register and augment categorized information in the database. Specifically, a person (e.g., restaurant owner) can contribute to the system by registering his/her item (e.g., restaurant) into a set of suitable categories (e.g., bathroom services, eatery, etc.). The registration is done by filling out the owner's identity (full name, contact address, phone, and email) as well as detailing the item to register and the category to classify. The information on the item includes name, address, phone, web URL, geo-position, capacity, up to 3 pictures, textual comment, and a link to the owner. The category can be chosen from those already in the database or newly created at the registration. There may be multiple categories to which the item needs to belong. For instance, restaurant can be in the categories of bathroom services and eatery.

The registration of the item is not immediately reflected in the database, but becomes pending at first. An administrator of the system needs to inspect if the requested reg-istration is valid or not. Email is generated to the owner right after the administrator's decision. Category classification is not static. The administrator can reorganize it by merging and splitting branches. The registered items whose locations are close to the suggested course of travel are selectively shown in the Google Map interface (see Fig-ure 6).

5   Related Work and Future Work Plan

The public acknowledgment of people with disabilities and progress toward enhanced care has developed in the last few decades along three parallel tracks of activities [16]—these are legislation spurred by the disability rights movement, barrier-free design to universal design movement, and advances in rehabilitation and assistive technology.

Universal design is a design paradigm that aims to reduce the physical and attitudi-nal barriers between people with and without disabilities. This concept emerged from barrier-free design principles and assistive technology. The former provides a level of accessibility for people with disabilities, and the latter enhances the physical, sensory, and cognitive abilities of those people [22]. The concept of universal design gives a broad-spectrum of solutions that help everyone, not just people with disabilities, and it is now becoming one of the most important design elements that range in scale from product design to architecture and urban design, and from simple systems to complex information technologies [19]. The forthcoming transportation facilities are therefore likely to be in compliance with universal design principles.

Assistive technology [6] applies to devices that provide direct physical or mental aid

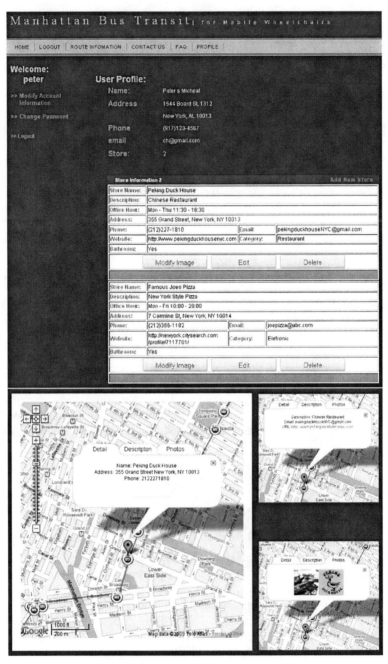

Fig. 6. Finding interest points with bus line

to people with disabilities. The element closely tied to mobility and mechatronics support is a smart wheelchair [26] or an augmentative mobility aid that accepts a variety of different controls tailored to the riders needs, and complements the riders efforts by expanding and interpreting their limited control commands to provide safe transit [4]. A smart wheelchair has a collection of sensors to work with several cognitive techniques similar to those developed in mobile robotics, but it is not necessarily acting autonomously because the aim is to complement and extend the user's abilities, not replace them.

The majority of the smart wheelchairs that have been developed to date have been tightly integrated with the underlying power wheelchair, thereby requiring significant modifications to function properly [25]. The forthcoming research on the extension of smart wheelchairs, enhanced with path-planning, behavioral learning, and cognitive capabilities will have a significant impact on the outcome of the mechatronics implementation. As an example, there is a study to systematically utilize and extend mechatronics-based assistive services, an emerging field devoted to engineering personal devices that enhance the physical, sensory, and cognitive performance of people with disabilities and help them function more independently in environments oblivious to their needs [11,12,13,14,20]. This field lies as a support technology centered on mechanics, electronics, and computing. The mechatronics support in our vision is meant to emphasize a synergistic integration of the latest techniques in cross-disciplinary fields.

Paratransit is another mode of passenger transportation increasingly offered for handicapped commuters and travelers, which in general does not follow fixed routes or schedules, but typically uses vans or mini-buses for the higher flexibility of picking up or discharging passengers on request. Many vehicles are specially equipped with wheelchair lifts or ramps to facilitate access, thus allowing people with disabilities to have greater employment opportunities by providing transportation to and from their workplaces [24]. A sub-sector of private business is on the rise to meet the growing interest in the paratransit strategy, but the cost for serving low-density areas and dispersed trip patterns do not balance with today's declining financial conditions, which may instead create an urgent need for public transit operators to maximize all available transportation resources.

General Transit Feed Specification (GTFS) originally developed by Google defines a common format for pubic transportation schedule and associated geographic information. The instance recently prepared by MTA NY would be used to populate the database for more extensive travel path computations. We are investigating the presence of entities sharable with GTFS format. This incorporation contributes to higher data portability in provision of data exchange in future development and wider-scale area support for bus and subway accessibility enhancement. In addition, the City of New York DataMine project (http://www.nyc.gov) has started providing the access to public data generated by the various New York City agencies and other City organizations. The data is machine-readable and is classified based on the category such as community service, public safety, events, etc. Availability of this kind of information facilitates the activation of our system significantly with a substantial amount of information already gathered. We plan to incorporate these two data sets into our system for the immediate offering of real services.

6 Conclusions

The subject of this paper is a high-level discussion to address the problem of physical mobility in our society in the coming age. The issue has powerful effects on the living conditions of those with physical disadvantage who seek to maintain mobility, wish to continue or broaden community and social activities, conserve strength and energy, and enhance their general quality of life. The community-based approach outlined here is a basic framework to cope with the influx of vulnerable people in mobile wheelchairs. The concept of information sharing gives the opportunity to understand and promote any resulting benefits in broader developmental contexts.

An abundance of information is available and sharable through the computer medium. The ultimate goal of our on-going work is to make electric powered wheelchairs predict and avoid risky situations and navigate safely through the congested areas and confined spaces, by exchanging the terrain and location information in real-time. To accomplish a more future oriented view of this class of services, today's information systems must be expanded to incorporate the community support and to objectively evaluate whether or not the public transportation services fit the user's needs. The community-based approach we proposed encompasses these views and shares a common spirit with the universal design ideal.

Acknowledgements. This work is partially supported by the research funds provided by the New York State Department of Transportation and New York City Environmental Protection. Our thanks go to City College's graduate students in database classes who have contributed to and worked on the data population and conceptual study of this work.

References

1. Appel, H.: Home-hunt help for disabled. November 14's article in am New York News (November 2007)
2. Bancilhon, F., Ramakrishnan, R.: An amateur's introduction to recursive query processing strategies. In: Proceedings of ACM SIGMOD, pp. 16–52 (1986)
3. Brault, M.W.: Americans with disabilities: 2005. Household Economic Studies, U.S.Census Bureau, pp. 1999–2013 (December 2008)
4. Learning through smart wheelchairs. Final report, Univ. of Edinburgh (1994)
5. The voice of people with disabilities in new york city. Center for Independence of the Disabled, New York, 2007 Annual Report (2007)
6. Cook, M.: Assistive technologies: principles and practice, 2nd edn. Mosby (2002)
7. Affiliate update. Cerebral Palsy Associations of New York State 13(11) (July 2007)
8. Medical supplies and devices. Industry report, First Research Inc. (2007)
9. Facts on disability in the world of work. International Labour Organization (2007)
10. Jones, M., Sanford, J.: People with mobility impairments in the united states today and in 2010. Assistive Technology 8(1), 43–53 (1996)
11. Kawaguchi, A., Noda, Y., Sato, Y., Kondo, Y., Terashima, K.: Mechatronics support for mobile wheelchairs. In: Proceedings of the 10th International Conference on Applications of Advanced Technologies in Transportation, AATT 2008 (2008)

12. Kawaguchi, A., Noda, Y., Sato, Y., Kondo, Y., Terashima, K.: A mechatronics vision for smart wheelchairs. In: Proceedings of the 4th International Conference on Assistive Technologies, pp. 145–150 (2008)
13. Kawaguchi, A., Chan, C.: Community support for disabled bus riders: What can we do? In: International Conference of Computing in Engineering, Science and Information (ICC 2009), pp. 100–103 (April 2009)
14. Kawaguchi, A., Wei, J., Noda, Y., Miyoshi, T., Terashima, K.: A study on the safety and drivability enhancement of mobile wheelchairs. In: International Conference of Computing in Engineering, Science and Information (ICC 2009), pp. 384–386 (April 2009)
15. Ministry of Land, I., Transport: General principles of universal design policy (2006)
16. Longmore, P.K., Umansky, L.: The New Disability History: American Perspectives. University Press, New York (2001)
17. Addressing the service and support needs of new yorkers with disabilities: Report of the most integrated setting coordinating council. Most Integrated Setting Coordinating Council, New York State (November 2006)
18. Mta guide to accessible transit, brochure of new york city metropolitan transportation authority. NYC MTA (2006)
19. Removing barriers: Planning meetings that are accessible to all participants. North Carolina Office on Disability and Health (2005)
20. Noda, Y., Kawaguchi, A., Terashima, K.: In: A Mechatronics Vision for Smart Wheelchairs. I-Tech Press (2009) (in press)
21. 2009 disability priority agenda. New York Association on Independent Living (April 2009)
22. Orpwood, R.: Design methodology for aids for the disabled. Journal of Medical Engineering & Technology 14(1), 2–10 (1990)
23. Paterson, D.A.: Find your way home (2009), www.nysaccessiblehousing.org
24. Simon, R.M.: Integrating americans with disabilities act paratransit services and health and human services transportation. Transportation Research Board 4(10) (1997)
25. Simpson, R., LoPresti, E., Hayashi, S., Nourbakhsh, I., Miller, D.: The smart wheelchair component system. J. Rehabilitation Res. & Dev. 41(3B), 429–442 (2004)
26. Simpson, R.C.: Smart wheelchairs: A literature review. J. Rehabilitation Res. & Dev. 42(4), 423–438 (2005)
27. Medical equipment and supplies manufacturing industry in the u.s. and its foreign trade (1997-2009) (2007)
28. Mta trip planner system. New York City Metropolitan Transportation Authority (2009), http://tripplanner.mta.info/
29. World population ageing. United Nations (2007)

An Empirical Study on Machine Learning-Based Sentiment Classification Using Polarity Clues

Ulli Waltinger

Artificial Intelligence Group, Cognitive Interaction Technology Excellence Center (CITEC)
Bielefeld University, Bielefeld, Germany
ulli_marc.waltinger@uni-bielefeld.de

Abstract. In recent years a variety of approaches in classifying the sentiment polarity of texts have been proposed. While in the majority of approaches the determination of subjectivity or polarity-related term features is at the center, the number of publicly available dictionaries is rather limited. In this paper, we investigate the performance of combining lexical resources with machine learning-based classifier for the task of sentiment classification. We systematically analyze four different English and three different German polarity dictionaries as a resources for a sentiment-based feature selection. The evaluation results show that smaller but more controlled dictionaries used for feature selection perform within a SVM-based classification setup equally good compared to the biggest available resources.

Keywords: Machine learning, Support vector machine, Sentiment analysis, Polarity classification, Polarity resources.

1 Introduction

With the enormous growth of digital content arising in the web, document classification and categorization receives more and more interest in the information retrieval community. This relates to content-based models [14] as well as to structure-orientated approaches [19]. While a majority of approaches focusses on a thematical or topical differentiation of textual data, the task of sentiment analysis [23] refers to the (non-topical) opinion mining. This area focuses on the detection and extraction of opinions, feelings and emotions in text with respect to a certain subject. A subtask of this area, which has been extensively studied, is the sentiment categorization on the basis of certain polarities. That is, being able to distinguish between positive, neutral or negative expressions or statements of extracted textual [24,7,12,40,2] or spoken elements [3]. Moreover, finer-grained methods additionally explore the level or intensity of polarity inducing a rating inference (e.g. a rating scale between one and five stars) model. In the majority of approaches on sentiment polarity identification, the determination of subjectivity or polarity-related term features is in the center in order to draw conclusions about the actual polarity-related orientation of the entire text. Since positive as well as negative expressions can occur within the same document, this task is challenging. Considering the following example of an Amazon product review:

J. Filipe and J. Cordeiro (Eds.): WEBIST 2010, LNBIP 75, pp. 202–214, 2011.

Product-Review[1]: <u>Wonderful</u> when it works... I owned this TV for a month. At first I thought it was <u>terrific</u>. <u>Beautiful</u> <u>clear</u> picture and <u>good</u> sound for such a <u>small</u> TV. Like others,however, I found that it did not always retain the programmed stations and then had to be reprogrammed every time you turned it off. I called the manufacturer and they <u>admitted</u> this is a <u>problem</u> with the TV.

Although most of the polarity-related text features contribute to a positive review (e.g. wonderful, terrific, beautiful...), this user-contribution is classified as a negative review. This example clearly shows that classical text categorization approaches (e.g. bag-of-words) need to be extended or seized to the domain of sentiment analysis. Though, we consider polarity identification as a binary classification task, the determination of semantically oriented linguistic features on different structural levels (words, sentences, documents,...) is at the core of attention. With respect to the task of term feature interpretation, most of the proposed unsupervised or (semi-)supervised sentiment-related approaches make use of annotated and constructed lists of subjectivity terms.

While there are various resources and data sets proposed in the research community, only a small number are freely available to the public – most of them for the English language – most recently also with respect to the German language [6,26]. In terms of coverage rate, the number of comprised subjectivity terms of these dictionaries varies significantly - ranging between $8,000$ and $140,000$ features. The questions that arise therefore are: How does the significant coverage variations of the English sentiment resources correlate to the task of polarity identification? Are there notable differences in the accuracy performance, if those resources are used within the same experimental setup? How does sentiment term selection combined with machine learning methods affect the performance? And finally, are we able to draw conclusions from the results of the experiments in building a German sentiment analysis resource?

In this paper, we investigate the effect of sentiment-based feature selection combined with machine learning algorithms in a comparative experiment, comprising the four most widely used subjectivity dictionaries. We empirically show that a sentiment-sensitive feature selection contributes to the task of polarity identification. Further, we propose based on the findings a subjectivity dictionary for the German language, that will be freely available to the public.

2 Related Work

In this section, we present related work on sentiment analysis. A focus is set on comparative studies and different algorithms applied to the task of polarity identification. Tan and Zhang (2008) presented an empirical study of sentiment categorization on the basis of different feature selection (e.g. document frequency, chi square, subjectivity terms) and different learning methods (e.g k-nearest neighbor, Naive Bayes, SVM) on a Chinese data set. The results indicated that the combination of sentimental feature selection and machine learning-based SVM performs best compared to other tested sentiment classifiers.

---

[1] http://www.amazon.com/

Chaovalit and Zhou (2005) published a comparative study on supervised and unsupervised classification methods in a polarity identification scenario of movie reviews. Their results confirmed also that machine learning on the basis of SVM are more accurate than any other unsupervised classification approaches. Hence, a significant amount of training and building associated models is needed.

Prabowo and Thelwall (2009) proposed a combined approach for sentiment analysis using rule-based, supervised and machine learning methods. An overview of current sentiment approaches is given, compared by their model, data source, evaluation methods and results. However, since most of the current attempts based their experiments on different setups, using mostly self-prepared corpora or subjectivity resources, a uniform comparison of the proposed algorithms is barely possible. The results of the combined approach show that no single classifier outperforms the other, and the hybrid classifier *can* result in a better effectiveness.

With respect to different methods applied to the sentiment polarity analysis, we can identify two different branches. On the one hand - rule-based approaches, as for instance counting positive and negative terms [33] on the basis of semantic lexicon, or combining it with so called discourse-based contextual valence shifters [15]. On the other hand - machine-learning approaches [32] on different document levels, such as the entire documents [24], phrases [40,29,1], sentences [21] or on the level of words [18], using extracted and enhanced linguistic features from internal (e.g. PoS- or text phrase information) and/or external resources (e.g. syntactic and semantic relationships extracted from lexical resources such as WordNet [10]) [20,5]. Most notably, sentence-based models have been quite intensively studied in the past, combining machine learning and unsupervised approaches using inter-sentence information [41,16], sentence-based linguistic feature enhancement [39] or most famous by following a sentence-based minimum cut strategy [21,22].

In general, sentence-based polarity identification contributes to a higher accuracy performance, but induces also a higher computational complexity. Nevertheless, depending on the used methods the reported increase of accuracy of document and sentence classifier range between $2 - 10\%$ [21,39], mostly compared to the baseline (e.g. Naive Bayes) implementations. However, in the majority of cases, only slightly better results could be achieved [16,39]. At the focus of almost all approaches, a set of subjectivity terms is needed, either to train a classifier or to extract polarity-related terms following a bootstrapping strategy [41].

3 Background

3.1 Modeling Opinion Orientation

Following Liu (2010)[17, pp. 5] we formally define an opinion oriented model as follow: A polarity-related document d contains a set of opinion objects $\{o_1, o_2, \ldots, o_q\}$ from a set of opinion holders $\{h_1, h_2, \ldots, h_p\}$. Each opinion object o_j is represented by a finite set of sentiment features, $F = \{f_1, f_2, \ldots, f_n\}$. Each feature $f_i \in F$ is represented in d by a set of term or phrases $W = \{w_{i1}, w_{i2}, \ldots, w_{im}\}$, which correspond to synonyms or associations of f_i and are indicated by a set of feature indicators $I_i = \{i_{i1}, i_{i2}, \ldots, i_{ip}\}$ of the feature. The direct opinion of o_j is expressed through the polarity of the opinion (e.g. positive, negative, neutral) defined as oo_j with respect to the comprised set of features f_j of o_j, the opinion holder h_i and the time or position within the text t_j, an opinion is expressed. The feature indicator i_j reflects thereby the strength of the opinion (e.g. rating scale). Following this definition, contrary opinions within a text document (e.g. phrase or sentence-based) correlate to a (dis-) similarity S of two opinion objects $S(o_j, o_k)$, while a concordance of a polarity is indicated by a high similarity value. At the center of the opinion-oriented model, a mapping from the input document to the corresponding sentiment features with associated indicators $(W \mapsto F)$ needs to be established. Meaning, an external resource is needed that embodies not only a set of term or phrase features, but also incorporates the polarity orientation at least as a boolean (positive, negative), preferably on a rating scale (positive, negative, neutral). We refer to these resources as *subjectivity dictionaries*. As we use machine learning classifiers, the similarity function $S(o_j, o_k)$ refers to the similarity between the supervised trained SVM-based opinion models (o_j) and the evaluation set of document opinions (o_k).

3.2 Subjectivity Dictionaries

In recent years a variety of approaches in classifying sentiment polarity in texts has been proposed. However, the number of comprised or constructed subjectivity resources are rather limited. In this section, we describe the most widely used subjectivity resources for the English language in more detail.

Adjective Conjunctions
As one of the first, Hatzivassiloglou et al. (1997) proposed a bootstrapping approach on the basis of adjective conjunctions. Thereby, a small set of manually annotated seed words (1,336 adjectives) were used in order to extract a number of 13,426 conjunctions, holding the same semantic orientation i.e. 'and' indicates an agreement of polarity (nice and comfortable) and 'but' indicates disagreement (nice but dirty). Subsequently, a clustering algorithm separated the sum of adjectives into two subsets of different sentiment orientation (positive or negative). This approach follows the notion that a pair of adjectives (e.g. conjunction in a sentence) will most likely have the same orientation (81% of the unmarked member will have the same semantic orientation as the marked member).

WordNet Distance
Maarten et al. (2004) presented an approach measuring the semantic orientation of adjectives on the basis of the linguistic resource *WordNet* [10]. A focus was set on graph-related measures on the syntactic category of adjectives. The geodesic distance is used as a measurement to extract not only synonyms but also antonyms. As a reference dataset, the manually constructed list of the General Inquirer [27] was used, comprising $1,638$ polarity-rated terms. Since the evaluation focused on the intersection of both resources (General Inquirer vs. *WordNet*), no additional corpus could be gained.

WordNet-Affect
A related approach in building a sentiment resource, Strapparava and Valitutti (2004) [28] studied the synset-relations of *WordNet* with respect to their semantic orientation. Following a bootstrapping-strategy, manually classified seed words were used for

constructing a list of 'reliable' relations (e.g. antonym, similarity, derived-from, also-see) out of the linguistic resource. The final dataset, *WordNet-Affect*, comprises $2,874$ synsets and $4,787$ words.

Subjectivity Clues
In 2005, Wiebe et al. (2005) presented the most fine-grained polarity resource. Within the Workshop on Multi-Perspective Question Answering (2002) the MPQA corpus was manually compiled. This corpus consists of 10,657 sentences comprising 535 documents. In total, 8,221 term features were not only rated by their polarity (positive, negative, both, neutral) but also by their reliability (e.g. strongly subjective, weakly subjective).

SentiWordNet
Esuli and Sebastiani (2006) introduced a method for the analysis of glosses associated to synsets of the *WordNet* data set. The proposed subjectivity resource *SentiWordNet* thereby assigns for each synset three numerical scores, describing the objective, negative, and positive polarity of interlinked terms. The used method is based on the quantitative analysis of glosses and a vectorial term representation for a semi-supervised synset classification. Overall, *SentiWordNet* comprises 144,308 terms with polarity scores assigned.

SentiSpin
Takamura et al. (2005) proposed an algorithm for extracting the semantic orientation of words using the *Ising Spin Model* [4, pp. 119]. Their approach focused on the construction of a gloss-thesaurus network inducing different semantic relations (e.g. synonyms, antonyms), and enhanced the built dataset with co-occurrence information extracted from a corpus. The construction of the gloss-thesaurus is based on *WordNet*. With respect to the co-occurrence statistics, conjunctive expressions from the Wall Street Journal and Brown corpus were used. The available subjectivity resource offers a number of $88,015$ words for the English language with assigned Part-of-Speech information and a sentiment polarity orientation.

Polarity Enhancement
Waltinger (2009) proposed an approach to term-based polarity enhancement using a social network. His approach focuses on the reinforcement of polarity-related term features with respect to colloquial language. Using the entries of the *SpinModel* dataset as seed words, associated phrase and term definitions were extracted from the *urban dictionary* project. The enhanced subjectivity resource comprises $137,088$ term features for the English language.

4   Methodology

With respect to the described approaches in the construction of subjectivity dictionaries, we can identify two different branches. The majority of proposals induce the lexical network *WordNet* as a foundation for either extending or extracting polarity-related semantic relations. Therefore, the constructed term set is limited to the number of entries within *WordNet*, comprising up to $144,308$ polarity features. Other approaches, focused on the manual creation of a subjectivity thesaurus by inducing expert knowledge (manually annotated). These costly built resources consist of a rather small set of polarity features, inducing a dictionary size of up to $6,663$ entries. The questions that arise therefore are: How does the different subjectivity resources perform within the same experimental setup of polarity identification? Does the significant difference (quantity) of used polarity features affect the performance of opinion mining applications? Our methodology focuses on the most widely used and freely available subjectivity dictionaries for the task of sentiment-based feature selection.

4.1 SVM-Classification

The method we have used for the polarity classification is a document-based hard-partition machine learning classifier [24,5,31,25,34] using Support Vector Machines (SVM) [14]. This supervised classification technique relies on training a set of polarity classifiers, each of them capable of deciding whether the input stream has a positive or negative polarity, $C = \{+1, -1\}$. The SVM predicts a hyperplane, which separates a given set into two divisions with a maximum margin (the largest possible distance) [14]. We make use of the $SVM^{LightV6.01}$ implementation [13], using *Leave-One-Out* cross-validation, reporting *F1-Measure* as the harmonic mean between *Precision* and *Recall*. The reported *Accuracy* measures are based on a *5-fold cross-validation*. In each case of the SVM-Classifiers, *Linear-* and *RBF-Kernel* were evaluated in a comparative manner.

4.2 Subjectivity-Feature-Selection

Using SVMs for classifying the sentiment orientation, each input text needs to be converted into a vector representation. This vector consists of a set of significant term features representing the associated document. With respect to the opinion-oriented model, this task corresponds to a mapping between subjectivity features from the particular dictionary, and the textual features of the input document. That is, only those features are selected that occur in the subjectivity lexicon. Since the polarity features can consist of single words as well as multi-word expressions, a sliding window is used, when extracting textual data from the input text. As the feature weighting function, we have used the normalized term frequency ($tf_{i,j}$), defined as

$$tf_{i,j} = \frac{f_{i,j}}{\sum_{k=1}^{n} f_{k,j}} \qquad (1)$$

where the number of occurrences of feature i in document j is normalized by the total number of features n in j. While various subjectivity resources have been proposed in recent years, only a few of them are freely available. In this paper, we evaluate the four most widely used and available resources (see Table 2):

1. Subjectivity Clues [38]
2. SentiSpin [30]
3. SentiWordNet [9]
4. Polarity Enhancement [34]

4.3   German Subjectivity Resource

As described in Section 3.2, the majority of subjectivity resources are based on the English language. Different to the approach of [8], by translating a German input text into the English language (*SentiWordNet* as a resource), we rather focused on building a new German dictionary by translating polarity features only. Since a goal of this paper is to evaluate the correlation between the size of subjectivity dictionaries and the accuracy performance, we have built three different German polarity resources of different size [35]. The construction of these dictionaries is based on a semi-supervised translation of existing English polarity term-sets. That is, we automatically translated each polarity feature into the German language – using an English-to-German translation software[2], and manually reviewed the translation quality. We have used the following English datasets: First, the *Subjectivity Clues* [38,40,37] dictionary, comprising $9,827$ term features, further called *German Subjectivity Clues*. Second, we translated the dataset of *SentiSpin* [30], comprising $105,561$ polarity features. We will refer to this resource as the *German SentiSpin* dictionary. While there are in many cases more than one possible translations available, we decided to take a maximum number of three translations for dictionary construction into account. Therefore, the size of the built German resources differ to their English pendant. With respect to polarity feature weights, each aggregated German feature has inherited the sentiment orientation score (e.g. positive, negative, neutral) of the initial seed word from the English resource (e.g. English: "brave"—"positive" ↦ German: "mutig"—"positive"). This approach clearly leads to a problem of term ambiguity. We therefore decided to compile in a third step the *GermanPolarityClues* dictionary, by *manually* assessing each individual term feature of the *German Subjectivity Clues* dataset by their sentiment orientation (See Table 1). In addition, we added to this resource a number of 290 German negation-phrases (e.g. "nicht schlecht" = "not bad") and the most frequent positive and negative synonyms of existing term features, which previously had not been in there[3] - inducing a total size of $10,141$ polarity features. All resources are freely available for research purposes[4].

5   Experiments

5.1   Corpora

We have used two different datasets for the experiments. For the English language we conducted the polarity identification classification using the movie review corpus initially compiled by [24]. This corpus consists of two polarity categories (positive and negative), each category comprises 1000 articles with an average of 707.64 textual features. With respect to the German language, we manually created a reference corpus by extracting review data from the Amazon.com website. Reviews at Amazon.com correspond to human-rated product reviews with an attached rating scale from 1 (worst) to 5 (best) stars. For the experiment, we have used 1000 reviews for each of the 5 ratings, each comprising 5 different categories. All category and star label information

---

[2] We have used the online service of dict.leo.org for the translation of term features.
[3] Note, these features were extracted from the dataset of the de.wiktionary.org project.
[4] The constructed resources can be accessed at: http://hudesktop.hucompute.org/

Table 1. Overview of the GermanPolarityClues data schema by (A) automatic- and (B) corpus-based polarity orientation rating after [35]

Id:	Feature	PoS	A(+)	A(−)	A(○)	B(+)	B(−)	B(○)
5653	Begründung	NN	0	0	1	0	0.5	0.5
7573	Katastrophe	NN	0	1	0	0	0.68	0.32
7074	ideal	ADJD	1	0	0	0.76	0.13	0.11

Table 2. The standard deviation (StdDevi) and arithmetic mean (AMean) of subjectivity features by resource, text corpus (Text) and polarity category (Positive, Negative)

Resource:	Subject. Clues	Senti Spin	Senti WordNet	Polarity Enhance	German SentiSpin	German Subject.	German Polarity Clues
No. of Features:	6,663	88,015	144,308	137,088	105,561	9,827	10,141
Positive-AMean:	76.83	236.94	241.36	239.25	53.63	27.70	26.66
Positive-StdDevi:	30.81	84.29	85.61	84.98	6.90	4.59	5.01
Negative-AMean:	69.72	218.46	223.11	221.25	50.18	25.68	24.14
Negative-StdDevi:	26.22	74.08	75.37	74.68	10.40	5.88	5.41
Text-AMean:	707.64	707.64	707.64	707.64	109.75	109.75	109.75
Text-StdDevi:	296.94	296.94	296.94	296.94	24.52	24.52	24.52

but also the name of the reviewers were removed from the documents. All textual data (term features in the document) were passed through a pre-processing component, that is lemmatized and tagged by a PoS-Tagger. The average number of term features of the comprised reviews is 109.75. With respect to the experiments on the German corpus, we evaluated different "Star" combinations as positive and negative categories (e.g classifying Star1 against Star5, but also Star1 and Star2 against Star 4 and Star 5).

5.2 Results

With respect to the English polarity experiment (see Table 3 and 4), we have used not only the published accuracy results of [24], using the Naive Bayes (NB), the Maximum Entropy (ME) and the N-Gram-based SVM implementation, but also the results of [34], a feature-enhanced SVM implementation as corresponding baselines. As Table 3 shows, the smallest resource, Subjectivity Clues, performs best with $acc = 84.1$. However, SentiWordNet ($acc = 83.9$), SentiSpin ($acc = 83.8$) but also the Polarity Enhancement ($acc = 83.1$) dataset used for feature selection, perform almost within the same accuracy.

It can be stated that all subjectivity feature selection resources clearly outperform not only the well known NB and ME classifier but also the N-Gram-based SVM implementation. Not surprisingly, with respect to the feature coverage of the used subjectivity resources (see Table 2), we can argue that the size of the dictionary clearly correlates to the coverage (arithmetic mean of polarity-features selected varies between $76.83 - 241.36$). Interestingly, the biggest dictionary with the highest coverage property does not outperform the resource with the lowest number of polarity-features. In contrast, we can state

Table 3. Accuracy results comparing four subjectivity resources and four baseline approaches

Sentiment-Method	Accuracy
Naive Bayes - unigrams [24]	78.7
Maximum Entropy - top 2633 unigrams [24]	81.0
SVM - unigrams+bigrams [24]	82.7
SVM -unigrams [24]	**82.9**
Polarity Enhancement - PDC (without feature enhancement) [34]	81.9
Polarity Enhancement - PDC (with feature enhancement) [34]	**83.1**
Subjectivity-Clues SVM Linear-Kernel	**84.1**
Subjectivity-Clues SVM RBF-Kernel	83.5
SentiWordNet SVM Linear-Kernel	**83.9**
SentiWordNet SVM RBF-Kernel	82.3
SentiSpin SVM Linear-Kernel	**83.8**
SentiSpin SVM RBF-Kernel	82.5

Table 4. F1-Measure evaluation results of an English subjectivity feature selection using SVM

Resource	Model	F1-Positive	F1-Negative	F1-Average
Subjectivity Clues	SVM-Linear	.832	.823	**.828**
	SVM-RBF	.828	.823	.826
SentiWordNet	SVM-Linear	.832	.828	**.830**
	SVM-RBF	.816	.812	.814
SentiSpin	SVM-Linear	.831	.827	**.829**
	SVM-RBF	.815	.811	.813
Polarity Enhancement	PDC	.828	.827	**.828**
	SVM-Linear	.841	.837	**.839**

that operating in the present settings, on 6, 663 term features (in contrast to 144, 308 of *SentiWordNet*), seem to be a sufficient number for the task of document-based polarity identification. This claim is also supported by the evaluation F1-Measure results as shown in Table 4. All subjectivity resources nearly perform equally well (F1-Measure results range between 82.9 − 83.9). In this *Leave − One − Out* estimation, the polarity-enhanced implementation performs with a touch better than the other resources. Table 5 shows the results of the new build German subjectivity resources, used for the document-based polarity identification. With respect to the correlation of subjectivity dictionary size and classification performance, similar results can be achieved. Using the *German SentiSpin* version, comprising 105, 561 polarity features, lets us gain a promising F1-Measure of 85.9. The *German Subjectivity Clues* dictionary, comprising 9, 827 polarity features, performs with an F1-Measure of 84.1 almost at the same level. However, the *GermanPolarityClues* dictionary, comprising 10, 141 polarity features, outperforms with an F1-Measure of 87.6 all other German resources. In addition, with respect to the number of polarity features actually used within the Amazon-based SVM-classification experiments (see Table 6), we can identify that a number of 2, 700

Table 5. F1-Measure evaluation results of a German subjectivity feature selection using SVM

Resource	Model	F1-Positive	F1-Negative	F1-Average
German SentiSpin	SVM-Linear	.827	.828	.828
Star1+2 vs. Star4+5	SVM-RBF	.830	.830	**.830**
German SentiSpin	SVM-Linear	.857	.861	**.859**
Star1 vs. Star5	SVM-RBF	.855	.858	.857
German Subjectivity	SVM-Linear	.810	.813	**.811**
Star1+2 vs. Star4+5	SVM-RBF	.804	.803	.803
German Subjectivity	SVM-Linear	.841	.842	**.841**
Star1 vs. Star5	SVM-RBF	.834	.834	.834
GermanPolarityClues	SVM-Linear	.875	.730	**.803**
Star1+2 vs. Star4+5	SVM-RBF	.866	.661	.758
GermanPolarityClues	SVM-Linear	.875	.876	**.876**
Star1 vs. Star5	SVM-RBF	.855	.850	.853

Table 6. Number of polarity features used for the SVM-Classification by comprised resources

German SentiSpin:	10,802
German Subjectivity:	2,657
German Polarity Clues:	2,700

features only within the *GermanPolarityClues* dictionary exhibits the best performance. It seems that this newly created sentiment resource, which induces a rather small feature size (10-times smaller than the *German SentiSpin*), is due to its manual controlled vocabulary and its introduced negation- and synonym-pattern, of high-quality for the task of polarity identification. In general, in terms of Kernel-Methods, we can argue that RBF-Kernel are inferior to the Linear-Kernel SVM implementation, though only to a minor extend. With reference to the coverage of subjectivity dictionaries for a polarity-based feature selection - *size does matter*. However, the classification accuracy results indicate - for both languages - that a smaller but controlled dictionary contributes to the accuracy performance (almost equally to big-sized data) of opinion mining systems.

6   Conclusions

This paper proposed an empirical study to machine learning-based sentiment analysis. We systematically analyzed the four most widely used English-based subjectivity resources for the task of sentiment polarity identification. In addition, we proposed and evaluated three new polarity resources for the German language. The evaluation results showed that the size of subjectivity dictionaries does not correlate with classification accuracy. Smaller but more controlled dictionaries used for a sentiment feature selection perform within a SVM-based classification setup equally good compared to the biggest available resources. We can conclude, that combining a polarity-based feature selection with machine learning, SVMs using Linear-Kernel exhibit the best performance ($acc = 84.1, f1 = 83.9$). The results of the German polarity identification experiments, with an F1-Measure of 80.3 - 87.6 are quite promising.

Acknowledgements. This paper is based on work that was first reported in [36]. The GermanPolarityClues resource was first reported in [35]. We gratefully acknowledge financial support of the German Research Foundation (DFG) through the EC 277 *Cognitive Interaction Technology* at Bielefeld University.

References

1. Agarwal, A., Biadsy, F., McKeown, K.: Contextual phrase-level polarity analysis using lexical affect scoring and syntactic n-grams. In: EACL 2009, Athens, Greece (2009)
2. Annett, M., Kondrak, G.: A comparison of sentiment analysis techniques: Polarizing movie blogs. In: Canadian Conference on AI, pp. 25–35 (2008)
3. Becker-Asano, C., Wachsmuth, I.: Affective computing with primary and secondary emotions in a virtual human. In: Autonomous Agents and Multi-Agent Systems (2009)
4. Chandler, D.: Introduction to Modern Statistical Mechanics. Oxford University Press, Oxford (1987)
5. Chaovalit, P., Zhou, L.: Movie review mining: a comparison between supervised and unsupervised classification approaches. In: Hawaii International Conference on System Sciences, vol. 4, p. 112c (2005)
6. Clematide, S., Klenner, M.: Evaluation and extension of a polarity lexicon for german. In: Proceedings of the 1st Workshop on Computational Approaches to Subjectivity and Sentiment Analysis, WASSA (2010)
7. Dave, K., Lawrence, S., Pennock, D.M.: Mining the peanut gallery: opinion extraction and semantic classification of product reviews. In: WWW 2003: Proceedings of the Twelfth International Conference on World Wide Web, pp. 519–528. ACM Press, New York (2003)
8. Denecke, K.: Using sentiwordnet for multilingual sentiment analysis. In: ICDE Workshops, pp. 507–512. IEEE Computer Society, Los Alamitos (2008)
9. Esuli, A., Sebastiani, F.: Sentiwordnet: A publicly available lexical resource for opinion mining. In: Proceedings of the 5th Conference on Language Resources and Evaluation (LREC 2006), pp. 417–422 (2006)
10. Fellbaum, C. (ed.): WordNet. An Electronic Lexical Database. MIT Press, Cambridge (1998)
11. Hatzivassiloglou, V., McKeown, K.R.: Predicting the semantic orientation of adjectives. In: Proceedings of the Eighth Conference on European Chapter of the Association for Computational Linguistics, pp. 174–181. Association for Computational Linguistics, Morristown (1997)
12. Hu, M., Liu, B.: Mining and summarizing customer reviews. In: KDD 2004: Proceedings of the tenth ACM SIGKDD International Conference on Knowledge Discovery and Data Mining, pp. 168–177. ACM Press, New York (2004)
13. Joachims, T.: SVM light (2002), http://svmlight.joachims.org
14. Joachims, T.: Learning to Classify Text Using Support Vector Machines: Methods, Theory and Algorithms. Kluwer Academic Publishers, Norwell (2002)
15. Kennedy, A., Inkpen, D.: Sentiment classification of movie reviews using contextual valence shifters. Computational Intelligence 22(2), 110–125 (2006)
16. Kugatsu Sadamitsu, S.S., Yamamoto, M.: Sentiment analysis based on probabilistic models using inter-sentence information. In: Calzolari, N., Choukri, K., B.M.J.M.J.O.S.P.D.T. (eds.) Proceedings of the Sixth International Language Resources and Evaluation (LREC 2008), European Language Resources Association, Marrakech (2008)

17. Liu, B.: Sentiment analysis and subjectivity. Handbook of Natural Language Processing 2, 568 (2010)
18. Maarten, J.K., Marx, M., Mokken, R.J., Rijke, M.D.: Using wordnet to measure semantic orientations of adjectives. In: National Institute for, pp. 1115–1118 (2004)
19. Mehler, A., Geibel, P., Pustylnikov, O.: Structural classifiers of text types: Towards a novel model of text representation. Journal for Language Technology and Computational Linguistics (JLCL) 22(2), 51–66 (2007)
20. Mullen, T., Collier, N.: Sentiment analysis using support vector machines with diverse information sources. In: Lin, D., Wu, D. (eds.) Proceedings of EMNLP 2004, pp. 412–418. Association for Computational Linguistics, Barcelona (2004)
21. Pang, L.A.: sentimental education: Sentiment analysis using subjectivity summarization based on minimum cuts. In: Proceedings of the ACL, pp. 271–278 (2004)
22. Pang, B., Lee, L.: Seeing stars: exploiting class relationships for sentiment categorization with respect to rating scales. In: ACL 2005: Proceedings of the 43rd Annual Meeting on Association for Computational Linguistics, pp. 115–124. Association for Computational Linguistics, Morristown (2005)
23. Pang, B., Lee, L.: Opinion Mining and Sentiment Analysis. Now Publishers Inc. (2008)
24. Pang, B., Lee, L., Vaithyanathan, S.: Thumbs up?: sentiment classification using machine learning techniques. In: EMNLP 2002: Proceedings of the ACL 2002 Conference on Empirical Methods in Natural Language Processing, pp. 79–86. Association for Computational Linguistics, Morristown (2002)
25. Prabowo, R., Thelwall, M.: Sentiment analysis: A combined approach. J. Informetrics 3(2), 143–157 (2009)
26. Remus, R., Quasthoff, U., Heyer, G.: Sentiws – a publicly available german-language resource for sentiment analysis. In: Proceedings of the 7th International Language Resources and Evaluation (LREC 2010), pp. 1168–1171 (2010)
27. Stone, P.J., Dunphy, D.C., Smith, M.S., Ogilvie, D.M.: The General Inquirer: A Computer Approach to Content Analysis. MIT Press, Cambridge (1966)
28. Strapparava, C., Valitutti, A.: WordNet-Affect: an affective extension of WordNet. In: Proceedings of LREC, vol. 4, pp. 1083–1086 (2004)
29. Taboada, M., Brooke, J., Stede, M.: Genre-based paragraph classification for sentiment analysis. In: Proceedings of the SIGDIAL 2009 Conference, pp. 62–70. Association for Computational Linguistics, London (2009)
30. Takamura, H., Inui, T., Okumura, M.: Extracting semantic orientations of words using spin model. In: ACL 2005: Proceedings of the 43rd Annual Meeting on Association for Computational Linguistics, pp. 133–140. Association for Computational Linguistics, Morristown (2005)
31. Tan, S., Zhang, J.: An empirical study of sentiment analysis for chinese documents. Expert Syst. Appl. 34(4), 2622–2629 (2008)
32. Turney, P.D.: Thumbs up or thumbs down?: semantic orientation applied to unsupervised classification of reviews. In: ACL 2002: Proceedings of the 40th Annual Meeting on Association for Computational Linguistics, pp. 417–424. Association for Computational Linguistics, Morristown (2001)
33. Turney, P.D., Littman, M.L.: Unsupervised learning of semantic orientation from a hundred-billion-word corpus. CoRR cs.LG/0212012 (2002)
34. Waltinger, U.: Polarity reinforcement: Sentiment polarity identification by means of social semantics. In: Proceedings of the IEEE Africon 2009, Nairobi, Kenya, September 23-25 (2009)

35. Waltinger, U.: Germanpolarityclues: A lexical resource for german sentiment analysis. In: Calzolari, N., Choukri, K., B.M.J.M.J.O.S.P.D.T. (eds.) Proceedings of the Seventh conference on International Language Resources and Evaluation (LREC 2010), European Language Resources Association, Valletta (2010)
36. Waltinger, U.: Sentiment analysis reloaded: A comparative study on sentiment polarity identification combining machine learning and subjectivity features. In: Proceedings of the 6th International Conference on Web Information Systems and Technologies (WEBIST 2010), Valencia (2010)
37. Wiebe, J., Riloff, E.: Creating subjective and objective sentence classifiers from unannotated texts. In: Gelbukh, A. (ed.) CICLing 2005. LNCS, vol. 3406, pp. 486–497. Springer, Heidelberg (2005)
38. Wiebe, J., Wilson, T., Cardie, C.: Annotating expressions of opinions and emotions in language. Language Resources and Evaluation 1(2), (2005)
39. Wiegand, M., Klakow, D.: The role of knowledge-based features in polarity classification at sentence level
40. Wilson, T., Wiebe, J., Hoffmann, P.: Recognizing contextual polarity in phrase-level sentiment analysis. In: HLT 2005: Proceedings of the conference on Human Language Technology and Empirical Methods in Natural Language Processing, pp. 347–354. Association for Computational Linguistics, Morristown (2005)
41. Yu, H., Hatzivassiloglou, V.: Towards answering opinion questions: Separating facts from opinions and identifying the polarity of opinion sentences. In: Proceedings of EMNLP 2003(2003)

The Generalist Recommender System GRSK and Its Extension to Groups

Inma Garcia, Laura Sebastia, Sergio Pajares, and Eva Onaindia

Dpt. Computer Science, Technical Univ. of Valencia
Camino de Vera s/n, 46022, Valencia, Spain
{ingarcia,lstarin,spajares,onaindia}@dsic.upv.es

Abstract. This paper presents a Generalist Recommender System Kernel (GRSK) and describes the differences of the recommendation process when it is applied to groups. The GRSK is able to work with any domain as long as the domain description is represented within an ontology. Several basic techniques like demographics, content-based or collaborative are used to elicit the recommendations, as well as other hybrid techniques. The GRSK provides a configuration process through which to select the techniques and parameters that best suit the particular application domain. The experiments will show the success of the GRSK in different domains. We also outline the changes and new techniques required by the GRSK when it is used in a group recommendation.

Keywords: Recommender systems, Group recommenders, Tourism, Movies.

1 Introduction

Every day, new data appears on the Web. Everyone browsing on the Internet can have the perception of the huge amount of information available, which can lead to a situation of information overload, that is the situation where there is far too much information at people disposal so that useful information could be hidden by other data. In this case, techniques to retrieve *useful* information become more and more important. The usefulness of information depends on the users and their objectives, so retrieval systems have to try to understand the purpose of a user search in order to propose information he could be interested in. A special kind of information retrieval techniques that focuses on this issue is named *information filtering*. As the name suggests, starting from a big set of information, this technique identifies a small subset which should include the useful/interesting information.

Recommendation systems are a specific type of information filtering technique that attempts to present information items (e.g. movies, songs, activities, etc.) that are likely of interest to the user. A **recommender system** (*RS*) [13] is a personalization tool that attempts to provide people with lists of information items that best fit their individual tastes. A RS infers the user's preferences by analyzing the available user data, information about other users and information about the environment.

RS are used to either predict whether a given user will like a particular item or identify the top N items that will be of interest to the user. In RS, how much a particular user likes an item is represented by a *rating*. Basically, a RS estimates ratings for the

J. Filipe and J. Cordeiro (Eds.): WEBIST 2010, LNBIP 75, pp. 215–229, 2011.

items that have not been seen by a user and recommends to the user the items with the highest estimated ratings.

Being an instance of information filtering, recommendation systems can be based on the demographic filtering algorithm, the content-based filtering algorithm or the collaborative filtering algorithm[1]. All these approaches have advantages and disadvantages [1]; a common solution adopted by many RS is to combine these techniques into an hybrid RS [11,4] thus improving recommendations by alleviating the limitations of one technique with the advantages of others.

Recently, some researchers have been focusing on enhancing recommendations by exploiting a semantic description of the domain in which recommendations are provided [16],[15]. In general, items handled by the system are semantically described through an ontology. Then, the recommendations are based on the semantic matching between the user profiles and the item descriptions. The main disadvantage of these approaches is that a semantic representation of the domain has to be available and, up to now, user profiles and items are described manually.

This paper summarizes the main characteristics of the *Generalist Recommender System Kernel (GRSK)*. It is a RS based in a semantic description of the domain that uses a hybrid recommendation technique, fed by the recommendations obtained from different algorithms. The task of GRSK is to generate the list of the top N items that will be of interest to the user. GRSK can be parameterized to adjust the system working model, i.e. to use the desired recommendation techniques. Besides, it is prepared to include as many techniques as desired by simply developing new modules. On the other hand, it is a domain-independent engine, able to work with different catalogs of items to recommend.

This paper is organized as follows. Section 2 gives an overview on the GRSK architecture, the information GRSK needs (ontology and user information) and, finally, the GRSK recommendation process. Section 3 explains the process of GRSK configuration to be integrated into a system. Section 4 presents the results we have obtained when working with a tourism domain and with a movies domain. We finish with some conclusions and future work.

2   GRSK: Generalist Recommender System Kernel

2.1   GRSK Ontology

The GRSK behaviour relies on the use of a **ontology** to describe the user's preferences and the items to recommend. It has been designed to be *generalist*, so GRSK is able to work with any application domain as long as the data of the new domain can be defined through an ontology representation.

An ontology is a formal representation of a set of concepts within a domain and the relationships between those concepts. The GRSK ontology contains the **features** that describe the items in the domain. For example, in the tourism domain, the ontology is composed of terms describing architectonic styles or types of buildings. Figure 1 shows an example of this ontology. In the movies domain (figure 2), the feature denote the

---
[1] These algorithms will be detailed later on.

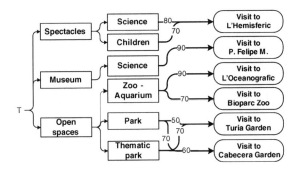

Fig. 1. Part of the *e-Tourism* ontology

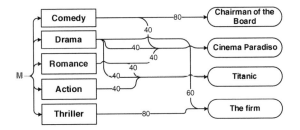

Fig. 2. Part of the *e-Movies* ontology

film genres. It is important to remark that GRSK is able to work from simple ontologies (such as the movies ontology, which is basically a list of genres) to more complex ontologies (with several levels of refinements, for example).

The **items** in the domain are described by the features of the ontology. Moreover, each pair item-feature is associated a value to indicate the **degree of interest** of the item under the feature, i.e. as a member of the category denoted by the feature. An item can also be categorized by more than one feature in the ontology. Formally, an item i is described by means of a list of tuples of the form (i, f, d^{if}), where f is a feature defined in the ontology and $d^{if} \in [0, 100]$ is the degree of interest of the item i under the feature f. Additionally, items are associated a numeric value AC^i (**acceptance counter**) to represent how popular the item i is among users; this value indicates how many times this item has been accepted when recommended.

2.2 User Information

In order to compute a recommendation, GRSK records a profile of each user, which models the user tastes and preferences as well as his historical interaction with the system. The **profile** of a given user u records, in first place, personal and demographic details about the user like the age, the gender, the family or the country. Second, the user profile also contains the user general-likes model, denoted by GL^u, which is a list of the features f in the ontology the user is interested in along with the user ratings r^{uf} for those features: $GL^u = \{(u, f, r^{uf})\}$, where $r^{uf} \in [0, 100]$. A user profile in GRSK also contains information about the historical interaction of the user with the RS,

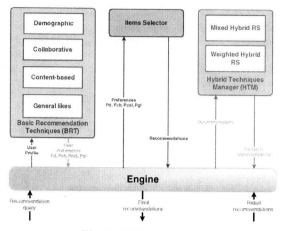

Fig. 3. GRSK Architecture

namely the set of items i the user has been recommended and his degree of satisfaction r^{ui} with the recommended items: $RT^u = \{(u, i, r^{ui}\}$, where $r^{ui} \in [0, 100]$.

2.3   The GRSK Architecture

Figure 3 shows an sketch of the GRSK architecture. The **Engine** module is the core of GRSK. The first task of the Engine is to capture and store the user profile when the user logs in the system for the first time. Then, the information obtained during the interaction of the user with the system *after* the recommendation (*rated recommendations*) will be used to update his profile to better capture his preferences.

The Engine is also in charge of controlling the recommendation process, which consists of two steps: first, each basic recommendation technique calculates a set of preferences for the user profile; and then, the items selector obtains the items that match the user preferences which are combined by the hybrid technique to obtain the final list of recommended items. The modules used by the engine to obtain the recommendation are:

- **Basic Recommendation Techniques** (BRT) [4] (demographic RS, content-based RS, collaborative RS and general likes-based filtering) are used to obtain the *user preferences* by analyzing his own profile, the profiles of other users and the items selected by the users that have utilized the system before. For a given user, each BRT creates a different list of preferences according to the parameters and data handled by the technique. The system configuration allows to select the set of BRT to use in the recommendation process (see section 3).
- **Items Selector:** receives the lists of *user preferences* and, for each list, it returns the set of items that better match the elements in the list.
- The **Hybrid Techniques Manager** (HTM) combines the lists of items in a single list, that conform the final user recommendation list. The hybrid techniques are applied on items, not on preferences. At this moment, GRSK includes two hybrid recommendation methods: the mixed hybrid technique and the weighted hybrid

technique. The system configuration allows to select *only one* hybrid technique to use in the recommendation process.

At this moment, GRSK includes several BRT and two hybrid techniques, but it is prepared to work with as many techniques as desired by simply developing new modules. We opted for these techniques because we considered them more suitable for the most common domains.

2.4   GRSK Recommendation Process

The recommendation process in GRSK is divided in two steps. The first one is to obtain the preferences that define the items that will be of interest to the user (section 2.4). The user introduces his query, which is sent joint with his profile to the BRT to produce a list of individual preferences for each technique. The second step is to obtain the list of items to recommend (section 2.4). This second step includes to obtain the list of items that match the preferences and to apply an hybrid recommendation technique to obtain the final ranked list of recommended items.

Modeling of User Preferences.   This step consists of analyzing the user profile and eliciting the corresponding list of preferences. It is important to note that, unlike most RS, GRSK is a semantic RS that does not initially work with the items that will be later recommended to the user. In contrast, GRSK makes use of the concept of feature to elicit the user preference model, which is a more general and flexible entity. This makes GRSK able to work with any application domain as long as the data can be represented through an ontology.

A *preference* (which is a tuple of the form (u, f, d^{uf})) is a feature f in the ontology with a interest-degree of d^{uf} for a user u, selected by one of the four basic recommendation techniques: demographic recommendation, content-based recommendation, collaborative recommendation and general likes-based filtering. Each BRT generates a different set of preferences, an independent list of preferences and hence the lists may contain different features or the same feature with different degrees of interest. We will call these lists P_d^u for the demographic preference list, P_{cb}^u for the content-based preference list, P_{col}^u for the collaborative preference list, and P_{gl}^u for the general-likes-based preference list.

The **demographic BRT** classifies the user into a demographic category according to his profile details. Each demographic category is associated a list of preferences (P_d^u) during the system configuration because they depend on the application domain. The success of the demographic recommendation is strongly dependant of this user classification. We opted for a demographic BRT because it is a good alternative to solve the problem of the *new user* since it is able to always give a recommendation.

The **content-based RS technique** computes a set of preferences by taking into account the items previously rated by the user (historical interaction). This technique will allow us to increase the user satisfaction by recommending items similar to those already accepted by the user. Let f be a feature and I a list of items described under the feature f in the ontology; I will be a list of tuples of the form (i, f, d^{if}) for a particular feature f. Let $RT^u = \{(u, i, r^{ui})\}$ be the set of items valued by user u with respective ratings of r^{ui}; a preference (u, f, d^{uf}) is added to the list P_{cb}^u where:

$$d^{uf} = \frac{\sum\limits_{\forall i \in I \cap RT^u} d^{if} * r^{ui}}{|RT^u|}$$

The value d^{uf} denotes the interest-degree of a user for the items described under the feature f amongst the whole set of items rated by the user.

The **collaborative RS technique** suggests those items preferred by people with a profile most similar to the given user profile (i.e. the user will be recommended items that people with similar tastes and preferences liked in the past). This technique is only useful when there is a great amount of data concerning items rated by other users. In order to obtain the corresponding list of preferences P_{col}^u, this technique decides whether a user v is similar to the given user u ($s_{u,v}$) by applying the Pearson Correlation with respect to the items that have been rated by both users. Then, by taking into account all the users v similar to u, a preference (u, f, d^{uf}) is added to P_{col}^u for each f that describes an item i rated by v, where:

$$d^{uf} = avg(d^{if} * r^{vi}), \forall v : s_{u,v}$$

The **general-likes-based filtering** is an information filtering technique that obtains the preferences that match with the main user interests specified by the user in his profile (GL^u). The accuracy of this technique depends on the information provided by the user. However, GRSK is able to work with few information. In this case, the set of preferences P_{gl}^u is simply built as $P_{gl}^u = GL^u$; that is, the interest-degree of the preferences in P_{gl}^u will be the ratings given by the user to that particular feature in his profile ($d^f = r^f$).

Obtention of the List of Recommended Items. In the second step of the recommenda-tion process, the **Items Selector** selects, among all of the items in the domain, those that best match the preferences in the lists P_d^u, P_{cb}^u, P_{col}^u and P_{gl}^u. Afterwards, the selected **Hybrid Technique** obtains a single list of ranked recommendations that we will denote as $RI^u = \{(u, i, d^{ui})\}$, where i is the item, and d^{ui} is the estimated interest-degree of the item i for the user u.

The method for selecting an item is quite simple: an item i represented by the tuple (i, f, d^{if}) matches a preference in P_{brt}^u if there is a tuple (u, f, d^{uf}) in P_{brt}^u such that the item has not previously rated by the user. The outcome of the Items Selector is a set of lists of ranked items, one list per BRT. The lists of recommended items computed by the Items Selector are then processed by the selected Hybrid Technique and returns a single list of ranked items (RI^u). The value d^{ui} of a tuple in RI^u depends on the selected Hybrid Technique. At this moment, GRSK includes two hybrid techniques: mixed and weighted techniques.

The **Mixed Hybrid Technique** mixes the items in the lists of all the BRT. All items are handled in the same way with independency the BRT they belong to. In this case, the value d^{ui} of a tuple in RI^u is calculated as follows:

$$d^{ui} = percentile(AC^i) + avg_{\forall f}(d^{if} + d^{uf})$$

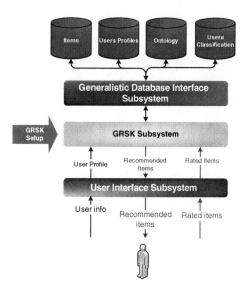

Fig. 4. GRSK Integration into a System

where $percentile(AC^i)$ refers to the percentile of the acceptance counter of i (AC^i) with respect to the whole set of items rated by the users. The second part of the formula considers the average interest-degree of all the features that describe the item i in both the ontology (d^{if}) and in the user preferences (d^{uf}).

The **Weighted Hybrid Technique** mixes the items in the lists, but the value d^{ui} is computed according to the weight of the BRT that selected the preference for which the item has been recommended. The weight of each BRT, defined in the configuration process, is denoted by ω_d for the demographic RS, ω_{cb} for the content-based RS, ω_{col} for the collaborative RS and ω_{gl} for the general-likes filtering. In this case the value d^{ui} of a tuple in RI^u is calculated as:

$$d^{ui} = percentile(AC^i) + avg_{\forall f}((d^{if} + d^{uf}) \times \omega_{brt})$$

The Hybrid Technique obtains a list of ranked items and retrieves the best N ranked elements.

3 GRSK Integration Process

This section describes the GRSK requirements to be integrated into any system (figure 4).

3.1 Database and External Subsystems

In first place, GRSK needs a **database** of the particular application domain containing: (1) *the domain ontology*; (2) *the set of items that can be recommended:* these items must be classified according to the ontology and the quality of the recommendation depends, in part, on the accuracy of the classification of items; (3) *the user profiles with the demographic user information* (if the demographic RS is used in GRSK) *and the user general likes GL^u* (if the general-likes filtering is used): the quality of the recommendation also depends on the information provided by the user - the more information, the more accurate the recommendation -, but it is possible to obtain a recommendation with a minimum amount of data; (4) *demographic classification of users* according to the ontology.

In order to obtain a complete recommender system, two external modules must be plugged to GRSK: the Database Interface and the User Interface. The **Database Interface subsystem**, which is the interface between GRSK and the database, processes the queries coming from GRSK, such as obtaining the user profile of the current user or the list of items that match a given preference. On the other hand, the **User Interface Subsystem** initiates the execution of GRSK and centralizes the exchange of information between the user and GRSK. This includes converting the user data into a user profile, showing the list of recommended items and recording the ones that are selected and discarded by the user joint with the rating of the user satisfaction with a given recommended item. The User Interface Subsystem is also in charge of deciding which information must be initially introduced by the user (which depends on the particular application domain).

3.2   GRSK Setup

GRSK requires an initial configuration to adjust the GRSK behaviour to the current application. First, it is possible to select *which BRT* among all the available BRT (demographic RS, content-based RS, collaborative RS and general likes-based filtering), will be used in GRSK to give a recommendation. Second, it is necessary to select only *one hybrid recommendation technique*. Moreover, for all hybrid techniques, it is possible to select the way to compute the interest-degree of items in case an item is selected by more than one preference. The techniques are: maximum ratio, median ratio and several techniques to compute the average.

On the other hand, some other computations can be parameterized. For example, a threshold of the interest-degree can be defined to consider or not a given preference. Or the acceptance counter can be computed in several ways.

4   Case Studies

This subsection discusses the experiments conducted to evaluate the behavior of GRSK.

Two domains have been used to evaluate GRSK: a tourism domain and a movies domain. Through these case studies, we will show that GRSK has been successfully used in both cases.

In order to test GRSK, we selected two classical Information Retrieval metrics: *precision* and *recall*. In an Information Retrieval scenario, precision is defined as the number of retrieved relevant items divided by the total number of items retrieved by that search; and recall is defined as the number of retrieved relevant items divided by the total number of existing relevant items. That is, precision represents the probability that a retrieved item is relevant to the user and recall is the probability that a relevant item is retrieved by the search.

Specifically, we call Ns the number of retrieved items by GRSK, that is, the number of recommendations solicited by the user. The number of relevant items is denoted by Nr and Nrs is the number of relevant items retrieved in the recommendation, that is, $Nrs = Nr \cap Ns$. Then, precision and recall are calculated as follows:

$$P = \frac{Nrs}{Ns} \qquad\qquad R = \frac{Nrs}{Nr}$$

Often, there is an inverse relationship between P and R, where it is possible to increase one at the cost of reducing the other. For example, R can be increased by increasing Ns, at the cost of increasing the number of irrelevant items retrieved (decreasing P). For this reason, P and R ratios are not discussed in isolation.

We run our experiments in terms of two parameters, Ns the number of retrieved items, and the information about past visits in the user profile. As for Ns, we run tests with $Ns = 10$ and $Ns = 25$. In both experiments, we obtained the same list of retrieved items, but in the first case, the system considered the first 10 items and, in the second case, the first 25 items were considered. Regarding the second parameter, we took into account four levels of historical information in the user profile; a new user and user profiles that store 25%, 50% and 75% of (randomly selected) rated items, respectively.

4.1   E-Tourism: A Touristic Recommender System

e-Tourism is a web-based recommender system that computes a user-adapted leisure and tourist plan for a given user. The system does not solve the problem of traveling to an specific place but it works on recommending a list of the activities that a tourist can perform in the city of Valencia (Spain). It also computes a time schedule for the list of recommended activities taking into account the distance between places, the opening hours, etc. - that is, an agenda of activities [14]. It is intended to be a service for foreigners and locals to become deeply familiar with the city and plan leisure activities.

Data Warehouse E-Tourism. As this is a new domain, a survey was filled by 58 people in order to obtain data for testing the system. Personal data like name, age, marital status and tourist profile (cultural, business, family, etc.) were collected. They also identified sites already visited along with a degree of interest (rating) for each site. There are 115 preferences structured in the ontology (see figure 1), 141 sites stored and 58 user profiles. Each user rated (positively or negatively) all sites (RT^u) and an average of 110 preferences (GL^u).

E-Tourism Experimental Results. When performing the experimental results in this domain, we divided the user profiles database into two sets: 48 users were the training users and 10 users were the test users. Then, as all users rated all sites, we considered as relevant items (Nr) those visits that the test users marked as visited with a positive degree of satisfaction in the survey.

Figure 5 shows a comparison between the average of precision (P) and recall (R) for all the different cases of user feedback. When $Ns = 10$, the difference between the precision and the recall is remarkable, and the precision decreases as the recall increases, as

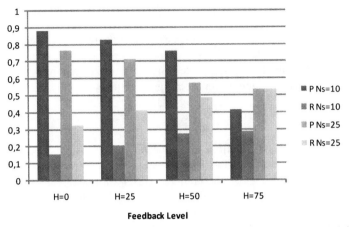

Fig. 5. Comparison of the P and R values obtained when Ns=10 and Ns=25 and for the four degrees of historical information for the tourism domain

expected. However, when $Ns = 25$, this difference is not so noticeable. When $Ns = 10$ and the information provided to the system increases ($H = 25$, $H = 50$), GRSK improves the quality of the recommendations if we consider P and R together. However, in some of the cases in which the user feedback is rather high ($H = 75$), the quality of the recommendation worsens. This is because the database does not contain a large number of items and, therefore, GRSK is not able to recommend places other than those ones already visited by the user. When $Ns = 25$, the general impression is similar. However, in this case, the relation $P - R$ is better because, although the precision is a bit lower, the recall increases in a higher order. Here again, the more feedback, the better the quality of the recommendation, and, unlike the previous case, the worsening in the case of $H = 75$ is not as noticeable.

4.2   E-Movies: A Movies Recommender System

e-Movies is a application-based recommender system that computes user tastes regarding preferences movies for a given user, in order to obtain the best list of movies for the user. It is intended to be a service for any cinephile, working with a multitude of movies.

Data Warehouse E-Movies. In this case, we selected a well-known movies database, MoviLens[2], which has been created by the GroupLens research group at the University of Minnesota. It contains 900 user profiles with their respective histories of interaction with the system and a set of 1682 films. A user has scored between 20 and 700 movies. Each film is described by a title, number of people who were recommended the film and watched it, the year was recorded, etc. All the films have been cataloged through an ontology of twenty preferences (see figure 2). Each user has an average of 15 preferences associated with several ratios (GL^u) and has rated an average of 45 movies

---

[2] http://www.grouplens.org/

(RT^u). Moreover, each movie has been rated by 57 different users in average and has been described by 2 preferences in average.

E-Movies Experimental Results. When performing the experimental results in this domain, we divided the user profiles database into two sets: 890 users were the training users and 10 users were the test users. We considered as relevant items (Nr) those movies that the test users have marked with a value between 2 and 5.

Figure 6 shows a comparison between the average of precision (P) and recall (R) for all the different cases of user feedback. In all cases, the difference between the precision and the recall is quite remarkable. The reason behind is that the number of relevant items (Nr) is quite high compared to the number of retrieved items as each test user has rated up to 685 movies and has an average of 551 movies. On the other hand, we expected (as in the tourism domain) that both measures (considered together) increased as the user history also increased (except when H=75, as explained above). However, figure 6 shows that when H = 50 the precision decreases slightly. The reason is the following. The precision P is calculated by taking into account a user history. Remember that the possibility that a retrieved relevant item in Nrs was not included in this Nr is not considered in P, therefore it must be satisfied that $Nrs \subseteq Nr$. Thereby the more feedback level, the lower Nr is observed, being Ns constant. This is the reason why P with 25% is a little bit better than P with 50%, because it is easier to find a retrieved relevant item within the 75% user history (25% feedback) than with 50%. If we could ask the user about his satisfaction with respect to a given recommendation, we would have a better picture of the GRSK performance in this domain. This does not happen in the tourism domain because we have a complete feedback for all users. We also have the intuition that a more complex ontology and a more complete description of items (such as in the tourism domain) improves the quality of the recommendations. However, we need to perform further experiments to confirm this intuition.

5 Extension of GRSK to Groups

RS usually give a recommendation for a single user considering his/her interests and tastes. However, many activities such as watching a movie or going to a restaurant involve a group of users, in which case recommendations must take into account the likes and tastes of all members in the group, thus giving rise to a Group Recommender System (GRS). In GRSs, individual profiles are merged so as to elicit a single set of preferences that represents the preferences of the group as a whole, and elicit a set of recommendations as if the group were a single user.

The first task of a GRS is to identify the individual preferences and then find a compromise that is accepted by all the group members. This is the crucial point in GRSs because how individual preferences are managed to come up with the group preferences will determine the success of the recommendation [12,7]. The purpose is that of elicitng a recommendation that equally satisfies, as much as possible, all the users and that no member is particularly satisfied or dissatisfied with the final recommendations.

This section outlines how our system is able to provide a recommendation for a group. When the GRSK receives a recommendation request from a group, it redirects

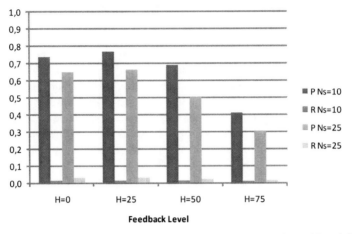

Fig. 6. Comparison of the P and R values obtained when Ns=10 and Ns=25 and for the four degrees of historical information for the movies domain

the request to the *Group Preference Manager* (GPM) which is in charge of controlling the group recommendation process. This process is composed of the following steps:

1. **Elicit the Individual Preferences.** The individual profiles of the users in the group are analyzed, and a list of preferences for each user in the group is elicited by using the Basic Recommendation Techniques (BRT). Each BRT returns a different list of individual preferences. Thus, after this stage, we have, for each user u in the group, four lists of individual preferences ($P^u_{demographic}$, $P^u_{collaborative}$, $P^u_{content-based}$, $P^u_{general-preferences}$) which describe the usual tastes of the user according to the criteria used by the BRT.

2. **Elicit the Group Preferences.** The aim of this process is to elicit a group preference model that reflects the preferences of all group members. Once the individual preferences are modeled (P^u_{brt}), they are merged in order to elicit the group preference model (P^G). This process is performed through the application of methods like *Aggregation, Intersection, Incremental Intersection* or *Incremental Collaborative Intersection*, which combine the individual preferences and generate the final group preference model P^G, composed of as many lists as applied BRT (one group preference list per BRT). From this point on, the GRSK follows the usual steps to make the final recommendations, as if P^G were the profile of a single user.

3. **Elicit the List of Recommended Items.** The Items Selector selects the items that match the group preference model and elicit the final recommendations. The Hybrid Technique joins the lists of group preferences into a single list, and the best recommendations are finally elicited for the group.

At this moment, the GPM makes use of four disjunctive methods to elicit the group preferences: *Aggregation, Intersection, Incremental Intersection* and *Incremental Collaborative Intersection*. These methods differ on the way the lists of individual preferences are merged. The work in [6] presents some comparison results on the application of these techniques.

The **Aggregation** mechanism is a common technique that is used in several GRSs. Aggregation gathers the preferences of all members in the group computed by each BRT, and builds a single set of preferences. A preference is included in the group profile if it belongs to the individual profile of at least one of the members in the group.

The **Intersection** finds the preferences that are shared by all the members in the group to build the group preference model. The advantage of this mechanism is that all of the users in the group will be equally satisfied with the resulting group model. However, the risk of using intersection is that we might end up with an empty list of preferences if the group is rather heterogeneous.

The **Incremental Intersection**, based on a voting strategy, incrementally lessens the number of users that should satisfy a particular preference, and hence it is always able to calculate a recommendation for a group. This mechanism reports good results as it brings together the benefits of the Aggregation and the Intersection techniques.

The **Incremental Collaborative Intersection** selects the preferences that better match the group among the preferences included in the Intersection list of the group. This technique does not consider all the preferences shared by all group members but only the ones with a higher ratio. From these preferences, and by using a collaborative RS, the Incremental Collaborative Intersection elicits a new set of preferences for the group. This technique makes recommendations that incrementally satisfy the group satisfaction in contexts like a tourism domain, thus alleviating the limitations of the basic recommendation techniques.

As [6] shows, the selection of the appropriate group modeling techniques depends on issues such as the characteristics of the application domain or the available information about the users.

6   Related Work

Some general-purpose domain independent open source libraries and engines have been developed in order to reuse the effort to design recommender systems. Some of these systems are: *RACOFI* [2], *SUGGEST* [5], *Vogoo* [9], *Taste*[3], *CoFE* [10], *ColFi* [3], *Duine Toolkit* [16] and *Aura* [8].

Most of these engines are Java-based, with the exception of *SUGGEST* (C) and *Vogoo* (PHP). At this moment, we have two versions of the GRSK, one written in Java and the other in C#. GRSK Java version is agent-based like *RACOFI* and *Aura*.

Duine Toolkit, *RACOFI* and *ColFi* are developed with a modular architecture that allows developers to change and add algorithms easily, in the same manner than GRSK. The GRSK configuration process allows to select which techniques to use and to parameterize different aspects of the recommendation process, in order to adjust the GRSK behavior to the particular application domain.

Most of these systems are collaborative recommendation engines (*ColFi, Cofi, Taste, SUGGEST* and *Vogoo*). *RACOFI, Aura* and *Duine Toolkit* are hybrid recommendation engines. *RACOFI* adjusts a collaborative filter prediction with mechanisms coming from content-based approaches. *Aura* uses collaborative recommendation but uses a

---

[3] http://www.opentaste.net/

mechanism that assigns and processes a set of tags to items to improve the recommendation. *Duine Toolkit* uses collaborative and content-based techniques.

GRSK is an hybrid recommendation engine that employs different basic and hybrid recommendation techniques. The purpose of including these different recommendation techniques is to make GRSK able to work with any application domain, independently from the number of users, the available user information, etc. On the other hand, it is based on the semantic description of the items in the domain.

7   Conclusions and Further Work

The GRSK, a *Generalist Recommender System Kernel*, relies on a specification of the domain represented within an ontology, thus being able to apply to any domain as long as there exists such an ontological representation. This makes the GRSK be *generalist* or domain-independent. The GRSK uses four Basic Recommendation Techniques (demographic, content-based, collaborative and general likes filtering), and two different Hybrid Techniques (mixed and weighed) to create the final ranked list of recommended items. The GRSK allows selecting the techniques and parameters that best suit the particular application domain. We have also shown the results obtained when applying the GRSK to two different application domains, e-Tourism and e-Movies, highlighting the adaptability of the GRSK, and showing the strengths and weaknesses on each domain.

Currently, we are working on the extension of GRSK to group recommendation [6]. Different innovative techniques like Incremental Intersection and Collaborative Incremental Intersection are being developed to compute the group preference model. Additionally, we are also working on the use of agreement techniques for group recommendations. The members of the group are modeled as agents who attempt achieving a reconciled solution for the whole group maximizing the user satisfaction. The inclusion of this technique will allow us to incorporate more sophisticated human-like behaviors into the group.

Acknowledgements. Partial support provided by Consolider Ingenio 2010 CSD2007-00022, Spanish Government Project MICINN TIN2008-6701-C03-01 and Valencian Government Project Prometeo 2008/051.

References

1. Adomavicius, G., Tuzhilin, A.: Toward the next generation of recommender systems: A survey of the state-of-the-art and possible extensions. IEEE Transactions on Knowledge and Data Engineering 17(6), 734–749 (2005)
2. Anderson, M., Ball, M., Boley, H., Greene, S., Howse, N., Lemire, D., McGrath, S.: Racofi: Rule-applying collaborative filtering systems. In: IEEE WIC COLA (2003)
3. Brozovsky, L.: Recommender system for a dating service. Master's thesis, KSI, MFF UK, Prague, Czech Republic (2006)
4. Burke, R.: The Adaptive Web, chapter Hybrid web recommender systems, pp. 377–408. Springer, Heidelberg (2007)
5. Deshpande, M., Karypis, G.: Item-based top-n recommendation algorithms. ACM Transactions on Information Systems 22(1), 143–177 (2004)

6. Garcia, I., Sebastia, L., Onaindia, E., Guzman, C.: A Group Recommender System for Tourist Activities. In: Di Noia, T., Buccafurri, F. (eds.) EC-Web 2009. LNCS, vol. 5692, pp. 26–37. Springer, Heidelberg (2009)
7. Jameson, A.: More than the sum of its members: Challenges for group recommender systems. In: Proceedings of the International Working Conference on Advanced Visual Interfaces, pp. 48–54. ACM, New York (2004)
8. Lamere, P., Green, S.: Project aura - recommendation for the rest of us. JavaOne (2008)
9. Lemire, D., McGrath, S.: Implementing a rating-based item-to-item recommender system in php/sql. D-01, On delette.com (2005)
10. Ogston, E., Bakker, A., van Steen, M.: On the value of random opinions in decentralized recommendation. In: Eliassen, F., Montresor, A. (eds.) DAIS 2006. LNCS, vol. 4025, pp. 84–98. Springer, Heidelberg (2006)
11. Pazzani, M.J.: A framework for collaborative, content-based and demographic filtering. Artificial Intelligence Review 13, 393–408 (1999)
12. Plua, C., Jameson, A.: Collaborative preference elicitation in a group travel recommender system. In: Proceedings of the AH Workshop on Recommendation and Personalization in eCommerce, Malaga, Spain, pp. 148–154 (2002)
13. Resnick, P., Varian, H.: Recommender systems. Communications of the ACM 40(3), 56–58 (1997)
14. Sebastia, L., Garcia, I., Onaindia, E., Guzman, C.: e-Tourism: a tourist recommendation and planning application. International Journal on Artificial Intelligence Tools (WSPC-IJAIT) 18(5), 717–738 (2009)
15. Li, T., Anand, S.S.: Exploiting Domain Knowledge by Automated Taxonomy Generation in Recommender Systems. In: Di Noia, T., Buccafurri, F. (eds.) EC-Web 2009. LNCS, vol. 5692, pp. 120–131. Springer, Heidelberg (2009)
16. van Setten, M., Reitsma, J., Ebben, P.: Duine toolkit - user manual. Technical report, Telematica Instituut (2006)

Extending User Profiles in Collaborative Filtering Algorithms to Alleviate the Sparsity Problem

Toon De Pessemier, Kris Vanhecke, Simon Dooms,
Tom Deryckere, and Luc Martens

Ghent University - IBBT, Department of Information Technology
Gaston Crommenlaan 8, B-9050 Ghent, Belgium
{toon.depessemier,kris.vanhecke,simon.dooms,
tom.deryckere,luc.martens}@intec.ugent.be
http://www.wica.intec.ugent.be

Abstract. The overabundance of information and the related difficulty to discover interesting content has complicated the selection process for end-users. Recommender systems try to assist in this content-selection process by using intelligent personalisation techniques which filter the information. Most commonly-used recommendation algorithms are based on Collaborative Filtering (CF). However, present-day CF techniques are optimized for suggesting provider-generated content and partially lose their effectiveness when recommending user-generated content. Therefore, we propose an advanced CF algorithm which considers the specific characteristics of user-generated content (like the sparsity of the data matrix). To alleviate this sparsity problem, profiles are extended with probable future consumptions. These extended profiles increase the profile overlap probability, thereby increasing the number of neighbours used for calculating the recommendations. This way, the recommendations become more precise and diverse compared to traditional CF recommendations. This paper explains the proposed algorithm in detail and demonstrates the improvements on standard CF.

Keywords: Collaborative filtering, Recommender system, Personalisation, Algorithm, Sparsity.

1 Introduction

Various Web 2.0 sites (like YouTube, Digg, Flickr, Google Video...) have an over-whelming bulk of user-generated content available for online consumers. Although this exploding offer can be seen as a way to meet the specific demands and expectations of users, it has complicated the content selection process to the extent that users are overloaded with information and risk to 'get lost': though an abundance of content is available, obtaining useful and relevant content is often difficult. Traditional filtering tools, like keyword-based or filtered searches, are not capable to weed out irrelevant content or provide too much search results. An additional filtering based on the overall popularity (expressed by consumption patterns or user ratings) can assist, but requires

J. Filipe and J. Cordeiro (Eds.): WEBIST 2010, LNBIP 75, pp. 230–244, 2011.

a broad basis of user feedback before it can make reasonable suggestions. Furthermore, this technique does not consider personal preferences and individual consumption behaviour, since only the most popular content will be suggested. This situation reinforces the role of (collaborative) filtering tools and stimulates the development of recommender systems that assist users in finding the most relevant content.

The remainder of this paper is organized as follows: Section 2 provides an overview of related work regarding recommender systems in various application domains. Section 3 discusses collaborative filtering techniques and the problems related to sparse data sets. In Section 4, we present an extended version of the CF to overcome these problems. Our evaluation methodology and utilized datasets are described in Section 5. Section 6 elaborates on the obtained results and compares the proposed algorithm with the traditional CF. Optimisations and potential drawbacks of the proposed algorithm are discussed in Section 7. Finally, we offer a brief conclusion on our research results and point out interesting future work in Section 8.

2   Related Work

The overabundance of information and the related difficulty to discover interesting content have already been addressed in several contexts. Online shops, like Amazon [14], internet radios, like Last.FM [4], and video sharing website, like YouTube [6] apply recommendation techniques to personalize their website according to the needs of each user. Purchasing, clicking and rating behaviour are valuable information channels for online retailers and content providers to investigate consumers' interests and generate personalized recommendations [13].

Netflix is an online, mail-based, DVD rental service in the United States. Customers have the possibility to express their appreciation for a rented movie by a star-rating mechanism on the Netflix website. These user ratings, representing the user's preferences, are used as input for the Netflix recommender to generate personalized movie suggestions. Convinced by the potential of an accurate recommendation system, Netflix published a large dataset and started a competition to find the most suitable recommendation algorithm for their store in October 2006. In this context, many research groups have competed to find the best movie recommendation algorithm based on the Netflix dataset [1].

The introduction of digital television entails an increase in the number of available TV channels and the information overload linked thereto. Consequently, new standards to describe this content, e.g. TV-Anytime [7], and advanced electronic program guides, which simplify the navigation and selection of TV programs, become necessary . Several personalized TV guide systems which filter and recommend TV programs according to the user's preferences, have been developed for set-top boxes and personal digital recorders [21].

Besides these traditional premium content sources (i.e. provider-generated content), user-generated content (like personal photos, videos, or bookmarks) has received a more prominent role on the web in recent years. These Web 2.0 applications use more pragmatic approaches, like tagging, to annotate content than the traditional metadata standards. Moreover, user-generated content services are characterized by an immense content growth, which introduces sparsity problems for recommender systems.

3   Collaborative Filtering

3.1   Traditional Collaborative Filtering Algorithms

Most commonly-used recommendation algorithms are based on Collaborative Filtering (CF) techniques because they generally provide better results than Content-Based (CB) methods and require no metadata of the content [9]. To describe these recommendation algorithms, the 'item' concept is introduced as a general term for any kind of content or information (e.g., a book, video or picture) and accordingly, 'consumption behaviour' is a more general expression for user feedback (like ratings or purchases) on these items. Most literature reviews distinguish two important classes of CF: user-based and item-based, supplemented with several optional variations on them. To generate personal recommendations for a target user, user-based CF algorithms start by finding a set of neighbouring users whose purchased or rated items overlap this target user's purchased or rated items. To identify these neighbours, users are represented as an N-dimensional vector of potential consumptions, where N is the number of distinct catalogue items. Consumptions of items (like purchases or ratings) are recorded in the corresponding components of this vector. However, this profile vector may remain extremely sparse (i.e. containing a lot of missing values) for the majority of users who purchased or rated only a very small fraction of the available catalogue items. Subsequently, the composition of neighbourhoods of like-minded users is based on user similarity values.

The similarity of two users, j and k, symbolized by their consumption vectors, U_j and U_k, can be measured in different ways. A commonly-used method to determine the similarity is measuring the cosine of the angle between the two consumption vectors [17].

$$Similarity(\boldsymbol{U}_j, \boldsymbol{U}_k) = cosine(\boldsymbol{U}_j, \boldsymbol{U}_k) = \frac{\boldsymbol{U}_j \cdot \boldsymbol{U}_k}{||\boldsymbol{U}_j|| \, ||\boldsymbol{U}_k||} \tag{1}$$

Next, the algorithm aggregates the items consumed by these neighbours while taking into account the similarity values. The items that the target user has already purchased or rated are eliminated, and the remaining items are candidate recommendations for this user [14]. An alternative for this user-based CF technique is item-based CF, a technique that matches each of the user's purchased or rated items to similar items and then combines those similar items into a recommendation list. For measuring the similarity of items, the same metrics can be used as with the user-based CF. Because of scalability reasons, this technique is often used to calculate recommendations for big online shops, like Amazon, where the number of users is much higher than the number of items [14].

3.2   Collaborative Filtering based on Sparse Datasets

Despite the popularity of CF, its applicability is limited due to the sparsity problem, which refers to the situation that the consumption data in the profile vectors are lacking or insufficient to calculate reliable recommendations. This sparsity problem is a big concern for user-generated content systems, since the content offer is rapidly growing and most users only consume a small fraction of the available items.

As a direct consequence of this sparsity problem, the number of similar users, i.e. the neighbours of the target user, might be very limited with a user-based CF technique. Indeed, to determine the similarity, almost all metrics rely on the profile overlap, which might be very incomplete or even nonexistent. In addition, because of this sparsity, the majority of these neighbours might have a profile vector containing a small number of consumed items. Because the prospective personal recommendations are limited to the set of items consumed by neighbours, the variety, quality and quantity of the final recommendation list might be inadequate. A comparable reasoning is applicable to item-based CF techniques that work on sparse profile data. Users might have consumed a small number of items, which in turn also have a limited number of neighbouring items. Again, the CF algorithm is restricted to a narrow set of neighbouring items to generate the personal suggestions, which is pernicious for the efficiency of the recommender.

In an attempt to provide high-quality recommendations, even based on sparse consumption data, various solutions are proposed in literature [16]. Most of these techniques use trust inferences, transitive associations between users that are based on an underlying social network, to deal with the sparsity and cold-start problems of CF[20]. Nevertheless, these underlying social networks are often insufficiently developed in content-delivery systems or even nonexistent for (new) web-based applications that desire to offer personalized recommendations.

'Default voting' is an extension to the traditional CF algorithms which tries to solve this sparsity problem without exploiting a social network. A default value is assumed as 'vote' for items without an explicit purchase or rating[2] . Although this technique enlarges the profile overlap, it can not identify more contributory neighbours than the traditional CF approach. Other approaches to deal with sparse data profiles, such as link analysis techniques [11] or spreading activation algorithms [12] are too computationally intensive to be applied on large datasets.

3.3 Recommendations for User-Generated Content

Because of the inherent characteristics of user-generated content systems, the size of the content catalogue (i.e. the number of items) is often significantly bigger compared to provider-generated content systems. User-generated content requires less production efforts. Consequently, the content production rate and the number of distinct publishers are massive. For example, YouTube enjoys 65,000 daily new uploads [5]. Due to these varied content (production) characteristics, the sparsity problem is a major concern for user-generated content systems. As a result, the recommender accuracy might be inadequate if the traditional CF techniques are ported from provider-generated content systems to user-generated content systems without any adaptation.

Therefore, we developed an advance CF algorithm that extends the user profiles based on the probability that an item will be consumed in the future. The denser profile vectors increase the profile overlap probability, which increases the number of neighbours in a CF algorithm. These extended profiles and additionally identified neighbours, in response to the sparsity problem, lead to more precise and varied content recommendations.

4   Probability-Based Extended Profile Filtering

4.1   Algorithm Details

To increase the number of neighbours for a target user, and to strengthen the existing similarities, the profile overlap has to be augmented. This can be achieved by a larger amount of consumption behaviour. Because stimulating the users to consume more content is not an option in most cases, we opted for an artificial profile extension based on the future consumption probability. Our developed algorithm (called probability-based extended profile filtering) is an iterative process consisting of four phases.

In the first phase, a traditional CF algorithm is employed to generate a top-N recommendation list with a corresponding confidence value for each recommendation based on the existing, sparse profiles [18]. These recommendations, which might be inaccurate due to the sparsity, are not used as the final suggestions but only as an information source for subsequent calculations.

In the second phase, all the initial profiles that do not contain a minimum number of consumptions are extended. To make these sparse profiles denser, presumable future consumptions are inserted into the profile vectors. These additional consumptions are based on two information sources: the general probability and the profile-based probability that the item will be consumed in the near future.

In the user-based version of the proposed algorithm, existing user profiles are extended with the items that have the highest probability to be consumed by the user in the near future. The general probability that a specific item will be consumed by a specific user without a priori knowledge of that user is proportional to the current popularity of the item. So, this probability is estimated by a linear function of the popularity of the item: $f(x) = a \cdot x + b$, in which f(x) is the probability of consumption, x is the popularity of the item and a and b are parameters that can be optimized according to the content type. Especially for user-generated content systems, the popularity of the 'top items' can vary rapidly in time. Additionally, the probability that a specific item will be consumed by a user can also be calculated based on the user's profile as a priori knowledge. This probability is inversely proportional to the index of the item in the personal top-N recommendation list, and can be estimated by the confidence value which is calculated by the traditional CF system in phase 1. In fact, this top-N recommendation list is a prediction of the items which the user will like or consume in the near future.

In the item-based version of the extended CF, item profiles, which contain the users who consumed the item in the past, are supplemented with the most likely future consumers. The general probability that a specific user will consume a specific item, without any knowledge of the item, is proportional to the present intensity of the consumption behaviour of that user. Again, a linear function can be used to estimate this probability. With additional a priori knowledge of the item, the calculations can be repeated. Then, the probability is inversely proportional to the index of the specific user in the top-N list of users who are the most likely to consume the item in the future. This list and the associated confidence values can be generated based on the results of the traditional item-based CF algorithm [18].

Based on these general and profile-based probabilities, the user or item profiles are completed, if possible, until the minimum profile threshold is reached. Therefore, the predicted future consumptions resulting from the two methods (without and with a priori knowledge) are merged via an aggregator function. (In the bench-marks we used the maximum as an aggregator operator.) However, these predicted consumptions are marked as 'uncertain' in contrast to the initial consumptions which are linked to the user behaviour (i.e. the ratings or purchases). For example for a web shop, the real purchases are indicated by a value of 1, which refers to a 100% guaranteed consumption, whereas the potential future consumptions are represented by a decimal value between 0 and 1, according to the probability value, in the profile vector. This first and second phase may consist of several successive iterations until a minimum threshold for the profile size is reached.

Based on these extended profile vectors, the similarities are recalculated with the chosen similarity metric, e.g. the cosine similarity (equation 1), in a third phase. Because of the additional future consumptions, the profile overlap and accordingly the number of neighbours will be increased, compared to the first phase. In the item-based version, these similarities can be used as an extended 'related item' section (like on Amazon: customers who bought this item also bought...).

To produce personal suggestions, a recommendation vector is generated based on these extended profile vectors, in a fourth phase. For the user-based algorithm, the recommendation vector, R_j, for target user j can be calculated as:

$$R_j = \frac{\sum_{k=1,k\neq j}^{M} U_k \cdot Similarity(U_j, U_k)}{\sum_{k=1,k\neq j}^{M} Similarity(U_j, U_k)} \tag{2}$$

where M stands for the number of users in the sysem. U_j and U_k represent the extended consumption vectors of users j and k respectively, which might contain real values. Subsequently, the top-N recommendations are obtained by selecting the indices of the components with the highest values from the recommendation vector, R_j, and eliminating the items which are already consumed by user j in the past.

4.2 Algorithm Example

The following concrete example of a small content delivery system (e.g. a video sharing website) can give more insights in the proposed recommendation algorithm. Table 1 illustrates the watching behaviour of 5 users and 8 videos in the system via the consumption matrix. The watched videos are indicated by a 'one' in the column of the user. E.g., user A has watched the videos 3, 6 and 8 in this example. Personal recommendations for the end-users can be calculated based on the data in this matrix. By way of illustration, the recommendations for user A are calculated in this example. Therefore, a traditional user-based CF algorithm is used in the first phase. To start, the neighbours of user A in the system are calculated based on the cosine similarity metric as illustrated in Table 2. Since all standard similarity metrics are based on the profile overlap between a couple of users, only 1 neighbour of user A can be identified, namely user B. Next, the personal recommendations are discovered by selecting the videos that neighbours watched in the past. Because the system does not suggest videos that the user has already watched, only 1 new video can be recommended to user A, namely video 5.

Table 1. The consumption matrix of the example. Videos watched by the end-user are indicated by a 'one'

Watching Behaviour	User A	User B	User C	User D	User E
Video 1			1		
Video 2				1	1
Video 3	1	1			
Video 4			1		
Video 5		1	1	1	
Video 6	1	1			
Video 7					1
Video 8	1	1			

Table 2. The similarity matrix that is calculated based on the original consumption matrix. Missing values indicate a zero similarity between two users.

Similarity	User A	User B	User C	User D	User E
User A	1	0.8660			
User B	0.8660	1	0.2887	0.3536	
User C		0.2887	1	0.4082	
User D		0.3536	0.4082	1	0.5000
User E				0.5000	1

In contrast, our proposed algorithm tries to extend the profile vectors with potential future consumptions, before generating the recommendations. The general probability that a video will be watched, without a priori knowledge, is proportional to the current popularity of the video. In this small example, video 5 is the most popular video (3 views). So, this video might be added as a potential future consumption to the profile vector of user A and E (i.e. the users who have not yet watched the video). However for simplicity of the example, this general probability of watching a video is not considered during the selection of potential future consumptions.

Additionally, the probability of watching a video can be calculated based on the confidence value of the user's traditional CF recommendations. This confidence value is derived (e.g. by a linear combination) from the similarity values of the identified neighbours who consumed the recommended video. Table 3 illustrates the consumption matrix after the addition of the confidence values calculated by a simple CF algorithm. This matrix contains decimal values for the potential future consumptions making it less sparse than the former. This extended consumption matrix is the input for recalculating the user similarities, which are illustrated in Table 4. Subsequently, these updated user similarities are used in equation 2 for calculating the final recommendations. The recommendations for user A, together with the accompanying prediction values are listed in Table 5. The prediction values show that the most interesting suggestion for user C is still video 5 (just like the CF predicted). However, additional video recommendations can be provided based on Table 5. In descending order of prediction value: video 5, 2, 1, 4 and 7.

Table 3. The consumption matrix after extending the profiles with potential future consumptions

Ticketing	User A	User B	User C	User D	User E
Video 1		0.2887	1	0.4082	
Video 2		0.3536	0.4082	1	1
Video 3	1	1	0.2887	0.3536	
Video 4		0.2887	1	0.4082	
Video 5	0.8660	1	1	1	0.5000
Video 6	1	1	0.2887	0.3536	
Video 7				0.5000	1
Video 8	1	1	0.2887	0.3536	

Table 4. The similarity matrix that is calculated based on the extended consumption matrix. Missing values indicate a zero similarity between two users.

Similarity	User A	User B	User C	User D	User E
User A	1	0.9637	0.4839	0.5785	0.1491
User B	0.9637	1	0.6758	0.7437	0.2747
User C	0.4839	0.6758	1	0.7961	0.3276
User D	0.5785	0.7437	0.7961	1	0.7752
User E	0.1491	0.2747	0.3276	0.7752	1

Table 5. The recommendations with the accompanying prediction values for user A, calculated with the probability-based extended profile filtering algorithm

Prediction	Prediction Value
$R_{a,1}$	0.4589
$R_{a,2}$	0.5820
$R_{a,4}$	0.4589
$R_{a,5}$	0.9657
$R_{a,7}$	0.2015

Alternatively, in addition to the traditional CF, the general popularity of the videos could be used to generate more recommendations (e.g., suggestions besides video 5 for user A). However, such a popular-item recommender can make no distinction between equally popular videos (like 1, 4 and 7 which are each watched by one user). In contrast, the proposed algorithm based on extended profiles can provide a (partial) ordering of these equally popular videos (video 1 = video 4 > video 7).

5   Evaluation Methodology

To estimate the accuracy of personal recommendations, two different evaluation methods are possible. On the one hand, online evaluation methods measure the user interactivity (like clicks or buying behaviour) with the recommendations on a running service. On the other hand, offline evaluation methods use a test set with consumption behaviour which has to be predicted based on a training set with consumption history. Although online evaluation methods are closest to reality, we opted for an offline evaluation based on datasets because such an evaluation is fast, reproducible and commonly used in recommendation research.

Therefore, we compared the proposed extended CF algorithm with the traditional CF algorithm based on evaluation metrics which are generated by an offline analysis using a dataset with consumption behaviour. Because the datasets that are commonly used to bench-mark recommendation algorithms (like Netflix, Movielens or Jester) contain too little sparse profiles and handle only provider-generated content, we evaluated our algorithm on a dataset of PianoFiles[1]. Pianofiles is a user-generated content site that offers users the opportunity to manage their personal collection of sheet music they like to play. Currently, users can manage their personal collection of sheet music on PianoFiles but they do not yet receive personal recommendations. The main consumption behaviour, used to feed the recommendation algorithm, consists of the personal collections of the users. Each addition to a personal collection is used to populate the consumption matrix. The dataset contains 401,593 items (music sheets), 80,683 active users and 1,553,586 distinct consumptions (individual additions of sheets to personal collections) in chronological order.

For evaluation purposes, we use 50% of the consumptions that are the most recent ones as the test set and use the remaining 50% of the consumption records as the input data. To analyse the performance of the algorithm under data of different sparsity levels, we compose 10 different training sets by selecting the first 10%, 20%, 30%, until 100% of the input data. The recommendation algorithm used these different training sets in successive iterations to generate personal suggestions. As commonly done for the evaluation of recommendations under sparse data [11], the test set was first filtered to include only consumptions that are possible to predict with the input data as a priori knowledge. A consumption of a sheet that is not contained in the input data or a consumption of a user without any consumption behaviour in the input data is not possible to predict with CF techniques. By eliminating the users and items without a priori knowledge, the CF algorithms can be compared more precisely based on the users (and items) which have specified preferences. Then, all users in this filtered test set were included into a set of target consumers. For each of these target consumers, the algorithm generated five ordered lists of 10, 20, 30, 40 and 50 recommendations respectively, which were compared with the test set. (Only the results for 10, 30 and 50 recommendations per user are shown in this paper, since the other results illustrate the same conclusions.) This offline evaluation methodology, in which a dataset is chronologically split into training set and test set, is commonly used for evaluating recommendation algorithms [8].

6 Results

6.1 Evaluation Metrics

One of the most used error metrics is the Root Mean Squared Error (RMSE) [19,10], which is also adopted by the official Netflix contest. However, the Netflix contest is

---

[1] http://www.pianofiles.com/

mainly focused on predicting accurate ratings for an entire set of items, while web-based content-delivery applications are most interested in providing the users with a short recommendation list of interesting items [3]. To evaluate this top-N recommendation task, i.e. a context where we are not interested in predicting user ratings with precision, but rather in giving an ordered list of N attractive suggestions to the users, error metrics are not meaningful. As a result, information-retrieval classification metrics, which evaluate the quality of a short list of recommendations, are the most suitable.

The most appropriate classification accuracy metrics for evaluating recommendations are precision and recall [3]. The precision is the ratio of the number of recommended items that match with future consumptions, and the total number of recommended items. In offline evaluations, the consumptions of the test set represent the future consumptions and the recommendations that match with these consumptions are called the *relevant recommendations*.

$$Precision = \frac{\# \; Relevant \; recommendations}{\# \; Recommendations} \tag{3}$$

The recall stands for the ratio of the number of relevant recommendations and the total number of future consumptions. Only the 'future consumptions' in the test set are considered as *relevant items* for the end-users in offline evaluations.

$$Recall = \frac{\# \; Relevant \; recommendations}{\# \; Relevant \; items} \tag{4}$$

It has been observed that precision and recall are inversely related and dependent on the length of the result list returned to the user [10]. If more recommended items are returned, precision decreases and recall increases. Therefore, to understand the global quality of a recommendation system, precision and recall is combined by means of the F1-measure.

$$F1 = \frac{2 \cdot Precision \cdot Recall}{Precision + Recall} \tag{5}$$

6.2   Bench-marked Algorithms

Since the item-based algorithms (the traditional item-based CF and the proposed item-based algorithm which extends profiles) generally achieved a very low performance on the PianoFiles dataset, we did not include the results of any item-based technique in the evaluation. This poor performance is mainly due to the nature of the dataset, which contains many more items than users. As a result, forming item neighbourhoods is actually much more difficult than forming user neighbourhoods [11]. Additionally, this ratio of users and items induces the big risk that item-based algorithms will trap users in a 'similarity hole', only giving exceptionally similar recommendations; e.g. once a user added a sheet of Michael Jackson to her collection, she would only receive recommendations for more Michael Jackson sheets [15]. Compared to this item-based CF, a user-based strategy achieved much better results based on the PianoFiles dataset.

6.3   Complete Training Set

In a first evaluation, we bench-marked the standard user-based CF algorithm (UBCF), which operates on the initially existing profiles [18], against the user-based version of our probability-based extended profile filtering (UBExtended), which extends the sparse profiles before generating the actual recommendations. In this accuracy evaluation, the UBExtended algorithm was configured to extend sparse profiles to a target size of 6 consumptions and the cosine similarity (equation 1) was used as a measure to compare profile vectors in both algorithms. The graphs in Figure 1(a), 1(c) and 1(e) illustrate the evaluation metrics (precision, recall and F1) for these two algorithms (UBCF and UBExtended). Due to the large content offer (401,593 items) and the sparsity of the dataset, the recommendation algorithms have a hard job to suggest the most appropriate content items for each user. Because of this, the absolute values of the evaluation metrics seem rather low. However, precision and recall values between 1 and 10% are very common in bench-marks of recommendation algorithms [12], [11].

The graphs illustrate that the most accurate results are obtained for iterations which are based on a large quantity of training data. As the size of the training set increases, more data about user behaviour becomes available. This supplementary training data can refine the user preferences, which leads to a higher precision. However, after the profile size has reached a critical point, supplementary training data have no more additional information value, which leads to a stagnating precision value. Besides additional information of existing users, the extra data contain information about the behaviour of new users for which no information was available in the first part(s) of the training set. These additional data make it possible to generate recommendations for more users, which explains the increasing recall value. However, the recommendations for these new users, which generally have a lower precision value because of a limited early profile, strengthen the stagnation of the general precision. At last, the F1 metric follows the progress of this precision and recall graph closely because of its definition. Besides these general trends, the graphs prove that the UBExtended algorithm outperforms the standard UBCF in all three evaluation metrics (precision, recall and F1) and for different sizes of the recommendation list. This improvement is especially noticeable for small training sets, which mainly consist of sparse user profiles.

6.4   Filtered Training Set: Sparse Profiles Only

To illustrate this superiority of the UBExtended algorithm for sparse profiles, a second evaluation was performed. To study the recommender performance on the subset of users with a sparse profile, the training set was submitted to an extra filter. This filter removed all the users with more than x consumptions from the training set to simulate the situation of a very novel content delivery system without 'well-developed' user profiles. In accordance with the first evaluation in which we extended sparse profiles to a target size of 6 consumptions, we chose in this second analysis for a filter that removes all users with a profile that is larger than 6 consumptions. In this way, a standard UBCF that operates on a dataset with only sparse profiles (profile size $\leq$ 6 consumptions), was compared with the UBExtended algorithm which extends these profiles to the target size (profile size $=$ 6 consumptions) before generating recommendations. Given the long-tail distribution of the profile size in content delivery systems, this subset of

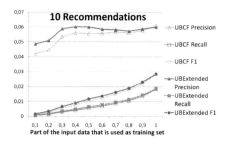

(a) 10 recommendations based on the initial training set

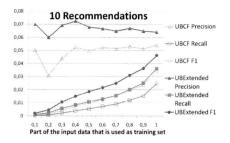

(b) 10 recommendations based on the training set which contains only sparse profiles

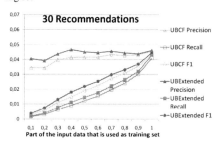

(c) 30 recommendations based on the initial training set

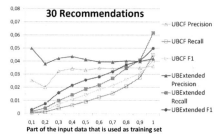

(d) 30 recommendations based on the training set which contains only sparse profiles

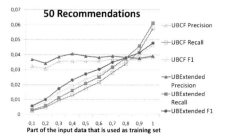

(e) 50 recommendations based on the initial training set

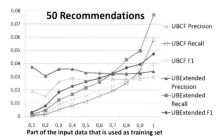

(f) 50 recommendations based on the training set which contains only sparse profiles

Fig. 1. The evaluation of the UBCF and UBExtended algorithm based on the precision, recall and F1 metric

sparse-profile consumers constitutes a considerable segment of the system users. This is illustrated in Figure 1(d) which visualizes the histogram of the profile size at PianoFiles, showing that the big majority of users only have a limited number of sheets in their collection.

Since the extra filter modifies the training and test sets, the absolute values of this evaluation can not be compared with the absolute values of the first evaluation, which is based on the unfiltered datasets. However, the differences between the UBCF and the UBExtended algorithm in this second evaluation, illustrated in Figure 1(b), 1(d)

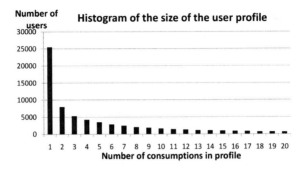

Fig. 2. Histogram of the number of sheets in the user profiles (i.e. the profile size) for the PianoFiles dataset. Profile sizes larger than 20 are not showed, because of the limited number of users that have such a profile.

and 1(f), compared with the differences between these algorithms in the first evaluation (Figure 1(a), 1(c) and 1(e)), confirm that the performance improvement of the UBExtended algorithm increases for sparser datasets. Finally, the graphs of this second evaluation show that for small training sets the precision might slightly fluctuate because of insufficient data and lots of new users.

7   Optimisations and Drawbacks

Since the parameters of the UBExtended algorithm are not yet optimized in this evaluation, the performance difference between the two bench-marked algorithms might even increase considerably. The UBExtended algorithm extends sparse profiles until each profile contains a predefined number of consumptions. This target profile size is an important parameter that has to be optimized as a function of the performance metrics. Although we have chosen a fixed size of 6 consumptions for the extended profiles in our evaluation, we believe this parameter might be a function of the general characteristics of the dataset, namely the overall sparsity of the data matrix, the number of items, and the number of users. Moreover, the procedure of extending the profiles, which is based on general and profile-based influences, can be fine-tuned. An optimal balance between this general and profile-based information to extend the profiles might result in more precise recommendations. Finally, some typical CF parameters have to be determined, such as the similarity metric and the number of neighbours used to calculate the recommendations.

Unfortunately, the accuracy improvement acquired with the UBExtended algorithm is associated with an extra calculation cost. Compared to the standard UBCF, the UBExtended algorithm consists of 2 extra phases: extending the profiles and recalculating the similarities after this extension. Especially the similarity calculation can be time-consuming due to its quadratic nature and therefore it may pose problems for systems that calculate the recommendations in real-time (i.e. generating recommendations when the web page is requested). However, since most recommender systems schedule the calculations and update their recommendations periodically, the additional calculation time is no major problem.

8   Conclusions and Future Work

In this research, we proposed an advanced collaborative filtering algorithm which takes into account the specific characteristics of user-generated content systems. The algorithm extends sparse profiles with the most likely future consumptions based on general and personal consumption behaviour. Our experimental study, using a dataset from a user-generated content site (PianoFiles), proved that the user-based version of the proposed algorithm achieves more accurate results than the standard user-based collaborative filtering algorithm, especially on sparse datasets. These results confirm the need to adapt traditional collaborative filtering techniques to the specific characteristics, such as the sparsity, of user-generated content systems. In future research, we will try to optimise the algorithm parameters to further improve the performance results. Besides, we will investigate if the principle of profile extension is applicable in other types of collaborative filtering algorithms.

Acknowledgements. We would like to thank the Research Foundation - Flanders (FWO), for the research position of Toon De Pessemier (Aspirant FWO). We would also like to express our appreciation to Thomas Bonte, the founder of PianoFiles, for putting the dataset of his website at our disposal.

References

1. Bell, R.M., Koren, Y.: Lessons from the netflix prize challenge. SIGKDD Explor. Newsl. 9(2), 75–79 (2007)
2. Breese, J.S., Heckerman, D., Kadie, C.: Empirical analysis of predictive algorithms for collaborative filtering, pp. 43–52. Morgan Kaufmann, San Francisco (1998)
3. Campochiaro, E., Casatta, R., Cremonesi, P., Turrin, R.: Do metrics make recommender algorithms? In: International Conference on Advanced Information Networking and Applications Workshops, pp. 648–653 (2009)
4. Celma, O., Cano, P.: From hits to niches?: or how popular artists can bias music recommendation and discovery. In: NETFLIX 2008: Proceedings of the 2nd KDD Workshop on Large-Scale Recommender Systems and the Netflix Prize Competition, pp. 1–8. ACM, New York (2008)
5. Cha, M., Kwak, H., Rodriguez, P., Ahn, Y.Y., Moon, S.: I tube, you tube, everybody tubes: analyzing the world's largest user generated content video system. In: IMC 2007: Proceedings of the 7th ACM SIGCOMM conference on Internet measurement, pp. 1–14. ACM, New York (2007)
6. Davidson, J., Liebald, B., Liu, J., Nandy, P., Van Vleet, T., Gargi, U., Gupta, S., He, Y., Lambert, M., Livingston, B., Sampath, D.: The youtube video recommendation system. In: RecSys 2010: Proceedings of the Fourth ACM Conference on Recommender Systems, pp. 293–296. ACM, New York (2010)
7. Evain, J.P., Martínez, J.M.: Tv-anytime phase 1 and mpeg-7. J. Am. Soc. Inf. Sci. Technol. 58(9), 1367–1373 (2007)
8. Hayes, C., Massa, P., Avesani, P., Cunningham, P.: An on-line evaluation framework for recommender systems. In: Workshop on Personalization and Recommendation in E-Commerce. Springer, Malaga (2002)

9. Herlocker, J.L., Konstan, J.A., Borchers, A., Riedl, J.: An algorithmic framework for performing collaborative filtering. In: SIGIR 1999: Proceedings of the 22nd Annual International ACM SIGIR Conference on Research and Development in Information Retrieval, pp. 230–237. ACM, New York (1999)

10. Herlocker, J.L., Konstan, J.A., Terveen, L.G., Riedl, J.T.: Evaluating collaborative filtering recommender systems. ACM Trans. Inf. Syst. 22(1), 5–53 (2004)

11. Huang, Z., Zeng, D., Chen, H.: A link analysis approach to recommendation with sparse data. In: AMCIS 2004: Americas Conference on Information Systems, New York, NY, USA (2004)

12. Huang, Z., Chen, H., Zeng, D.: Applying associative retrieval techniques to alleviate the sparsity problem in collaborative filtering. ACM Trans. Inf. Syst. 22(1), 116–142 (2004)

13. Karypis, G.: Evaluation of item-based top-n recommendation algorithms. In: CIKM 2001: Proceedings of the Tenth International Conference on Information and Knowledge Management, pp. 247–254. ACM, New York (2001)

14. Linden, G., Smith, B., York, J.: Amazon.com recommendations: item-to-item collaborative filtering. IEEE Internet Computing 7(1), 76–80 (2003),
    http://ieeexplore.ieee.org/xpls/abs_all.jsp?arnumber=1167344

15. McNee, S.M., Riedl, J., Konstan, J.A.: Being accurate is not enough: how accuracy metrics have hurt recommender systems. In: CHI 2006: extended abstracts on Human Factors in Computing Systems, pp. 1097–1101. ACM, New York (2006)

16. Papagelis, M., Plexousakis, D., Kutsuras, T.: Trust Management. Springer, Heidelberg (2005)

17. Sarwar, B., Karypis, G., Konstan, J., Riedl, J.: Analysis of recommendation algorithms for e-commerce. In: EC 2000: Proceedings of the 2nd ACM Conference on Electronic Commerce, pp. 158–167. ACM, New York (2000)

18. Segaran, T.: Programming collective intelligence. O'Reilly, Sebastopol (2007)

19. Shani, G.: Tutorial on evaluating recommender systems. In: RecSys 2010: Proceedings of the Fourth ACM Conference on Recommender Systems, pp. 1–1. ACM, New York (2010)

20. Weng, J., Miao, C., Goh, A., Shen, Z., Gay, R.: Trust-based agent community for collaborative recommendation. In: AAMAS 2006: Proceedings of the Fifth International Joint Conference on Autonomous Agents and Multiagent Systems, pp. 1260–1262. ACM, New York (2006)

21. Yu, Z., Zhou, X.: Tv3p: an adaptive assistant for personalized tv. IEEE Transactions on Consumer Electronics 50(1), 393–399 (2004)

Automatic Short Text Annotation
for Question Answering System

Gang Liu, Zhi Lu, Tianyong Hao, and Wenyin Liu

Dept of Computer Science, City University of Hong Kong
83 Tat Chee Avenue, HKSAR, China
{gangliu,luzhi2,tianyong}@student.cityu.edu.hk
csliuwy@cityu.edu.hk

Abstract. Semantic annotation for text is a well-studied topic. However, little contribution has been engaged in the application of short text annotation. In this article, an automatic annotation approach is proposed for such purpose, which annotates short text with semantic labels for question answering systems. In the first step, keywords are extracted from a question and then a semantic label selection module is used to select semantic labels to tag keywords. If there is no appropriate label, WordNet is employed to obtain candidate labels to annotate those keywords by calculating the similarity between each keyword in the question and the concept list in our predefined Tagger Ontology. To improve the accuracy of annotation, we also design a naïve Bayesian based method to distinguish multi-senses and assign best semantic labels by referring to historically annotated questions. Preliminary experiments on 6 categories show our approach achieves the precision of 76% in average.

Keywords: Text annotation, Similarity, Question answering, Tagger ontology.

1 Introduction

It has been shown that annotating text with appropriate tags may benefit many applications [1]. Such annotated information could provide clues for many information retrieval (IR) tasks to improve their performance, such as question answering, text categorization, topic detection and tracking, etc. In this paper, we address the problem of automatically annotating a special kind of text which is referred to as unstructured questions in question answering (QA) systems.

The past decade has seen increasing research on the usage of QA for providing more precise answers to users' questions. As a consequence, there are some automatic QA systems designed to retrieve information for given queries, such as Ask Jeeves[1]. In addition, more and more user interactive QA systems have been launched in recent years, including Yahoo! Answers[2], Microsoft QnA[3] and BuyAns[4]. These QA systems

---

[1] http://uk.ask.com/
[2] http://answers.yahoo.com/
[3] http://qna.live.com/
[4] http://www.buyans.com/

J. Filipe and J. Cordeiro (Eds.): WEBIST 2010, LNBIP 75, pp. 245–258, 2011.

provide the opportunities for users to post their questions as well as to answer others' questions. With the accumulation of a huge number of questions and answers, some user interactive QA systems may be able to automatically answer users' questions using text-processing techniques. However, due to the complexity of the human languages, most of the current QA systems are difficult to effectively analyze users' free text questions. Hence the accuracy of the question searching, classification and recommendation in these systems is not very satisfactory and the performance of these systems cannot outperform those well-known search engines, such as Google.

To solve these problems, many researchers are engaged in the efforts for improving the capability of machine understanding on questions. Cowie et al. [16] use the Mikrokosmos ontology in their method to represent knowledge about the question content as well as the answer. A specialized lexicon of English is then built to connect the words to their ontological meanings. Hao et al. [2] propose an approach to using semantic pattern to analyze questions. However, processing of natural language text is complicated especially when a word may have different meanings in different context. For example, given two questions "What are the differences between Apple and Dell?" and "What are the differences between apple and banana?", the word "Apple" in the first question represents a company name while "apple" in the second question refers to a kind of fruit. It is usually difficult for a computer to determine suitable meanings of words under the question context with only several words.

Furthermore, in a real QA system, questions are usually asked in an informal syntax. Some questions are submitted in long sentence while others are posted only with a few words. This kind of irregularity could increases the complexity of analyzing such questions. In a question, keywords are the core semantic units and can be viewed as main point for the given question. If a keyword is misunderstood by the machine, it is hard for the machine to extract right answers from the corpus for this question. Thus, the quality of recognizing and semantically annotating the keywords has significant effect on question understanding and answer retrieval.

Considering the importance of semantics of keywords, in this paper, we propose a new approach to acquiring keywords structures and automatically annotating keywords in questions with semantic labels to facilitate machine understanding. This method first uses a part of speech (POS) tool, such as MiniPar [3], to acquire keywords of a given question. A statistical technique is developed to unambiguously estimate and assign the most appropriate semantic labels for these keywords which contain more than one meaning. We make use of a two-word list named Semantic Labelled Terms (SLT), in which each item records the occurrence of a word's latent semantic labels with the condition that another word occurs at the same time. A naïve Bayesian model is developed to estimate the semantic label of each keyword, with the hypothesis that each word in a sentence is considered to be independently distributed. If there is no corresponding label extracted from SLT, WordNet[5] is then employed to obtain the upper concepts of the keyword by measuring the similarity between the keyword and its candidate labels in a semantic label list defined by the Tagger Ontology mapping table. In addition, an automatic semantic label tagging method is developed to estimate the most semantically related label from the candidates. All keywords in the original question are annotated with semantic labels selected using

---

[5] http://wordnet.princeton.edu/

the above method. In our experiment, we implement our method as a service in our user-interactive QA system – BuyAns. Six groups of words from different domains are chosen to be annotated with semantic labels and their annotated results are also evaluated. Experimental results show that in average 76% annotations are correct according to our evaluation method.

The rest of this paper is organized as follows: we briefly review related work in Section 2. Section 3 introduces the mechanism of the approach proposed in this paper. The experimental results and evaluation are presented in Section 4. Finally, we draw a conclusion and discuss future work in Section 5.

2 Related Work

In the past few years, annotation of documents as a tool for document representation and analysis are widely developed in the field of Information Retrieval (IR). Semantic Annotation is about assigning to the entities in the text links to their semantic descriptions [9]. Many approaches of semantic annotation are employed for tagging instances of ontology classes and mapping them into the ontology classes in the research of semantic web [10]. Carr et al. [6] provide an ontological reasoning service, which is used to represent a sophisticated conceptual model of document words and their relationships. They use their self-defined data called metadata to annotate the web resources. In a webpage, metadata provides links into and from its resources. With metadata, such a web-based, open hypermedia linking service is created by a conceptual model of document terminology. Users could query the metadata to find their wanted resources in the Web. Handschuh et al. [7] present the semantic annotation in the S-CREAM project. The approach makes use of machine learning techniques to automatically extract the relations between the entities. All of these entities are annotated in advance. A similar approach is also taken within the MnM [8], which provides an annotation method for marking up web pages with semantic contents. It integrates a web browser with an ontology editor where semantic annotations can be placed inline and refer to an ontology server, accessible through an API. Kiryakov et al. [9] proposed a particular schema for semantic annotation with respect to real-word entities. They introduce an upper-level ontology (of about 250 classes and 100 properties), which starts with some basic philosophical distinctions and then goes down to the most common entity types (people, companies, cities, etc.). Thus it encodes many of the domain-independent commonsense concepts and allows straightforward domain-specific extensions. On the basis of the ontology, their information extraction system can obtain the automatic semantic annotation with references to classes in the ontology and to instances.

In the field of computational linguistics, word sense disambiguation (WSD) in sentence annotation is an open problem, which comprises the process of identifying which sense of a word is used in any given sentence, in which the word has a number of distinct senses (polysemy). Solution of this problem impacts such other tasks of computation linguistics, such as discourse, improving relevance of search engines, reference resolution, coherence (linguistics), inference and others. These approaches normally work by defining a window of N content words around each word to be disambiguated in the corpus, and statistically analyzing those N surrounding words.

Two shallow approaches used to train and then disambiguate are Naïve Bayes classifiers and decision trees. In recent research, kernel based methods such as support vector machines have shown superior performance in supervised learning.

In the application of QA systems, approaches of annotation are developed to analyze text of questions and extract the structure of questions. Veale [11] uses the meta-knowledge to annotating a question and generate an information-retrieval query. With this query, the system searches an authoritative text archive to retrieve relevant documents and extracts the semantic entities from these documents as candidate answers to the given question. In his annotation method, non-focal words in a question would be pruned and focus words would be expanded by adding synonyms and other correlated disjuncts. All these possible disjunctions combined by the conjunction operators (e.g. #add, #or) are presented as annotations in stand of the focus word. Prager et al. [4] present a technique for QA called Predictive Annotation. Predictive Annotation identifies potential answers to questions in text, annotates them accordingly and indexes them. They extract the interrogative pronouns such as what, where and how long as Question Type. They choose an intermediate level of about 20 categories, which correspond fairly close to the name–entity types of [5]. Each category is identified by a construct called *QA-Token*. The *QA-Token* serves both as a category label and a text-string used in the process. For example, the query "How tall is the Matterhorn" gets translated into the new format of "*LENGTH$*" is the Matterhorn. Thus the question is converted into a form suitable for their search engine and then the relative answers are returned to the users. In the question process, all the interrogative pronouns are treated as the *Question Type*. If a question posted is not well-formed or without the interrogative pronoun, their system might fail to process it. Thus it might not flexible for the query analysis process and question representation. Prager et al. [12] also propose another method called virtual annotation for answering the *what-is* questions. They extract Question Type and target word from a user well-form question. They look up the target word in a thesaurus such as WordNet and use *hypernyms* returned by WordNet as the answers for the given *what-is* question. To obtain best suitable answer from these hypernyms, they use each hypernym with its target word as the query to search in their database. The hypernym which has the most frequently co-occurring with the target word is selected as the answer. This method is not flawless. One problem is that the hierarchy in WordNet does not always correspond to the way people define the word. Another one causing the error resource is *polysemy*. In these circumstances, the hypernym is not always suitable for the answer.

In the User-Interactive QA field, the mentioned approaches of annotation are not widely used for the text-processing of the questions. Partly because current methods are limited in analyzing informal questions and could not effectively distinguish polysemous keywords in the questions automatically. Therefore, this paper has proposed a new automatic annotation method of identifying and selecting the most related semantic labels for tagging the keywords of the questions. This method employs an effective technique in indicating the word-senses of the polysemous words. Moreover, the new format structure with such semantic annotation is well formed to represent the original question and could be easily recognized and understood by the machine.

3 The Approach

To annotate a free text question, the process of our proposed approach consists of three main modules: keywords extraction module, semantic label selection module and semantic label tagging module. Given a new free text question, the keywords extraction module firstly pre-processes the question using stemming, Part-of-Speech and Name Entity Recognition to acquire all the key nouns (also referred to as keyword). In the semantic label selection module, our system uses keywords as a query to match the records in Semantic Labelled Terms (SLT) to obtain the suitable semantic labels to annotate the keywords extracted in the keywords extraction module.

SLT is built as a kind of semantic dictionary, which uses a formatted two-word list to record the occurrences of two words co-occurred in the same question with their corresponding semantic labels [18]. SLT consists of two parts: one-word list and two-word list. In the one-word list, each item contains one word, its corresponding semantic labels and the occurrences of this word tagged by the semantic labels historically. Each element in the one-word list is formatted as follows:

$$([Word_i] \text{ \textbf{HAVING} } [Semantic\_labels]): Occurrence$$

On the other hand, the two-word list considers the semantic label to each word in the context of a question. In the two-word list, each item records the occurrences of semantic labels for every pairs of words in a question. We format each element in the two-word list as follows:

$$([Word1] \text{ \textbf{HAVING} } [Semantic\_labels1] \text{ \textbf{WITH} } [Word2]$$
$$\text{\textbf{HAVING} } [Semantic\_labels2]): Occurrence$$

where the *Semantic_labels* can be added and the *Occurrence* can be increased and updated when there are new semantic labels used for the current word.

For the keywords in the given free text question, if there are records matched in SLT, the system retrieves the related semantic labels for them. Since some keywords are polysemous and several related records may be matched, the system employs a naïve Bayesian model to select the most relevant semantic label from those candidate records. If the keywords are not matched in SLT, the semantic label tagging module is called, in which each keyword is queried in WordNet to obtain its upper concepts and then corresponding concepts are retrieved with the Tagger Ontology (cf. 3.3). Since all the concepts in this ontology are mapped to WordNet, the related semantic labels in this ontology can be acquired by calculating the similarity between the keyword and each matched concept and finally are used for annotating the keywords of the question. The related workflow is shown in Fig. 1.

3.1 Finding Key Nouns Extraction

Given a new free text sentence, it is important to analyze key nouns, which is the nouns in the main structure of the sentence, by using nature language processing techniques. There are many Part-of-Speech methods and tools such as TreeTagger[6].

---

[6] http://www.ims.uni-stuttgart.de/projekte/corplex/TreeTagger/

Most of these tools identify all the words without considering the importance of them in the sentence. Therefore, the nouns even in attributive clauses are also identified. Such nouns actually decrease the accuracy of the semantic representation of main point in the sentence. In our research, we only consider the nouns in the main structure of a sentence and call them key nouns.

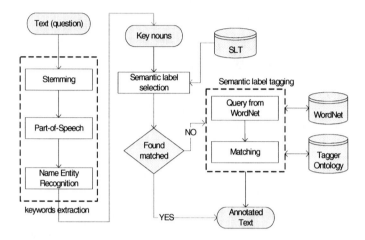

Fig. 1. Workflow of automatic text annotation with semantic labels

Dependency Grammar (DG) is a class of syntactic theories developed by Lucien Tesnière. The sentence structure is determined by the relation between a word (a head) and its dependents, which is distinct from phrase structure grammars[7]. The dependency relationship in this model is an asymmetric relationship between a word called head (a.k.a., governor) and another one called modifier [13]. This kind of relationship can be used to analyze the dependency thus to acquire the main structure and key nouns effectively. MiniPar is a broad-coverage parser for the English language [3]. An evaluation with the SUSANNE corpus shows that MiniPar achieves about 88% precision and 80% recall with respect to dependency relationships[8].

E0	(() fin C	*	)			
1	(What	~ N	E0	whn	(**gov** fin))	
2	(is be VBE	E0	i	(gov fin))		
E2	(() what N	4	subj	(**gov** *density*)	(antecedent 1))	
3	(the ~ Det	4	det	(gov *density*))		
4	(*density*	~ N	2	pred	(**gov** *be*))	
5	(of ~ Prep	4	mod	(gov *density*))		
6	(water	~ N	5	pcomp-n (**gov** of))		
7	(? ~ U	*	punc)			

Fig. 2. Dependency relationship of "*What is the density of water?*" processed by MiniPar

---

[7] http://en.wikipedia.org/wiki/Dependency_grammar
[8] http://www.cs.ualberta.ca/~lindek/downloads.htm

Therefore, we use MiniPar to discover and acquire the key nouns by analyzing the dependency relationship. An output of MiniPar mainly consists of three components in the form of *"[word, lexicon category, head]"*. Fig. 2. shows the output with an example of "What is the density of water?".

In this example, the key noun "density", which indicates that the asker concerns one property "density" of the liquid "water", can be acquired firstly in this short text by the dependency grammar. As a result, the word "density" is regarded as a key noun for the following process.

3.2 Semantic Label Selection Based on Naïve Bayesian Model

Since the high diversity of language expression, a text sentence could be described in many ways and the same word in different contexts would have totally different meanings. Thus annotation of the multiple meaning words is a challenging research work. For better annotating keywords in a text paragraph (e.g., a question) from multiple meanings, we employ a naïve Bayesian formulation with the hypothesis that each word in a question is thought to be independently distributed when determining the semantic label of each word. Given a new question, the system first removes stop words and then acquires all keywords $<Word_1, Word_2,..., Word_n>$. For any two words $Word_i$ and $Word_j$, the probability of $Word_i$ assigned with the semantic label $label'$ can be calculated by Equation (1).

$$P(Word_i \rightarrow label'|Word_j) = \frac{P(Word_i \rightarrow label')P(Word_j|Word_i \rightarrow label')}{\sum_{k=1}^{m} P(Word_i \rightarrow label_k)P(Word_j|Word_i \rightarrow label_k)}, (i \neq j) \quad (1)$$

where $P(Word_i \rightarrow label'|Word_j)$ denotes the probability of $Word_i$ assigned with semantic label $label'$ in the condition that $Word_i$ co-occurs with $Word_j$; $P(Word_i \rightarrow label')$ is the probability of $Word_i$ assigned with semantic label $label'$; $P(Word_j|Word_i \rightarrow label')$ represents the probability of occurring $Word_j$ when $Word_i$ is assigned with $label'$. $\sum_{k=1}^{m} P(Word_i \rightarrow label_k)P(Word_j|Word_i \rightarrow label_k)$ is the prior probability and it is a constant value. Hence we only need to calculate the product of $P(Word_i \rightarrow label')$ and $P(Word_j|Word_i \rightarrow label')$ to determine the semantic label of $Word_i$ using the following equation:

$$label* = \underset{label' \in LABEL}{\arg \max} \{P(Word_i \rightarrow label') \times P(Word_j|Word_i \rightarrow label')\} \quad (2)$$

For a given $Word_i$, $label'$ represents any label in the label set LABEL, which refers to all labels in Tagger Ontology. $label*$ is the most suitable label for the $Word_i$. Hence, $Word_i$ is annotated by $label*$ on the condition that $Word_i$ co-occurs with $Word_j$.

3.3 Tagger Ontology

The fundamental task of the question annotation is to annotate keywords with appro-appropriate semantic labels in a given question. WordNet are large lexical resources freely-available and widely used for annotation [17]. It provides a large database of English lexical items available online and establishes the connections between four types of Parts of Speech (POS) - noun, verb, adjective, and adverb. The basic unit in WordNet is *synset*, which is defined as a set of one or more synonyms. Commonly, a word may have several meanings. The specific meaning of one word under one type of POS is called a sense. Each sense of a word is in a different synset which has a gloss defining the concept it represents. Synsets are designed to connect the word and its corresponding sense through the explicit semantic relations including hypernym, hyponym for nouns, and hypernym and troponym for verbs. Holonymy relations constitute *is-a-kind-of* hierarchies and meronymy relations constitute *is-a-part-of* hierarchies respectively.

However, WordNet has too many upper concepts and complicated hierarchy levels for a given concept. Therefore it is difficult to organize and maintain semantic labels in controllable quantity, especially when these semantic labels are used for common users in a user interactive QA system. The concise representations of semantic labels have many advantages such as effectively simplifying the hierarchical structure of ontology as well as reducing complexity of the calculation of similarity between words and labels. Consequently, we propose a Tagger Ontology with only two levels to maintain these semantic labels.

Since the construction of the concept nodes in the ontology is for all open domains, we use a well defined standard taxonom[9] to build the core structure. The ontology is organized as containing certain concepts at the upper levels of the hierarchy of WordNet and it can be mapped to WordNet by a mapping table (samples are shown in Table 1). For better understanding and easy usage by users, it just includes two-level concepts, which have IS_A relationship used to represent hyponymy relationship between two semantic labels.

The semantic labels in the Tagger Ontology are defined as *[Concept1]\[Concept2]*, where these two concepts Concept 1 and Concept 2 have the relationship of *SubCategory(Concept1, Concept 2)*. Our Tagger Ontology consists of 7 first level concepts and 63 second level concepts in total. Table 1 shows some examples of semantic labels and their corresponding labels in WordNet.

The ontology is mainly used to extract a semantic label of a word in the following way. For a given question, we first obtain its syntactic structure and find all nouns using POS tagger. We then retrieve its super concepts of each noun in WordNet. We finally retrieve these super concepts in the Tagger Ontology to find a suitable semantic label for annotating each of nouns.

For example, for a given free text question "What is the color of rose?", the system first analyzes the question and obtains all the nouns "color" and "rose" by simple syntax analysis using POS tagger. The super concepts of each noun can be retrieved from WordNet. In this example, the super concepts of "rose" are "bush, woody plant, vascular plant, plant, organism, living thing, object, physical entity, entity". Among

---

[9] http://l2r.cs.uiuc.edu/~cogcomp/Data/QA/QC/definition.html

these concepts in WordNet, by mapping with the Tagger Ontology using the mapping table, only "plant, physical entity" are acquired. Hence, the semantic label of "rose" is tagged as *"[Physical_Entity\Plant]"* finally.

3.4 Semantic Label Tagging Based on Similarity

In our User-Interactive QA system – BuyAns, a mapping table, which represents the bijection between the two-level concepts in our Tagger Ontology and the upper level of hierarchy in WordNet [14], is manually constructed. In Table 1, a partial mapping table is given as an example.

Table 1. Examples of semantic labels and mapped words in WordNet

Semantic labels	Mapped words in WordNet
[human]\[title]	[abstraction]\[title]
[location]\[city]	[physical_entity]\[city]
[location]\[country]	[physical_entity]\[country]
[location]\[state]	[abstraction]\[state]
[numeric]\[count]	[abstraction]\[count]
[numeric]\[date]	[abstraction]\[date]
[numeric]\[distance]	[abstraction]\[distance]

To assign the best semantic label, we use similarity between words in WordNet and semantic labels in our Tagger Ontology to evaluate the candidate labels. To calculate the similarity, we first employ a traditional distance based similarity measurement [15], which is shown in Equation (3).

$$S(word_i, word_j) = \frac{1}{-\log(\frac{1}{Dis\tan ce}) + 1} \qquad (3)$$

Based on this distance based similarity method, we propose a new similarity measurement considering the word depth in the WordNet hierarchy structure. In this measurement, the semantic labels are mapped to the concepts in WordNet firstly. The similarities between each candidate noun acquired from the question by Minipar and all the concepts already mapped are calculated to find the maximum value. The equation of this measurement is shown as follows.

$$S'(word_i, word_j) = \frac{(Depth_{word_i} + Depth_{word_j})}{36} \times \frac{1}{-\log(\frac{1}{Distance}) + 1} \qquad (4)$$

where *Depth* refers to the quantity of concept nodes from the current concept to the top of the lexical hierarchy. *Distance* is defined as the quantity of concept nodes in the shortest path from *Word_i* to *Word_j* in the WordNet. Since the maximum value of *Depth* for the whole hierarchy in WordNet is 18, we use 36 to represent the double value of maximum *Depth*.

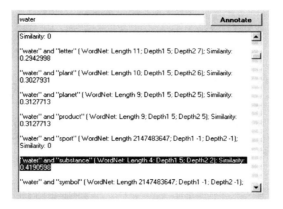

Fig. 3. Similarity calculation for the word "water"

Since a semantic label is defined as two related concepts (referred to as Section 3.3), the similarity between a given word and a semantic label can be obtained by representing the semantic label with the concepts. The label with the highest similarity value is selected as the most appropriate label for this word. Figure 3 shows an example of the similarity calculation for the word "water".

In this example, the label "substance" has the highest similarity in this measurement. Accordingly, the semantic label *"entity\substance"* in our Tagger Ontology is matched with its counterpart *"physical_entity\substance"* in WordNet. Therefore, the semantic labels *"entity\substa*nce" is assigned to the word "water" as the best annotation finally.

3.5   Application of Question Annotation

As we have discussed, question annotation can be used for many aspects in QA system, such as question classification and question recommendation. In our system, the annotated questions are mainly used on question classification and pattern-based automatic QA.

For the question classification, given a new question q, after acquiring m semantic labels of key nouns, which are the meaningful nouns obtained by sentence processing, we can calculate the score of each category C_j for each semantic label $Score(C_j,Label_n)$ by using LCMT [18]. The number of occurrence of category C_j containing $Label_n$ is also considered in the whole SLT. $Score(C_j,q)$, the score of each category C_j, for all m semantic labels in question q is calculated and the scores for all C_j are then compared and the categories are ordered according to their scores to obtain the top x categories.

For the pattern based automatic QA, we annotate questions with patterns and semantic labels. For a new question q, we can acquire a best matched pattern with Pattern matching technique. After that, since each question is assigned a unique pattern ID in our pattern database, we can acquire related questions and answers easily by query pattern ID in the QA Database with Pattern. For each question in such related question set QC $(qc_1, qc_2 \ldots qc_n)$ we can obtain its key nouns KNC (knc_1, knc_2, knc_m) $(0<m)$ easily since it is associated with a certain pattern. The similarity

$Sim(kn_i, knc_i)$ between each key noun k_n in q and knc_i in QC can be calculated. Thus the final similarity between them can be used to identify the most similar questions.

4 Experiments

To evaluate the proposed method, we develop a Windows application where a question can be annotated with semantic labels automatically. In our system, given a new question, MiniPar is used to identify key nouns. Afterward, with the Tagger Ontology, each noun selected is tagged with a semantic label. Two similarity measurements mentioned above are employed to acquire most appropriate semantic label for each of key nouns. The first similarity measurement only concerns the distance parameter of concepts in WordNet. The second measurement improves the first one by considering the depths of concepts. It also takes into account the whole depth of the WordNet hierarchical structure to normalize the similarity value. A user interface of the program including keywords extraction, two similarity measurements, and semantic label tagging is implemented.

Since MiniPar is used to extract keywords for a given question and the evaluation result is already provided in official website, it is unnecessary to test the performance of keywords extraction. In our experiment, we selected different categories of keywords and predefined them with semantic labels manually to build the ground truth dataset for semantic label annotation evaluation.

To evaluate the performance of annotation, the standard measurements such as recall, precision and F1-measures are used. Recall and precision measures reflect the different aspects of annotation performance. Usually, recall and precision have a trade-off relationship: increased precision results in decreased recall, and vice versa. In our experiment, recall is defined as the ratio of correct annotation made by the system to the total number of relevant keywords, which is greater than 0. Precision is defined as the ratio of correct annotations made by the system to the total number of keywords.

$$
RECALL = \frac{|Corrected\ annotation\ s|}{|R\,elevant\ keywords\,|},
$$
$$
PRECISION = \frac{|Corrected\ annotation\ s|}{|Total\ keywords\,|}
\tag{5}
$$

$$
F_1 = \frac{2 \times PRECISION \times RECALL}{PRECISION + RECALL}
\tag{6}
$$

In the experiment, since there is no open test data of question annotation available, we choose 6 categories and 50 nouns in each category from the Web as the test data to test the keywords annotation. Most of data are all from Wikipedia[10] and others are from open category list (e.g., animal category). Our system automatically annotates these words with semantic labels through two measurements. Since the ground truth in each category has already been defined, the correct annotations can be obtained by comparison of annotated labels and predefined annotations. The experimental results of keywords annotation for these categories with different similarity measurements

---

[10] http://en.wikipedia.org/wiki/Word_sense_disambiguation

are shown in Table 2. The average precision and recall for measurement 1 (M1, referred to equation 3) are 72% and 82%, respectively. For measurement 2 (M2, referred to equation 4), the precision and recall are 76% and 86%, respectively. For the category 4 (entity\planet), the annotation result is not very good. It is partly because many planets are named by religious gods like "Tethys" and "Jupiter" such that many of them are annotated as *"entity\religion"*. While in Category 2 (entity\vehicle), there is no description for some words like "quadricycle" and "Velomobile". Thus no annotation is for them. Other words like "toyota" and "benz" are car brands and also cannot find appropriate descriptions in WordNet. In Category 6 (entity\sport), some words like "canoe" and "yacht" are annotated as "entity\vehicle" while "throwing" and "fencing" are annotated as "entity\action".

To better measure the annotation performance, we also use the F1 measure which combines precision and recall measures, treated with equal importance, into a single parameter for optimization. Its definition is presented in equation (6) and its experimental results are shown in Figure 4. From the results, we can see that both two measurements achieve good performance over four categories (C1, C2, C3 and C5). Our proposed measurement 2 has a better performance than that of measurement 1 (traditional distance based method) in annotating the words from all of these categories.

Table 2. Experimental results of keywords annotation with two similarity measurements

		C1 entity\ animal	C2 entity\ vehicle	C3 location\ country	C4 entity\ lanet	C5 entity\ food	C6 entity\ sport	Avg.
Precision	M 1	0.98	0.64	0.92	0.38	0.9	0.5	0.72
	M 2	1	0.64	0.92	0.38	0.9	0.7	0.76
Recall	M 1	0.98	0.97	0.94	0.59	0.9	0.54	0.82
	M 2	1	0.97	0.94	0.59	0.9	0.76	0.86

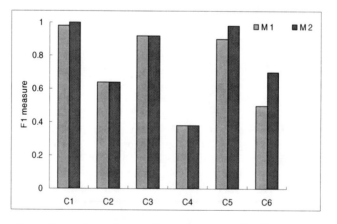

Fig. 4. Comparison of annotation performance using F1 measure

Given a question set $Q = \{q_1, q_2, \ldots q_m\}$, for each q_i $(1 \leq i \leq m)$, suppose there are n key nouns in q_i. $S(KN_j)$ $(1 \leq j \leq n)$ represents whether a key noun KN_j is selected for keyword annotation correctly. $A(KN_j)(1 \leq j \leq n)$ means whether a key noun is annotated with appropriate semantic label correctly. The values of $S(KN_j)$ and $A(KN_j)$ are either 0 or 1. Therefore, the average annotation precision of q_i can be calculated by equation (7).

$$PRECISION(q_i) = \frac{1}{n} \sum_{j=1}^{n} S(KN_j) \times A(KN_j) \tag{7}$$

Since all the key nouns are extracted by MiniPar and the average precision of MiniPar is 88%, which is provided in the official website, we can regard the precision of key nouns selection for annotation as 88%. Therefore, we can calculate the average precision of question annotation and the results are 63.4% and 66.9% using measurement 1 and measurement 2, respectively.

5 Conclusions and Future Work

In this paper, we propose a novel method to automatically annotate short text, questions with semantic labels. Given a new free text question, the keywords extraction module first processes the question to acquire all the keywords. In the semantic label selection module, we use each keyword as a query to match and retrieve the appropriate semantic labels from the semantic labelled terms (SLT) using a naïve Bayesian method. In the semantic label tagging module, each keyword is assigned with the best suitable label by calculating the similarity between the keyword and each mapped concept in WordNet and the Tagger Ontology. We implement the proposed method and evaluate it with a ground truth dataset. Six categories of nouns are tagged automatically and preliminary results show that the proposed automatic annotation method can achieve a precision of 76% in keywords annotation and 66.9% in question annotation.

However, some categories such as "planet" are difficult to be annotated precisely as analyzed in the experiments part. There are also some categories need to be improved in recognition of words with multiple senses. In future work, we will intend to investigate and evaluate more accurate and compatible method to identify the meaning of keywords in the given question thus to further improve the overall performance of the proposed method. We will also explore the applications of the proposed method to more tasks, such as question categorization and recommendation.

Acknowledgements. We thank Mr. Xiaojun Quan for his comments and suggestions on this work.

References

1. Cheng, P.J., Chiao, H.C., Pan, Y.C., Chien, L.F.: Annotating text segments in documents for search. In: Proceedings of the 2005 IEEE/WIC/ACM International Conference on Web Intelligence, pp. 317–320 (2005)

2. Hao, T.Y., Hu, D.W., Liu, W.Y., Zeng, Q.T.: Semantic patterns for user-interactive question answering. Journal of Concurrency and Computation: Practice and Experience 20(1) (2007)
3. Lin, D.: Dependency-based evaluation of MINIPAR. Treebanks: Building and Using Parsed Corpora (2003)
4. Prager, J., Brown, E., Coden, A.: Question-answering by predictive annotation. In: Proceedings of the 23rd Annual International ACM SIGIR Conference, Athens (2000)
5. Sfihari, R., Li, W.: Question answering supported by information extraction. In: Proceedings of the Eighth Text REtrieval Conference (TREC8), Gaithersburg, Md (1999)
6. Carr, L., Bechhofer, S., Goble, C., Hall, W.: Conceptual linking: ontology-based open hypermedia. In: Proceedings of the 10th International World Wide Web Conference, Hong Kong, pp. 334–342 (2001)
7. Handschuh, S., Staab, S., Ciravegna, F.: S-CREAM – semi-automatic cREAtion of metadata. In: Gómez-Pérez, A., Benjamins, V.R. (eds.) EKAW 2002. LNCS (LNAI), vol. 2473, p. 358. Springer, Heidelberg (2002)
8. Vargas-Vera, M., Motta, E., Domingue, J., Lanzoni, M., Stutt, A., Ciravegna, F.: MnM: Ontology driven semi-automatic and automatic support for semantic markup. In: Gómez-Pérez, A., Benjamins, V.R. (eds.) EKAW 2002. LNCS (LNAI), vol. 2473, p. 379. Springer, Heidelberg (2002)
9. Kiryakov, A., Popov, B., Ognyanoff, D., Manov, D., Goranov, K.M.: Semantic annotation, indexing, and retrieval. Journal of Web Semantics, 49–79 (2004)
10. Reeve, L., Han, H.: Survey of semantic annotation platforms. In: Proceedings of the 2005 ACM Symposium on Applied Computing, Santa Fe, New, Mexico, March 13 -17 (2005)
11. Veale, T.: Meta-knowledge annotation for efficient natural-language question-answering. In: O'Neill, M., Sutcliffe, R.F.E., Ryan, C., Eaton, M., Griffith, N.J.L. (eds.) AICS 2002. LNCS (LNAI), vol. 2464, pp. 127–128. Springer, Heidelberg (2002)
12. Prager, J., Radev, D., Czuba, K.: Answering what-is questions by virtual annotation. In: Proceedings of the first International Conference on Human Language Technology Research 2001, San Diego, March 18 - 21 (2001)
13. Hays, D.: Dependency theory: a formalism and some observations. Language, Linguistic Society of America 40(4), 511–525 (1964)
14. Miller, G.A.: WordNet: a lexical database for English. Communications of the ACM 38(11) (1995)
15. Li, Y.H., Bandar, Z.A., McLean, D.: An approach for measuring semantic similarity between words using multiple information sources. IEEE Transactions on Knowledge and Data Engineering 15(4) (July/August 2003)
16. Cowie, J., Ludovik, E., Molina-Salgado, H., Nirenburg, S., Sheremetyeva, S.: Automatic question answering. In: Proceedings of the Rubin Institute for Advanced Orthopedics Conference, Paris (2000)
17. Álvez, J., Atserias, J., Carrera, J., Climent, S., Laparra, E., Oliver, A., Rigau, G.: Complete and consistent annotation of wordNet using the top concept ontology. In: Proceedings of Sixth International Language Resources and Evaluation (LREC 2008), European Language Resources Association, ELRA (2008)
18. Hao, T.Y., Ni, X.L., Quan, X.J., Liu, W.Y.: Automatic Construction of Semantic Dictionary for Question Categorization. In: Proceedings of The 13th World Multi-Conference on Systemics, Cybernetics and Informatics: WMSCI 2009, Orlando, July 10-13, pp. 220–225 (2009)

Ad-Hoc Georeferencing of Web-Pages
Using Street-Name Prefix Trees

Andrei Tabarcea[1], Ville Hautamäki[2], and Pasi Fränti[1]

[1] Speech and Image Processing Unit, University of Eastern Finland, Joensuu, Finland
[2] Human Language Technology Department, Institute for Infocomm Research
A*STAR, Singapore 138632, Singapore
{tabarcea,franti}@cs.joensuu.fi,
vmhautamaki@i2r.a-star.edu.sg

Abstract. A bottleneck of constructing location-based web searches is that most web-pages do not contain any explicit geocoding such as geotags. Alternative solution can be based on ad-hoc georeferencing which relies on street addresses, but the problem is how to extract and validate the address strings from free-form text. We propose a rule-based pattern matching solution that detects address-based locations using a gazetteer and street-name prefix trees created from the gazetteer. We compare this approach against a method that doesn't require a gazetteer (a heuristic method that assumes that street-name has a certain structure) and a method that also uses data structures created from the gazetteer in the form of street-name arrays. Experiments using our location based search engine prototype (MOPSI) for Finland and Singapore, show that the proposed prefix-tree solution is twice as fast and 10% more accurate than its rule-based alternative and 10 times faster if an array structure is used when accessing the gazetteer.

Keywords: Search engine, LBS, Database, prefix tree, Georeferencing, Mobile device, Location information, Personal navigation, WWW.

1 Introduction

Location-based services (LBS) have become popular during recent years due to increasingly wide availability of GPS positioning in multimedia mobile phones. For instance, according to Nokia's own estimate more than half of their phones would include GPS by 2010-2012. In case of lacking GPS, positioning can also be based on cellular network or even on IP address for rough estimation. It is therefore expected that location-based services are emerging very fast to our everyday life via mobile phones and other consumer electronics.

Locations-based services such as YellowPages[1] , Google Maps[2] and Nokia Ovi Services[3] are traditionally based on databases where all entries have been explicitly georeferenced when stored in the database. An alternative approach has been outlined

---

[1] http://en.02.fi/yellow+pages/
[2] http:/maps.google.com/
[3] http://www.ovi.com/services/

J. Filipe and J. Cordeiro (Eds.): WEBIST 2010, LNBIP 75, pp. 259–271, 2011.
© Springer-Verlag Berlin Heidelberg 2011

in [10] and [8] based on web search and using ad-hoc georeferencing of the web-pages. We denote this approach as *location-based search engine* and emphasize it has seemingly small but significant distinction from traditional location-based services.

The bottleneck of this approach is that only very few pages have explicit georeferencing in form of geotaging, using address field or by other means. On the other hand, it is rather common that web-pages include street or postal addresses as free (non-tagged) text. According to [15], most of relevant services (especially commercial ones) can be found in this way. The main problem however, is how to find valid address elements from the web-pages both reliably and efficiently.

In this paper, we propose a method for extracting street names based on street-name prefix tree and a gazetteer. A potentially relevant web-page (by its content) is first analyzed by extracting all potential street address elements. The hypothesized addresses are then validated by the gazetteer. The pages (or part of them) with validated address are attached by the exact location obtained from the gazetteer and a prototype solution can be found at the *MOPSI Search* website[4].

Extraction of the potential street-name portion of the address field in most languages is very regular. It usually ends to *way, drive, road*, or in Finnish language to a suffix such as *-katu, -kuja, -tie*. A simple *heuristic*, used earlier in [8], performs a search for regular expressions with predefined endings (suffixes). However, not all street-names follow the predefined pattern and street-names that have a different suffix, such as *Neulavahe*, would not be detected. We therefore process all strings from the web-page since it can be done at the same cost when parsing the document.

Another problem is that we might detect as an address a portion of text that is not an actual address, causing a false detection. We therefore validate all hypothesized addresses by a gazetteer and discard the false detections. Our gazetteer is a *geocoded* database that contains geographical coordinates attached to address strings. As a side-product, the validation process provides the geocoding, i.e. converts the given address to a pair of coordinates. The process of recognizing geographic context is referred to as *geoparsing* and the process of assigning geographic coordinates to an address is known as *geocoding*.

One way to detect addresses from free form text is to build a classifier and let it detect addresses from the web-pages as in [21]. However, customizing the classifier to other languages and countries takes a considerable work as new ground truth tagged text corpus must be created by hand. In our approach, no ground truth tagging is needed. The only things needed are a gazetteer and simple rules on how the street name appears in relation to other address fields. Efficient use of the gazetteer is possible because we know the user's current location and its interest area consists only on those services that are close to him. Therefore, we can build fast access structure to that partial gazetteer.

Matching of the potential address strings can be done *brute force* by comparing each word in the document to the retrieved table of street-names. However, this can be rather inefficient if the database is large. We therefore use the prefix tree as a search structure, which is critical for the performance of the matching. A set of prefix trees is constructed from all street-names in a given municipality and the ones in the

---

[4] http://cs.joensuu.fi/mopsi/

proximity of the user's location are used. The proposed solution is faster and more accurate than the heuristic solution alone and much faster than the brute force.

2 Related Work

There has been a lot of progress in location-based search during the last years, starting with commercial services like Google Maps, Yahoo! Local[5], Bing Maps[6] and Yellow Pages, or with research projects such as [12], [17] and [1].

A spatially-aware search engine (SPIRIT) was developed in [12] using geographic ontology, textual and spatial indexing of web-pages. In [17], a system for extracting geographic information from web-pages gathered by crawling programs is presented, whilst the system in [1] relies on web crawling which is targeted to create topical web indices. Our approach differs from these since we don't rely on explicit indexing, but apply ad-hoc georeferencing by detecting postal addresses from free-text.

A categorization scheme of web queries is defined in [9] based on global or local geographic locality. In this view, our search engine handles local queries. In [22], three types of locations from web resources are defined: *provider location* (physical location of the provider who owns the web resource), *content location* (the geographic location of the content) and *serving location* (the geographical scope it can reach). Our goal is to search for the content location.

Methods of detecting tagged location of a web resource are found in [5] and [15]. In [5], "whois" records are analyzed and phone numbers of network administrators are used jointly with zip code and area database to assign coordinates to so-called Class A and B domains and to determine the "globality" of a web-site. In [15], the sources for geospatial context are classified as being for the hosts of a web-page (usually found in "whois" databases and the way the traffic is routed on the Internet), and for its content (postal addresses and codes, telephone numbers, geographic feature names). Additional geographical information is found from hyperlinks and meta tags.

In [11], a gazetteer is defined as a geospatial dictionary of geographic names and its minimum components as a geographic name, a geographic location represented by coordinates, and a type designation. Our gazetteer is a geocoded database which contains postal addresses and their corresponding coordinates.

On the other hand, *name entity recognition* without gazetteers is discussed in [16] and it turns out to work well with people and organizations, but bad with locations. Our solution of postal address detection without a gazetteer (the heuristic method) is much simpler and exploits structural characteristics of postal addresses.

The majority of location-based search systems use gazetteers. For example, the system in [3] uses a three-step process: spotting, disambiguation and focus determination. Our address detection algorithm uses the first two steps.

In [4], an ontology-based approach that extracts geographic knowledge is presented. The address is divided into 3 parts: basic address (street and building number), complement (optional, may be neighborhood name) and location identifiers (phone number, postal code, city name). It can be complete, incomplete or partial.

---

[5] http://local.yahoo.com/
[6] http://www.bing.com/maps/

The address recognition consists of the processes of geoparsing and geocoding, which uses a gazetteer as described in [20]. A spatial index (geoindex) is built for each page. The geoparsing process relies on a set of rules and creating patterns implemented as regular expression from four elements: *basic address*, *postal code*, *phone number* and *city/state*. Our approach is different in a sense that it relies merely on text matching, although our heuristic uses matching via regular expression.

In [7], a syntactic approach to postal address detection is proposed. It consists of two steps: a vision-based text segmentation and a syntactic pattern recognition method. The text segmentation analyses the html tags and detects cue blocks (for the purpose of indications, annotation, and explanation) and body blocks (main text body content). The recognition of postal address relies on calculating the confidence of the detected blocks, which in turn is based on tokenization of the words, which uses city names, state names, street and organization suffixes, but not street names. Our approach is simpler, as we filter out all the html tags before the matching process, and different, as our address detection relies on street-name detection.

In [6], location-based data is retrieved by recognizing postal addresses. The method is ontology-based conceptual information retrieval combined with graph matching. The concepts (knowledge/address elements) in a document are identified and linked in the graph by semantic relations. A set of rules is used on the graph and graph matching methods are used to compute similarity and map concept nodes. The concept set used is actually a gazetteer.

In [19], a graph-ranking algorithm for assigning the geographic scope of a web-page is proposed. Georeferencing is aided by a geo-ontology knowledge base, which uses a set of rules, relationships and heuristics.

In [14], regular expressions are used to detect patterns of typical address elements and database to validate results. The detected street name candidate is then retrieved from the address database to compare all street names for a specific area. In case of a positive match, house numbers are searched and the final address is validated through the database. Our heuristic address detection algorithm is similar to this solution.

In [2] a geoparser that identify address level location is built using a database rather than rely on metadata or other structured annotation. The database used by the geoparser contains postal codes, city names, street names, and also every city-postal code combination is also used for validation. The address detection assumes that the address blocks have a certain structure, and that there are certain dependencies between the address elements. We utilize the idea of identifying a number of address elements in our geoparsing algorithm, and validating the address by geocoding it. However, our contribution is that we use own geocoded database and rely on street-name detection based on prefix-trees data structures, while [1] uses freely available geocoders.

3   Location-Based Search Engine

3.1   System Description

A location-based search engine is one of the practical applications of the proposed ad hoc georeferencing of web-pages. The basic idea behind the location-based search engine has been presented already in [10] and the first prototype application, *MOPSI Search*, has been described in [13] and [8]. It consists of the following components:

1. User interfaces for mobile devices and web.

2. Core server software: search engine and database administrator.

3. Geocoded street-name database with spatial indexing: the gazetteer of the project.

Our approach to the location-based search is to use an external search engine for query-based searching and to post-process the search results provided by that engine, extracting the street or postal addresses. These addresses are then translated into coordinates using a geocoded street-name database for result validation and ranking.
The core server software (Figure 1) is the key component in the system as it implements the georeferencing module. It consists of:

1. Relevant municipalities detector

2. Page parser

3. Address and description detector

4. Address validator

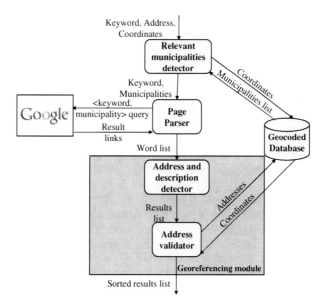

Fig. 1. Architecture of the core server software

The *Relevant municipalities detector* uses the Geocoded database to find all the municipalities that are within a predefined search range (e.g. 10 km square) centered in the user's location.

The *Page parser* uses an external search engine to perform a *<keyword, municipality>* query for every municipality detected at the previous step. It downloads the web-pages found, strips the html tags, and extracts the text.

The *Address and description detector* searches for address blocks, descriptions and telephone numbers in the web-pages found by the Page parser.

The *Address validator* uses the Geocoded database to convert street addresses from the previous step to geographical coordinates, then validates and filters the addresses according to a distance threshold. The validated addresses are used to georeference the web-pages.

3.2 Street-Address Detection

Current prototype uses a rule-based pattern matching algorithm, which starts with the detection of street-names (Figure 2).

If a street-name is found, an address-block candidate is constructed by detecting other typical address elements, such as street numbers, postal codes and municipal names. The application looks for these elements in the vicinity of the found street-name. Variations about how addresses are constructed are taken into account. An address-block candidate is validated using the Geocoded database. If the detected address has corresponding coordinates in the database, it is considered as valid; otherwise it is discarded.

```
StreetNameDetection(words)
{
WHILE i < count(words) DO
    {
    IF words[i] = street name THEN
        {
        Search for street number, postal code and other
        IF address elements found THEN
          {
          Create address block
          Get coordinates using Geocoded database
          IF coordinates found THEN
             Add address block to address list
          }
        }
    i = i + 1;
    }
}
```

Fig. 2. Pseudocode for address detection

Since a plain address without any additional information is not a useful search result alone, the application extracts descriptive information relative to the address. The current implementation employs a set of heuristic rules to the text before the detected addresses to extract descriptive information. This information is used to create a search result, which is composed of the following: *descriptive phrase, telephone number* (if detected), *address, web link, map link* and *Euclidian distance* between user and the target location.

3.3 Street-Name Detection

Street-name detection is the starting point of the address detection. One practical issue is the availability of a gazetteer, as it can be used as a street-name database. Such databases are commonly available, but not necessarily free for commercial purposes. Our application uses a gazetteer of National Land Survey of Finland, and for Singapore, we use the street data from OpenStreetMap[7].

The methods that don't use gazetteer usually assume that a street-name has a certain structure, whilst the methods which use a gazetteer rely on fast word matching. For comparison, we implemented both approaches: a *heuristic method* that does not use a gazetteer, and two text matching methods that use data extracted from a street-name database.

3.3.1 Heuristic Method
Our heuristic method relies on regular expression matching. The structure of most of the addresses has certain particularities. For example, street-names can start with the same prefix or end with the same suffix, they can be in the vicinity of standard words and they are always followed or preceded by a number. In this case, the address block detection also starts with the street-name detection and relies on a set of regular expressions.

According to our experiments, this approach has very good results for Finnish street-names, because most of them end in words like "katu" (street), "tie" (road), "kuja" (lane) or "polku" (path) and has the advantage that it does not need any database or other data structures to store the street-names, and it is reasonably fast.

The accuracy may vary from country to country and the main disadvantage is that the method has to be tailored for every country and language because of the various ways an address block can be constructed. For example, in Finland it is common that the address block has *<street-name, street number, postal code, municipality>* structure, with the street type (e.g. road, lane, street, avenue) as a suffix, whilst in Singapore the *<street number, street name, street type, municipality, postal code>* is more common, but more variations exist. For example, in Singapore a street-name can be written using abbreviations such as Av. instead of Avenue, which is much rarer in Finnish addresses.

3.3.2 Brute-Force Matching Using Street-Name Arrays
A brute-force text matching method checks every word in a web-page against a street-name database. We use an optimized brute-force solution that checks the word against all street-names in the proximity of the location the query is made, for example the street-names in the municipality where the user location is.

---

[7] http://www.openstreetmap.org/

We use arrays of street-names that are created beforehand from the gazetteer. Each array is used to store all the street-names in a municipality and the search is done using language-specific functions. Since our search engine is written using PHP scripts, we use the *array_search* and *in_array* functions optimized to find an object in an array.

3.3.3 Text Matching Using Street-Name Prefix Trees

This method uses prefix trees of street-names, which are created beforehand using the information in our gazetteer. The gazetteer used in the project is a geocoded database which contains all the postal addresses in Finland with their corresponding coordinates. For Singapore, the prefix trees were constructed from street names extracted from freely available map data. Statistical data about both gazetteers are detailed in Table 1.

Table 1. Gazetteer statistics

	Finland	Singapore
Number of municipalities	410	1
Total number of street names	92 572	573
Number of streets per municipality	474	573
Average street name length	11.6	6.1
Total size (MB)	2 982	0.18

In general, the postal addresses are not unique, and the same street-name can be found in many cities. A prefix tree is therefore built for each municipality and just the prefix trees corresponding to the search area are loaded during a search.

4   Street-Name Prefix Tree

The prefix tree (or *trie*) is a fast ordered tree data structure used for retrieval [18]. The prefix tree stores a collection of strings, indexed from the beginning of a word (i.e. prefix). The root node represents an empty string and its children store the first letter of the string. The same principle is applied at every level of the tree so that the internal nodes describe all the sub-strings (prefix) of the particular string. The recursive version of the algorithm is presented in Figure 3.

The nodes of the prefix tree can also have values associated with them, although the only values that are commonly used are the values of the leaf nodes and the values of some inner nodes. In our case, we use the values to mark the end of a street name in the tree structure. Usually, only the leaf nodes are the end of a street name, but if a street name is a prefix of another street name, then an inner node can also be the end of a street name.

```
ConstructTrie(streetnames)
{
    Create empty node root
    FOR i = 1 TO count(streetnames) DO
      AddString(root, streetnames[i], i);
}

AddString(node, string, index)
{
    IF (length(string) > 0) THEN
      IF (string[0] is not the key of a child of node) THEN
         Create new node child with the value string[0]
      ELSE
         Set child as the child of node with the key string[0]
      AddString(child, substring(string, 1), index);
    ELSE   //node is a terminal node
      node.index = index;
}
```

Fig. 3. Prefix tree generation pseudocode

Dictionary search is one of the most common applications of the prefix tree. It traverses the prefix tree until it reaches a leaf node, or when a node does not have any children whose key contains the desired letter. The recursive version of the prefix tree search algorithm is presented in Figure 4.

In our implementation, we create prefix trees from street-names of each municipality. Therefore, the street-name detection becomes a dictionary search using prefix tree. Because the Finnish street-names usually end with a limited number of suffixes, the names were introduced in the prefix-tree in reverse order and the search in the prefix-tree is done starting from the last letter. Figure 5 gives an example of a prefix tree pre-computed from the Geocoded database.

```
FindString(root, string)
{
    IF (strlen(string) == 0) THEN
      RETURN root.index;  //we have reached last node
    ELSE
      IF (string[0] is not the key of a child of root) THEN
      RETURN -1; //string is not found
      ELSE
         Set child as the child of root with the key string[0]
         RETURN FindString(child, substring(string,1))
}
```

Fig. 4. Pseudocode of the Prefix Tree search

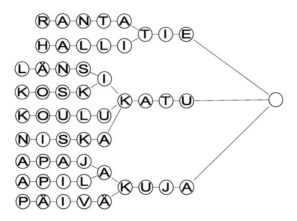

Fig. 5. A sample prefix tree built from street-names

Table 2 summarizes the computed Prefix Trees for Finland and Singapore. It highlights the fact that the gazetteer obtained from the OpenStreetMap is not complete. One of the main advantages of using prefix trees or other pre-built data structures to access street-name data from the gazetteer is the fact that the storage size is reduced (from 3 GB to 74 MB) and the gazetteer is used only for address validation and geocoding.

Table 2. Prefix tree statistics

	Finland	Singapore
Maximum tree depth	34	14
Average tree depth	12.7	7.4
Average tree width	105	167
Average number of nodes per tree	2338	2335
Total size (MB)	74.4	0.18

5 Experiments

We tested the proposed MOPSI location-based search engine using 20 different search locations and 10 keywords to construct *<keyword, municipality>* queries. We downloaded the content of the first 10 search results for each query of Google search engine and the downloaded content was used as data input for the MOPSI prototype.

The search locations were divided into 2 groups: 10 rural 10 urban municipalities (Figure 6), and the test keywords were divided into 5 commercial and 5 non-commercial ones (Table 3).

Table 3. Keywords used for experiments

Commercial	hotel, restaurant, pizzeria, cinema, car repair
Non-commercial	hospital, museum, police station, swimming hall, church

The addresses detected by each method were validated using our geocoded database. The size of the downloaded data in the rural and urban municipalities is 13.9 and 11.2 MB, respectively.

Table 4 shows the average time for address detection and the number of detected addresses for the considered municipalities. The average time is calculated per query over all searches. According to the results, the proposed Prefix Tree method is considerably faster than the Brute Force method, and 2-3 times faster than the Heuristic approach, which does not use the gazetteer. Typical search times of the Prefix Tree are less than 1 second per query.

The detected addresses are validated using our gazetteer. The accuracy (number of validated addresses) of the Brute Force and Prefix Tree methods are higher than that of the Heuristic method. The biggest difference between urban and rural municipalities is that the number and the density of streets are much larger in the urban municipalities and, therefore, the methods using gazetteer (Prefix Tree and Brute Force) are slower in rural municipalities. Nevertheless, the Prefix Tree method is the fastest even in this case.

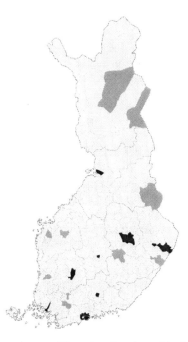

Fig. 6. Locations used for experiments. The urban locations (blue): Espoo, Helsinki, Joensuu, Jyväskylä, Kuopio, Lahti, Oulu, Tampere, Turku, Vantaa; the rural locations (orange): Forssa, Kitee, Kuhmo, Laihia, Lapua, Pieksämäki, Salla, Sodankylä, Somero, Ulvila.

The results also show that, for the Heuristic solution, street density and city size do not affect much the search times. In case of Prefix Tree method, the average search time is somewhat bigger in rural municipality (0.51 vs. 0.87 seconds). The Brute Force method is affected most by the street density as the search times in the street array are bigger than the ones in the prefix tree, resulting in more than 3 times longer search time in urban areas.

Table 4. Average search times for the address detection

Method	Time (s)	Standard deviation	Number of validated addresses
Rural municipalities			
Brute-Force	3.01	2.43	3.7
Heuristic	1.54	1.15	2.5
Prefix Tree	0.51	0.35	3.7
Urban Municipalities			
Brute-Force	10.18	7.11	19.8
Heuristic	1.70	1.24	18.6
Prefix Tree	0.87	0.85	19.8
Total			
Brute-Force	6.59	6.40	11.8
Heuristic	1.62	1.20	10.5
Prefix Tree	0.69	0.68	11.8

In total, the proposed Prefix Tree method is twice as fast as and 10% more accurate than the Heuristic method, on average. It reaches the same accuracy than the Brute Force search but using only 10% of the processing time.

6   Conclusions

Our main goal to design a gazetteer-based street address detector was to increase the accuracy in comparison to the fast heuristic method that was used in the earlier implementation [8]. This goal was achieved, as the proposed prefix tree solution is 57% faster and 10% more accurate, on average, than the heuristic solution. In comparison to Brute Force, it is 10 times faster.

The resulting solution improves the speed and quality of web-page georeferencing and removes one bottleneck for creating efficient location-based search engine as the prototype *MOPSI search.*

Acknowledgements. The research was supported by EU/EAKR and the work of Ville Hautamäki by the Academy of Finland, under project 131298.

References

1. Ahlers, D., Boll, S.: Retrieving address-based locations from the web. In: Int. Workshop on Geographic Information Retrieval, Napa Valey, CA, pp. 27–34 (2008a)
2. Ahlers, D., Boll, S.: Urban Web Crawling. In: ACM Int.workshop on Location and the web., Beijing, China, vol. 300, pp. 25–32 (2008b)
3. Amitay, E., Har'El, N., Sivan, R., Soffer, A.: Web-a-where: geotagging web content. In: ACM SIGIR Conf. on Research and Development in Information Retrieval, Sheffield, UK, pp. 273–280 (2004)

4. Borges, K., Laender, A., Medeiros, C., Davis Jr., C.: Discovering geographic locations in web pages using urban addresses. In: ACM Workshop on Geographical Information Retrieval. Lisbon, Portugal, pp. 31–36 (2007)
5. Buyukkokten, O., Cho, J., Garcia-Molina, H., Gravano, L., Shivakumar, N.: Exploiting geographical location information of web pages. In: WebDB (Informal Proceedings) (1999), http://dbpubs.stanford.edu
6. Cai, W., Wang, S., Jiang, Q.: Address Extraction: Extraction of Location-Based Information from the Web. In: Zhang, Y., Tanaka, K., Yu, J.X., Wang, S., Li, M. (eds.) APWeb 2005. LNCS, vol. 3399, pp. 925–937. Springer, Heidelberg (2005)
7. Can, L., Qian, Z., Xiaofeng, M., Wenyin, L.: Postal address detection from web documents. In: Web Information Retrieval and Integration. Int. Workshop on Challenges in Web Information Retrieval and Integration, pp. 40–45 (2005)
8. Fränti, P., Kuittinen, J., Tabarcea, A., Sakala, L.: MOPSI Location-based Search Engine: Concept, Architecture and Prototype. In: ACM Symposium on Applied Computing, Sierre, Switzerland (2010)
9. Gravano, L., Hatzivassiloglou, V., Lichtenstein, R.: Categorizing web queries according to geographical locality. In: Int. Conf. on Information and Knowledge Management, New Orleans, LA, pp. 325–333 (2003)
10. Hariharan, G., Fränti, P., Mehta, S.: Data mining for personal navigation. In: SPIE Conf. on Data Mining and Knowledge Discovery, vol. 4730, pp. 355–365 (2002)
11. Hill, L., Frew, J., Zheng, Q.: Geographic names: The implementation of a gazetteer in a georeferenced digital library. D-Lib Mag. 5(1) (January 1999)
12. Jones, C.B., Abdelmoty, A.I., Finch, D., Fu, G., Vaid, S.: The SPIRIT spatial search engine: Architecture, ontologies and spatial indexing. LNCS. Springer, Heidelberg (2004)
13. Kuittinen, J.: Using location information in search engines. MSc thesis, Univ. of Joensuu (2006) (in Finnish)
14. Lee, H.C., Liu, H., Miller, R.J.: Geographically-Sensitive Link Analysis. In: IEEE/WIC/ACM Int. Conf. on Web Intelligence, Silicon Valley, CA, pp. 628–634 (2007)
15. McCurley, K.S.: Geospatial mapping and navigation of the web. In: Int. Conf. on WWW, pp. 221–229 (2001)
16. Mikheev, A., Moens, M., Grover, C.: Named entity recognition without gazetteers. In: Conf. on European Chapter of the Association for Computational Linguistics, Bergen, Norway, pp. 1–8 (1999)
17. Morimoto, Y., Aono, M., Houle, M.E., McCurley, K.S.: Extracting spatial knowledge from the web. In: Symposium on Applications and the Internet, pp. 326–333 (2003)
18. Navarro, G., Raffinot, M.: Flexible Pattern Matching in Strings. Cambridge University Press, Cambridge (2002)
19. Silva, M.J., Martins, B., Chaves, M., Afonso, A.P., Cardoso, N.: Adding geographic scopes to web resources. Computers Environment and Urban Systems 30(4), 378–399 (2006)
20. Souza, L.A., Davis Jr., C.A., Borges, K.A.V., Delboni, T.M., Laender, A.H.F.: The role of gazetteers in geographic knowledge discovery on the Web. In: 3rd Latin American Web Congress, vol. 9 (2005)
21. Viola, P., Narasimhan, M.: Learning to extract information from semi-structured text using a discriminative context free grammar. In: ACM SIGIR Conf. on Research and Development in Information Retrieval, Salvador, Brazil, pp. 330–337 (2005)
22. Wang, C., Xie, X., Wang, L., Lu, Y., Ma, W.Y.: Detecting geographic locations from web resources. In: Workshop on Geographic Information Retrieval, Bremen, Germany, pp. 17–24 (2005)

Web Page Classification Using Image Analysis Features

Viktor de Boer[1], Maarten W. van Someren[1], and Tiberiu Lupascu[2]

[1] Informatics Institute, Universiteit van Amsterdam
Science Park 107, 1098 XG Amsterdam, The Netherlands
[2] EURO IT&C B.V., Haarlem, The Netherlands
{v.deboer,m.w.vansomeren}@uva.nl,
tiberiu.lupascu@euroitc.com

Abstract. Classification of web pages is usually done by extracting the textual content of the page and/or by extracting structural features from the HTML. In this work, we present a different approach, where we use the visual appearance of web pages for their classification. We extract generic, low-level visual features directly from the page as it is rendered by a web browser. The visual features used in this document are simple color and edge histograms, Gabor and texture features. These were extracted using an off-the-shelf visual feature extraction method. In three experiments, we classify web pages based on their aesthetic value, their recency and the type of website. Results show that these simple, global visual features already produce good classification results. We also introduce an online tool that uses the trained classifiers to assess new web pages.

Keywords: Web design, Computer vision, Image analysis, Machine learning.

1 Introduction

The "Look and Feel" or is an important property of a website. Most research and development that is aimed at analysis of websites focuses on the content, in particular on the words and their meanings. In addition to the content the form of a webpage is used to convey or even to induce emotional aspects. Individuals and organizations attach much importance to the image that is created by their presence on the web. A bank should appear reliable, an artist creative, an IT company technically advanced and user friendly. Designers use their creativity to find a form that conveys and evokes emotion, trust, authority or a range of impressions like creativity, innovation, political or environmental awareness, religious background, etc. etc. In this paper we describe preliminary experiments with several dimensions of Look and Feel.

Look and feel can take many forms, as can easily be seen by reviewing for example home pages of persons and organizations. In the design of a website the visual appearance or look and feel is constructed by colors and color combinations, type fonts, images and videos, dimensions of page layout such as contrasts. Look and Feel is produced by designers in an intuitive way, using design tools that enable manipulation of visual elements.

Our goal is to enable automatic analysis of this visual appearance of web pages. This goal is part of a wider effort to achieve automated analysis of websites. In earlier

J. Filipe and J. Cordeiro (Eds.): WEBIST 2010, LNBIP 75, pp. 272–285, 2011.

studies methods and tools were developed that analyze websites by their content, in particular their vocabulary and structure. The practical goal of this is to develop a tool that supports the design of web-based information systems by constructing a first draft of the information architecture or by critiquing a first draft. This is done by modeling a given collection of sites and comparing the model with the draft. The first version of the tool only considered the content, the way in which this is organized over pages and the hyperlinks between pages [8].

Our approach is based on using the page as it appears to the user. Analysis of documents on the web is normally based on data that are extracted from the HTML. This is the approach that is typically followed for analyzing the content of web pages. The HTML is removed and the natural language words are used as properties of the page and used for classification or extracting information [5,9, e.g.]. For analysis of Look and Feel this approach seems hardly feasible because Look and Feel elements are difficult or impossible to identify in the HTML code.Some systems allow selection of Look and Feel elements in the form of possibilities for color schemes or the shape and layout of menus, buttons, etc. but many designers construct their own layout, colors and style for objects. For this reason we decided to use low level features of a page, taken as an image. This makes it independent of how the page is produced and analyzes it directly in terms of how the user sees it.

In [1], the authors describe a study into the perceived quality of web sites. The results show that the number of images on a web site is one of the five features that has the highest correlation with high quality web sites as perceived by users. Research into the perceived quality of web pages has shown that the visual appearance of web pages is also important for the perceived credibility [7].

In [11] the author describes the AQUAINT system, a quality based search engine. The system uses 113 features to describe web pages, which are extracted at runtime. Among these features are also color features: notably the number of colors, the number of unique colors, the RGB values of most frequent color, the text color and the background color. Other visual features include the number of graphics on a page, the number of links to graphics, the relation between the number of graphics and the file size. These features are at least partially derived from the underlying HTML. In our approach, we extract the visual features from the pages, as rendered by a web browser. These visual features were combined with other features (e.g. textual content) to train a classifier that distinguishes between high and low quality web pages. The relation between the number of graphics and the file size was among the most important distinguishing features.

Below we summarize our method for training classifiers, the evaluation procedure and the results of experiments with visual attributes of web pages.

2   Visual Features

We use the Firefox web browser to render an image for a web page. Of each page, we save a screen shot using the Fireshot plugin[1] for the Firefox web browser. These screen shots are stored as .PNG files.

---

[1] http://screenshot-program.com/fireshot/

ugly   beautiful

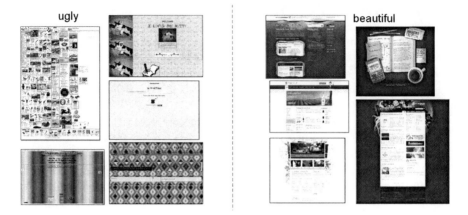

Fig. 1. Example Screenshots of 5 ugly and 5 beautiful pages

2.1 Attributes of Pages

For each page a number of low-level features are computed. For this, we use the Lire image feature library for content-based image retrieval [10]. This Java library offers a number of different feature extraction modules, including MPEG-7 standard features. In this study we used the following features:

Simple Color Histogram. The default RGB color histogram. The histogram is produced by discretization of the colors in the image into 32 of bins, and counting the number of image pixels in each bin. A bin corresponds to part of the color intensity spectrum. High frequencies in low bins indicate that the image has a lot of dark colors. High values in the bins with a higher number indicate images with more light colors.

Edge Histogram. The MPEG-7 edge histogram descriptor represents the spatial distribution of five types of edges (four directional edges and one non-directional) [14]. Specifically, the image space is divided into 16 (4x4) non-overlapping sub-images and for each sub-image a histogram with five edge bins is generated. This results in a descriptor with 80 attributes.

Tamura Features. In [15] the authors propose a number of features of texture that they claim to correspond to human visual perception. The Tamura module in Lire extracts the features describing the coarseness, contrast and directionality of an image. The first two are represented by single values, while directionality is split into 16 bins. This results in a Tamura feature vector of 18 attributes.

Gabor Features. Gabor filters have been used extensively as a model of texture for image interpretation tasks. We here use the Gabor feature extraction model as implemented in Lire. This results in 36 attributes.

For each pages this results in total of (32+80+18+36=) 166 variables that characterize the image of the page.

2.2   Feature Selection and Learning

The machine learning process consists of two steps. The first is to select relevant features. This was done using chi-square as a criterion. Attributes are ranked based on their chi-square value. The top M attributes are then selected, the rest are discarded. In this research, we experimented with values 20, 15, 10, 5 and 1 for M. In the second step a classifier is constructed using the Navc Bayes classifier and a decision tree learning algorithm (J48). In both cases the default implementations in the WEKA toolkit were used.

3   Evaluation Methodology

In this paper, we present the results of three different web page classification experiments. These are two binary classification tasks: on aesthetic value and on recency. In the third experiment we classify the web pages on the web site topic, this task uses four classes. All comparisons used sets of 30 pages for each class. Pages have different sizes and a page may not fit on a single screen. In each case the complete page was used.

To evaluate which features are the most predictive for the different tasks, we evaluate the classification accuracy with three feature vector subsets: the whole feature vector (166 attributes), just the Simple Color Histogram, just the Edge Histogram and the subset indicated by the feature selection procedure. For the latter, we present the results with the highest accuracy for each experiment.

The results were evaluated using 10-fold cross-validation. For each cross validation experiment we report the mean accuracy over the 10 runs and the features that were selected.

4   Experiment 1: Aesthetic Value

In the first experiment, we define two classes: that of ugly web pages and beautiful web pages. With our notion of Aesthetic Value, we only consider the visual design of a web page. This does not need to reflect the quality of the information, the usefulness or the popularity of a page. Neither do the classes represent the quality of the interaction of information design of a page. This classification is of course quite subjective. We decided to use pages on which most people would agree that they are beautiful or ugly, which results in pages that have rather extreme position on this dimension.

4.1   The Data

For the ugly pages, we downloaded 30 pages listed in the article "The World's Ugliest Websites" from a popular design weblog [2]. The web pages were listed either in the article or in the comment section of this article. An informal opinion poll resulted in unanimous agreement with this classification. Among these are the use of color, animated gif's, tiled backgrounds or a cluttered page design. Figure 1 shows screenshots of a number of these ugly web pages.

For the beautiful pages, we also consulted a design web log, listing the author's selection of the most beautiful web pages of 2008 [4]. From this list, we retrieved 30 web pages. Inspection of these pages shows that they include many web designers home pages. The web pages feature a lot of visual design, many colors, pictures and Adobe Flash elements. In that sense they differ from a more minimalistic design that popular web sites use. Figure 1 shows screenshots of a number of these ugly and beautiful web pages.

We note that pages from both categories use a lot of color, both include pages with many visual elements. It appears that the beautiful web sites make more use of softer color schemes and edges, while in the ugly pages, the colors are brighter and the edges are sharper.

4.2   Results

The results are shown in Figure 2. The Naive Bayes Classifier, trained on all features predicted the class for 41 web pages correctly, while the trained J48 decision tree classifier predicted 48 pages correctly, resulting in accuracy of 68% and 80% respectively, which is well over chance level. To evaluate the influence of the two basic features, Simple Color Histogram and Edge Histogram, we trained the model with these two subsets individually. For the Simple Color Histogram subset, this resulted in models that correctly classified 41 (Naive Bayes) and 40 (J48 tree) pages correctly. For Edge Histogram, 42 (Naive Bayes) and 32 (J48 tree) pages were classified correctly.

We applied feature selection, as explained in Section 2.2. All the selected features are either from the Simple Color Histogram or the Edge Histogram. The best predicting features are the 74th Edge Histogram attribute. A high value for this attribute indicates that there are many non-directional edges in the bottom-right of the image. Ugly web sites have relatively more of these non-directional edges in this sub-image. Other selected features include the Simple Color Histogram attributes 22-25. High values in these bins indicate that a website has a higher probability of being 'beautiful'. These high values correspond to images with relatively light colors. Analysis of the data showed that instances from both classes have high values in the extreme bins (1 and 80, indicating the use of black and white respectively), but that beautiful pages use more colors that are in between these extremes.

We again trained the model using the top 20, 15, 10, 5 and the top 1 ranked attributes. Of these, the best result was obtained when the top 5 attributes are used and those results are also shown in Figure 2. The best results are obtained when the J48 decision tree is used, trained on the top 5 attributes. Here 50 pages are classified correctly, resulting in a 83% accuracy. The result for a classification based on only one feature (in this case the 74th Edge Histogram attribute), produces relatively good results (73% and 62% for Naive Bayes and J48 tree respectively). The reduced number of features most likely prevents the models from overfitting. Overall, the results show a surprisingly high prediction accuracy which can be achieved using only a few simple global color and edge frequency features.

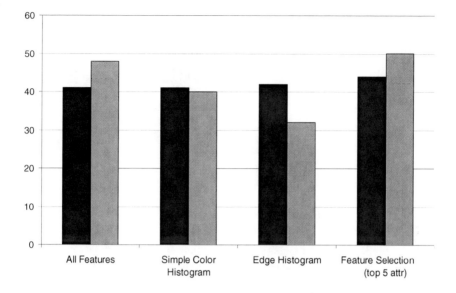

Fig. 2. Class prediction results for different feature subsets for the ugly vs beautiful web pages task. The black bars in the histogram show the number Naive Bayes classifiers correct predictions, the gray bars that of the j48 decision tree.

5   Experiment 2: Recency

For the second experiment, we look at old and new pages. Web design has changed a lot over the years and our visual classification method should be able to identify old or new pages. While the aesthetic quality of a web page is subjective, the time at which it was created is not.

5.1   The Data

We extracted pages from 1999 and from 2009. For the 1999 pages, we selected the 16 popular US web sites of 1999. We also included 8 of the most popular Dutch and 6 of the most popular German sites of the same year. We used the Internet Archive web site [16] to retrieve the 1999 versions of the web pages. We made sure that the web page was fully loaded and displayed all visual elements. The most popular pages of 2009 were selected using the Alexa.com web page popularity rankings[2]. Even though the look and feel of most web pages changes a lot over ten years, the modern versions often still resemble the old versions. The final set of 30 2009 web pages consisted of 15 top US pages, 9 Dutch and 6 German web pages.

Inspection of the screenshots of the 60 web pages shows that there is indeed a difference in visual appearance between the two classes. The older web pages in general seem to have fewer colors than the new web pages. Hyperlinks in old pages are generally blue and underlined, while hyperlinks in new pages have arbitrary colors. Because

---

[2] www.alexa.com

old (1999)   new (2009)

Fig. 3. Example Screenshots of 5 old and 5 new pages

of technical limitations, older pages generally contain few images and video thumbnails compared to newer pages, which is also visible in the visual appearance.

Figure 3 shows a sample of the web pages.

5.2 The Results

Figure 4 show the results of this experiment. Using the complete feature vector, the Naive Bayes and J48 classifiers predict the correct class for 49 and 51 web pages, resulting in accuracies of 82% and 85% respectively. This is again well above chance level. This indicates that this classification can also be learned by using simple visual features. When only the color histogram subset of the attributes is used, the Naive Bayes classifier performed slightly less than the baseline and the J48 tree slightly better. Using only edge information, both models performed slightly worse than the baseline, but still with a accuracy of 72% (Naive Bayes) and 78% (J48).

Feature selection showed that the best predicting features for this problem were again the use of lighter, non-extreme colors: Simple Color Histogram bins 21-29. A higher value in these bins indicates a higher probability of a web page being 'new'. This corresponds to an increased use of both digital photographs on web sites and tot the intuition that advancements in both display monitor capabilities and web design tools will cause newer web pages to employ a wider color spectrum. Tamura directionality features are also among the selected features. On average, the newer web pages have higher scores in the Tamura directionality bins, more specifically in directionality bins 7-13. These bins correspond to the frequencies of diagonal, slanted edges of which there are more in the newer web pages. This difference can be explained by the increased use of graphics and photographs on web pages.

Using a subset of 10 feature-selected attributes resulted in the best predicting models: The average accuracy over 10 cross-validation runs was 87% and 93% for Naive Bayes and the Decision Tree respectively. Using only the features of the Simple Color Histogram gives more or less the same accuracy as using all features. The same is true for features of the edges. Using the entire feature set probably causes overfitting and this

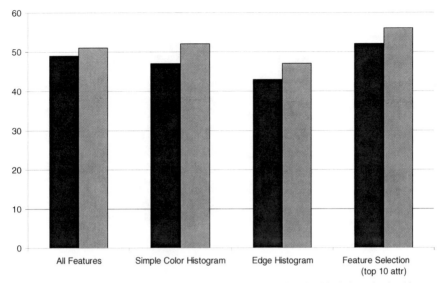

Fig. 4. Class prediction results for the new vs. old pages task. The black bars in the histogram show the Naive Bayes classifiers correct predictions, the gray bars that of the j48 decision tree.

removes the potential benefit of using extra features. Here again the data represented extreme cases rather than a representative sample and average classifications will have lower accuracy.

6 Experiment 3: Web Page Topic

The third experiment involves classification on web page *topic*. The topic of a web site is of course reflected first of all in its content and does not automatically dictate the visual appearance. Numerous methods for classifying web pages by their verbal content were developed and tested successfully. However, in addition to their content, many topics have a characteristic visual appearance. For example web design blogs have a highly designed visual appearance themselves, while newspaper sites will have a lot of text and images. The goal of this experiment is to see if it is possible to classify web pages by topic based on their visual appearance. A practical advantage of the use of visual features is that they can be used independent of the language. Although there is research that shows how cultural differences are reflected in interface and web design [6], the visual design of web pages from the same web site topic is appears to be very much similar across different countries. To demonstrate this we included web pages in different languages in our experiment.

6.1 The Data

We define four classes, corresponding to web site topics. These classes are *newspaper sites*, *hotel sites*, *celebrity sites* and *conference sites*. For each of these classes we retrieved 30 homepages:

newspaper	hotel	celebrity	conference

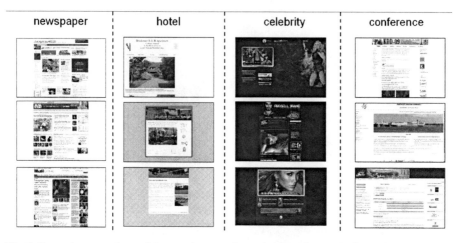

Fig. 5. Example screenshots of three web pages for each of the four web site topic classes. The images shown here are representative of the look and feel in for those web site topics.

- For the newspaper class, we retrieved 30 homepages of well-known newspapers from the US, UK, the Netherlands, Germany, France, Belgium, Russia, Japan, India and China, all in their native language.
- For the conference class, we retrieved the homepages of 30 of the highest ranked computer science conferences.
- The celebrity sites class consists of 30 web pages for celebrities. For this we consulted the Alexa.com popularity ranking of celebrity sites. These included a number of fan sites. We excluded multiple sites from the same domain or sites about the same celebrity.
- For the hotel class, we retrieved 30 home pages from small British bed-and-breakfast businesses. We here included only businesses with their own domain, so that the visual design was determined by that business.

Inspection of the pages suggests that there is indeed a difference in visual appearance of the sites: newspaper homepages have a lot of text on a semi-white background and some photographs. The conference pages mainly conform to the 'three column' design and have a clear, simple, two-color design with one colorful banner on the top of the page. Celebrity pages have a lot of visual design, images and video thumbnails. The hotel sites often have a minimalistic design, but do include photographs. Figure 5 shows for each class three representative web pages.

6.2 Results

Figure 6 shows the classification results. When all features are used, the Naive Bayes and J48 classifiers predict the correct class for 65 and 67 web pages out of 120, resulting in accuracy of 54% and 56% respectively. This is a significant improvement over the 25% prior probability of correct classifications. Using the subset of Simple Color Histogram features results in much worse performance for both classifiers. Apparently,

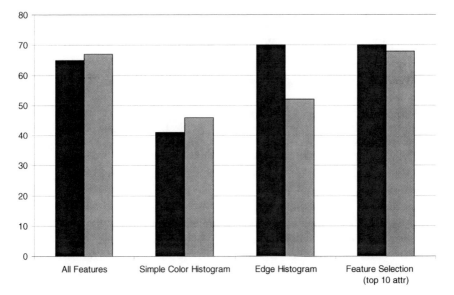

Fig. 6. Class prediction results for the classification of web site topics. The black bars in the histogram show the Naive Bayes classifiers correct predictions, the gray bars that of the j48 decision tree.

using only color information is not sufficient for this type of classification task. When only the Edge Histogram attributes are used, the difference between the two classifiers is very large: the Naive Bayes classifier performs very well, predicting 70 pages correctly (58% accuracy), whereas the J48 decision tree only predicts 52 pages correct (43% accuracy). This suggests that in fact many edge frequencies are predictive and their effects are relatively independent of other features.

The feature selection shows that the best predicting attributes are all from the Tamura and Gabor feature vectors. For the Tamura features, these include the same directionality attributes as in the previous experiment but here the coarseness of the image is also indicative of the newspaper class. An explanation for this is that the newspaper sites have a lot of recurring components (such as photograph thumbnails) that are recognized as being part of a very coarse texture.

The fact that simple color and edge histogram features are no longer among the best predicting features indicates that this classification task is more difficult. More sophisticated visual information, which is at least partly provided by the Tamura and Gabor feature, produces a better classification. The best classification results after feature selection are obtained with the top 10 attributes. Here, the Naive Bayes model classifies 70 pages correctly (43% precision) and the J48 tree predicts the correct class for 68 pages (43% precision). These results are also shown in Figure 6

Analysis of the accuracy by class shows that learned models perform much worse for the *hotel* class than for the other three classes. Only five instances were correctly classified as hotel web pages, the rest were mostly classified as conference sites. Both web page topics have relatively simple designs, especially when compared to the other classes, thus making it harder to distinguish between these two classes. A more specific example of a classification error is the misclassification of the German 'Bild Zeitung' web page as a celebrity site. A look at the homepage shows that indeed it looks more like a celebrity site (large photographs, a lot of dark colors and large visual elements).

7 Conclusions and Discussion

The experiments showed that low level features of webpages are able to distinguish between several classes that vary in their Look and Feel, in particular aesthetically well-designed vs. badly designed, recent vs. old sites and different topics. These features are obtained directly from pages as they are rendered by web browsers and displayed on the screen. This approach is therefore independent of the environment and format in which the site was constructed.

As we have noted in Section 5, a visual difference between older and newer web pages is the use of blue underlined text. Our simple RGB color histogram cannot distinguish the use of the specific color blue, its bins only count number of pixes of a certain brightness. More specific color features such as the adherence to 'good' design color schemes can produce better results. Combinations with the visual features described for example by [11] can also improve the results. In the next section, we show that mid-level features specifically focusing on color and composition improve the classification results.

Our future work will focus on the integration of these visual features with other features of web pages. This includes the textual context and the underlying HTML, the used technologies and functionalities of a web page. By combining visual and the underlying HTML, we can better identify elements on a web page, which can be used as better features for classification.

This paper presents a first step towards an advice system that assists the design and assessment of web sites. From a research perspective it is interesting because it shows that objective and operational analysis of Look and Feel of websites is possible. This enables a wide range of possibilities for research on the relations between features of websites and the effect that this has on different types of users. At the technical side it seems likely that more abstract features will be needed for finer discrimination between different types of sites as in for example [6,12].

8 Mid-Level Color and Composition Features

In this document found that for classification based on aesthetic value and recency, simple features such as a color histogram and edge histograms provide very good results. For the more difficult task of classifying web pages by their topic, more elaborate visual features provide better results. Although these simple, global features already provide good classification results, using more specific visual features can significantly boost the accuracy. In [3], the experiments from this work are repeated with mid-level features representing the color use and and composition of the web page. The color feature extractors consist of a method for extracting a color palette from a web page and analyzing this palette. For example, one important feature is the distribution of brightness

Fig. 7. A screenshot of the current beta-version of the online visual web site assessment tool. For this Dutch news site the topic is correctly classified, it's recency is misclassified as 'old'. The correctness of the aesthetic classification (ugly) can be debated.

of colors across the page. Research on color perception has shown that people prefer distributions that are closer to natural distributions [13]. Other features such as mean chroma, color balance and hue spread were extracted.

The composition feature extractors detect photos and columns on a page. The average number of photo's, the average photo size and the total percentage of the page occupied by photo's were used as features. A 'column detector' for web pages was also built, with extracted features being the sizes of page margins, number of content columns and column widths.

In total, 45 mid-level color and composition features were extracted to repeat the experiments described in sections 4, 5 and 6. The results show that these mid-level features are even better capable of classifying web pages. Here, feature selection also proved effective. In total, using mid-level features improved the accuracy by 8-13% with respect to the experiments described above.

9   Application: A Site Assessment Tool

The resulting classifiers described in this paper are used for an online site assessment tool. In previous work, we have developed a tool that is able to analyze a website based on the content and topics on that website's pages. This research provides us with the means to analyze the visual appearance of a target site. Using the best classifiers resulting from the three experiments described in this paper, we can classify a new page on three orthogonal dimensions: beauty/ugliness, up-to-dateness of the design and whether or not the site looks like one of the four web site topics introduced in Section 6. We expect that this information can be of value to (amateur) web designers or web site owners.

Figure 7 shows a screenshot of the current version of the tool. The site allows a user to enter a URL. The web page is then retrieved and classified in three dimensions, corresponding to those presented in sections 4-6. For this we use the best models learned from the data presented here. The three classes are presented to the user. An example output for an analyzed page is: "your website looks like a beautiful, new celebrity website", which depending on the actual type of the page might or might not be a good thing.

We also included a feedback feature on the website where the user can reinforce or correct the classifications. This information is then used to update the models iteratively. We are currently looking at possible expansions of this online tool. The analysis of the visual appearance of a web page can be combined with analysis based on textual content, technological implementation, functionalities or usage data. Another possible expansion of the tool's functionality is that users can define their own web site topics. Through this web site we are looking towards gaining much more data and user evaluations of that data.

References

1. Amento, B., Terveen, L., Hill, W.: Does "authority" mean quality? predicting expert quality ratings of web documents. In: Proc. ACM SIGIR 2000, pp. 296–303. ACM, New York (2000)
2. Andrade, L.: The worlds ugliest websites (2009), http://www.nikibrown.com/designoblog/2009/03/03/the-worlds-ugliest-websites/ (retrieved October 2009)
3. van den Berg, T.: Using Color and Composition to Classify Web Pages. Master's thesis, Universiteit van Amsterdam, the Netherlands (June 2010)
4. 40 most beautiful and inspirational website designs of 2008 (2009), http://www.crazyleafdesign.com/blog/top-40-beautiful-and-inspirational-website-designs-of-2008/ (retrieved October 2009)
5. Ester, M., Kriegel, H.P., Schubert, M.: Web site mining: a new way to spot competitors, customers and suppliers in the world wide web. In: KDD, pp. 249–258. ACM, New York (2002)
6. Evers, V., Day, D.L.: The role of culture in interface acceptance. In: Howard, S., Hammond, J., Lindgaard, G. (eds.) INTERACT. IFIP Conference Proceedings, vol. 96, pp. 260–267. Chapman & Hall, Boca Raton (1997)
7. Fogg, B.J., Marshall, J., Laraki, O., Osipovich, A., Varma, C., Fang, N., Paul, J., Rangnekar, A., Shon, J., Swani, P., Treinen, M.: What makes web sites credible?: a report on a large quantitative study. In: CHI 2001: Proceedings of the SIGCHI Conference on Human Factors in Computing Systems, pp. 61–68. ACM, New York (2001)
8. Hollink, V., de Boer, V., van Someren, M.: Siteguide: An example-based approach to web site development assistance. In: Filipe, J., Cordeiro, J. (eds.) WEBIST, pp. 143–150. INSTICC Press (2009)

9. Kwon, O.W., Lee, J.H.: Text categorization based on k-nearest neighbor approach for web site classification. Inf. Process. Manage. 39(1), 25–44 (2003)
10. Lux, M., Chatzichristofis, S.A.: Lire: lucene image retrieval: an extensible java cbir library. In: MM 2008: Proceeding of the 16th ACM International Conference on Multimedia, pp. 1085–1088. ACM, New York (2008)
11. Mandl, T.: Implementation and evaluation of a quality-based search engine. In: HYPER-TEXT 2006: Proceedings of the Seventeenth Conference on Hypertext and Hypermedia, pp. 73–84. ACM, New York (2006)
12. Moss, G., Gunn, R., Heller, J.: Some men like it black, some women like it pink: consumer implications of differences in male and female website design. Journal of Consumer Behaviour 5, 328–341 (2006)
13. Müller, A.: Die Moderne Farbenharmonielehre. Chromos Winterthur (1948)
14. Park, D.K., Jeon, Y.S., Won, C.S.: Efficient use of local edge histogram descriptor. In: MULTIMEDIA 2000: Proceedings of the 2000 ACM Workshops on Multimedia, pp. 51–54. ACM, New York (2000)
15. Tamura, H., Mori, T., Yamawaki, T.: Textural features corresponding to visual perception. Systems, Man, and Cybernetics Society 8, 460–473 (1978)
16. The internet archive wayback machine (2009), http://www.archive.org

Towards a Better Semantic Matching for Indexation Improvement of Error-Prone (Semi-)Structured XML Documents

Arnaud Renard, Sylvie Calabretto, and Béatrice Rumpler

Université de Lyon, CNRS,
INSA-Lyon, LIRIS, UMR5205, 7 Avenue Jean Capelle
F-69621 Villeurbanne Cedex, France
{arnaud.renard,sylvie.calabretto,beatrice.rumpler}
@insa-lyon.fr

Abstract. Documents containing errors in their textual content (which we will call noisy documents) are difficultly handled by Information Retrieval systems. The same observation is verified when it comes to (semi-)structured IR systems this paper deals with. However, the problem is even bigger when those systems rely on Semantics. In order to achieve that, they need an additional external semantic resource related to the documents collection. Then, ranking is made possible thanks to concepts comparisons allowed by similarity measures. Similarity measures assume that concepts related to the words have been identified without ambiguity. Nevertheless, this assumption can't be made in presence of noisy documents where words are potentially misspelled, resulting in a word having a different meaning or at least in a non-word. Semantic aware (semi-)structured IR systems lay on basic concept identification but they don't care about spelling uncertainties. As this can degrade systems results, we suggest a way to detect and correct misspelled terms which can be used in documents pre-processing of IR systems. First results on small datasets seem promising.

Keywords: Information retrieval, (Semi-)structured documents, XML, Semantic resource, Thesaurus, Ontology, Fuzzy matching, Error detection, Error correction, OCR.

1 Introduction

Today's society is evolving and relies on more tools and practices related to information technologies. This is mostly due to the evolution of communication infrastructures. Indeed, the difficulty no longer lies in information availability but rather in access to relevant information according to the user. In order to help in information management, the Web is growing according to two tendencies.

On one side, the first one deals with the larger availability of more structured data. That means that large amounts of data which were formerly stored in flat textual files are now frequently stored in (semi-)structured XML based files. That is the reason why we choose to deal this kind of documents.

On the other side, the second one brings semantic aware techniques in order to achieve better machine level understanding of those data. Semantics consists in the

J. Filipe and J. Cordeiro (Eds.): WEBIST 2010, LNBIP 75, pp. 286–298, 2011.

study of words meaning and their relationships like: homonymy, synonymy, antonymy, hyperonymy, hyponymy. The use of semantics in IR systems can be an efficient way to solve data heterogeneity problems: both in terms of content and data structure representation (documents follow neither the same DTD nor the same XML schema). Most of the time, heterogeneity is due to the lack of a common consensus between information sources, which results in global end users incapacity to have a whole knowledge of documents content and structure in a given collection. As a consequence, semantics can be considered as a key factor in search engine improvement. This observation can be made for both domain specific as well as public at large search engines (like Google, Yahoo ...). Indeed, there are an increasing amount of attempts to take semantic into accounts and recently Google integrated some kind of semantics to fill the semantic gap between user real needs and what he has typed as a query. In the same way Microsoft launched recently a new semantic search engine known as "Bing".

It is commonly accepted that the use of semantic resources like ontologies, thesauri and taxonomies of concepts improve IR systems performances [1]. Thus, to use a semantic resource, it is necessary to perform matching between terms of documents and concepts instances in a semantic resource. Some systems already try to achieve (semi-)structured IR by using semantic resources but they are still few. Our goal is to improve results by making a fuzzy semantic matching to take into account common mistakes in indexed documents such as typos or wrong words spelling. In fact, none of semantic aware IR systems currently take into account these anomalies.

The article is structured as follows: we present in section 2 some semantic resources, similarity measures, different approaches proposed in the literature about (semi-)structured IR which consider the semantic aspect, and some error correction systems proposition. After, we present our proposal in order to improve semantic indexing of structured documents in section 3. Then, we discuss briefly about prototype design in and the evaluation process in section 4, to finish with evaluation results we obtained in section 5. Finally, we conclude and debate about future works in section 6.

2 Related Works

A common characteristic of semantic aware IR systems is the necessity of external semantic resources as well as similarity measures allowing for comparisons between concepts. It leads Bellia [2] to define the notion of semantic framework, which relies on two complementary concepts: an external semantic resource and a model for measuring similarity between concepts.

2.1 Semantic Resources

Semantic resources can be split in two categories according to the range of knowledge they represent: domain specific resources, and general resources. Given the nature of documents collections which are as we indicated before very heterogeneous, only general resources are considered here. Indeed, domain specific semantic resources do not cover a sufficiently broad area and would provide fine grained but fragmentary knowledge about collections. We plan to use general semantic resources: thesaurus like Wordnet, ontologies like YAGO [3] which is a large and extensible ontology built on top of Wikipedia and Wordnet, or DBpedia which is resulting from a community effort to extract structured data from Wikipedia [4]. DBpedia "uses cases" indicate that it can be used as a very large multilingual and multidomain ontology. DBpedia has the advantage of covering many domains and containing many instances. Moreover, it represents real community agreement and "automatically" evolves as Wikipedia changes. Kobilarov [5] works about interconnection of many domain specific BBC sites by using DBpedia resources seem to be promising. However, there seems to be a lack of semantic similarity measures available on DBpedia data, which makes it difficult to use. As we can see in the next section, semantic similarity measures are very useful to use semantic resources.

2.2 Semantic Similarity Measures

Similarity measures are required to be able to evaluate the semantic similarity of concepts included in a semantic resource such as a thesaurus or ontology. These measures provide estimations about strength of relations between concepts (which queries terms and documents terms are related). It is particularly useful in the semantic disambiguation process, in terms weighting process and when querying by concepts. An almost complete survey of disambiguation may be found in [6].

Two types of semantic similarity measures can be distinguished. The first type is based on the structure of the semantic resource and counts the number of arcs between two concepts. In contrast, the second type of measures is based on the information content. Information content reflects the relevance of a concept in the collection according to its frequency in the whole collection and the frequency of occurrence of concepts it subsumes. However, Zargayouna [7] showed that the first type of measure could be as efficient as the second one. Moreover, the second type of measures requires a learning phase dependent on the quality of the learning collection. So it is more difficult to carry out (especially because of the difficulty to find a suitable collection for the learning phase). Examples in this area, are Resnik [8] works who brought the information content, as well as those of Jiang [9] and Lin [10] using a mixed approach, and more recently of Formica [11]. In this work, we will only discuss the first type of measurement.

Rada [12] suggested that the similarity in a semantic network can be calculated by relying on links expressing taxonomic *hypernym/hyponym* relationships, and more specifically of "is-a" type. Then, the semantic similarity can be measured in taxonomy by calculating the distance between concepts by following the shortest path between them. It is mentioned in this article that this method is valid for all hierarchical links ("is-a", "sort-of", "part-of" ...), but it may be modified to take into account other types of relationships.

Wu and Palmer developed in [13] a measure of similarity between concepts for machine translation. Their method is defined according to the distance of two concepts with their smallest common ancestor (the smallest concept that subsumes both of them), and with the root of the hierarchy. The following formula allows computing of similarity between two concepts C_1 and C_2:

$$Sim_{WP}(C_1, C_2) = \frac{2 * depth(C)}{dist(C, C_1) + dist(C, C_2) + 2 * depth(C)}. \tag{1}$$

Where, C is the smallest common ancestor of C_1 and C_2 (according to the number of arcs between them), $depth(C)$ is the number of arcs between C and the root, and $dist(C, C_i)$ the number of arcs between C_i and C.

In Zargayouna [7], the proposed similarity measure is based on Wu-Palmer's [13]. The "father-son" relationship is privileged over other neighborhood links. To achieve that, Wu-Palmer's measure needs to be modified, because in some cases it penalizes the son of a concept compared to its brothers. Adaptation of the measure is made thanks to the specialization degree function of a concept (*spec*) which represents its distance from the anti-root. This helps to penalize concepts which are not of the same lineage.

$$Sim_{ZS}(C_1, C_2) = \frac{2 * depth(C)}{dist(C, C_1) + dist(C, C_2) + 2 * depth(C) + spec(C_1, C_2)}. \tag{2}$$

$$spec(C_1, C_2) = depth_b(C) * dist(C, C_1) * dist(C, C_2). \tag{3}$$

Where, $depth_b(C)$ is the maximum number of arcs between the lowest common ancestor and anti-root "virtual" concept: $\perp$.

In Torjmen [14] works on multimedia structure based IR, they assume that the structure of an XML document can be assimilated to ontology. Consequently, they proposed a new refinement of Wu-Palmer [13] and Zargayouna [7] measures applicable directly on documents structure.

Various works designed to manage semantics in IR systems require the use of tools and resources we have introduced. However, most approaches take only the semantic of documents textual content into account and not the semantic of their structure but some IR systems tend to take semantic into account in both content and structure of documents. The XXL system is the first one which incorporated ontology in the indexing process.

2.3 (Semi-)Structured Semantic IR Systems

The XXL query language system allows querying XML documents with syntax similar to SQL. Indeed, it is based on XML-QL and XQuery query languages and adds a semantic similarity operator noted "~". This operator allows expressing constraints of semantic similarity on elements and on their textual content. Query evaluation is based on similarity calculations in ontology as well as terms weighting techniques. The XXL search engine architecture is based on 3 index structures [15]: element path index, element content index, ontological index. This approach, which consists in semantic indexing by ontology, seems to be interesting.

Van Zwol studies on XSee IR system [16] are interesting because it confirmed that semantic improves the performance of structured IR systems.

Zargayouna [7, 17] works on semantic indexing led to SemIndex prototype (dedicated to the semantic indexing) and SemIR (dedicated to the retrieval). In this system, the semantic dimension is taken into account at both terms and structure levels. The previously defined similarity measure is used for terms sense disambiguation. This is performed favoring the meaning attached to the concept that maximizes the density of the semantic network. The originality of the approach is primarily in the similarity measure used to enrich terms weighting method.

Mercier-Beigbeder measure [18] is merged by Bellia [2] with a previous version of Zargayouna's works [17] to take semantic into account. This measure is then enriched to consider XML formalism and latent similarity links between documents.

Other semantic aware structured IR systems may be cited such as CXLEngine [19], which is derived from previous works that led to OOXSearch.

Nevertheless, neither system takes terms uncertainty into account during the indexing process.

2.4 Documents Error Management Mechanisms

Terms uncertainty Errors may have several sources. They can be caused by bad quality documents which results in wrong characters recognition by OCR. Distribution of this kind of errors across documents is somewhat unpredictable a priori. Errors can be caused by human errors in particular when those are dyslexics, or when they come from foreign countries and learn a new language, or when they write documents on portable devices ... Damerau [20] established a list of different kind of resulting errors.

According to [21] two error types can be distinguished: non-words errors which can be easily detected thanks to a dictionary, and real-words errors which are harder to detect while they represent real existing words. Indeed, to be able to detect the second type of errors, the spellchecker must be able to understand (thanks to semantics) the context in which the syntaxically but not semantically correct term is misused.

Error correction problem has been challenged in the Text Retrieval Conference (TREC-5 Confusion Track). Three versions of a collection of more than 55000 documents containing respectively error rates of 0%, 5%, and 20% have been used to run different approaches in the management of those errors for information retrieval systems. A paper which describes this track [22] indicates the different methods followed by five of the participants. It shows a drop in performances of every IR systems in presence of corrupted documents containing errors. Three of them used query expansion with altered terms and two of them tried to correct documents content. Comparison of these methods indicates that the second approach seems to offer better results and constitute a good starting point. Introduction of semantics in these error correcting systems could be a way to achieve better results. This is the in which our proposal evolves.

3   Proposal: Fuzzy Semantic Weighting

During our study of related works, we could identify that Zargayouna's [7, 17] weighting method introduces good concepts for semantic (semi-)structured IR so that we extends [17] semantic weighting formula. The objective is to eliminate mistakes and typos in content by making a fuzzy term matching.

3.1 Term Semantic Weighting

In Zargayouna [17], the semantic weight $SemW(t, b, d)$ of a term t in a tag b of a document d in the semantic vector corresponds to the sum of its weight and semantically close terms TFITDF weights.

$$SemW(t, b, d) = TFITDF(t, b, d) + \frac{\sum_{i=1}^{n} Sim_{ZS}(t, t_i) * TFITDF(t_i, b, d)}{n}. \qquad (4)$$

However, TFITDF is better suited for structured XML documents than for (semi-) structured XML documents as it considers specific tags models. Thus, in $SemW_{mod}(t, b, d)$, TFITDF is replaced with standard TFIEFIDF weighting formula.

3.2 Terms Fuzzy Matching

Our idea is to enrich the semantic weighting formula proposed in [17] by taking into account errors in terms spelling leading to uncertainty in written terms. To manage this purpose we were inspired by Tambellini's works on uncertain data management [23].

Since we rely on a lexicalized semantic resource where concepts are represented by terms, we believe it may be interesting to perform a fuzzy matching between documents terms and terms reflecting concepts in the lexicalized semantic resource.

According to [23], two terms t_1 and t_2 can be paired according to: their concordance i.e. their relative positioning that we note $Conc(t_1, t_2)$, and their intersection i.e. common areas between two terms that we note $Inter(t_1, t_2)$.

Table 1. Adapted Allen's spatial relations

Relations scheme	Signification	Notation
	x *starts* y	$Conc(x,y) = starts$
	x *during* y	$Conc(x,y) = during$
	x *finishes* y	$Conc(x,y) = finishes$
	x *overlaps* y	$Conc(x,y) = overlaps$
	x *equals* y	$Conc(x,y) = equals$
	x *not_equals* y	$Conc(x,y) = not\_equals$

The concordance value noted $ValConc(t_1, t_2)$ is determined according to terms characterization. It depends on spatial relationships derived from Allen's relations [24, 25]: "*starts*", "*during*", "*finishes*", "*overlaps*", "*equals*" and "*not_equals*". Each characterization is then associated with a value α_i.

$$ValConc(t_1, t_2) = \begin{cases} \alpha_1 = 0.8, & if\ Conc(t_1, t_2) = starts \\ \alpha_2 = 0.6, & if\ Conc(t_1, t_2) = during \\ \alpha_3 = 0.8, & if\ Conc(t_1, t_2) = finishes \\ \alpha_4 = 0.2, & if\ Conc(t_1, t_2) = overlaps \\ \alpha_5 = 1, & if\ Conc(t_1, t_2) = equals \\ \alpha_6 = 0, & if\ Conc(t_1, t_2) = not\_equals \end{cases} \qquad (5)$$

It should be noted that in [23] these values seem to be determined empirically.

We respectively note terms common areas of t_1 and t_2, st_1 and st_2 (cf. Table 1).

The intersection value $ValInter(t_1, t_2)$ is highest i.e. 1 if terms common areas are equals i.e. $st_1 = st_2$ and otherwise its value is $ValInter(st_1, st_2)$.

$$ValInter(t_1, t_2) = \begin{cases} 1, & if\ st_1 = st_2 \\ 0 \le ValInter(st_1, st_2) < 1, & else \end{cases}. \qquad (6)$$

The problem of uncertainty is present in many areas including systems which determine if two words are phonetically identical (like *Soundex* algorithm and its derivatives: *Metaphone* ...). Spelling correction systems rely on the problem of data uncertainty in the manner they try to compare two words according to their common letters. This kind of algorithm is used to determine $ValInter(st_1, st_2)$. Indeed, terms common areas are phonetically encoded and we note them respectively cst_1 and cst_2:

$$ValInter(st_1, st_2) = 0.75 * \left(1 - \frac{distHamming(cst_1, cst_2)}{max\ (length(cst_1), length(cst_2))}\right). \qquad (7)$$

The proximity between encodings is computed using a *normalized Hamming distance* and then leveraged with a factor of 0.75 which reflect intersection uncertainty relative to the phonetic encoding.

Thus, the matching value $ValApp(t_1, t_2)$ can be defined from $ValConc(t_1, t_2)$ and $ValInter(t_1, t_2)$:

$$ValApp(t_1, t_2) = ValConc(t_1, t_2) * ValInter(t_1, t_2). \qquad (8)$$

A term t_1 in a document may be considered to be *present* in the semantic resource RS if there is a term t_2 in the semantic resource and $Conc(t_1, t_2) = equals$ among concordance relations defined above, and if $ValInter(t_1, t_2) = 1$. In the same way if $Conc(t_1, t_2) = not\_equals$ then it is *missing* from the semantic resource.

Therefore, it is possible to define an approximation of each term in the documents collection as: all concepts instances of the ontology, which are neither *missing* nor *present*:

$$\sim t = \{t_{RS} \in C_{RS} | t \approx t_{RS}\}. \qquad (9)$$

Where, $\sim t$ is the set of terms t_{RS} representing close concepts C_{RS} in the semantic resource RS to a document term t.

3.3 Misleading Terms Detection

It is evident that a fuzzy semantic weighting could introduce noise if applied on correct (not misspelled) terms. Therefore, it is needed to detect off-board terms which can be considered as being misleading terms first. We propose to use Semantic frequency to achieve this by calculating the frequency of the term and that of all semantically close terms:

$$FreqSem(t, b, d) = TF(t, b, d) + \frac{\sum_{i=1}^{n} Sim_{ZS}(t, t_i) * TF(t_i, b, d)}{n}. \qquad (10)$$

Indeed, if a term t is out of context, its semantic frequency will probably be very low as it will be isolated. Thus, terms whose semantic frequency is below a threshold can be considered as misleading terms. A *Context Presence Indicator* function tries to determine if a term t is a wrong term, or not:

$$CPI(t,b,d) = \begin{cases} 1, & if\ FreqSem(t,b,d) > threshold \\ 0, & else \end{cases}$$
(11)

The threshold estimation has been experimentally determined and fixed at:

$$\frac{1}{n} + 0.4 * \frac{1}{n}.$$
(12)

Where n is the number of terms in the considered element b. In order to adapt the threshold to different profile of elements textual content (for example when there is not a prevailing thematic in the element), we plan to use an outlier identification data-mining algorithm. The drawback of our error detection method is that it can't detect misleading terms when they are alone in an element. Indeed in that case there is no context in the elements that is why surrounding elements should be used instead.

3.4 Terms Fuzzy Semantic Weighting

Misleading terms detected have to be corrected with best possible substitutes. Our proposition can be considered as fuzzy (imprecise and uncertain) the replacing term selected $t_j \in \sim t$ (among approximations of term t) is the one which seems the most relevant in the context. For this, we select the term t_j whose semantic frequency penalized by its matching value with the term t obtains the highest score:

$$\left\{ t_j \in \sim t \middle| \max_{1 \leq j \leq n'} \left(ValApp(t,t_j) * FreqSem(t_j,b,d) \right) \right\}.$$
(13)

To confer more fuzziness to our proposition we could have considered building a vector of best replacing terms instead of choosing the best one according to our criteria. The new occurrence of the selected replacing term can then be weighted: from nothing if it is not present elsewhere in the element or its occurrence can be added to the semantic weight of this term if it exists already. Obviously, the matching value is used to weight the significance of the selected term owing to term matching uncertainty. Our terms weighting formula derived from [17] is:

$$SemW_{fuzzy}(t_j,b,d) = \begin{cases} ValApp(t,t_j) * SemW_{mod}(t_j,b,d), & if\ t_j \notin b \\ ValApp(t,t_j) * SemW_{mod,corrected}(t_j,b,d), else \end{cases}$$
(14)

Where $SemW_{mod,corrected}(t_j,b,d)$ is the same formula as $SemW_{mod}(t_j,b,d)$ except the fact that its TFIEFIDF factor is updated to take new possible term occurrence into account.

$$TF_{updated} = \frac{n + ValApp(t,t_j)}{N}.$$
(15)

$$IEF_{updated} = log \frac{|E|}{|e : t \in e| + ValApp(t, t_j)} \tag{16}$$

$$IDF_{updated} = log \frac{|D|}{|d : t \in d| + ValApp(t, t_j)} \tag{17}$$

We have presented terms fuzzy semantic weighting formula for terms belonging to a document which has been integrated within a semantic aware (semi-)structured IR system to be evaluated.

4   Prototype

The prototype we have developed to validate our weighting formula should have multiple index structures to access the collection through the structure, the content, and especially the concepts. In addition, it should create a Soundex index of terms in the lexicalized semantic resource in order to make fast comparisons of documents and semantic resources terms phonetic forms. During prototype development phase, we performed a survey of existing libraries and platforms dedicated to IR with the objective to allow the prototype to scale-up on large documents collections. The following tools have been considered: Zettair, Lemur Toolkit, Dragon Toolkit, Terrier, Lucene, GATE. Although none of evaluated systems responds to semantics and (semi-)structured documents constraints, GATE platform has been considered because of its high level of modularity. Thus, it provides many useful tools and libraries to improve prototype development speed, so some of them were used in our prototype (cf. Fig. 1). Index persistence problem has been managed through Java Persistence API and a MySQL/InnoDB relational database.

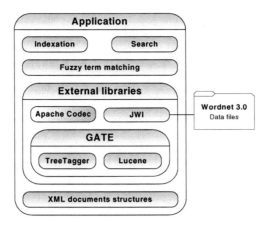

Fig. 1. Global application architecture

5 Evaluation

The developed prototype allowed us to study the behavior of our proposal against a collection of documents according to the kind of anomalies we wish to correct.

Table 2 is a representation of textual elements of a collection of four documents. Only items with text content are represented as they would result after selection and stemming of words achieved through a morphosyntactic analyzer.

Table 2. Terms distribution per document and element

Markup	*Doc1*	*Doc2*	*Doc3*	*Doc4*
name	Anne, Frank	concert	supermarket, grocery, store	movie, theater
sect/title	introduction	introduction	introduction	introduction
sect/par	book, writings, *dairy*, girl, family, diary, journal	concert, music, musician, recital, ensemble, orchestra, choir, band, show, tour	food, merchandise, meat, produce, dairy, pharmacy, pet, medicine, clothes	movie (x2), theater (x2), theatre (x2), picture, film, cinema, motion, picture, ticket, projector, screen, auditorium

We have deliberately introduced an error in « Doc1/sect/par » element to highlight the interest of our proposal. Indeed, the term "diary" has been replaced by the word "dairy", shown in red bold italic in Table 2.

5.1 Terms Semantic Frequency

In order to identify off-board terms requiring fuzzy weighting, we calculate the semantic frequency of each term. The calculated threshold value is 0.2 and is symbolized by a red horizontal line. Each term which semantic frequency is below that point is considered as being off-board, and consequently as misleading.

We can observe on Fig. 2 histogram that only one term has a semantic frequency below the threshold. The term "dairy" can be identified as being out of context (it has indeed been introduced as an error on the word "diary"), and therefore the fuzzy semantic weighting formula has to be applied to correct the mistake.

5.2 Terms Fuzzy Semantic Weighting

It is necessary for detected wrong terms to identify the best term in the set of terms approximation. The term of the semantic resource which achieves the best score according to the matching value (*ValApp*) and to its semantic relatedness in the element will be considered as being the best substitute. In the considered case, the best replacing term retrieved for "dairy" is "diary". So the weight of the term "diary" is enriched with "dairy" occurrence. Hence, we have increased the importance of the term "diary" almost as if no mistake occurred on it. Its importance is still lowered due to the uncertainty in terms fuzzy matching.

We can observe on Fig. 3 histogram that none of the first two weighting schemes (solid bars and hollow bars) is able to detect the erroneous writing of an occurrence of

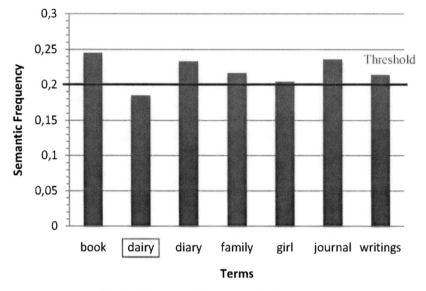

Fig. 2. Histogram of terms semantic frequencies

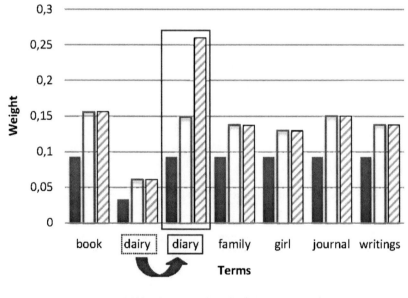

Fig. 3. Terms weighting comparison according to the weighting formula

the term "diary" spelled as "dairy". This is the normal behavior expected from these formulas. However, we note that the third weighting formula affects to the term "diary" a weighing greater than other terms thanks to enrichment (modulo the confidence of the matching between "dairy" and "diary") of the weighting of this term with the occurrence of erroneous term "dairy". This is what we want to achieve in order to weight terms beyond errors which can be found in original documents. This can be seen as a semantic corrector which runs during indexation process.

6 Conclusions and Further Works

In this paper, we have presented a state of the art about useful tools to make semantic aware (semi-)structured IR systems. In particular, semantic similarity measures which allows for concepts comparisons. We then talked about related IR systems and exposed some considerations about error management mechanisms. We finally ended with a proposal for a misleading terms detection method and a fuzzy semantic weighting formula that can be incorporated in an existing system.

The fuzzy matching and weighting formula we propose can be used in conjunction with semantic resources such as Wordnet. An interesting evolution would be to use YAGO or DBpedia instead of Wordnet while they represent much richer resources. Our first evaluations show index quality improvements.

The first short-term development is the implementation of a more scalable prototype allowing us to evaluate error detection/correction and the weighting formula with richer semantic resources on very large datasets like INEX evaluation campaign documents collection.

As indicated before, many other refinements can be considered at different stages. For the misleading term detection, we plan to use data-mining algorithms in order to detect outlier values and avoid the use of empirical thresholds. We plan to include surrounding elements in context definition to help in populating elements context. For the correction phase, we could consider vector of replacing terms instead of choosing the "best" replacing one.

Acknowledgements. This work has received support from the National Agency for Research on the reference ANR-08-CORD-002.

References

1. Rosso, P., Ferretti, E., Jimenez, D., Vidal, V.: Text categorization and information retrieval using wordnet senses. In: Proc. of 2nd GWC, Czech Republic, pp. 299–304 (2004)
2. Bellia, Z., Vincent, N., Kirchner, S., Stamon, G.: Assignation automatique de solutions à des classes de plaintes liées aux ambiances intérieures polluées. In: Proc. of 8th EGC, Sophia-Antipolis (2008)
3. Suchanek, F., Kasneci, G., Weikum, G.: Yago – A Core of Semantic knowledge. In: 16th International World Wide Web Conference (2007)
4. Auer, S., Bizer, C., Kobilarov, G., Lehmann, J., Cyganiak, R., Ives, Z.G.: DBpedia: A nucleus for a web of open data. In: Aberer, K., Choi, K.-S., Noy, N., Allemang, D., Lee, K.-I., Nixon, L.J.B., Golbeck, J., Mika, P., Maynard, D., Mizoguchi, R., Schreiber, G., Cudré-Mauroux, P. (eds.) ASWC 2007 and ISWC 2007. LNCS, vol. 4825, pp. 722–735. Springer, Heidelberg (2007)

5. Kobilarov, G., Scott, T., Raimond, Y., Oliver, S., Sizemore, C., Smethurst, M., Bizer, C., Lee, R.: Media Meets Semantic Web – How the BBC Uses DBpedia and Linked Data to Make Connections. In: Aroyo, L., Traverso, P., Ciravegna, F., Cimiano, P., Heath, T., Hyvönen, E., Mizoguchi, R., Oren, E., Sabou, M., Simperl, E. (eds.) ESWC 2009. LNCS, vol. 5554, pp. 723–737. Springer, Heidelberg (2009)
6. Navigli, R.: Word sense disambiguation: A survey. ACM Computing Surveys (CSUR) 41, 1–69 (2009)
7. Zargayouna, H.: Indexation sémantique de documents XML. Phd thesis. Université Paris-Sud (Orsay), Paris, 227 (2005)
8. Resnik, P.: Using information content to evaluate semantic similarity in taxonomy. In: Proc. of 14th IJCAI, pp. 448–453 (1995)
9. Jiang, J.J., Conrath, D.W.: Semantic similarity based on corpus statistics and lexical taxonomy. In: Proc. of International Conference on Research in Computational Linguistics (1997)
10. Lin, D.: An Information-Theoretic Definition of Similarity. In: Proc. of 15th ICML, pp. 296–304. Morgan Kaufmann Publishers Inc., San Francisco (1998)
11. Formica, A.: Concept similarity by evaluating information contents and feature vectors: a combined approach. Commununications of the ACM 52, 145–149 (2009)
12. Rada, R., Mili, H., Bicknell, E., Blettner, M.: Development and application of a metric on semantic nets. IEEE Transactions on Systems, Man and Cybernetics 19, 17–30 (1989)
13. Wu, Z., Palmer, M.: Verbs semantics and lexical selection. In: Proc. of 32nd annual meeting of ACL, ACL, Las Cruces, New Mexico, pp. 133–138 (1994)
14. Torjmen, M., Pinel-Sauvagnat, K., Boughanem, M.: Towards a structure-based multimedia retrieval model. In: Proc. of 1st ACM MIR, pp. 350–357. ACM, Vancouver (2008)
15. Schenkel, R., Theobald, A., Weikum, G.: Semantic Similarity Search on Semistructured Data with the XXL Search Engine. Information Retrieval 8, 521–545 (2005)
16. van Zwol, R., van Loosbroek, T.: Effective Use of Semantic Structure in XML Retrieval. In: Amati, G., Carpineto, C., Romano, G. (eds.) ECiR 2007. LNCS, vol. 4425, pp. 621–628. Springer, Heidelberg (2007)
17. Zargayouna, H., Salotti, S.: Mesure de similarité dans une ontologie pour l'indexation sémantique de documents XML. In: Proc. of IC (2004)
18. Mercier, A., Beigbeder, M.: Application de la logique floue à un modèle de recherche d'information basé sur la proximité. In: Proc. of 12th LFA 2004, pp. 231–237 (2005)
19. Taha, K., Elmasri, R.: CXLEngine: a comprehensive XML loosely structured search engine. In: Proc. of 11th EDBT workshop on Database technologies for handling XML information on the Web, vol. 261, pp. 37–42. ACM, Nantes (2008)
20. Damerau, F.J.: A technique for computer detection and correction of spelling errors. Communications of the ACM 7, 171–176 (1964)
21. Pedler, J.: Computer Correction of Real-word spelling Errors in Dyslexic Text. Phd thesis. Birkbeck, London University, 239 (2007)
22. Kantor, P., Voorhees, E.: The TREC-5 Confusion Track: Comparing Retrieval Methods for Scanned Text. Information Retrieval 2(2/3), 165–176 (2000)
23. Tambellini, C.: Un système de recherche d'information adapté aux données incertaines: adaptation du modèle de langue. Phd Thesis. Université Joseph Fourier, Grenoble, 182 (2007)
24. Allen, J.F.: Maintaining knowledge about temporal intervals. Communications of the ACM 26(11), 832–843 (1983)
25. Allen, J.F.: Time and time again: The many ways to represent time. International Journal of Intelligent Systems 6(4), 341–355 (1991)

Author Index